THRING OF UPPINGHAM

VICTORIAN EDUCATOR

THRING OF UPPINGHAM

VICTORIAN EDUCATOR

Nigel Richardson

The University of Buckingham Press

First published in Great Britain in 2014 by

The University of Buckingham Press
Yeomanry House
Hunter Street
Buckingham MK18 1EG

A CIP catalogue record for this book is available at the British Library

ISBN 978-1-908684-0-59

In memory of Cormac Rigby
1939-2007

'If children are precious,
and human lives not to be bought and sold,
and to educate well requires all the knowledge of the trained intellect,
all a good man's patience and a brave man's heart,
believe and act on this belief.'

Edward Thring, *Education and School* (1864)

An archbishop was once asked:
'What kind of man was Edward Thring?'

The archbishop was about to poke the fire.
He paused, and holding out the poker, said:
'Why, he was this kind of man: if he were poking a fire,
he would make you believe that the one thing worth living for
was to know how to poke a fire properly.'

From Parkin, G R (ed.), *Edward Thring, Headmaster of Uppingham School: Life, Diary and Letters* (1898)

TABLE OF CONTENTS

LIST OF ILLUSTRATIONS

ILLUSTRATIONS – 2

ILLUSTRATIONS – 3

ILLUSTRATIONS - 4

ACKNOWLEDGEMENTS

This book grew out of a Ph.D. thesis and monograph on Uppingham's typhoid outbreak (1875-7), completed in 2007. I am grateful to many former colleagues and others for their help as it has evolved over the years.

Geoffrey Frowde and the late Bryan Matthews first encouraged me to contemplate it. When it began to take shape five years ago, Stuart Proffitt OU helped me to structure the proposal for its publisher. At Uppingham School Richard Harman (headmaster) and Stephen Taylor (bursar), have given me both moral and practical support.

Three people have given me particular support in bringing this project to fruition. Malcolm Tozer's Ph.D. thesis 'Manliness: The Evolution of a Victorian Ideal', his book *Physical Education at Thring's Uppingham* (1976) and his journal articles helped me a great deal. He has been a generous-spirited critic: unstinting with his time in commenting on my first draft; setting the record straight on Thring's views on games and philathleticism, and increasing my knowledge of Thring's curriculum and his preaching. No one could have been more patient and accommodating than Jerry Rudman, the Uppingham School archivist, who played the major role in assembling the illustrations. I have also been highly fortunate in having Christopher Woodhead, of the University of Buckingham Press, as an expert, calm and ever-encouraging editor and mentor.

I am also very grateful to the following: John Thring (descended from Godfrey Thring) and Sue Kalaugher (descended from Charles Thring) over family matters; Sally Rotheray (Ben Place, Ambleside) in my pursuit of the Thrings in the Lake District; Peter Attenborough, David Fotheringham (Highgate School) and Stephen Kern (the Perse School, Cambridge) for advice on classical issues; John Hodgkinson in connection with his ancestor; Peter Colville for perspectives on Uppingham since 1945; Sarah and the late Colin Forsyth for help over local buildings.

There has been valuable advice from further afield: in Canada, from Terry Cook and William Christian with their expertise on Thring's friendship with George Parkin, and Robert Fisher (Library and Archives Canada, Ottawa) who provided information about the Parkin archive; at Glenalmond, from Elaine Mundill in response to my enquiries about John Skrine; at Westminster School, Connecticut, from Douglas Allen as I traced Thring's transatlantic influence; from Christopher Bearman OU who gave me advice on Uppingham's musical significance.

In Cambridge I have been guided by Christine Corton, Peter Cunningham, Kenneth Edwards, Simon Goldhill, Patricia McGuire

(King's College archivist), Anne Thomson (Newnham College archivist) and the ever-helpful staff at the Cambridge University Library. Other sources of advice have included: at Eton, Penny Hatfield (archivist); at the University of Buckingham, John Clarke; at the London University Institute of Education, Gary McCulloch; at HMC, successive general secretaries Vivian Anthony, Geoff Lucas and William Richardson, and chairman Tim Hands. I have been fortunate in the patience of staff in record offices in Aberystwyth, Gloucester, Leicester, Northampton and Taunton. Karen Gibson helped me in the early stages by scanning key documents.

I owe particular debts of gratitude too to the late Cormac Rigby, for reasons explained in the introduction, and to my wife, Joy Richardson, who helped me to transcribe many of the documents in the Parkin archive in Ottawa; to assess Thring's legacy to the education of primary-age children, and to refine my text in its later stages. For much of her thirteen-year period as a member of a body which caused Thring so much difficulty, the trustees of Uppingham School, she has also had to live vicariously with Thring and his family.

Nigel Richardson
Harston, Cambridge,
February 2014

AUTHOR'S NOTES

Footnotes and sources

Footnotes are explanations of the text rather than a detailed guide to sources. A select bibliography appears at the end of the book. The Uppingham School archive also holds a working draft of the text, annotated with much more extensive footnotes and sources.

Financial figures

For ease of reading, many of the figures quoted are approximate, or are expressed as percentages rather than in numbers of £s.

English coinage in Thring's time was divided into pounds (£), shillings (s) and pence (d): there were 20 shillings to the pound and 12 pence to the shilling – expressed as (e.g.) £12.4s.8d.

Comparing the prices and wages of 130 years ago with those of today is much more complex than it might seem. Price rises vary so much from item to item that attempts to make overall comparisons are almost meaningless. Nevertheless it may be helpful to assume that £1 in Thring's time equates *very* approximately to between £90 and £100 at today's values (based on figures produced by the Office for National Statistics).

It is also hard even to compare figures between different years within Thring's own time because of incomplete documentation; his frequent shifts of ground about how costs should be categorised, and changes made to various fees and charges – especially during his final decade.

Uppingham: governors and trustees

Thring's employers were known as 'governors' at the time of his arrival in Uppingham, and remained so until the New Scheme for the school was introduced in the early 1870s, at which point they became known 'trustees'. I have designated them accordingly.

Distances

A kilometre is approximately five-eighths of a British mile. As a rough guide, distances quoted in miles should therefore be doubled in any conversion to kilometres.

THE THRING FAMILY TREE

INTRODUCTION

WHEN Edward Thring died in October 1887 the *Pall Mall Gazette* described him as 'a man of striking gifts and singular strength and separateness of character: the ablest and most original educationalist since Arnold; a great schoolmaster and a born leader of men'. Twelve years after Arnold left Rugby, and only thirty miles away, in 1853 Thring began his 34 years in Uppingham, a little-known market town in England's East Midlands. There he used his 'singular strength' to transform its small three-hundred-year-old grammar school into a large boarding school with a national reputation.

Arnold is still revered as the most influential headmaster of his day, but for over a century Thring's life and legacy have received little attention beyond his immediate locality. This relative obscurity is surprising. Beyond Uppingham Thring challenged the prevailing educational ideas of the post-Arnold generation, becoming 'the man who most determined the shape of things to come' as he set the tone for many of the new or re-founded schools catering for the sons of the expanding middle class.[1] During the 1860s and 70s he fought local and national government over educational and public health matters and he became the founding father of the Headmasters' Conference of leading British independent schools (HMC).

'Educator' might seem a strange word for Thring but his friends used it to describe him: 'No one was ever more convinced than Thring that he was an honest educator doing God's work'. He used it himself to denote the best type of teacher in two books on which he brought the *Gazette's* 'striking gifts' to bear: *Education and School* (1864) which outlined his guiding principles for boarding schools, and *Theory and Practice of Teaching* (1883) which showed teachers how to develop child-centred teaching by recognising the world as young minds saw it, rather than merely lecturing pupils or 'hammering' information into them.

In his final decade his writings, speeches and letters touched many lives: friends, former pupils and, more widely, teachers on several continents. An obituarist in the *Guardian* declared that his ideas acted as 'life-giving rain which seeped underground and ran through hidden channels to emerge in fresh and revivifying channels elsewhere'. The

---

[1] Newsome, David: *Godliness and Good Learning: Four Studies on a Victorian Ideal* (1961), pp. 220-1. Newsome (1929-2004) was a Fellow of Emmanuel College, Cambridge and later headmaster of Christ's Hospital and Master of Wellington.

organising committee for his memorial included the Archbishop of Canterbury and three bishops; peers, masters of Oxford and Cambridge colleges, headmasters from the best-known schools and, significantly, both the most celebrated headmistresses of his day.

Thring embarked on his career at a propitious time. Mid-Victorian Britain was buoyant with economic and social optimism: its expanding empire and innovative entrepreneurship proclaimed by the Great Exhibition of 1851. Large cities, factories and railways were transforming the landscape, as imaginative, energetic individuals from Brunel to Pugin created visible symbols of Victorian confidence. Major advances in science, public health, and social reform resulted from the work of men such as Charles Darwin, Joseph Bazalgette and William Booth. Thanks to new railways, boarding schools drew pupils from a wide area as the new professional and business classes became socially and educationally ambitious for their children, recognising the need to prepare them for the new world order.

Uppingham was an untypical Victorian boarding school insofar as Thring re-fashioned it without any famous sponsors or corporate backers. He had limited capital of his own and he received scant help from his governors who were sometimes deeply hostile. His dogged determination to go it alone, recruiting housemasters to build their own houses as satellite enterprises with their own feeding arrangements, resulted in his school being more geographically dispersed around its local town and less administratively centralised than many of its counterparts. Ultimately he would pay a high price for this independence, but he was impelled through every setback by the unswerving conviction that he was doing God's work.

****

Casting his eye over his colleagues at the inaugural meeting of the Headmasters' Conference in Uppingham in 1869, Thring noted their 'superior style'.[1] According to historian David Newsome, 'the nineteenth century headmaster is now almost a legend: a symbol of an educational system that has passed away... a Titan in an age of Titans: undisputed monarch of his kingdom, spiritual leader of his flock, mentor and chastiser of his charges, feared and respected by governors, parents, masters and

---

[1] Alicia Percival adapted this phrase for the title of *Very Superior Men: Some Early Public School Headmasters and Their Achievements* (1973). She also wrote *The Origins of the Headmasters' Conference* (1969).

pupils alike. We shall not see his like again'.[1] However, few of these Titans went on to become household names except Arnold (who died in 1842, only five years into the new Queen's reign) and W E Forster, architect of the great Education Act of 1870. This fact has prompted other writers to see the headmasters rather less flatteringly. For one, the shortage of biographies of these Victorian school leaders merely confirms their limitations and their obscurity: 'Remove them from the exaggerating memories of the tiny subjects in their kingdoms (i.e. their Old Boys) – and how they dwindle' – although he conceded that two of them (Temple of Rugby and Benson of Wellington) went on to be Archbishops of Canterbury, but 'for the rest, have we ever heard of them?'[2]

This negative view ignores the fact that the Victorian headmasters were part of a distinguished and diverse network of individuals and ideas. The ancient-world values that they represented re-emerged in the Victorian concept of true manliness which they sought to instil in their boys. Arnold, Benson, F W Farrar at Marlborough, Temple, Thring and many others shared a strong admiration for Plato's notions about the ideal state and the virtues required by the capable and unselfish citizen – and a desire to recreate these qualities in their pupils. They saw that happiness was the reward of virtue; that it consisted in the good use of one's talents; that the well-being of a man's soul depended on the quality of the society in which he lived and that education was the means to improve it. They were also steeped in the romantic writings of Coleridge and Wordsworth, Tennyson and Sir Walter Scott.

Many provided a curriculum still dominated by classics, but while this might stimulate the high-flyer it often did little for the average or struggling boy. Thring was committed to classical languages as the curricular corner-stone, but he added a huge range of subjects and activities alongside them, determined to help every boy to build his self-confidence by doing *something* well.

The headmasters' convictions were shared by men in a range of other fields: Thomas Hughes (who helped to perpetuate Arnold's memory and reputation through his novel *Tom Brown's Schooldays);* Charles Kingsley (clergyman, academic and author of *The Water Babies*, as well as a friend of Charles Darwin); F D Maurice (theologian and Christian socialist); Daniel and Alexander Macmillan (publishers, whose authors included Kingsley) and John Ruskin (artist, critic, social thinker and philanthropist). Their reading of each others' work; their overlapping friendships; their mutual god-children; their love of nature and especially

---

[1] Newsome, David: *A History of Wellington College* (1959) p.15.

[2] Gathorne Hardy, Jonathan: *The Public School Phenomenon* (1977), p.86.

of the Lake District all sustained them and many others across several decades.

Thring met Ruskin only once, but he frequently acknowledged the artist's influence and his enthusiasm for the teaching power of art and other visual images. This impelled Thring to display portraits of heroes and scenes from ancient life all around his school. His contemporaries at Eton included William Cory, another Romantic poet deeply influenced in his social views by F D Maurice. It was Maurice and the Macmillans who persuaded two young Cambridge men, William Witts (Thring's near-contemporary at Eton and King's and later an Uppingham housemaster) and Harvey Goodwin (later Dean of Ely and Bishop of Carlisle and an enthusiastic Uppingham parent) to spend their early careers working in a deprived area of Cambridge.

The Macmillans also had much to do with Thring's decision to embark on the curacy in the Gloucester docks which helped to shape his subsequent life. Their circle included Kingsley, of whom it has been said that 'if [he] had been a headmaster, he would have taught his boys to jump five-barred gates, to climb trees, to run like hares over difficult country; and there would have been nature rambles, a school museum stocked with specimens collected by the boys, science lessons and occasional lectures on hygiene and drains'.[1] This description of what Kingsley *might* have been and done is remarkably close to what Thring actually was and did, and it helps to explain how Thring became a friend for over twenty years of Kingsley's wife, to whom (amongst others) he owed the concern for women's education that he developed in the final decade of his life.

Moulded by others, the Victorian headmasters became formative influences in their pupils' lives. Their schools were distinctive communities with influential housemasters (a role that Thring combined with being headmaster) and pupil hierarchies led by prefects and captains of games. Institutionally they shaped the cultural and moral attitudes and the leadership styles of several generations of boys who went on to hold high positions in state, church, business, the law, the press and the armed forces right through to the early 1960s - including prime ministers such as Churchill (Harrow), Attlee (Haileybury) and Macmillan (Eton). Thring's love of Grasmere led his godson and pupil, Hardie Rawnsley, to become a founding figure in the National Trust, and his interest in the moral and educational possibilities of Empire did much to impel a young Canadian headmaster, George Parkin, to spend his later years developing the Rhodes Trust scholarship scheme and Rhodes House in Oxford.

---

[1] Newsome: *Godliness* p.211. Temple did in fact climb the trees in the Close at Rugby, to check their safety for the boys.

Within the schools, the chapel, usually presided over by the headmaster, was a focal point. More than in most comparable institutions, Uppingham pupils' future careers were shaped by what they learned in chapel – and by the pioneering Mission that Thring established in the East End of London. Other schools followed: Attlee, the founder of the modern welfare state, spent three years working with the Haileybury Boys' Club and as manager of Haileybury House in Stepney (1906-9), an experience which he never forgot. Many pupils of the late Victorian era were sustained by their chapel experiences as they mourned sons who perished on the battlefields of the Great War, where Uppingham's dead included the brother and the fiancé of Vera Brittain, author of *Testament of Youth*.

****

In an article in the *British Journal of Educational Studies* in 1984, Robert Protherough echoed Newsome's description of the Victorian headmasters in his analysis of their stereotypes in fictional literature: 'Majestic figures, creating a godlike effect of awe and terror, outsize in terms of physique and personality, and separated from ordinary mortals by their powers of speech and by a special rhetorical style... never seen except in academic cap and gown... with little humour or light touch'. There were stereotypical adjectives too: 'dignified', 'grave', 'stern', and 'impressive'. Protherough contrasted this fictional picture with the reality: many of the Victorian headmasters were not only highly energetic, but also liberal, witty, reformist, progressive, kindly and understanding. [1]

Thring differed from the factual and fictional stereotypes in just as many ways as he conformed to them – not least in his modest height. The 'separateness of character' identified by the *Pall Mall Gazette* reflected the fact that he was a man of great contrasts. His weaknesses are as interesting as his strengths. At his best he was warm, full of fun, confident and inspirational. In his energy, vision and conviction of God's special calling, he exemplified the Victorian ideal. Yet he could also be angry, abrasive, autocratic and pessimistic – even paranoid – towards those who disagreed with him. He suffered from anxiety throughout his adult life

---

[1] Protherough, Robert: 'Shaping the Image of the Great Headmaster', *British Journal of Educational Studies* Vol. XXXII No 3 October 1984. He studied twenty school novels, including *Fathers of Men* (1912), E W Hornung's novel based on Uppingham. See also the description of a typical headmaster in Hay, Ian: *The Lighter Side of School Life* (1914): 'An Olympian, having none of the foibles or soft moments of a human being, he dwells apart, in an atmosphere too rarefied for those who intrude into it'.

which made him vulnerable, sometimes aggressive, yet also sensitive to the fears of others. He often infuriated his staff but in his greatest hours of need they gave him their unqualified support.

Although educated at Eton and Cambridge he was more homespun in speech and attitudes than many of his professional contemporaries, who were sometimes amused by his eccentricities. In one sense he was child-like, blessed with a greater empathy with young minds than most of his fellow-headmasters: 'King of Boys' to one former pupil and colleague and 'thoroughly a boy in all his feelings' to another. Yet he also had childish limitations: petulance and impatience. If he had been allowed to take Cambridge degree examinations they would have confirmed his academic ability. However, his intellectual curiosity was selective and patchy. He could be diffuse and eclectic in his writing and he tended to dismiss or sidestep new ideas which caused him to feel threatened.

His preoccupation with action rather than abstraction reflected the large range of skills that his role demanded. Victorian headmasters had to be hugely versatile and sometimes daringly entrepreneurial. Technical expertise and support – for finance, administration, communication, recruitment and building development – was in short supply. In our own time school headship has been described as 'a cross between an accountant, lawyer, fundraiser, jailer, PR expert, punchbag and Butlin's redcoat', demanding the skills of a 'commander, counsellor, academic, judge, ambassador, mentor, dinner-lady, manager, performer, accountant and workaholic'.[1] For Thring and his headmaster-colleagues it is an equally apt description: they needed to be exceptional leaders and managers.

****

The Victorians mourned their leaders with lengthy, effusive tributes and much of what we know about Thring comes from what was written by friends in the period immediately after his death.[2] This biography uses their memories – and Thring's own words – extensively. It is primarily an account of his life, ideas and influence rather than a history of his school.

---

[1] The first description was by Professor Ted Wragg. The second appeared in a *Times 2* article: 29 March 2007.

[2] Goldhill, Simon: *Victorian Culture and Classical Antiquity: art, opera, fiction, and the proclamation of modernity* (2011) p.246: 'The two-volume 'Life and Letters' became a particularly prevalent Victorian production. Usually written by somebody close to the subject... [it was] nearly always written with an air of pious celebration... the public recognition of the significance of the life...'

It includes the first attempt to explain Thring's personal finances, and how it was that his wife and children inherited so little, despite the fact that his combined sources of income may have amounted to £450,000 per year (at modern values) in his final decade.

Limitations of space preclude deconstruction of his poetry or his sermons, whose convolutions and challenging handwriting are not for the faint-hearted, or a lengthy comparison between Thring and Arnold. Those seeking further examples of Thring's vivid maxims and aphorisms may refer to his books or to Sir George Parkin's two-volume selection of his diaries, letters and speeches published in 1898: the only previously published survey of Thring's life.[1]

Parkin enjoyed a 35-year correspondence from Canada not only with Thring himself but with his wife and daughters, his younger son and three of his brothers. Parkin omitted virtually all of these personal letters from his books, and they were eventually lodged with his own papers in the Canadian National Archive in Ottawa. They reveal much that was previously little-known about the family's domestic life in term time and on holiday.

Because most of Thring's original diaries were destroyed, modern writers travel in Parkin's footsteps – and those of three rival writers: J H Skrine and the brothers W F and H D Rawnsley, all of whom published memories of him between 1890 and 1926. Twenty years later (1946) Geoffrey Hoyland, a preparatory school headmaster, produced a brief narrative, hard on the heels of the momentous 1944 Education Act. Hoyland asserted that 'the ideals of our greatest Victorian schoolmaster are well worth reconsidering'; he was able to talk to some of Thring's surviving pupils and his book is insightful in parts despite its cloying sentimentality.[2]

By the time Cormac Rigby began work on his Oxford D.Phil. thesis 'The Life and Influence of Edward Thring' (1968), only a handful of Thring's pupils were still alive. Rigby expanded his research over the next two decades as he rose to be chief announcer on BBC Radio 3 before becoming a catholic priest in the mid-1980s. He intended to title his biography of Thring *The Teacher's Teacher* but he never completed it, leaving behind a substantial unpublished manuscript when he died in

---

[1] Parkin, G R, (ed): *Edward Thring, Headmaster of Uppingham School: Life, Diary and Letters* 2 vols. (1898). See ch. 22 for details.

[2] Hoyland, Geoffrey: *The Man who made a School: Thring of Uppingham* (1946).

2007.[1] All writers about Thring since the 1960s have been influenced by Rigby's work: examples include Malcolm Tozer, an expert on Thring's contribution to physical education and on how he stood out against the harsher version of Victorian manliness which emerged in the decades leading up to the Great War;[2] Bryan Matthews, who included two learned chapters summarising Thring's life and career in a history of Uppingham School entitled *By God's Grace* which he wrote for its quatercentenary in 1984, and Donald Leinster-Mackay, who wrote a study of Thring in 1987 to mark the centenary of his death.[3]

Above all, Rigby was very generous with his time and advice, and it was his express wish that his research should be used after his death. Sadly he did not live to be this book's critical friend, but it draws extensively on his work.[4] It is also dedicated to his memory.

---

[1] Unlike Parkin, Rigby studied Thring's sermons in some detail. A tribute at Rigby's funeral suggested mischievously that 'some might think that he had served his purgatory rather early' in this respect.

[2] Tozer, Malcolm: *Physical Education at Thring's Uppingham* (1976). See bibliography for Ph.D. thesis and other publications.

[3] Leinster-Mackay, Donald: *The Educational World of Edward Thring: A Centenary Study* (1987).

[4] Particularly for details about his early life, his sermons and his interest in music.

CHAPTER ONE

ALFORD, ILMINSTER AND ETON

IN March 1871 Edward Thring spent a weekend at Harrow School, then still in the country some miles out of London. At the height of his powers, he was the guest of its Head Master, Montagu Butler, who (like him) was something of a boyish enthusiast.[1] After a halcyon weekend spent catching up with old friends and crowned by news of a major university award for one of his pupils, he returned home full of it all.

During his visit Thring preached at evensong in the chapel, greatly enjoying the 'hearty singing' which preceded his sermon. Alas, the young Harrovians were less impressed: they regarded their own school as famous and long-established, and Uppingham as something of an upstart. As a result, although not always their own Head Master's greatest admirers, they quickly decided that he was superior in every respect to his visitor. Taking against the rustic tone of Thring's voice and the way in which he 'bellowed out with such vigour' his text from Psalm 78 ('He chose David his servant, and took him from the sheepfolds'), they immediately nicknamed him 'Old Sheepfolds'.

The incident reveals two aspects of Thring. He was not always sensitive to how others reacted to his passionate manner, and he was a quintessential countryman.

The second of these is unsurprising, for the Thrings were originally a Wiltshire family. John Thring, Edward's grandfather and a successful lawyer, moved to East Somerset in 1807 on buying Alford House, a fine property with a wooded and agricultural estate which included the fifteenth-century church in which he is commemorated. Edward's father, known as John Gale (Thring), went from Winchester College to Cambridge University, where he was a contemporary of Palmerston at St John's. He was ordained priest in 1808, and promptly installed as Rector

---

[1] According to Christopher Tyerman's *A History of Harrow School* (2,000) pp. 304-5, 'Butler never really grew up... a puppyish naive enthusiasm for interests shared by the young rendered him a powerful force'. The description is strikingly similar to the description of Thring as 'King of Boys'.

of Alford, a good living consolidated with the adjoining parish of Hornblotton in 1836 which he held for well over fifty years.[1]

In 1811 John Gale married Sarah, the second daughter of the Revd. John Jenkyns, Vicar of nearby Evercreech. She spent almost her entire life thereafter in one spot, devoting much of her later years to planting cedars, yews and shrubs around her house and church, but her siblings all became significant figures in Oxford. Her sister married the Dean of Christ Church; one brother was Master of Balliol and Vice Chancellor (and later returned to Somerset as Dean of Wells); another became a Fellow of Oriel.

Edward, the fifth of the seven Thring children, was born on 29 November 1821, after Theresa (1815), Theodore (1816), Henry (1818)[2] and Elizabeth (1819), but ahead of Godfrey (1823), known as 'Goo' because his father called him a 'silly goose' when he kept falling off his horse as child, and John Charles, usually called Charles or Charlie (1824). For Edward's first nine years the family lived in the Old Manor House, known as 'The Cottage', but when his father became squire and inherited most of the Alford estate, they moved into Alford House.

The parish was situated ten miles south of the Mendip hills in an area deep in history – including Cadbury castle with its overtones of King Arthur's Camelot, and the route of the Roman Fosse Way at Ilchester. It consisted of only 722 acres, with seven farms and a dozen cottages, and its population varied between 100 and 150, mostly employed on good arable and pasture land. Castle Cary was two miles away with a population of 1600, a weekly market and a daily coach service to London.

John Gale was a sound classical scholar, a county magistrate and a man said to be the best and boldest horseman in Somerset: no mean accolade in a strong hunting county. However, Alford was too small a stage for him, and he was not an easy acquaintance. Villagers fled for their houses when he walked down the street. When a curate came to dine and admitted that he did not know how to play whist, his carriage was summoned forthwith. To his children, John Gale could seem formidably grim, and in describing life at Alford as 'just, but hard', friends suggested that it was only the boys' religious upbringing with its strong sense of respect for authority – reinforced, no doubt, through their father's weekly sermons – that prevented them from challenging his overbearing manner.

[1] The estate comprised over 700 acres in the parish of Alford, but several thousand more in neighbouring Hornblotton, Lovington and Charlton Adam.
[2] An earlier son also named Henry was born in 1817 but lived for only a few months.

John Gale's marriage was an attraction of opposites. While Edward inherited some of his father's autocratic traits, his more tender side came entirely from his gentle, unassuming mother. He admired her faith and her saintly inner strength; she acted as the go-between for the children with their father in his more difficult moods. She bequeathed to him a life-long love of the psalms, and he rarely spoke of her without a quiver in his voice. She also encouraged her third son's love of reading. A visiting neighbour found him one day, aged six or seven, lying on the floor in the library and completely absorbed in a huge volume of Indian history. When it was suggested that perhaps he should not be reading an adult book, Sarah replied that any book which awakened such deep interest was suitable for a child. He often said later that his most vivid conceptions of India were gained from reading it.

He also had a great love of the outdoor life. The mill (mentioned in the Domesday Book) was on the banks of the river Brue, which he recalled whimsically in later life: 'Companion of my boyhood, my manhood's living friend, I fain would know thy rising, I fain would know thy end'. He took from it one of his favourite metaphors: 'The stream makes music as it ripples over its hindrances; the pebbles bring out its music'. Among Alford's elms and apple orchards, dogs and horses, fields and lanes, Edward, Godfrey and Charles developed a deep affinity with nature as they sent ferrets after rabbits, fished, travelled down the river in makeshift coracles, and occasionally shot birds which they stuffed and preserved. The trio also saw plenty of their cousins, the Hobhouse boys at nearby Hadspen House: Henry (ten years older than Edward),[1] Edmund and Arthur. Their ties were close – although in adult life Edward (Thring) and Arthur (Hobhouse) would find themselves on opposite sides in one of the great educational controversies of the day.[2]

These experiences were deeply formative influences for the young Thring. 'You cannot think', he wrote to his mother, at the age of 59 and at a difficult time in his life, 'how [much] my feelings are bound up in Alford – so much that I can never allow myself to dwell on the dream of those old days. I could not bear it here with the incessant battle of life'. His childhood also gave him an appreciation of something which was to be his watchword in education and his consolation in times of trouble: the notion of *True Life*: 'the sight of life everywhere: the rush of life in the trees and the grass. That is a wonderful comfort: that thought'. He remembered it all as 'a boyhood gemmed with flowers'.

---

[1] In 1826 Henry Hobhouse left Eton; he was subsequently taught at Laleham by young Dr. Thomas Arnold.
[2] See chs. 8 and 9.

3

****

Although John Gale taught Theodore and Henry at home until they were thirteen, in 1829 he sent eight-year-old Edward as a boarder to Ilminster Grammar School sixteen miles away – possibly because his third son already showed a strong independence of mind. The school dated from 1550 and its motto was *Learninge gaineth Honor*. The Revd. John Allen, himself the son of a headmaster, had entered Christ Church, Oxford aged 15, taking a First in mathematics and starting to teach at the age of 22. He had been running the school for seven years when Thring arrived, and its reputation was growing. Numbers reached 85 (71 boarders, 13 free scholars and one fee-paying day boy) by 1831. Allen provided better washing facilities, a playground and – as a believer in exercise – a games field. He urged his governors to support subjects which went well beyond the traditional classical curriculum: Hebrew; 'some continental language'; science, mechanics and mathematics; natural history and natural philosophy.

Despite his success, Allen's pupils had conflicting memories of him. Some remembered his engaging manner and fine tenor voice. His predecessor entrusted his own son to him, and Henry Alford, later Dean of Canterbury, became his 'ever attached friend and pupil', dedicating a learned book 'in grateful recollection of the happy time spent in acquiring under him the first knowledge of the [Greek] poets'. However, Thomas Baker, a day boy in Thring's time, remembered Allen as 'a small man, a very sprig of conceit... a most self-satisfied, important little person, and exceedingly severe in his discipline', and the school for its parrot-learning rather than any educational originality: 'Going to school meant terror, and escape was elysium'.

C Kegan Paul, later to found a famous publishing house, agreed: 'Allen and his wife were the least fitted to train the young... we children were never helped to learn for ourselves; we never heard a word of kindness or encouragement; [there were] furious floggings for the majority, the grossest favouritism for the few'. In old age Paul retained graphic memories of the little cupboard containing the canes, which was opened by a spring mechanism operated from Allen's desk. There were canings on most days, and Allen 'flogged till he was tired, and then locked the boy in for an hour or two to recover as best he might'. Mrs. Allen helped her husband with some of the teaching, but Paul remembered her as hard and coarse, with 'no grain of motherly kindness'; he was always cold and the food was bad. One of his contemporaries claimed that his only pleasurable time at the school was when he was allowed to go to bed.

4

Fortunately for Thring, he was one of Allen's favourites, partly because what his fellow-pupils called his 'fondness for acting the schoolmaster' impelled him to get small groups of younger boys together for impromptu lunchtime coaching, thus reducing Allen's workload. Even so, it was a far cry from the freedom of Alford. Over fifty years later (1881), Thring became very emotional on hearing that a pupil, convalescing from illness at home, had burst into tears because he could not return to Uppingham with his brothers. It seemed to confirm the school's humanity: 'Something worth living for, when I think what bitter tears I shed at having to go back at his age'. He also tearfully recalled envying a little chimney sweep walking past Ilminster's boarding house because the boy did not have to go to school.

Even late in life Thring puzzled over Ilminster's 'light-hearted liberty gone, and a prison in exchange... full of blind fears, daily task-work, sharp and constant checks', but he accepted that the Allens had meant well, however misguided their methods. Mrs. Allen continued to take an interest in his work for forty years, and he sent her a book of Uppingham photographs in the 1870s via a friend, commenting that 'both she and her husband worked very hard and never spared themselves, [although] the school was dreadfully mistaken'. However, nothing could wipe out the bitter recollections, and in the last year of his life he told a friend, as they travelled along the Ilminster road, that his time with Allen still gave him feelings of dread: 'It was my memories of that school and its severities which first made me long to try if I could to make the life of small boys at school happier and brighter'.

In his presidential address to the Education Society in 1885 he looked back on Ilminster as 'an old-fashioned private school of the flog-flog, milk-and-water-at-breakfast type'. He saw its 'prim misery [as] the misery of a clipped hedge, with every clip through flesh and blood and fresh young feelings; its snatches of joy, its painful but honest work... and its prison morality of discipline'. It had taught him that suspicion and severity were no basis on which to run a school, and that a teacher must 'get inside the boy-world'. He never stopped believing that there was a better way than the Allens' unimaginative preoccupation with conformity and order, and this image of the clipped hedge shaped his teaching life:

'It is doubtless a fascinating sight to some people to see a charming uniformity, a trim perfection... It is a pleasanter, at least a less vexatious life, for the master to clip the boys to a pattern, and never allow a bramble to be seen, than to trust to growth, to let the brambles grow too, and then pull them out as they appear; for this makes the fingers bleed; it makes the heart bleed, and the lookers-on scoff, but the work once done, [it] is done'.

5

****

If Ilminster had been a clipped hedge, Eton College under the notorious Dr. John Keate was a wilderness of near-anarchy. Thring began his nine years there in September 1832, two months before his eleventh birthday: three years behind Theodore and two years before Keate was finally forced out. Although Thring was spared some of Eton's worst excesses (and appears to have played no part in them, either), he could not avoid its prevailing atmosphere. Even if he saw it only through young eyes, memories of its deficiencies would shape his adult life.

Situated across the Thames from Windsor Castle and founded by King Henry VI in 1449, the famous school had close links with the monarchy, and a significant proportion of its boys came from families of the aristocracy. Boys entered aged 10-13 and were placed in one of three divisions (forms) of twenty or so in the Lower School. Progression could be rapid for the successful, but others were merely left to struggle: the masters had little understanding of how to teach boys so young, and they valued flair more highly than diligence. Pupils too showed contempt of any boy 'who surpasses the rest, and beats the boy of superior talents, by sheer labour and poring over his books'. At 13+ the divisions were swelled by new recruits, from which an elite dozen or so each year eventually graduated into the sixth form – but only as spaces became available.

Latin and Greek predominated, although wealthier families could pay extra for lessons in French, drawing and science. Younger boys might have only twenty lessons (schools) per week, and many of their free periods were spent doing Latin verse composition in masters' houses. Periodically their work was 'called up' (tested) in school, but the classes were so large that this took place only spasmodically. There were also tutorial periods known as 'private business': these took place either one-to-one or in small groups, but tutors varied greatly in their effectiveness.

Otherwise there were vast swathes of free time. Official activities included team sports, river swimming and boating, and the famous Wall Game. There were unofficial pastimes, too: hunting, fist fighting, night-time poaching, and hare coursing in Windsor Park. The boarding houses were widely scattered: boys passing through the town to lessons and games faced the temptations of nearly a dozen inns, a workshop making clay pipes, three gunsmiths and various billiards and betting establishments. Unsurprisingly, the boys' behaviour was distinctly free-range. They frequently passed the time at chapel services by noisily consuming food or releasing rats.

6

These problems had accumulated over many years. The supine Joseph Goodall (Head Master 1802-9) adopted a blind-eye policy - even when pupils ended up in jail. When floods swept away a local bridge, he left boys to their own devices in their houses for five days. Keate (1809-34), a man whose unprepossessing appearance and demeanour made him a figure of fun, inherited a school with only eight assistant masters for 500 pupils, and he gave unquestioning support to weaker masters while ignoring the wayward behaviour of their more robust and maverick colleagues.[1] His dealings with pupils mixed blind-eye tactics with large-scale floggings for issues which could not be evaded. Stories about his injustices and mistakes abound: he once flogged a group of boys sent to him not for punishment but for confirmation preparation. Initially he was surprisingly popular, perhaps because (as one former pupil believed) 'he had no favourites, and flogged the son of a duke and the son of a grocer with perfect impartiality'.

Eventually, however, the boys came to resent his inconsistency and heavy-handedness. As he steadily lost control, a war of attrition developed: the boys started hissing him and setting booby traps, so the floggings increased. He survived several full-scale rebellions and the scandal surrounding a pupil's death in a fight in 1825, but in 1834 he was finally driven out, exhausted, after a campaign by hostile parents. His successor, Edward Hawtrey (1834-53) was generally respected by the boys because he was more inclined to see their successes than their failures, and was prepared to admit his own mistakes. He gradually embarked on a reform programme but most of it would take place only after Thring's time.[2]

Thring was intelligent and academically inclined – and fortunate to be tutored by two conscientious men: first James Chapman (an Old Etonian, and previously tutor to his brother Theodore), and later Charles Goodford. Chapman found Thring bright and positive, reporting after a year that 'the little fellow goes on well, but is not quite so steady at any but his poetical work as I would wish'. The following year he wrote again: 'The little fellow goes on capitally. He is a sharp, clear-headed, good little boy, and will, I hope, turn out a tasteful and correct scholar'. In 1834: 'Since I last

---

[1] Keate was expected to teach all two hundred Upper School boys in one room. The house masters strongly resisted any attempts to restrict the number in houses to 24 as it would reduce their profits. Any additional assistant masters would mean fewer tutorial pupils for each and therefore less income.

[2] Hawtrey had been a pupil in 1799 and a master since 1814. Changes were only possible when the conservative Joseph Goodall ceased to be Provost (chairman of the governors) in 1840.

wrote little Edward has been doing well on all points, and has secured his reward'.

Thring spent his first three years as an Oppidan. Over the years Henry VI's original 70 scholars (known as Collegers), living in Long Chamber and fed in their own dining hall, had been joined by a larger number of fee-paying boys (Oppidans), living in dozens of houses run by assistant masters and local ladies (known as Dames) all over the town.

The Collegers in Thring's day were not yet the academic elite: they gained places in College by nomination. College status bestowed two advantages: a free education at Eton and an automatic passport afterwards to Cambridge as a scholar of King's College and possibly later a Fellow. Thring joined their ranks at the age of 14, reluctantly. Despite its material advantages, College was seldom full, because its conditions were so tough, and its discipline so uncontrolled, that many parents transferred their sons into it from other houses only at the last moment possible to secure entry to King's.

Whereas most Oppidans had a small room, which a brother might share, and their food was generally reasonable, Collegers' living conditions had been allowed to deteriorate over many years. There was no supervision between lock-up around 8pm and early school next morning. Hungry pupils bought extra food – and illicit drink – each evening from a tradesman hawking them outside a grated window. They had no privacy: 'Long Chamber', the huge, draughty four-chamber dormitory, had windows high up, many broken. It was infested with rats, which the boys trapped in stockings and then banged to death against the bedposts. Beds were in short supply, so junior boys slept on the floor – and rarely washed because sixth formers monopolised the few basins. There were limited numbers of desks and chairs, forcing some boys to wait until others were in bed before settling down to work, or to compete for spaces in the damp tower or in one of eight cupboards: large but cold, for which 'rent' had to be paid to older boys. More affluent boys (Thring included) paid for breakfast, study and washing facilities in local houses. Again the authorities turned a blind eye.

All the younger boys were expected to fag for their seniors.[1] Thring seems to have been fortunate in this, because his fagmaster was his

---

[1] Fagging (younger boys doing menial tasks for older ones) was especially severe in College. They made beds, fetched water and coal, and did many other tasks for senior boys. Those told to break bounds to procure forbidden alcohol for their seniors were ignored when they told masters about this after being caught. 'Cricket fagging', which Thring strongly disliked, involved fetching cricket balls hit by batsmen during practice to points all round the boundary. One local journal

8

Somerset cousin, Arthur Hobhouse. He kept his head down and got on with everyday life, avoiding the worst of the bullying and Long Chamber's fearsome initiation rites. The Collegers called him 'Quilp', claiming that in his diminutive height he resembled the character in Charles Dickens' *The Old Curiosity Shop*.[1] He kept two tadpoles as pets, trying to train them to move small quantities of water around their cage.

Friends later remembered with amusement his extreme self-confidence and honesty – and that while he loved teasing other boys, he never bullied them. One described him as 'sturdy – in build, in mind, in principle, in fidelity, in antagonism to all that was wrong and false'. If his sense of justice was offended, he stood his ground. When he once accidentally hurt another boy, the victim unleashed a stream of invective, and then threatened to complain to Thring's tutor. 'No', replied Thring, 'you have had your flings at me, and I deserved it. But you have no right to go further. This is quite enough, and now we must part friends'. A witness recalled: 'So the matter was made up. I never knew anyone more heroic in his courage, or more skilful and judgmatical (sic) in giving effect to that courage'.

He did not win a place in the first cricket team, but in this and other sports (notably football and fives)[2] his bravery made up for any lack of skill and height: 'He would take on all-comers, however good they might be, and he was seldom beaten'. Boys had to rush to claim the few fives courts available. Once when he got one, a much larger bully began to 'persuade' him to give way by kicking and punching him. Nothing daunted, Thring yelled out 'I'll die first' and refused to move. The nickname 'Little Die First' then stuck to him throughout his schooldays.

He had a strong sense of fun. Boys often sat on a favourite wall, flicking hard pellets of kneaded bread with finger and thumb at people passing by. He once tried it from his own room, targeting the open window next door, where its owner, a solicitor with a fiery temper, was sitting at his desk. Eventually the man stormed over to the house and demanded to see the culprit. Upstairs he found Thring, 'a model of

---

claimed that inmates of the local jail or workhouse were treated better than boys in Long Chamber: on average one boy died per year.

[1] Daniel Quilp was an evil hunchbacked moneylender.

[2] Eton Fives: a game played with the (gloved) hand and a hard ball, by two pairs in a three-sided court, not unlike a squash court but with no back wall. The walls have ledges, and there is a large buttress on the left-hand side. At Eton it was played in the space between the buttresses of the chapel.

attentive and absorbed industry deep in his books, pleading to be left in peace'.

The same mischievous spirit appeared in class, in an incident which tells us as much about Head Master Hawtrey as about Thring:-

'Thring... tying a string round the handle of the bell just behind Hawtrey, and passing the string under Hawtrey's chair to little Henry Coleridge on the other side. First pull, up came Finmore (the Head Master's servant), "Did you ring, sir?" "No". Second pull. Ditto. [It took] much pressure and pinching to make Coleridge pull it a third time, but he did so. Again Finmore, asserting that it had been rung three times. Hawtrey looked about him and caught sight of the peccant (i.e. sinful) string. "Thring, did you ring the bell?" "No, sir, I didn't ring it." "Thring, I'm ashamed of you: contemptible subterfuge."'

His closest associates would mostly turn out to be serious-minded men. His longest-standing friend, John Fielder Mackarness,[1] later became Bishop of Oxford. As schoolboys they went to the Sunday evening service in Windsor parish church, discussing how Eton might be reformed, and forty years later their two families would holiday together.

As with Ilminster, memories of Eton never left him. Twenty-five years later he sent £5 to Mrs. Joel, the 'good, kind woman' who had given him a room in her house. His first tutor, Chapman (by then Bishop of Colombo), would become the first subscriber to the Uppingham chapel. Later still, he sent Chapman one of his books, recognising his old tutor's unusual commitment for that era to boys beyond the academic elite: 'I have such a great respect for him, [and for] the efforts which he made to do his duty by each boy'.

Of Long Chamber he remembered 'the wild, rough, rollicking freedom and the fun of that land of misrule, with its strange code of boy-law, which worked rather well as long as the sixth form were well disposed or sober'. He recalled 'Olympic games' (long-jumping over a trail of mattresses spread out across the floor) and battles in which boys threw fireworks at each other, only for the Head Master suddenly to appear through the smoke like 'Titan on the misty mountain top, blazing with wrath'. He reminisced about one boy hungrily attacking an illicit piece of steak just as a squib was thrown into his lap: 'The heroic sufferer held to his steak, the squib burnt out, and victorious though

---

[1] Rt. Revd. John Fielder Mackarness (1820-89): later Fellow of Exeter College Oxford; Domestic Chaplain to his friend, Lord Lyttelton (see ch. 8); Diocesan Inspector of Schools; Bishop of Oxford from 1869. He played a major role in the founding of Culham theological college.

not unscathed, [he] solaced [his] wounds with mouthfuls of homeopathic beef'. He believed that Long Chamber rivalled anything described in *Tom Brown's Schooldays.*

Eton had been better than Ilminster, because 'freedom was better than slavery', but he regretted the lost opportunities and waste of talent, and he likened Eton's lack of structure to a farmer growing grass and corn with no proper drainage and careless ploughing. Above all, he regretted the complete lack of supervision: 'Cries of joy or pain were equally unheard; and, excepting a code of laws of their own, there was no help or redress for any one. A mob of boys cannot be educated'.

Despite all the hardships, he crowned his schooldays by becoming Captain of the School in 1841: a Montem year. The triennial Montem celebrations were a huge social festival whose origins stretched back to medieval times.[1] Royalty, government ministers, country gentry, Eton parents and friends gathered that year from far and wide for what was thought 'probably the gayest and most magnificent [Montem] ever seen', their numbers swelled by local onlookers and large crowds which arrived via the newly-opened railway to Slough.

Thring's parents came up from Alford. Sarah rose early, well before Edward called on them, accompanied by Henry who had travelled down from Cambridge to support him. The two brothers scaled the balcony wall of the lodging house to the astonishment of those staying next door, and their mother, wide-eyed with admiration, thought that Edward looked 'the hero of the day' in his special uniform. After he went off to the Captain's breakfast, she and John Gale went to the College Hall, filled with '200 of the youths, all dressed either in fancy costumes or in scarlet, while a military band played and the whole area was filled with genteel people'.

A guard of honour and the entire school greeted the recently-married Queen and Prince Albert at 11 a.m. and the long procession of troops, military bands, coaches and visitors began. Henry feared briefly that his brother might be trampled underfoot, but a tall soldier lifted him up and passed him over the heads of the crowd. The day ended with the Captain's dinner, and the writer of the customary *Montem Ode* was well satisfied: 'So drink his health, and praise his feast, And, when this holiday has ceased, Say, one and all, with grateful heart, THRING has played well the Captain's part'.

---

[1] Under Hawtrey's reforms Montem was scaled down and then abolished. As the Great Western Railway's new line to Windsor became increasingly popular, Eton could not control the crowds.

The day brought Thring a lucrative privilege: the 'salt' collection, taken for the captain's anticipated expenses on moving on to Cambridge and made by costumed 'salt-bearers' who collected a toll and sold tickets (programmes). His collection was the largest ever,[1] and he was subsequently praised for not being spoiled by all the adulation, nor tempted by the huge credit customarily offered by local shops and inns to Montem captains.

It was a great day. Sarah, who had seen the royal couple close-to at the Provost's Lodge, thought Prince Albert 'a gentlemanly, good-looking man, with a pleasing, but rather melancholy expression'. Eventually they returned to their lodgings, to entertain their friends to cold chicken pie. She noted with pleasure how popular her son was with the junior boys, and hoped that her family were 'truly grateful for the blessings conferred upon us'.

A decade later Eton's limited curriculum, excessive free time, weak supervision and loose organisation would be key reference points in Thring's re-creation of Uppingham. Meanwhile to his contemporaries, 'he had made goodness possible among Etonians of his own generation; he was determined to teach – and to prove... that boys could always be trusted'.

---

[1] Parkin gives some of the financial details (Vol 1, pp. 33-6). Over £1,250 was collected – although his calculations, and a letter from Thring's mother to a friend soon afterwards, suggest that well over two-thirds of the money went to pay expenses and tradesmen. It seems a huge sum – but Hawtrey regretted to Thring's father that it was not as much as had been anticipated.

CHAPTER TWO

CAMBRIDGE, GLOUCESTER AND ITALY

THRING was elected a scholar of King's College, Cambridge, on 5 June 1841 and arrived as an undergraduate in October. The University was still small by modern standards,[1] and (as at Eton) change was in the air though not imminent. Entrance requirements were undemanding and lectures often poor, with too many dons content to live a relaxed, comfortable life in their colleges. Undergraduates from public schools knew plenty of Latin and Greek but they struggled with the mathematics requirements, and many were happy enough to take the undemanding 'ordinary' degree in preference to honours.

King's College was especially insulated against the march of time. Like Eton, it had been founded by King Henry VI as a community of 70, comprising undergraduates and Fellows. The latter held office for life unless they married, and they no longer had to be resident. They therefore hung on to their positions into old age, in some years restricting undergraduate numbers to as few as ten, all of them former Eton pupils. Entry prospects had thus become a lottery, with aspiring undergraduates discovering all too often that they had endured Long Chamber for nothing.

To outsiders, Kingsmen had 'levity, and that kind of impudence which shows itself in ten Etonians talking to [other] Etonians at a party without caring for what is due to the other four men present'.[2] King's undergraduates also enjoyed one extraordinary privilege: they could graduate without taking examinations. With so little academic incentive the college tended to attract 'gentlemen of leisure, whiling away the years in careless indolence', and after graduation men could progress automatically to junior and then senior fellowships. Not surprisingly, many Fellows saw no reason to change things.

As an undergraduate (1841-4), Thring appeared untroubled by these issues. He won several college awards and a university prize for a translation from Shakespeare into Greek iambics, but to his great disappointment he came second in the major awards to an old Eton rival,

---

[1] Its number of admissions had doubled since 1800 to about 400 undergraduates per year.
[2] This was the description of them by an American: see Bristed, C A: *Five Years in an English University* (New York, 1852) p.269.

William Johnson. His friends remembered his hard work and his love of classics and, as at Eton, they remarked on his sense of responsibility: he told one of them that 'an upright, steady character was in itself a silent rebuke of vice'.

He continued to play fives and 'the Eton version of hockey' with fearsome energy, and he rowed in a King's boat. Defying college rules he owned a small terrier named Fan, which he lodged out with a servant who brought her to him each day. Thring trained the dog so thoroughly that if she met him within the College she would pass him without even wagging her tail. He described his three undergraduate years as a 'very quiet, powerful time', especially the two summer long vacation terms[1] when he could read without interruption and walk at dusk around Cambridge's beautiful buildings along the Backs. He began to compile a small, leather-bound commonplace book, his *Index Rerum,* of maxims, quotations and snatches of poetry.[2]

On becoming a Fellow in 1844 he unexpectedly threw himself into a campaign to end Kingsmen's exemption from examinations, by writing two passionate, anonymous pamphlets. He praised New College, Oxford for giving up a similar privilege: it was 'a wise and liberal policy, [to end] its monopoly of idleness' and, seeing how Hawtrey's reforms at Eton were bearing fruit, he contrasted Eton's 'innovation and wondrous vitality' with King's, which was 'paralysed and asleep'. He was especially contemptuous of those whose reform instincts subsided 'into a settled admiration when it comes to their turn to receive the port-wine'.

Thring also asserted the importance of learning mathematics as well as classics. He speculated mischievously that the College might be trying to negotiate an agreement with the University whereby Kingsmen would take university examinations but would receive exemptions in mathematics. He thought this quite wrong: it was a reflection of how, by poor or non-existent teaching, the College had 'enveloped mathematics in a sort of fog', even though in such scientific times it was 'a department of knowledge which no gentleman's education can be considered perfect without'.

A first vote failed in 1849, but the reformers knew that their day would soon come, prompting Thring to write to his mother that next time

---

[1] An optional extra (4th) term, in the summer between two academic years

[2] He included a memory of one of his walks in a poem, *Night at King's College*: 'A few dim shadowy clouds of snowy white/ Hang like a veil upon the brow of night/ And ever and anon the timid stars/ Peep through with furtive glances breathing love/ and inspiration to clear chastened thought/ upon their mortal levers as of yore...'

he would go to any lengths to vote, wherever he was living: it was time to remove King's 'last excuse for idleness'. Two years later (by which time he had left Cambridge) the Fellows reversed the original vote, and he agreed to become a mathematics entrance examiner for the College. He approached the role with characteristic enthusiasm despite his own lack of experience in the subject, declaring that 'the four first books of Euclid ought decidedly to be required. I believe a man who knows algebra and Euclid well is ready to turn with advantage to any work'.

****

Cambridge fashioned Thring's religious life, too. The University, along with Oxford, produced priests for the Church of England, with large numbers of graduates taking orders and then moving straight on to nomination to a parish. Evangelical Protestantism was strong in a city recently dominated by Charles Simeon, Fellow of King's and Vicar of Holy Trinity Church for over half a century. The high church Oxford movement also had its supporters, including many King's Fellows, but there was little of the party animus that would develop in later years.

Thring experienced both types of churchmanship through his associations with two such Fellows: an evangelical friend from Eton days, William Witts,[1] and a high churchman, Rowland Williams. In 1843 he joined the Cambridge Camden Society, recently founded to promote 'the study of Gothic Architecture, and of Ecclesiastical Antiques'. He saw faith as based not on intellectual knowledge but on the spiritual insight and understanding which could only come through familiarity with the Scriptures and a strong prayer-life. He regarded frequent communion and daily worship as a defence against the daily temptations of life: each day was a battlefield where heaven was lost or won.

His attitude to church issues was neither zealous nor indifferent. He noted a prophecy in his commonplace book by the moderate Elizabethan theologian Richard Hooker: 'There will come a time when three words uttered with charity and meekness shall receive a far more blessed reward than three thousand volumes written with disdainful sharpness of wit'. To

---

[1] As curate of St Giles, Cambridge (1844-61) Witts turned down smart London parishes and gave half his stipend to found an industrial school with his wife to reform 400 'youthful offenders'. This later became the Cambridge branch of the Working Men's College. His co-founder was Harvey Goodwin, later Dean of Ely and Bishop of Carlisle: he too became Thring's friend, sending two boys through Uppingham and speaking or preaching at special occasions there all through Thring's time.

this he added: 'Controversial bickerings [are] like gladiatorial shows... Intellect without moral excellence [is] like a dwarf with the head disproportionately large'. Although surely not yet aware that the great seventeenth-century Divine, Bishop Jeremy Taylor, had once been Rector of Uppingham, he also included in his book Taylor's definition of prayer: 'The key to open the day & the bolt to shut in the night', along with John Ruskin's idea that God wishes to be invoked even on small matters: 'We treat God with irreverence by banishing Him from our thoughts, not by referring to His will on slight occasions'.[1]

He began a strong and formative friendship with Daniel Macmillan (grandfather of Prime Minister Harold Macmillan) who, with his brother Alexander, was the founder of the great Macmillan publishing house.[2] The brothers opened their Cambridge bookshop at 1 Trinity Street in 1843, and their published list included works on education, religion and social reform as well as classical literature, journals and syllabus materials. Daniel Macmillan was a deeply religious man, and Alexander wrote for the *Christian Socialist*.[3] The room over their bookshop became an evening meeting place for their friends (Maurice, Kingsley *et al*) to discuss books, or God, or social reform. Thring warmed to their idealism: as a group they discussed late into the night how they might give practical support to the 'Black Dragoons': young clergy who took the message of the gospel and of social reform into city slums.[4]

Daniel was a consumptive from an early age, and knowing that his time was short he was determined to make it fruitful. He died in 1857 aged only 44, yet even in the 1880s Thring recalled him as 'the most distinct personality of my early manhood, an embodiment of gentle, thoughtful power [who] abides with me still'. In describing Daniel as a 'living presence', he articulated an idea that would come to dominate his whole educational philosophy: life-enhancement as one of the most important human qualities. For their part, the Macmillans believed strongly in Thring. They published his two anonymous reform pamphlets,

---

[1] Ruskin – *The Seven Lamps of Architecture*, p.6. Thring noted: 'It is easy to be magnanimous when one is happy'.

[2] Daniel: known to his friends as 'the grave black man'. The Macmillans were once Scots farmers; their father died young, and Daniel worked in the London book trade. He and Alexander moved to Cambridge in 1843. Like Thring, they felt the strong influence of a gentle mother.

[3] Under the pseudonym 'Amos Yates'. Thomas Hughes asked him for advice about *Tom Brown's Schooldays*.

[4] Daniel was deeply impressed by a letter from a young Derbyshire curate about a night-school for 70 all-age pupils there. Thring told him that it showed the Black Dragoons' potential for doing good in cities. See ch. 16.

and Alexander later told him that he and Daniel used to speculate about Thring's bright future, 'for you were the first of the Cambridge men whom [Daniel's] clear eye determined as fitted to do world work'.

Thring's friends believed that he would have done well in university examinations – if only he had been eligible to take them. As it was, King's moved too slowly for him and after five years he left, retaining his fellowship *pro tem*. He did not have the dispassionate qualities or singleness of intellectual purpose necessary for an academic career, but he was always grateful for his time at Cambridge, with its mixture of 'labour and hope... bringing great searching of heart, and much balancing of right and wrong, much anxious weighing of the value of education and life'.

He looked back on university as one of the best periods of his life: one which gave him a sense of future direction. Through the Macmillans and their circle he became convinced that 'the education of the people of this great country is one of the most engrossing topics of the present day'. The same contemporary who had described him 'working exceedingly hard' at King's, also recalled that 'what seemed to me to cheer him most of all was when he made his mind up to be a clergyman'.

****

Yet another deeply formative experience awaited Thring in Gloucester. In December 1846 he was ordained deacon by the Bishop of Gloucester and Bristol and licensed as curate at the city's St James' church. Exactly a year later, he became a priest. Although described in one gazetteer as 'delightfully situated on a gentle eminence rising on the East side of the Severn', Gloucester had another, seamier side. Canal construction and the subsequent arrival of railways had made it a commercial and industrial town boasting sizeable wharves, factories, warehouses, timber yards and sidings. Its population had grown rapidly, amid concerns about poor housing, rising crime, drunkenness and prostitution. Robert Raikes had opened his first Sunday school there in 1780, for children employed in the pin industry who ran wild in their leisure hours.

The parish of St James had been formed four years before Thring's arrival. An appeal to pay for its new church described its population as 'very poor, almost proverbial hitherto for ungodliness, vice, and outrage, and now rapidly increasing', but the Revd. Thomas Hedley, its incumbent, was a graduate of Trinity College, Cambridge and a dedicated supporter of education, undaunted by the challenge. His bishop, whilst concerned about 'the souls of multitudes now abandoned to error, to ignorance, and to heathenism', thought him too ambitious. The schoolrooms which he built at Barton End in 1844 were larger and more costly than the parish required or could afford, but within three years the school had 244 children, taught by one master who was helped by the curate and some parish ladies. A monitorial system was tried, with the monitors themselves being taught at lunchtime and helping younger pupils at other times of day, but the idea was abandoned because at mid-day the monitors had to run to the docks with their fathers' dinners.

Thring lived half a mile from the church in simple style. When Charles visited him he had to sleep in a makeshift bed rigged up on chairs. Parish life had a few lighter moments – with its 'pretty infantine processions' and plum cake at annual Sunday school treats – but mostly it was grim, and Thring's eyes were quickly and rudely opened to this unfamiliar world. His first funeral was that of an eighteen month old boy; the second, one month; the third, five weeks. The first child whom he baptised, he also buried five days later. Of the twenty-seven burials he conducted, twelve were of children under two years old. In a sermon in Uppingham (1882) he recalled one incident which had haunted him all his life:

'I remember visiting a woman in extreme old age, a pauper, friendless and homeless, lodged with strangers, bedridden, twisted and shrivelled almost out of human shape, no man can imagine a more desolate lot, a more dreary ending of a long life. Aye, brethren, but what did she think of it? Thanksgiving for blessings, praise of God, gratitude, heartfelt cheery interest for others, happiness and peace always came forth from her lips. Never has that memory been out of my mind'.

Every assumption about his faith was challenged by such confrontations with death and he struggled to discern their meaning. He included a description of one such encounter in his commonplace book:

'I stood beside the dying girl, a minister of prayer
God's censer in my hand to stay the plague of her despair
I gazed upon her livid face, more ghastly from the wreath
of dead white folds which seemed to mock the features black beneath
Her swollen flesh drawn tightly back from half shut sunken eyes
was crossed by one dark sluggish vein, blocked by her agonies.
I prayed, but from a heavy heart: 'God help the sinner', then
her deep-drawn answers gurgled forth, half prayer, half sobs of pain.
She died, and now the morning sun is shed upon her wave
not far from trodden streets and where the thoughtless daily rave'.

Still more formative of his educational thinking were the lessons he learnt from teaching scripture to the children in the school. The work involved constantly 'churning an idea' as he looked for new ways of presenting information:

> 'Everything I most value of teaching thought, practice and experience, came from that [encounter]... with its solemn problem, no more difficult one in the world, how on earth the Cambridge Honour Man, with his success and his brain-world, was to get at the minds of those little labourers' sons with their unfurnished heads, and no time to give... How hard it was to get into shape, their shape, and fit the twists and corners of blocked and ignorant minds. But it was a glorious work. There was wonderful freshness in these schools, a most exhilarating sense of life touching life, of freedom and reality'.

These young minds 'had to be got at, or I had failed'. He compared it all with the search for St Augustine's golden key 'which, though it be of gold, is useless unless it fits the wards of the lock', the challenge being 'unlocking the minds, and opening the shut chambers of the heart'.[1]

> 'They tried all my patience, called every power into play, and visited me with such searching of heart if they did not do well. Never shall I cease to be grateful to those... other-world boys, and that world of theirs which had to be got into.
> They called out the useful dictum with which I ever silently stepped over the threshold: "If these fellows don't learn, it's my fault." They disentangled all the loose threads of knowledge in my brain, and forced me to wind each separately in its place, with its beginning and its end'.

He came to recognise all the limitations of what he would later call 'lecturing' or 'hammering', in which teaching is delivered top-down:

> 'They bred in me a supreme contempt for knowledge-lumps, for emptying out knowledge-lumps in a heap, like stones at a roadside, and calling it teachings.
> They made me hate the long array of fine words, which lesson-hearers ask, and pupils answer, and neither really knows the meaning of.
> They taught me the more valuable lesson still, how different knowledge which can be produced to an Examiner is from knowledge which knows itself, and understands its own life and growth'.

These ideas became the basis of his views about what constituted proper teaching, and they were to recur over and over again in his later

---

[1] A warded lock uses obstructions, or *wards*, to prevent the lock from opening unless the correct key is used.

writings. They also gave him a key maxim: 'The worse the material, the greater the skill of the worker'.

Gradually, however, he became haunted by the daily succession of tragedies, and he began to experience the extreme mood-swings which would become such a feature of his later life. By the spring of 1848 his health and confidence were shattered and he had to leave, after a succession of throat infections and attacks of boils from which it took fifteen years to recover. A few months later Hedley also left, his health similarly broken. He later returned briefly to parish work but died in 1854, aged only forty-two.

Much later Thring wrote to Hedley's daughter: 'No epoch of my life has made half the impression on me that my Gloucester stay and your dear father did... he was the most single-minded Christian I ever met'. He also recalled Hedley's dictum: 'I never see a particularly disagreeable little boy come into my parish school without thinking: here is someone I have to learn to love for Christ's sake'. Two of Hedley's sons would be among Thring's first pupils at Uppingham.

****

During nearly two years of convalescence (1848-9) Thring initially moved back to Alford, acting as his father's curate at Hornblotton and teaching private pupils. He delighted his mother by starting a rose garden, although the family thought him too generous in what he paid his workmen. He acquired a pet raven, which was given his own Eton nickname, 'Quilp'.[1] There were occasional games of cricket, including one to which he and Charles travelled sixteen miles together. They played on opposite sides, Charles describing how 'we had made an unusually large score, and [Edward] was lying down after fielding, with a very bad headache. He went in and knocked up over 80 runs very rapidly, beat our side and got rid of his headache. Moral: when unwell, play cricket!'

After a few months Thring moved on to lodge at Seymour Court, near Marlow on the River Thames. There were new pupils and more rose growing. Local people welcomed his advice about their gardens and noted the many hours he spent patiently training his dogs. He burned off his

---

[1] According to Charles Thring: 'Quilp used to cause great fun... several wild ravens used to appear, anxious apparently to show her the polite attentions due to her subtle beauty. The cat sought to stalk a fine blackbird, who kept provokingly unsuspicious, yet always managed to avoid the murderous springs; or taking the offensive quickly put pussy to flight. Her imitation of a trotting horse was very deceptive and many of the noises and eccentric motions caused much merriment'.

nervous energy by walking, riding and rowing: gradually his self-confidence returned. He took on additional examining work and started making new friends, to whom he poured out his plans to return to teaching as soon as he could. Taking his obligations as a King's examiner seriously, he spent an autumn holiday with a group of friends at Tenby (in south-west Wales), filling gaps in his mathematical knowledge. Gradually he took on some parish work, assisting the Vicar of Bisham, Thomas Powell. In 1849 family friends in Somerset, the Skrines, decided to build a church at Stubbings, a few miles away near Maidenhead, to provide a living for their son. Thring acted as locum priest until the son arrived; designed altar rails for the church; worked with children in its new elementary school, and started some textbook writing.

Although he slowly learned to laugh when others poked fun at his passionate intensity, he was still very fragile. Powell noted his proneness to terrible attacks of nervous indigestion, and how much he relied on the man who treated him, Dr. Lionel Beale who (like Powell) became a lifelong friend. A note in Thring's bible shows that as he turned 30, his Gloucester experience had taught him not to be in too much of a hurry: 'Not before thirty years is any great public work to be done. Joseph. David. John the Baptist. Nothing known of Our Blessed Lord but His obedience till he was thirty years of age. All real power must follow this example and gather quiet experience... Frosts kill tender shoots'.

In September 1852 and now much better, he left Stubbings. The time was near to resume what he saw as real work. In his commonplace book he reflected on how he had changed:

'The dreams of childhood and of youth were pleasant dreams I wot
But they are gone for ever, gone and I lament them not.
Who would not change his aimless hopes for manhood's stirring strife?
For those who like it nursery milk, give me the wine of life'.

He applied unsuccessfully to be Principal of the new Oxford diocesan training college. Then, apparently content to let the future take care of itself, he set out on a long-planned journey to the Holy Land in September 1852. His journey was similar to many other Victorian Grand Tours, and he kept an exercise book of impressions and opinions. He progressed through Cologne, Leipzig, Dresden and Prague to Vienna, where he encountered 'some Americans: most intolerable people, especially the women', and was briefly delayed when his pistol was seized. He thought 'the women ugly enough to relieve Vienna from the charge of being the most dissolute capital in Europe'. In Trieste he lost his hat box. As he approached Venice by steamer, it filled him with 'a feeling of dreamy magnificence more unearthly than anything I had ever felt', but its officials objected to the colour of his new (brown) hat as being republican.

At Ferrara his prints of Venice were taken by customs officials, and in Padua he was deeply moved by the painting of Giotto. On 20 October 1852 he reached Florence and found that his brother Godfrey was also there. In the church of San Marco he marvelled at the masterpieces of Fra Angelico. At Santa Croce, the rose window was 'I think, the best I ever saw', but he was disappointed by Fiesole's much-vaunted scenery and the leaning tower of Pisa: 'Its proportions won't do after Giotto's tower' (at Florence cathedral). He thought the beggars in Pisa a great nuisance, and the Duomo in Siena a vulgar mistake. In Perugia he gazed on 'the finest window I ever saw', and he delivered a similar verdict in Assisi's lower church on Giotto's frescoes.

He reached Rome on 22 November. The city captivated him, and he sketched it by moonlight. He disliked the external appearance and music of St Peter's, and the Sistine Chapel offended his protestant sensibilities, Michaelangelo's work being 'on the whole the most marvellous instances of power misapplied and self-glorification conceivable'. On 6 December he saw the Pope (Pius IX) driving out into the city: 'A rather pleasant looking old man', but the elaborate Mass in the Sistine Chapel two days later was 'as void of religious solemnity as anything well could be'.

He was still in Rome for Christmas, but shortly afterwards this breathless recording of new discoveries and opinions petered out. He was suddenly in love. One reason for being in Italy was his parents' wish that he keep an eye on Godfrey, whom they feared had become attracted by a young German girl there, Marie Koch, the daughter of an official in the Prussian customs service. Whether or not an engagement to Godfrey was in the offing, Thring pre-empted it most effectively and with characteristic impulsiveness by proposing successfully to Fräulein Koch himself.[1]

Marie's sudden appearance in his life made it imperative to return to England and find a job which would enable him to marry. He wrote to a Fellow of Trinity College asking for a testimonial 'for the headmastership of one of the schools... Besides general blarney, you might put in with advantage something about my National School practice [in Gloucester]; it will be sufficient, I feel'. However, with few influential contacts he would have to travel to interviews around the country.

Soon he was in Durham, 'seeing canons, and trying for the school'. After a day of interviews, the final choice lay between him and Dr. Henry Holden, headmaster of the grammar school in Uppingham. The

---

[1] Tradition in Godfrey's family suggests that he was never really in love, and that his parents over-reacted.

experienced man inevitably had an advantage over someone seven years his junior: Holden was duly offered the post on 20 July, whereupon Thring applied for Uppingham. In mid-August he was on tenterhooks, explaining to friends that such headmasterships (unlike those in famous public schools) went mostly to men with previous experience. He dreaded a long-drawn-out engagement to Marie, and his parents had vetoed his request for financial help to set up a preparatory school for Eton. He might yet have to return to Stubbings to undertake more tutoring.

Despite his pessimism, Uppingham appointed him on 30 August 1853 and two days later he visited the school for the first time. Changing trains at Didcot station on the way back to Buckinghamshire, he met an acquaintance who rashly asked him what on earth he hoped to achieve in such an obscure place as Rutland. Ignoring another passenger looking on, Thring confronted his questioner across the table of the waiting room and poured out his hopes and plans: 'Yes, I have a work before me, but I am engaged to marry a lady whose affection it would be an honour for any man to engage: and you know, my dear fellow, self-confidence is not a deficiency in the Thring family'.[1]

The acquaintance noted how the third man turned his face to the wall and laughed: 'It was most humorous: Thring's animation, his screwed-up courage, his perfect estimate of his own powers'. Daniel Macmillan, who had just published Thring's *Child's Grammar,* reacted with rather more conviction on hearing of his friend's success: 'It seems to me one of the surest ways of doing good. Mr. Thring is beginning to take in England! We have so much confidence in him. Very rash, you will say…. But I don't think so!'

---

[1] Parkin's book omitted the reference to Thring's engagement out of sensitivity to his grieving family.

CHAPTER THREE

UPPINGHAM 1853: 'FULL OF HOPE'

UPPINGHAM, situated on the intersection of the Nottingham-Northampton and Leicester-Peterborough roads,[1] was a town of 2,000 people in 1853: a mixture of gentry, professional classes, small tradesmen, shopkeepers and agricultural workers. The wealthier households (and the school) were in the town centre, with the rest confined to poorly-paved streets and tumbledown houses on its fringes. Local allegiances were strong. Nearly two-thirds of the population lived within 12 miles of where they had been born, and the thriving weekly market was a magnet for nearby villages.

Archdeacon Robert Johnson, an Elizabethan philanthropist, founded schools in Uppingham and nearby Oakham in 1584, along with some almshouses. During nearly three centuries the two schools enjoyed a cyclical prosperity, the one in decline as the other prospered. Uppingham initially had just twenty local boys, educated free of charge in a schoolroom next to the churchyard.[2] In the early 1700s fee-payers were added, some of them boarders living in a house two hundred yards away across the market place. Over time, this house gained extensions to its dining room and dormitories, and the boys were given some small studies, individual garden-plots and the use of a rented playing field.

Henry Holden, its headmaster from 1845, had been a great success. He made the school more widely known, improved its teaching and promoted good relationships between masters and boys. He also introduced praepostors (prefects) on the model of Thomas Arnold. When numbers briefly grew to 70, he further extended the boarding house, provided a library and more studies, and persuaded the governors to buy land for a covered play area (the *Tectum*) for ball games. However, in 1853 he left Uppingham hurriedly for his new post in Durham, taking eleven pupils with him and leaving around 40 others who resented his departure.[3] This remaining group quickly realised that the man overseeing the brief

---

[1] Leicester was the nearest large town. With a population of 60,000, it was well on the way to becoming an industrial city.

[2] Many grammar schools had similar origins. Johnson decreed that his schoolmasters should be honest, conscientious and learned, especially in Greek and Latin.

[3] Accounts vary between 36 and 43. Pupils transferring schools with Heads who were on the move was not unusual.

interregnum, the hapless Revd. Coker Adams, was no match for them. They put gunpowder into the keyholes of the boarding house to frighten him.[1]

When Thring arrived (to be housemaster as well as headmaster) they turned up late for his first lesson, saying that they did not think it mattered. They let off fireworks at prayer-time, whereupon Thring quickly restored order, but on his first night there were violent storms. The small diamond panes in all the bedroom windows rattled furiously, and in the small hours Adams knocked nervously on Thring's door to ask if they might sit together. Eventually the weather quietened down, and on the next day, as Adams departed for good: 'The tenth of September 1853, I entered on my headmastership with the very appropriate initiation of a whole holiday and a cricket match in which I recollect I got 15 by some good swinging hits to the great delight of my few pupils'.

Thring made two frequent and doubtful assertions about these early days: first, that the school he inherited had only 25 boys and was in a poor way;[2] secondly, that he had arrived with a blueprint clearly in his mind: 'A sketch, almost in detail, of everything I proposed to do'. Despite his optimism, this claim is hard to believe. Even if he had an outline plan in his mind, there would inevitably have to be plenty of experiment, improvisation and opportunism in acquiring extra land and property.

Most of the newly-founded mid-Victorian boarding schools were backed either by local community or corporate initiative.[3] Their capital came from a variety of sources: local resident shareholders or businessmen; the Church; particular interest groups or an energetic founder. The older, 'great' boarding schools favoured by the aristocracy

---

[1] Adams was a friend of Holden's. According to Thring's daughter, Margaret, 'They only did that once after my father came'.

[2] Thring may have ignored day pupils in his calculation: a revealing clue about his future priorities. Holden disputed Thring's figures. Although Holden remembered Uppingham as where 'the sunniest hours of his life' had been spent, he stayed away for most of Thring's three decades as his successor.

[3] E.g. local resident shareholders (Cheltenham, Clifton and Brighton College); local businessmen (Malvern); the Anglican Church (Marlborough, Radley and Rossall); the medical fraternity (Epsom); the East India connection (Haileybury). Wellington College began as a public memorial to the Duke, with a huge public subscription and royal support. Woodard's energy and connections created the schools that bear his name. Endowed boarding schools included Eton, Harrow and Winchester. City day schools included Manchester, Bradford and Bristol Grammar Schools and King Edward's, Birmingham. Some smaller grammar schools reinvented themselves through rising land values: e.g. Tonbridge, thanks to Sir Andrew Judde's property in London.

could often draw on endowments, and day schools benefited from the wealth of commercial networks of successful entrepreneurs in expanding cities.

Thring had none of these possibilities. His school was almost unknown and Uppingham was a very small town. The charitable trust established by Archdeacon Johnson had purely local aims and an income of only a few thousand pounds per year. He had very limited teaching experience and few financial resources of his own. Much would depend on external factors such as educational fashion and whether the national economy continued to expand.[1]

Despite all this, he felt that his time had come. The political and economic advances of recent decades had created a favourable public mood: 'A new epoch... for the first time in the history of the world, there was a demand that everybody should get some teaching of a regular kind... The air was full of hope, and bright with possibilities... everything pointed to a great new birth of teaching power'. With no powerful backers he had to depend on fee-paying parents, but he sensed a large demand for boarding education amongst the new middle classes: 'Hundreds go to schools now who thirty years ago would not have thought of doing so'. Once educated themselves, they could provide 'endowments [to] help forward the poorer and less powerful but intelligent workers' of future generations.

The rapidly expanding railways were 'a great connecter', making what would once have been major expeditions into quick and simple journeys for prospective parents and pupils.[2] Two stations had opened nearby in the previous five years:[3] 'We stand on the threshold of a new world. Railways and steamships and telegraphs have made this earth of ours to all intents and purposes another planet... all the nations are suddenly being poured together into one great tumultuous sea of stormy strife'. He was less certain about their wider impact on society, fearing that the pace of

---

[1] The school had taught two future bishops and the occasional aristocrat, but no important Old Boys were still alive. The Trust's income in the early 1870s (largely rental income on lands in neighbouring counties) was £4,280, of which 4/7 was spent roughly equally on the two schools and the rest on the almshouses. Many of Thring's contemporary-headmasters had either school or university teaching experience.

[2] Marlborough, Cheltenham and Rossall were examples of new 'proprietory' (as opposed to the smaller 'private') schools. They emphasised their accessibility by train.

[3] Seaton 1850: Manton 1848. The railway did not reach Uppingham until the 1890s. In 1838 there were only 250 miles of passenger railway open; by the early 1850s, over 5,000. Within two decades it would reach 12,000.

change might prove too rapid, because 'railway progress brings the old and new too quickly together'. Even so, he was sure that his small school was 'worthy of better things':

> 'I suddenly found myself brought face to face with all I had professed to believe... with a platform to make the attempt on, youth on my side, and faith... [but also] in an unfurnished house; my own bed, and a table and a few chairs the only things left: two boxes of books of my own were all the things I had time to bring... I had at once to enter on a new school, and make a start... And so the work began'.

As at Gloucester, Charles came to visit. He found his brother 'bursting with ideas', but all the unfamiliar demands on Thring soon revived his old attacks of boils.[1] As autumn gave way to winter, he made only minor adjustments to the curriculum and domestic arrangements, 'dragging through the dreary months as best I could till Xmas', with his mind often elsewhere. As his first term ended on 19 December, he resigned his Cambridge fellowship and headed for Bournemouth, where his parents were staying, and where he and Marie were married.[2]

****

Once back in Uppingham with Marie, he began to change things. He later bemoaned the universally poor quality of the three masters he had inherited, but this too was a dubious claim. William Earle, Usher (Deputy) since 1850, was a young Cambridge mathematician who was also curate of nearby Lyndon: conservative and cautious, but reliable in the classroom. However, the only other full-time appointment was quickly dismissed as incompetent, while Clarke, 'the writing master', was willing but very limited: 'His duties were to fill the ink pots, and mend pens, and tidy up the room after each school-time; in school he set copies and heard a little Latin grammar, or did the multiplication table with a few backward boys'. Clarke too, soon departed.

Right from the start Thring was intent on growing the school by increasing the boarding numbers. His only hope of doing this lay in persuading like-minded men to become co-investors: setting up houses at their own expense and running them as satellite enterprises providing

---

[1] Another example of Parkin's careful editing of Thring's diaries: he omitted the reference to boils.

[2] According to Charles, Bournemouth was then 'a quiet retired seaside place', but John Gale disliked more 'popular' watering places. No details survive of the wedding. Oxford and Cambridge Fellows were not allowed to be married.

accommodation and their own catering. This would mean adopting the Eton model of houses dispersed around the town, rather than the grand quadrangles and central feeding facilities then being built by wealthy backers in many of the 'new' Victorian schools such as Marlborough and Wellington.[1] However, he was determined that housemasters should work to *his* standards. They should not be allowed to run their houses frugally, with profit too much in mind; nor (after his experience of Long Chamber) should they live in buildings away from their pupils.

Under Thring, most housemasters began with a few pupils in a hastily converted property. If successful, they moved on to a larger house, selling their previous one to a successor: a process which often triggered a whole series of housemaster changes in the early years. In return for a housemaster's commitment, Thring guaranteed to find pupils for him, but if the housemaster started to fail, Thring could (and did) divert prospective parents to other houses. Then, if a housemaster left, either voluntarily or under duress, Thring might be forced to buy the man's house, retaining it for a time so that its boys could remain in the school. Much therefore depended on choosing the right housemasters, but in his early recruitment he showed how much he had to learn about managing adults. By his own admission, he initially assumed that a good degree automatically made a man a good teacher. He was also too attracted by force of personality, considering too little how well an individual might work within a team.

His first appointment (1854) was John Richard Blakiston, a twenty-five-year-old classicist from Trinity, Cambridge. Enthusiastic but impatient with small boys, Blakiston was also a man in a hurry – and prepared to challenge Thring's authority. He set up first a temporary, and within two years a more permanent, boarding house,[2] but was then dismissed. Thring blamed himself for years afterwards for Blakiston's 'fatal influence... he was a perpetual anxiety, a canker in our work and reduced us and our system to the brink of ruin'. Blakiston's subsequent career (headmaster of Giggleswick, chief inspector and educational writer) proved his ability, but the school was too small for both the vigorous young headmaster (Thring) and his ambitious assistant.

R J Hodgkinson (1855) was less personally ambitious. He gave Thring loyalty and financial support, extended Blakiston's temporary house and

---

[1] Eton and Uppingham were far from the only schools where pupils were fed in houses, although the number of such schools has steadily declined since Thring's day to a handful now. Some of the newer foundations began with a hostel system or adopted a mixture of centralised and house feeding – e.g. Marlborough.

[2] Bought by Holden as stables, and known as 'The Lodge'. Under Blakiston it stretched almost to the present chapel.

later built one of his own. He was also popular: a skilled football player who appeared in full clerical costume: white choker, black trousers and tall hat, throwing off the hat as the game warmed up. Thring recognised that 'Hoddy's' calm was a foil to his own impulsiveness: 'He threw himself heartily into the work [and] acted as a great check on [Blakiston]... he is true and large-hearted, whatever mistakes he may occasionally make'.[1]

John Baverstock, one of a pair of former Etonians recruited in 1858, was determined and deeply spiritual. 'Bav' contributed the first purpose-built house, but delicate health forced him to retire after only eight years. He arrived with G H D Mathias, who seemed initially to Thring to be 'an excellent worthy fellow, and a very good master, gaining experience daily'. The boys loved Mathias' lively lessons and sermons and they gave three cheers after his brilliant evening lectures, but his more routine teaching was eccentric and patchy. He sent boys to Thring for commendation with pieces of work full of mistakes, which led to stormy confrontations between them.

Thring came to see Mathias as 'naturally careless and unmethodical'; unrealistic about his own ability, and influenced too much by a wife who lacked commitment to the school. The couple were poor at boarding house management, and parents complained. One transferred his son to Thring's own house, which Thring hoped would be a good lesson: 'What a pity that with all his excellent qualities, the dead fly of a little conceit should damage so much, and make [Mathias] so self-willed and silly in little things'. Nothing improved, however, and in mid-November 1859 Thring began to divert parents away from Mathias, while letting him carry on in the house for another year to avoid being forced to buy it himself.[2]

It proved to be a mistake. During that year three of Mathias' boys contracted diphtheria, one fatally. Thring became alarmed that there would be parental panic, and the desperate Mathias made things worse by alleging to parents that his was not the only infected house. After a blazing argument Thring decided that they had reached a point of no return: 'We shall never have tolerable peace here till Mathias goes. He wants judgment and is full of self. He will go as soon as he thinks he can get a good headmastership'. Mathias did exactly that, but then demanded

---

[1] Hodgkinson's solicitor-father had been mayor of Newark. His brother-in-law was an Uppingham lawyer. He built a dining-hall and dormitories and turned stables into studies.

[2] He heard of two instances of parents who liked the school but not Mathias' house. He later admitted in his diary that, where housemasters were concerned: 'I expected too much rigid authority in the men and strained authority too tight'.

to be reimbursed for the house *and* for £400 allegedly spent on it. With great difficulty Thring paid up, in a desperate attempt to speed Mathias' departure,[1] discovering subsequently that the studies were filthy, with an open drain running directly underneath.

Twenty-five-year-old T E Stokoe (1859) was Thring's first Oxford recruit. Stokoe agreed to build a new house, but his father – presumably also his backer – vetoed Thring's conditions. This led over several months to a wholesale reallocation of houses, the situation being unlocked only when the selfless Hodgkinson offered to stay in the buildings which he had taken over when Blakiston left, rather than to move in to a larger property – one which Stokoe could now take over instead.

Thring was withering about Stokoe: 'Apparently he is to hold his mouth open whilst we drop guineas into it'. Worse still, Stokoe and Mathias jointly dared to dispute classical grammar with him: 'These fellows think nothing of criticising any thoughtful scholarship, which they about reach to my ancle (sic) in'. They came up with endless new ideas for the school, which he thought an impertinence: he knew better than they, and while they might be clever intellectually, they had no feel for the differing needs of each class and individual. Despite the brevity of his time in Gloucester, he reckoned that 'thanks to my National School experience, I am at no loss to estimate this priggishness at its proper value'.

Like Mathias, Stokoe gradually became tiresome to his colleagues. In 1861 he applied for the second mastership at Dulwich but Thring was asked for a testimonial only about Stokoe's academic achievements. Despite having once described Stokoe as 'an Oxford First, but a bad one', Thring thought this 'just the opportunity I wanted'; he wrote about what he had been asked, and no more. Dulwich duly appointed Stokoe, only for bitter recriminations to follow. Then, rather than gratefully letting Stokoe depart, Thring accused him of breaking an unwritten understanding about his notice period, whereupon Stokoe threatened legal action if Thring declined to provide future references. Stokoe's later career included two headships but he too could not bring himself to accept Thring's dominance.[2]

---

[1] £2,000: money that he must have borrowed. He probably made a loss when he sold the house to Mathias' successor.

[2] Hodgkinson acted as intermediary, and Stokoe resigned. Thring: 'I am so thankful, but I do pity his poor little wife so, beginning life so early with this sort of thing. She is only 18'. He claimed that Stokoe's successor found that the management of the house had been 'stingy and quite against the spirit and practice of the school'.

Thring's biggest disappointment (and the last of his early mistakes) was his brother Charles. Despite some misgivings he greatly looked forward to Charles' arrival in 1859: Charles was an outgoing man, genuinely interested in teaching; the boys admired his skill and interest in football,[1] and Thring thought his published *First Principles of Arithmetic Explained by Diagrams* 'ingenious and useful'. However, Charles had a temperament which was ill-suited to the more routine aspects of school life. Moreover Lydia, his wife, was intelligent, forceful and capable: as well as helping her husband to run his house, she produced four children (one still-born) between 1859 and 1863.

She also refused to toe any party line from her headmaster/brother-in-law, which inevitably led Thring to contrast Lydia's independence of mind with his own wife's obedient supportiveness. Difficulties began with a simple misunderstanding over whether boys could attend a party which Lydia and Charles gave on their arrival at the school: they did not know that Thring had vetoed the idea. Once they took over a house, he fell out with them over a succession of housekeeping issues, minor in themselves but (he claimed) 'the only instance since I have been here of a master who has openly refused obedience to an established law'. In 1861 he wrote to Lydia complaining that studies built for individuals were being allocated to boys in pairs: he objected on principle, and he was sure that it would cause friction between houses. Unless Charles and Lydia desisted he would never recommend another boy to their house.

Godfrey tried vainly to mediate from Somerset, but Charles and Lydia refused to submit. They were overheard criticising arrangements for football teams and for the choir. Thring accused Charles of talking 'rebellious humbug' at a masters' meeting and wrote in his diary that Charles was 'a fool and a traitor, cutting his own throat', painfully altered by a marriage which had tied him to Lydia's apron strings. Furious that she discussed her grievances openly with the boys, he remained baffled by the contrast between her 'impertinence, meddling and conceit' and the helpful demeanour of his own wife. He also resented having rescued them from a precarious curacy elsewhere, only to find that his generosity was now being thrown back in his face: 'They are my only enemies in the place'.

Eventually other housemasters began a whispering campaign about Charles' and Lydia's indulgence of their boys' idleness. In 1864 they too

---

[1] In 1846 Charles and an ex-Shrewsbury friend had founded the Cambridge University Football Club: an early attempt to bring standard rules to the game in schools. Whilst at Uppingham he drew up the rules for Uppingham football: similar to the Eton field game, but with an oval pitch and long fly kicks.

left, Thring defensively telling Godfrey that the experience had taught him some hard lessons but that if Godfrey felt like blaming him, he should be aware that 'while Charles is writing humbly to you, he is both writing and speaking haughtily to us. You have a very subtle politician to deal with in Lydia. Beware'.

Charles was the last of the serial housemaster dissidents, but meanwhile there had also been problems with Dr. Benguerel, who came from Switzerland to teach German.[1] Again Thring began with high hopes. He liked Benguerel's enthusiasm and he thought him 'a zealous, clever, trustworthy man with many good qualities'. He welcomed Benguerel's proposal to build a gymnasium (one of the first of its kind in the country): it would be excellent in winter and on rainy days. It opened with much celebration on Marie's birthday in November 1859.[2]

Unfortunately Benguerel proved a difficult colleague. Bitter words were exchanged when Thring failed to consult him over the recruitment of a gymnastics master.[3] Benguerel offered his resignation, which Thring eventually accepted. He was puzzled and depressed that Benguerel, 'so good a fellow, so sterling and trustworthy with the boys', had no job to go to, but he convinced himself that Benguerel had 'temper and conceit'; that his behaviour had been 'petty and contemptible', and that he had been manipulated by 'Blakiston and his baleful influence'. He unbent just a little in allowing the boys to collect money for a parting gift and Hodgkinson to organise a farewell supper, but his relief at Benguerel's departure was unconfined: 'I feared he would remain always nagging but always stopping short of any serious offence. But now I am delivered of him'.[4] He also believed that it had become a 'contest for power', and his

---

[1] Benguerel was one of the earliest of many German speakers at the school from 1855, following in Marie's footsteps. He played football until he tired, and then shrieked encouragement from the touchline in a garbled mixture of English, French and German. Thring appointed 18 German-speaking masters in all, notably George Beisiegel who oversaw the gym, and the inspirational music teacher, Paul David (see ch. 5). Thring used to attend annual festivities at David's house to mark the Kaiser's birthday.

[2] Thring later added gas lighting and a sand floor. The lower floor had gym apparatus; its upper floor was for standing exercises, drilling and fencing. It was replaced (1904) by a larger one: a memorial to victims of the Boer War. Wellington College (opened in 1859) included a gym – and Brighton College opened one in that year, too – so which was the first is a matter for debate.

[3] By modern standards, and given Benguerel's role in setting up the gymnasium, Thring's action might seem surprising – but also a sign of his autocratic nature.

[4] Earle tried briefly to mediate, but soon concluded that Thring's decision had been right.

own need for obedience came ahead of anything that Benguerel contributed to the school.

Thring never fully overcame a tendency to be disappointed by his colleagues' limitations rather than cheerful about their successes. This first generation were 'excellent fellows in many ways', but inexperienced and self-important, and they took financial security too much for granted: 'Unless you fling them plenty of corn, they peek (peck at) you'. Brooding on their failings prompted introspection about his own shortcomings. He was gradually adding to his self-knowledge, but he had still to learn how to get the best out of his subordinates.

****

None of these early setbacks deterred parents from sending Thring their sons. His optimism about the thirst of 1850s middle-class parents for education was well founded, and numbers began to grow almost from the day he arrived.

Of the 40 or so boys whom Thring inherited, his 25 boarders mostly came from Midland counties. Six of their fathers were doctors and seven were clergymen, some hoping that their sons might gain access to endowed (i.e. closed) scholarships at Oxford or Cambridge. By contrast, five day boys and one boarder had tradesmen fathers, suggesting that the pupil body was part-boarding and part-local-grammar school in nature.

Thring brought one boy with him, to whom he had previously promised private tuition. The first ten parents he recruited were a Kettering solicitor; gentlemen from Bath (Somerset) and Charmouth (Dorset); clergymen from Worksop (Nottinghamshire), Stony Stratford (Buckinghamshire), Linton (Cambridgeshire), Taunton (Somerset) and nearby Wing (Rutland); a Liskeard (Cornwall) solicitor, and a London architect. Twenty years later the intake was similar in background: a Wansford (Northamptonshire) solicitor; an Irish gentleman; a London surgeon; two Manchester physicians; gentlemen from Barnstaple (Devon) and Canada; clergy from Thrapston (Northamptonshire) and Wisbech (Cambridgeshire), and a land agent from Monmouth. He also benefited from the loyalty of some large families: Dr. Wroughton of Kettering (14 miles away, in Northamptonshire) sent seven sons to Uppingham between 1865 and 1882.

There were, however, three major changes in the complexion of the school's intake over the years. First, the school grew steadily – to 140 pupils in 1859; 200 in 1863 and 300 in 1865. Secondly, its catchment area noticeably expanded. Under Holden, 40% of the boys came from Rutland and neighbouring Leicestershire and Northamptonshire, along with a smattering from Yorkshire, Lincolnshire and London (see table below). Thring's formidable promotional skills drew in nearly 3,000 boys during his 34 years, including many from much further afield.

There were four main categories of 'new' parent: military and naval officers and diplomatic or colonial officials (especially from India) needing boarding education; landed proprietors living on large estates and concerned at their sons' possible isolation; men in political life, too peripatetic to provide stability, and – much the largest category – wealthy men looking for a better education for their sons than they could find in their own home area, whilst also keen to provide them with good connections for their later lives through membership of what were fast becoming known as the 'public schools'.[1]

Many in this last group were manufacturers, merchants and members of the expanding professions, including a sizeable network of doctors. The commercial group included several Brighton brewers: word of mouth recommendation was important.[2]

Distance was no object for these parents:

Intake figures: 1846-88: (NB: 1846-53 was under Holden)

Year	TOTAL NEW BOYS	Local %	c20-75 miles %	London area %	NW %	Other UK %	Ireland/ Foreign %	Not Known %
1846-53	139	37	31	4	1.5	23	1.5	2
1854-8	149	23.5	41.5	10.5	0	23	0.5	1
1859-63	320	10	34.5	13.5	2	31	4	5
1864-8	460	5	25.5	16.5	6	32.5	9	5.5
1869-73	469	7	18	12	19	32	8	4
1874-8	439	3.5	13	12.5	29	31	9	2
1879-83	472	4	10	15.5	24	36	8	2.5
1884-8	475	3.5	7	18	17	44	7	3.5

---

[1] The term 'public school' had long been used to denote schools which were principally for boarders. Ancient charity 'grammar' schools like Uppingham's might have a few boarders but they mainly educated local scholars, often of limited means. References to 'public schools' became more prevalent in the mid-nineteenth century as the number of boarding schools grew, and after the Clarendon Commission of the early 1860s which led to the Public Schools Act (1868): see ch. 8.

[2] As a class, they were described by Winston Churchill as 'the sons of merchants and manufacturers, of doctors, lawyers, clergymen, of authors, teachers and shopkeepers'.

Significant numbers came from the country's two wealthiest areas: London and the Home Counties,[1] and (from the late 1860s), cities in the industrial North such as Sheffield. Liverpool's shipping tonnage trebled between 1835 and 1870, enabling citizens who prospered by it to send their sons to boarding schools. Theodore, Thring's eldest brother, held senior posts in the bankruptcy courts in the city (1862-74) and persuaded a number of its parents to choose Uppingham. Others became aware of the school through business associates: a Mr. Gladstone of Cheetham Hill, Manchester heard it well spoken of in cotton circles in 1867. Liverpool talk reached out to an area from Cheshire to Kirby Lonsdale, from where Mr. Pearson sent two sons.[2]

Thring also gathered a personal following from every stage of his life: neighbours from Somerset such as the Newbolts and Cornishes,[3] and sons of Eton and Cambridge contemporaries. Several of his most significant parents were clergymen friends: seven of the eight Skrine boys (Somerset) came to him; Powell, the vicar of Bisham, sent all his sons and other Thames valley families followed; Rawnsley from Lincolnshire and Harman from Peterborough each sent five. There were former Black Dragoons too, following the example of Daniel Macmillan who had always wanted his sons to go to a public school and who had spoken of both Rugby and Uppingham. After Daniel's death Alexander Macmillan asked Thring about possible scholarships for his own sons – and his nephews, having discussed it with Daniel's widow: 'I understand that a boy must be entered years in advance if he goes to Rugby, and I suppose with your present prosperity you will be coming into this condition yourself soon'.[4]

The housemasters of the 1860s had sons, nephews and friends too. 'Westmacott has been here to inspect the school', recorded Thring in

---

[1] As late as 1865 there were so few boys from the North of England that in a match between 'North and South' it was decided that 'the line dividing the two parties must be fixed further to the south than Cambridge'.

[2] The 1880s Principal of Liverpool College appealed for new buildings, so that parents would educate their sons locally instead of 'boarding them away from home and home influence at enormous expense in unhealthy swamps and desolate hillsides in remote parts of England'. Ironically, Selwyn later became Thring's successor.

[3] Examples from Rigby's conversations with Old Boys in the 1960s. Somerset clergymen's sons were among his prominent alumni: Newbolt was later Canon of St Paul's and Cornish became Bishop of Madagascar.

[4] Frederick Macmillan arrived in 1861; Daniel's son, Maurice (named after his godfather, F D Maurice) came in 1866, the father of Prime Minister Harold Macmillan. The Thring and Macmillan families forged close links.

1860, 'he takes private pupils and he is also an old Eton friend of mine and Baverstock'. Approval from preparatory schools was important when parents were abroad: Mr. Feild, stationed in St Petersburg, left choosing the next school for his thirteen-year-old son to the boy's current headmaster. Other parents took immense trouble, and some were overwhelmed by choice. A widow, Mrs. Murray of Dartford, visited Thring in 1861, who thought her 'a nice poor woman, travelling about to the various schools in the wild hope of deciding on a right one. What a chaos her mind must be by the time she finishes'. Her sons duly came.[1]

The early parents especially felt the need to see the school and its headmaster in personal terms: as an extension of their family, headed by a man of strong character and clear aims. Thring fitted this role well. He retraced many times the three-mile journey taken on his own interview visit: walking with his sheep-dog Queer to meet parents at Seaton station; having their luggage loaded on to a horse-drawn cart, and walking with them back to Uppingham as he enthusiastically explained his educational principles. Frederic Barber (and many others) came 'simply because of Thring's reputation'. George Pilkington's elder brother had come to Uppingham on the advice of the Master of Queen's College, Cambridge. By then, Mrs. Pilkington had visited the school and was more than ever satisfied that it was right for George, too. She reported to her husband on Thring's religious conviction – and the power of his personality:

'Every time I hear him, I am struck with how remarkably Mr. Thring is one of those who "speak with authority." I never heard anything... so fine as his reading of the Commandments. Every vestige of a thought "is there any other school I should like better?" vanishes the instant I hear him say "I am the Lord thy God, thou shalt have none other gods but me". The intense force with which, with his whole being, he himself is loyal to that God comes out, and it is a thing that, in these days of unsettled belief, is invaluable'.

Once George had settled in, she wrote again:

'What we want for our boy is just precisely and exactly what [Mr. Thring] wants for him. I look with wonder at that large chapel perfectly full of boys, and reflect that, personally and by name and character, that man knows them every single one. "More than three or four hundred boys", he says, "no headmaster can possibly know, and he has no

---

[1] One was later Secretary of the Treasury; the other, Commandant of the Duke of York's Royal Military School.

business to have more boys than he can know." George says there's not a doubt that he <u>does</u> know them, both in their games and in their work'.

For others, the breadth of curriculum or music was the key factor, and some boys arrived complaining of bad experiences in other schools. In his first decade, however, despite Thring's preference for boys to stay for at least five years, Uppingham was sometimes used as preparation for elsewhere, or as second choice. The demands of recruitment were continuous: half of the first 28 boys left after less than two years, and the average stay was under three. Moreover the predominant age was low (12-15), suggesting that some older pupils departed for better-known schools.

Thring could not deny the implication in Alexander Macmillan's enquiry that the school might sometimes be seen as a poor alternative to Rugby. When the two Pease boys suddenly left Uppingham only to reappear at Rugby shortly afterwards, he reflected with annoyance that their father must 'secretly' have had their names down there for some time. Later, however, what had been a buyer's market became a seller's one, as Macmillan had predicted. When a Somerset clergyman told Thring openly that he would send his ward to Uppingham only if the boy failed to get a place at Rugby, Thring 'wrote to decline the honour', and by 1865, when Bishop Jeune of Peterborough applied, Thring remarked that attracting such a notable parent would once had cheered him, but now 'we are getting on so well that it takes great things to please me'.

By then his reputation for nurturing talents beyond the purely academic had brought one associated risk: that parents would send their cleverer sons to long-established schools, and only their less able ones to Uppingham. To counter this, in 1860 he persuaded the housemasters that they should each take one extra boy, the extra income gained being used to establish two boarder scholarships.[1] He hoped these awards would also help to secure Oxford and Cambridge places, seen by many parents as a certificate of success for the whole school. The Oxford successes of two of his ablest leavers (Wynford Alington and Lewis Nettleship) were a major stimulus to confirming the school's public reputation,[2] and the scholarship scheme kept the boarder numbers rising, but it signalled that he did not greatly mind if day boys were gradually squeezed out.

---

[1] Yearly value £70, tenable for five years. The first advertisement (1860), invited boys under 13 to come with a Latin dictionary at 7.15 a.m. for an exam of 4 translation papers and exercises in Latin Prose and Latin Verse.

[2] Both names were significant later. Thring noted a visit from the Vice-President of Magdalen College, Oxford at the time of Alington's examination: he came as a prospective parent and spoke admiringly of Alington's performance.

****

The day boy issue helped to make Thring one very powerful enemy: a new arrival in the town over whom he had no control. William Wales became Rector of the parish church in 1859, after 27 successful years at All Saints', Northampton. From his large and prominent rectory right in the centre of Uppingham, Wales exercised strong powers of patronage through rents and other payments from tenants of church land.[1] He exercised his legal skills as Chancellor of the Peterborough diocese, a school governor, a town poor law guardian and chairman or member of a string of local committees. Having married well, he was also a man of means.

Wales had two driving motivations. Orphaned at the age of six, he owed his education to the generosity of Christ's Hospital,[2] from which he later developed a strong interest in educational opportunity through the SPCK.[3] This had led him in Northampton to set up a 'religious and useful knowledge society', complete with an education programme of classes and lectures backed by a library, reading room and museum. From Uppingham he often went to preach at the nearby railway mission. He also strongly disapproved of dissenters and free-thinkers; in his previous parish they had drawn caricatures of 'Billy Wales, the black slug'. He determined to make his church the centre of religion in Uppingham, and he attracted congregations of over 500 each Sunday morning and evening.

Wales and Thring were as different in circumstances, temperament and churchmanship as it was possible to be: the austere, legalistic, humourless high-church parish priest with a rich wife but no children, and the hard-pressed evangelically-minded, charismatic and impulsive young headmaster with a growing family. Their joint presence in a small town would be a cause of rivalry and conflict, with Wales resenting Thring's growing success and self-advertisement, and Thring envying Wales' personal influence and financial resources.

At the start of the 1860s Thring could not yet realise how much Wales would dog his footsteps over the next twenty years. Perhaps this was just as well: with so many other challenges facing him, he likened his life after

---

[1] The Rectory was at No.2, London Road, where Wales lived in some style with his wife and sister-in-law, together with six servants including a footman. A century after he left it, it became the doctors' surgery.

[2] A sixteenth-century charitable foundation, it had (and still has) an unusually high proportion of its pupils educated free or at a greatly reduced rate. It seems likely that this influenced Wales' priorities for Uppingham.

[3] The Society for the Promotion of Christian Knowledge (1698).

a decade at Uppingham to the endurance test that he remembered facing a decade earlier on the Welsh holiday when he had been improving his mathematics:

'How often I feel as if I could sit down and let all go, so incessant is the struggle. Just as at Tenby when I climbed a very steep slope under a burning sun for half an hour or more, crawling over gorse bushes with my naked hands, and death to let go, now very much, it is the prolonged strain and the turning yourself body and soul into a pin cushion that is so trying. One gorse grasp is nothing, but a series is no joke'.

Ultimately, one thought kept him going: 'I felt confident that if the work was blessed there would be no want of numbers in time, though I kept this to myself, as I should have been set down as mad if I had disclosed my real views... My trust was in God and that it was His work'.

CHAPTER FOUR

TRUST, MANLINESS AND CONFRONTATION

EVEN if Thring had no precise blueprint in 1853, he arrived in Uppingham with some key expectations in mind for both masters and pupils. He began his first diary there with great optimism: 'May God keep our hearts fresh and childlike and not let them be hardened by the vexations which must happen. Boys mean well on the whole: let us trust to that [with] large liberal forgiving hearts'.

The education which he planned to provide should shape not merely brain and body but the spirit, too: it must inculcate 'duty and honour and grit' to ensure 'upright living'. Eton had given him a horror of 'moral miasma', which he defined as a combination of temptation, bullying, lying, cheating, rebellion and sensuality (homosexuality). He was clear about the causes of these things: harsh, remote and unsympathetic masters; boys herded together in 'promiscuous masses'; unimaginative teaching; arbitrary punishments; lack of self-respect and too much time poorly used. These evils must be eliminated, through an infusion of *Life-power*, or *True Life:* twin concepts which appeared in so many of his addresses and sermons that the boys mimicked them.

He saw boarding schools, whose origins he traced back to monastic times, as the fullest expression of that life.[1] Their success depended on a strong system of houses with top-quality accommodation. There must be high-calibre housemasters: preferably married with children and thus able to create a family atmosphere, because 'every boy who leaves home ought to go to a better than home place'. He was convinced that boarding schools helped to form the adventurous English national character, by giving boys a sense of responsibility and independence and enabling them 'to bear pain, to play games, to drop rank, and wealth, and home luxury'.

At all levels in the community there had to be a sense of mutual trust, with the headmaster and his assistants providing moral and religious leadership but also earning the boys' respect: 'Then you have a right to expect honour, but not otherwise'. Sanctions should improve as well as punish. Some punishment was necessary, but it could be kept to a

---

[1] Thring told Parkin: 'The first germ of the boarding school [was] sending lads into the families of the great nobles to be educated in knightly proficiency with the children of the house. Then the first endowments [arose from] the monasteries which always had schools for the education of the clergy. The public school is a cross between these two'.

minimum if boys respected each other.[1] He thought it unrealistic to ban fagging altogether, because its existence made bullying less likely, but it must be carefully controlled. Being allowed a fag must not be a privilege exclusively for the best sportsmen, and small boys must not become substitute housemaids.

All boys, young or old, must be imbued with qualities of true manliness. His definition of this concept would gradually change over the years. Initially it was essentially masculine, shaped by medieval chivalry as reflected in the writings of Tennyson and Sir Walter Scott. Later he added some more feminine attributes to it: qualities such as intuition, tenderness and sensitivity. This was partly in reaction to the extreme muscular Christianity which emerged in some schools in the 1860s, and partly through the influence of Charles Kingsley (author of *The Water Babies*) and his wife.

Thring recognised the uniqueness of each individual pupil as coming above the general *esprit de corps.* Boys kept busy and interested would be less tempted into trouble. As well as sound classical teaching he would provide a variety of activities – including sport and music – to develop their various skills: 'The whole efforts of school ought to be directed to making boys manly, earnest, and true by everything around them, all that they do and all that is done to them being of the best stamp'. There would be prizes for achievement, but he hoped that good work would be its own reward.

His ambition for his fledgling community was not to be achieved easily or overnight and there were spectacular early confrontations with pupils and parents. Holden had used praepostors (prefects) to set a good example in work and conduct; to help maintain good order and either to punish misconduct themselves or to report it at once to him. Thring saw them much more as role models than policemen, and he was determined not to allow them the excessive powers of punishment given to prefects in other schools. They were only to act collectively (as a court), and he and his school captains would work together to ensure that their decisions could stand the test of community opinion. Boys who were punished would have a right of appeal to him.

Many headmasters looked to their senior pupils to set the tone, but he wanted to go further, instilling self-responsibility right through the pupil body. Every boy should be responsible for breaches of trust. Convinced that the fewer rules he laid down for pupils, the more they were likely to live up to his expectations, he aimed to create a 'state of perfect truth and

---

[1] E.g. boys who broke rules about respecting the countryside had to use the main roads for their afternoon walks.

freedom', in which collective opinion would police the school rather than authority being imposed from above: 'Every society can, if it chooses, send any culprit to Coventry'.[1]

Because liberty implied responsibility, any infringement of the cardinal rules would be dealt with by punishing not only the individual, but entire classes, houses or even the whole school. According to one school captain: 'If anything went wrong, his first question was "*Who was there?*"':

> 'Whoever was head of anything, a house, a dormitory, a class, a ground, or, failing regular officers, whoever was senior of those present, had to answer in his own person... "Why did you permit this?" To the plea of human weakness, he would show an indifference that was sublime... "I don't know who the offenders are, and I don't want to know". When a fashion developed for [set-piece] fights, he threatened to flog both the fighters, all the seconds, and everyone who was looking on'.

Thring justified this by asserting the power of social pressure:

> 'When boys fell short: "I hold that the whole school is responsible for these wrong-doings. Any society can put down offences committed by individuals, if it chooses. Why don't thieves break the windows of jewellers' shops in Regent Street? The policeman, you say? Why, he may be safe round the corner. No, it's because the rogue knows that every honest hand in the crowd would be upon him. People don't like thieves. It's society that keeps down stealing. And your society can keep down cheating and lying. And I am going to help you. The form in which the cheats are will be excluded from the cricket field for a week or two."'

Any excuse that pupils elsewhere behaved in the same way cut no ice. He simply retorted that 'we are not other schools'. Nor would he ever take the line that 'boys will be boys' or 'I was young once myself'. Previous good character rarely counted. It was not a cause for mitigation but 'just the reason why I have got to punish him, to show that *no* good character can excuse the breach of law'.

He was especially uncompromising about cheating and cribbing: 'I hold that to cheat a master is inexpressibly base! You may call it what you

---

[1] 'For instance, if the boys are allowed absolute freedom to walk where they please, on the implied contract that they do not go into pot-houses, the public opinion of the school can prevent this being done... the great point of internal discipline is to make every boy interested in the conduct of his fellows. They are their own lawgivers, inasmuch as the more they show themselves worthy of trust, the more rules are relaxed'.

please: I call it sheer, unmitigated, contemptible lying'. He particularly hated the boys' honour-code of silence. When a parent wrote to him alleging (wrongly, as it turned out) that his son had been punished for not revealing the name of a fellow-pupil in trouble, and stating that the boy's loyalty 'shows the stuff of which our soldiers and sailors are made, and which is supposed to be the good result of public school training', Thring replied that 'we hold *thieves' honour* to be only fit for thieves, and no sneaking is worse than betraying the good and screening the bad'.[1]

Two boys who ran away present an interesting contrast. The first was a sixteen-year-old who warned friends of what he was planning. They assumed that he was joking and did nothing. After an anxious weekend for everyone, he returned, sheepish and glad to be back. It had been a reaction to his guardian repeatedly putting pressure on him to choose a career. He had an unblemished record, and Thring did nothing other than show relief that the disappearance had not been because the boy was unhappy at school. But when a second boy had help from his friends in getting money together to buy a railway ticket, Thring's anger was ballistic: the friends' action was 'conspiracy, rebellion, and high treason'.

To modern eyes some of his actions appear naive or inconsistent. Mass punishment seems to fly in the face of natural justice, and at times it did cause great unfairness. Yet many pupils thought him fundamentally fair-minded, and their tributes after his death suggest that many accepted his methods as a lesson for later life, even if they smarted under them at the time: 'It taught us that we are our brother's keeper'. On balance, they preferred self-policing to the overbearing masters who taught in many of their friends' schools.

Three years after quelling the mild demonstration that had marked his first evening there was a much more complex battle of wills. He recognised this as a defining moment, and decided to face the miscreants with a direct choice: either to accept his system or to leave the school. Four senior boys had been playing cards, a strictly forbidden act, and they were beaten. However, the praepostor body (seven in all) had known about it, so Thring dismissed them *en masse*. He then set punishments for every pupil in all the sections of the school which contained culprits, and

---

[1] 'Cribbing' was the use of a printed translation, hidden on a pupil's knees as he sat at his desk. It became a point of honour not to use cribs in construing work after Thring banned them. Skrine: 'Thring would sometimes say: "I don't know who the offenders are, and I don't want to know. They would not have done it if the rest of you disliked it enough. I hold that society can keep down any offences it disapproves of, and I mean to give you reasons for disapproving of this kind of thing"'.

made the entire school attend a roll call every hour. The action was disproportionate, but deliberately confrontational: 'I had always warned them that I would make the whole school responsible for any great breach of trust'.

The boys reacted immediately, refusing to take a call-over (register) of pupils. Treating it as only a moderate rebellion, Thring took the call-over himself and, after carefully explaining his earlier actions, held his ground and his peace for three weeks. Two praepostors had missed the call-over through being away from the school that day. When they eventually returned, he repeated his explanation to them and asked whether they supported him, adding that he was still determined to make the entire praepostor body admit its original misjudgement if he was to reinstate them. If they joined the rebellion, they would never be restored. After a night to consider, the pair sided with him. He immediately appointed some additional praepostors, reinstating them and two others who had back-tracked, and ending the other punishments.

There was then another disciplinary clash: insolence from a boy to a master. It is not clear whether it stemmed from the previous incidents, but again he treated it firmly, sending for the boy, who then refused to kneel down and was soundly caned standing up. The situation was snowballing. Two senior boys came to disturb his Sunday afternoon by telling him that he had acted wrongly. Their 'impertinence' led to a heated argument, after which they backed down. He sent them away with a message to the trio of former praepostors who were still holding out after the original incident: either they must reconsider or they would hear further from him. This ultimatum brought one decisive change of heart. That night, the captain of the school, Henry Barstow, 'the only one I cared about', came and apologised.[1]

By a mixture of boldness and patience Thring had wooed the seven, relying on their eventual good sense. The acceptance by most of them of the full code of collective responsibility was a major break-through, and he restored Barstow as school captain. However, to show the pupil body that he was not weakening, he then sent for the boy whom he had earlier beaten for insolence, telling him that he would now receive a second caning for refusing to kneel down. When the boy hesitated, Thring took out his watch and gave him two minutes – or he would return home for good, escorted by Thring's servant on the next train.

Finally he allowed the two remaining rebel praepostors a further evening to change their minds, but when they refused, he demoted them

---

[1] Barstow was eighteen: school captain and the captain of the XI. Winning him over was crucial.

for good, before making a trenchant speech to the entire school on the following morning and then expelling the pair for good measure. The five praepostor survivors signed a compact, pledging never to break the rules about drinking or smoking again and 'that should such a necessity arise we will do our best to prevent their being broken'. Barstow was so nervous that he signed in the wrong place and his first signature had to be scratched out. Thring countersigned, later writing in his diary that 'the question of authority was forever set at rest by the result of this contest'.

Where trusted senior boys had defied him because they thought him unjust, he had played a long game, eventually persuading three-quarters of them to submit. By contrast he had summarily dealt out two very sharp lessons to an insolent boy who had refused to take a punishment he deserved. He was learning fast.

****

It was inevitable, sooner or later, that such an uncompromising stand on discipline would be challenged by a parent. In 1859, less than three years after the card-playing incident, the praepostors reported two of their own number – the school captain, John Williams, and a boy in Thring's own house, Marmaduke Athorpe – for drinking and smoking. The pair promised that they had learned their lesson, and Thring barred them from competing for that year's prizes. Further enquiries then suggested that the ringleader was one Thomas Frederick Fowler, who was making illicit visits to a girl in the town. Fowler's belongings were searched, revealing a betting book. It transpired that for a year he had been carrying on what Thring called 'a system of organised profligacy', aided and abetted by one friend who lived locally and another who was at Marlborough.[1]

Thring expelled Fowler. At this point Williams' father, who had supported Thring's action against his son, suddenly decided that the original investigation had been mishandled; that the blame lay entirely with Fowler and that Thring had demonstrably lost control of the school. Williams demanded that all sanctions against his son be dropped. When Thring refused, he withdrew the boy and appealed to the governors, who declined to interfere.

Fowler's uncle then entered the fray, with a widely-circulated letter claiming that his nephew had previously had a good disciplinary record. He conceded that Fowler had been justly punished for this incident but asserted that the boy had accepted a caning on the understanding that this

---

[1] Possibly it was a betting ring. Thring was very annoyed that Marlborough declined to investigate the evidence he sent.

would be the end of it, only then to be expelled. Thring had acted 'hastily and unjustly', not least in opening a boy's private letters.[1]

Mr. Fowler backed up this appeal with testimonials from his nephew's teachers, who had found him 'generous, confiding, truthful, and temperate'. To Thring's fury, one of these, 'a flimsy, lying affair', was from the boy's first Uppingham housemaster, the disaffected Blakiston, now a headmaster elsewhere. Blakiston wrote glowingly of Fowler's work and conduct: he had been a boy 'likely to do me great credit. I am very sorry to hear that he has been so injudiciously treated'. Worse still, Blakiston suggested that Thring's actions smacked of the treatment that boys received in 'the lowest of private schools, and I sincerely trust that [Fowler's] future career may prove the folly and injustice of those who have so mismanaged him'. To Thring, it was 'the first time in my life that I have had to deal with real malice and deliberate untempted wickedness'.[2]

The attack from the Fowler camp continued for some time, and shook Thring far more than he cared to admit. He saw that he had acted against Williams before all the facts were known, but he had not anticipated how determinedly parents would seek to undermine his position: 'It is no wonder schools are what they are whilst parents are what they are'.[3] The affair dragged on for some time, but the governors stood firm, and the masters mostly supported him.

This confrontation had only two redeeming aspects for Thring. It added to the collection of complaints that he was already accumulating about Fowler's housemaster, Mathias. It also turned out to be the making of one of the original miscreants, Athorpe, whom (perhaps surprisingly) Thring appointed school captain later in 1859. In that role, during a long rain-break in a cricket match Athorpe was tempted into playing cards with other members of the team. Two evenings later he arrived in Thring's study in tears saying that he could not go to communion next day without confessing first. Thring praised his courage, which encouraged Athorpe to

---

[1] Probably also the boy's guardian. The school roll suggests that Fowler's father had died. The uncle seems to have thought the sanction was for playing cards: in fact it was for habitual drinking and smoking too.

[2] Blakiston subsequently took the Williams boy at Giggleswick, but soon fell out with him. In September, Thring heard with glee that Williams had been taken away from the school and put to work in his father's office.

[3] 'Who could have guessed the efforts made by parents to corrupt and degrade all good school life? I feel a serene rest when engaged in [teaching], and could do it ten times as well if parents would leave one in peace'.

return later with news of a suspected gathering of secret drinkers from several houses somewhere outside the school. He asked what to do.[1]

Thring told him not to act on an uncorroborated accusation. Athorpe should summon the suspects before the praepostors, warn them that they would be watched and that if they persisted, they risked expulsion. It had little effect: within a week Mathias came to report four of the same boys (from his house) for breaches of discipline, including 'indecency'. Even so, Thring refused to be rushed into expulsions. He mulled it over that evening, initially deciding to persuade the parents of one boy to withdraw him. However, he later changed his mind: he would merely punish the four for the proven misdemeanours and send a letter of warning to their parents. Despite the entreaties of both Athorpe and Mathias, he was reluctant to expel the boys, preferring to reform them if he could.[2]

Within a few days the local policeman reported that two of the boys were spending time in a small side-street tavern every Saturday. Thring asked Athorpe to find out who they were: one was caned and then removed by agreement; the other turned out to be the boy whose friends had bought a ticket to help him run away from school some years earlier. The praepostors wanted him expelled for ignoring every warning and lying his way out of trouble, but his guardian wrote pleading for a final chance. Thring gave it, not without misgivings: it was the first time that he had ever reversed an expulsion. He did so only because the boy was an orphan. His decision, and the faith which he had placed in Athorpe as school captain despite a chequered disciplinary past, both suggested a growing confidence.

****

In 1861 he faced another major challenge. After being frustrated for some time by boys casually returning late after the mid-half break,[3] he repeatedly warned that this must stop. In April several boys again ignored him. There were various justifications: one had been at a wedding; another had waited to see a brother off to the Far East; a third had missed his train. By now Thring's policy was to accept such excuses only if prior

---

[1] Some were in Baverstock's house, some in Mathias' and one in Earle's – but probably not Thring's.

[2] He may also still have been concerned about the impact on pupil numbers of the Fowler case. Athorpe died at only 29. Thring said: 'He was one of my most influential captains, much good, much evil mixed, but the good prevailed. He filled such an important epoch in my school life. Pray God we meet in heaven'.

[3] At this stage the school year was still divided into two halves. See ch. 5.

permission had been obtained, so he caned eight boys – including the Jackson brothers, George and Richard. They boasted to their friends that it had not hurt at all, but their father angrily demanded an explanation. He immediately received a very detailed one, perhaps because Thring could not ignore that fact that the Jacksons lived near Marlow, his own former home and now a fruitful recruiting ground.

The boys' indignant grandmother then weighed in, claiming that Thring had ignored the boys' explanations about the poor train service, and that her other grandson who was at Rugby would never have been treated so unfairly by *its* headmaster, Dr. Temple. Mr. Jackson conceded that the boys were at fault, but thought the punishment too severe. He carefully couched his protest in Thringian terms, appealing to Thring's 'conscience as a Christian [and as one] to whom the education of youth is entrusted'. Thring should have 'used that discretionary power upon which you lay so great a stress, on the side of mercy rather than its opposite'.

Thring was conciliatory, again patiently asserting that late-returners could not be ignored and that he had to punish all of them.[1] Unfortunately, Jackson took this as encouragement to demand a complete climb-down, while Thring felt himself being patronised by righteousness. He was sure that the boys had known the score, because they were 17 and 18 and had been in the school for five years, and he disagreed with their father's claim that they were too old to be caned. He could see no extenuating circumstances.

This hit the sanctimonious Mr. Jackson very hard. He threatened that unless Thring backed down, he would remove both his sons and make a formal complaint to the governors. When Thring gave him short shrift, he promptly carried out both threats. He also lobbied the new Bishop of London (Archibald Tait, Temple's predecessor as headmaster of Rugby), and persuaded one of his neighbours in Marlow to threaten to withdraw her son too. Thereafter he dragged out the dispute for over nine months, regularly writing letters to the national and local papers.

Thring especially hated the caricatures of him in those newspapers which reported each turn of the story with relish. The school's reputation was still fragile, and he felt bound to reply individually to every one of the abusive letters he received: on a single day in January 1862 he despatched nearly forty replies to prospective parents who were demanding explanations. Worse still, Jackson gleefully sent Thring every hostile press cutting, stoking the anxiety which was still Thring's Achilles' heel:

---

[1] Jackson had been a pupil at Shrewsbury. Thring added: 'Would *you* have come back late to Shrewsbury with impunity?' Having had brothers there himself, he knew that Shrewsbury sent out term dates with each term's bills.

'I feel so jaded, and badgered and faithless that a little (or much) of the old Adam rises and I almost long to plunge into some wild challenge of the world, set my teeth and die fighting'. Four days later: 'I could have sat down and cried today, I felt so vexed and wounded. A most bitter sarcastic satire on me in the *Saturday Review*'.[1]

He feared that the dispute would ruin nine years of hard, patient work. His gloom was not helped by 'the little superiorities and patronisings' that he received from his family at Alford: 'They are all so *wise*: that is perhaps the most painful part'. A sharp letter from his normally gentle mother suggested that he suffered from 'schoolmaster dogmatism'. He was frustrated that his two older brothers had no idea of the complexities of his job, and furious that Charles (still his employee) had written to the press about how the Jacksons might have been better handled: 'He is most wilful and she (Lydia) at the bottom of all the mischief'.

Not wishing to escalate his personal dispute with Mr. Jackson still more, he banned the masters from starting a press campaign on his behalf, but his old friend and a much respected parent, Harvey Goodwin (now Dean of Ely), came to his defence with a pithy letter to *The Guardian* which Thring circulated to parents. Better still, the *Morning Post* and the *Daily News* reprinted the Dean's letter, and *Punch* took the *Saturday Review* to task.[2] As the balance of incoming letters became more supportive, Thring was amused to hear that a parent had written to Jackson 'telling him that as his boys were so low in the school and stupid, he had much better have held his tongue, [and] that this was his opinion and everybody's about here and in Uppingham'.

The tide had turned, although it was much easier for the public to believe in a flogging headmaster than in a school based on trust and reasonability – and to perpetuate the saying: 'Dr. Thring's school, where

---

[1] Jackson published the correspondence as a pamphlet. Thring: 'I have been honoured with scurrilous leading articles or notices in sundry of the low papers. Mr. Jackson and the *Morning Star* bill and coo together, and lies float about. Private letters of the vilest abuse come in... a threatening letter, beginning "You d--d scamp" from some righteous individual... one can but bear it all as best one may. Some nice things too from friends'.

[2] The *Northampton Mercury* reprinted Jackson's letter to *The Field,* and Goodwin's riposte. Jackson sent copies to the masters, first cutting out Goodwin's letter. Thring circulated copies of Goodwin's letter himself. Godfrey tried unsuccessfully to persuade a friend, Edward Freeman, who wrote articles for the *Saturday Review*, to write a defence of Thring, but was told that he overestimated the importance of Uppingham and that the storm would soon blow over.

they whip the boys so'.[1] Together the Fowler and Jackson cases checked the steady growth in numbers. In just six years before these disputes, the school had grown from 40 to 140, and in three more years once they were over, it would grow from 174 to 300. However, while they were taking place (1859-62), numbers climbed only from 140 to 174: well short of the 200 places that the housemasters had optimistically provided. One of them experienced 'an almost absolute cessation of entries'; another took on a small house expecting sixteen boys, only to find that his actual numbers in his first five terms were 0, 1, 2, 4 and 8. For a third: 'It was no fun... studies vacant quarter after quarter made a sorry sight. I had fifteen vacancies for two years. But we had friends and slowly the clouds passed'.

For Thring, the most cheering aspect of his troubles was the way in which the boys rallied to his support. On 4 March 1862, the school captain brought him a memorial signed by 163 of the 174 pupils, expressing their sympathy in the 'false and unjust' attacks on him. He saw it as 'a great reward for truth to have carried the school so with me. I shall have it framed and kept in my drawing room'. Other messages followed from Old Boys at Cambridge and Oxford, which helped him to ignore the suggestion in the *Morning Star* that the boys' memorial (which the paper published) had been prompted by fear of a caning. *Punch* provided the best judgement on it all: 'We don't know whether Mr. Thring trains the boys' minds; but he makes them mind their trains'.

****

It is hard to determine just how much Thring's disciplinary decisions in this period were determined by his desire to reform boys; by a fear of losing parental confidence, or even by his psychological state at the time. After the Jackson case, he admitted in his diary: 'I have detected an oldish boy making a row in a bedroom, and concealing himself. I should have caned him soundly last half year, but in honest truth I dare not now. So he will get a long imposition instead, but I am sure this will cause evil and difficulty another day'. He tried increasingly to restrict expulsion to cases involving 'sins' (moral offences) or situations in which trust between the school and a pupil had irretrievably broken down.

---

[1] Eventually the newspapers were drowned out by encouraging letters. A Mrs. Murray made a point of calling on him, and a Canadian whose sons had joined the school on the advice of the Macmillans wrote to cheer him. Unlike many other headmasters of the day, Thring was not in fact a 'Dr.'.

During the smoking incident involving Williams, Athorpe and Fowler, some masters felt that he was too lenient towards Athorpe (in his own house)[1] whilst being uncompromising with Fowler (one of Mathias' boys). Even senior pupils sometimes found him unpredictable and quixotic: he liked to keep them guessing or to surprise them.

When he met a trio of praepostors on their way to a school concert one evening, they were breaking a rule by walking three abreast and arm-in-arm down the street.[2] He gave them a fearsome dressing-down; they protested, and he agreed to meet them later. They filed nervously into his study, knowing that he was quite capable of caning or expelling them all. They found the room in total darkness apart from a green reading light directed towards his face. When they protested that they had meant no harm, their diffident spokesman kept stuttering. At each pause Thring grimly intoned the word 'Well...?' Then he suddenly broke into laughter and the conversation became relaxed. When one of the boys then politely reminded him of some of the names he had called them in the street, he challenged him playfully: 'You great baby, did you think I meant them?'

Years later this same boy, now an adult, suggested that Thring had been less autocratic with the sixth form than with his masters, because he trusted the boys more. He may well have had a point, and it would certainly have been understandable if housemasters sometimes felt poorly supported. As he struggled to make them into a cohesive body, he realised that he must give them a degree of autonomy, but with their houses being so dispersed, he did not want to let them become too independent or baronial. He set strict limits on their discretion, insisting on common standards in accommodation and catering and as much consistency as possible over matters of trust and punishment.

He was very concerned that no master should punish boys to mask his own failings. Even though the cane saved time compared with setting lines or detentions, he insisted (on pain of dismissal) that no master should administer it except him – and then only under formal conditions: never in haste or anger.[3] He greatly irritated housemasters by telling them to be more patient with miscreants, or by saying that 'before I came here I

---

[1] Of the dozen boys most closely involved in these incidents described, houses can be identified for only about half. Of that group, only Athorpe was in Thring's house.

[2] He was keen to avoid confrontations with members of the town who had been edged off the pavements.

[3] Corporal punishment was the standard punishment of the day – although not on the scale of Keate at Eton. Holden had flogged with a birch, but Thring (though he called it flogging) only caned.

taught a rougher set than you have ever had, and under worse circumstances'. They had to make out their case to him for canings, and he regularly told them that the request seemed to be a result of their own inadequacies, or that they were coming to him for support too often. When they asked for a boy to be expelled, they were not happy to be challenged with questions such as: 'Have you facts and evidence of any magnitude? A false step might be very serious', or to be told that it was 'a failure in the training power if a boy has to be got rid of'.

He reminded them too of how easy it was to make even the most hardened boys into martyrs, and he sometimes made himself unpopular by taking a boy's side. One housemaster was told: 'I do not think we are concerned with his influence on others: you are too sensitive'; another that his boy felt very unjustly treated and would be allowed to stay for at least another term: 'You will kindly be conveniently blind to anything that does not force itself on your notice, and gentle with what does. I have promised that the boy shall meet with friendly treatment and consideration'.[1]

Publicly however, despite the temporary setbacks caused by Fowler or Jackson, by the mid 1860s Thring was admired by parents and most pupils as having uncompromising, if sometimes rigid, standards. He was seen as a man not lightly to be crossed: an image that he was happy to cultivate. Walking around the school one day he spotted a notice listing two teams for a cricket match. One team was labelled: 'Those who have been beaten by Mr. Thring' and the other: 'Those who have not'. He smiled, observing to those around him that 'if the game is played again, all the players will be on the same side'.

---

[1] One master told him that boy "A" needed caning for insolence. Thring agreed, and the boy was caned. A week later the master made exactly the same request. Thring told him: '"A" shan't be crushed; he is a very good boy, but at present he is standing at bay like a rat in a corner. Punish him slightly for this, and for the next month shut your eyes resolutely to everything you are not obliged to see.' This plan worked. To another master: 'I observe with much concern the number of boys you report for punishment, and the reasons you give. I know the boys, and I have no hesitation in saying that nothing but grave incapacity for management on your part can account for some of them having conducted themselves as you report them to have done'.

CHAPTER FIVE

WIDER HORIZONS: NARROWER VISIONS

IN 1880 a formidable Cheshire lady, Mrs. Jackson,[1] wrote to her second son, then at a small private school. She wanted to tell him about her investigations into possible future schools for him as far apart as Clifton, Repton and Sedbergh, and she summarized Uppingham in her letter: '[It] is a first rate public school where you could learn carpentry, drawing and German in addition to Latin and mathematics... The full number is about 300 boys: 30 in a house, each boy having a study and a cubicle to himself'.

She enclosed Thring's *Statement* of his aims (originally written for his governors, but now also being used as a prospectus), adding: 'Uppingham could afford you plenty in subjects which would be useful to you for business. Drawing, German, French, mathematics are all taught. There is also a science master there. You could take up any subject: Spanish, chemistry etc'. Possibly sensing something which might attract him rather more than all these lessons, she added: 'A healthy bracing situation and the longest holidays, 16 weeks...'

Thring's emphasis on a broad education, by then developed over many years, convinced both mother and son. In designing his curriculum he was less constrained by examinations and inspection than his modern counterparts, but parents needed reassurance that schools were academically sound: the most public indicator of success was still their results at Oxford or Cambridge. A rudimentary system of examinations began in the late 1850s, when schools approached the major universities to send them examiners: men who stayed for several days, and oversaw tests well into the evening.[2]

Thring inherited a school year of two halves, running from early February to late June and mid-August until Christmas. Morning lessons were from 7-8.30 and again from 10-12. There were 'extra subjects' for an

---

[1] No relation to the boys who missed their trains in the previous chapter. Her two sons arrived in 1880.
[2] Examiners wore full academic dress. Their vists were more like modern inspections (albeit through administered tests) than today's public examinations. School and Higher School Certificate examinations began in 1918.

hour before lunch and on non half-holiday afternoons, and 'private work' after tea on weekdays from 7-8.45.[1]

Holden's formal curriculum had been almost entirely classical. Thring changed its overall balance, but not (despite his strong interest in mathematics whilst at Cambridge) its core emphasis. Morning lessons were prime learning time, to be devoted mostly to Latin and Greek language and literature because they trained mental faculties and helped a boy to use accurate English. He held that 'a literary education contains the best thoughts of the best thinkers in the best shape, [and] is the most perfect training for [a boy], whatever he may be obliged to do later in life':

'If I wanted to train a soldier, I should not take a child and drill him every day and put him through the regimental movements; I should teach him to race, to climb, to swim, to be a gymnast, to play games, to make his body as strong, as active, as enduring as possible. It will be quite time enough to narrow this, and teach him the goose step, when he enlists. So also with the mind. If our literary and classical education is true... it makes the mind strong and ready'.

The mastery of language was one of the greatest gifts that each generation could pass on to the next,[2] and dead languages were better subjects of instruction than living ones: 'Once you are past sentence-structure, the more difficulties in a language, the better; because a dead language cannot be learned parrot-fashion from a governess'. Inflected languages, with their subtle variations in word-order, were most likely to train a pupil in the importance of accuracy.

Even so, he recognised that for academically limited boys an excess of Latin and Greek literature merely led to 'the unintelligent dealing with the unintelligible'. The complexities of language-development would be

---

[1] The termly pattern ran until the early 1870s, when a three-term pattern was developed: see chapter 12. The first lesson ended at 8.40 in winter. Afternoon lessons were from 2.30-4.00 in summer: in winter, games came first while the daylight held, with lessons from 4.00-5.25. There were half holidays on saints' days. Private work was akin to modern homework, or 'prep'.

[2] 'Perfectly easy [yet] perfectly hard; familiar to all and known to none; of universal use and universally strange to the users; so simple that babies learn it with ease, and so complicated that the ablest are ever clearing it unsuccessfully; the most fixed of all things and the most shifting; plain, yet infinitely obscure; the common property of ignorance and wisdom; the joint inheritance of the ploughboy and the poet; holding nothing and yet full of all things; all these and many more paradoxes are reconciled in language'.

beyond them, or little more than exercises in fact-cramming.[1] He allowed them to drop some, though not all, Latin verse composition, but ancient history was a different matter. He believed that studying it helped to build character, and he strove 'to make [it] a living thing, to join together the ages, and show how thought in heathen times worshipped form and beautiful shape, and how thought in Christian times worships expression and beautiful life'.

His core curriculum consisted of classics, scripture, English language and composition, and some arithmetic. There was a little chemistry, but he preferred science to be learned through practical work and observation, encouraging such initatives as the boys' garden plots, and the field naturalists' club, although in 1866 he found a part-time lecturer on the principles of physics, because pupils had pointed out that Rugby had such a teacher and demanded to know: 'Why should we be behind other public schools?' Prizes were offered for the best essays and projects in history and geography, but these subjects were not allocated periods in the timetable. There were occasional lessons in public speaking.

After mid-day boys could take two 'extra subjects' in which the atmosphere would be more relaxed, yet still purposeful. These included French, German, drawing, gymnastics, and metalwork and carpentry classes where Thring led by example, with huge concentration and notable skill.[2] He carved portraits of his children on the panels of a wooden casket, invented (and later patented) a smoke-preventing fire-grate for his study and designed a 'drop-gate' for the cricket field. Typically, he thought his fire-grate to be 'the best in the world', and his enthusiasm was only briefly dampened when his prototype for a slow combustion stove nearly suffocated him as he tested it out in his greenhouse. Facilities often had to be improvised: lessons took place in house dining halls; science in makeshift laboratories; carpentry and metalwork in tumbledown cottages. Music rooms were created in a disused alehouse.[3]

After mid-day boys could take two 'extra subjects' in which the
Afternoons and evenings saw an increasing variety of sporting and musical activities and voluntary societies, bringing pupils together from

---

[1] He regarded philology (the study of language in written historical sources) as 'totally unsuited to school'.

[2] Thring held that French was suitable only for 'conversational purposes' and that German, with its 'complete structure' constituted a better intellectual training. His carpentry reflected his manual dexterity: Skrine reckoned that 'no-one ever sharpened a pencil as beautifully as he did'.

[3] The Chequers Inn was bought as a music school: a rabbit-warren of small rooms. The sounds of competing pianos led Thring to give it a Lakeland name: Scale Hill.

across the whole age-range. There were debates on capital punishment and 'whether football is a better game than cricket', and lectures by masters about their scientific interests or holiday travels. Benguerel took boys on a bird-watching expedition to the Faroe Islands.[1]

Thring was keen to dispel any idea that these activities were of only secondary importance. Their range was highly unusual and they did not come cheap, but he thought them well worth the effort:

> 'Get rid for ever of the idea that painting, music, architecture, sculpture are less noble as mind-power, [just] because we do not put them into our hard-work time... We endeavour by encouraging subordinate studies, for the stupid especially, to make everyone capable of doing something – at least to give all some knowledge, and thus avoid the festering corruption of a heap of hopeless idlers... Every fresh interest in a school is a fresh barrier against evil... a net which catches someone and educates those who are usually neglected and left to rot'.

Above all, every child could do *something* well. One former pupil summed it up: 'If a stupid lad excelled in the carpenter's shop, or a fool in form made good hits to leg, or took his hurdles easily, or a duffer at Greek prose bowed his violin well, we had the feeling that the headmaster looked on him as a *good fellow*'.

****

In Holden's time there had been rudimentary cricket and local versions of fives, hockey and football, as well as swimming in the local brook; walks for bird-watching or to look at local churches; skating and snowballing; boys following hounds and paper-chasing. By mid-century many headmasters were starting programmes of more formalised activities: football, rowing and various racket games were all widespread, and gymnastics skills were being copied from Germany. Games were becoming more competitive, but they were still prized for their social and recreational value; masters sometimes joined in and senior boys often helped with their organisation.

---

[1] Witts described Vesuvius and Pompeii in 1868, and a trip around the Black Sea. Thring described Rome, Italy. Rowe (see ch. 11) spoke about geology, natural history and sciences, shooting stars and atmospheric electricity. There were demands for a museum and a tuckshop (both quickly realised); chess, croquet and quoits; a better library; straw hats in summer, and more prizes. Some were suggested because 'private' (i.e. proprietor) schools did not have such events, reflecting a desire for the school to have a stronger reputation and social cachet.

Thring's enthusiasm for games sprang not only from a desire to keep boys out of the mischief of 'hopeless idleness', but also from his childhood love of the outdoors, along with some personal skill and a belief that through sport his school could become better-known.[1] It gave un-intellectual boys the chance to develop self-confidence. *All* boys should aspire to 'the racer's spirit', yet they were also expected to show fairness and generosity. Visiting speakers were expected to praise the development of character, not just athletic success. Convinced that some doctors cosseted healthy boys too much,[2] Thring promoted the concept of sound mind in sound body, extolling the virtues of a healthy diet and denouncing the evils of tobacco. His pupils should strive for 'a proper balance between manliness and intellect'. Sport had character-building benefits because its pleasure was mixed with 'pain, possible disagreeables, blows, defeat, disappointment, mortified pride, trials of temper, trials of courage, trials of honesty'. It should never be approached with half-heartedness, but above all it should be fun: enjoyed for its own sake because 'merriment unlocks the heart', and not regarded as a tribal rite.

Ball games had special virtues for him. When his colleagues joined in, it reinforced the notion of a community united through ties of mutual competition and respect: 'Masters and boys mixed, both understanding a drive or good cut... [or] a stinging catch, which sends mutual respect into the tips of the fingers'. He led by example until well into middle age, although he always claimed that he played only by invitation, leaving all the organisation, field placings and umpiring to the boys – while adding disingenuously that they did sometimes consult him because of his greater experience.

Early on, he built a fives court within Holden's enclosed *tectum* play area, and he saw the gymnasium as a valuable asset which boys could use

---

[1] According to Dominic Erdozain: *The Problem of Pleasure: Sport, Recreation and the Crisis of Victorian Religion* (2010) p.108: 'Thring was the most representative exponent of moralising athleticism; [he] translated a Romantic delight in natural exuberance into the structured idiom of games, turning muscular Christianity into a practical system'. Erdozain accepts that Thring had a passion for nature and bodily exercise, but also suggests that 'Thring waged war on "the devil work of impurity" with the diversionary tactics of sport', and that 'games and the culture surrounding them amounted to an out-sourced remedy for vice and temptation'.

[2] Housemasters were expected to feed boys well, 'especially in the matter of beer'. Sound health was derived from 'gymnastics, games, pedestrianism, and other forms of bodily exertion'; staff were forbidden to smoke in front of boys, and he insisted that houses employ the school doctor, Thomas Bell.

in their spare time as well as during formal activities. He had to search much longer for a safe swimming area and permanent fields: it took four years of negotiation before the school could rent the 'Middle', a large field to the south of the town (1865), whereupon the masters paid for its levelling. Thereafter he gradually acquired additional fields as pupil numbers grew. He worked hard to keep on good terms with local farmers, drawing up detailed rules for cross-country running, steeplechases, paper-chases, and country walks – in which the masters sometimes joined – as well as donating annually to the agricultural show.

In theory the Committee of Games, formed of senior boys from 1857, published rules and results and acted as 'arbiter of all disputes', but Thring had to approve its members and he insisted on the captain of the XI holding the post for just one year. Only sixth formers could play in matches, and only with housemasters' permission. All games officials had to keep to his fundamental principles, which included a ban on games fagging which he saw as 'the curse of slavery for little boys'. *All* boys who played cricket were expected to help roll the pitch, whatever their seniority.

He drew up rules himself for athletic sports in 1859, insisting that they remain voluntary. Training was allowed, but nothing beyond 'normal exercise and abstinence from pudding'. In the next decade the athletics prize-giving in the new schoolroom (built in 1863) became an annual event with speeches. He thought it 'of wonderful importance in communicating and exemplifying our life', yet races remained far from obsessively competitive, and one boy who had been the champion for the previous two years was barred from competing a third time. There was even a short-lived proposal for handicapping previous winners.

Nowhere was the domestic, gentleman-amateur ethos more evident than in the very popular gymnastics.[1] Thring insisted that its prizes should be 'rather a joke [and] things that perished in the using', which in practice meant a goose for the winner (to be eaten in his house), a large pork pie for the runner-up, and a pot of jam for whoever came third. Thus the entire house shared the pleasure of winning.

A revealing photograph of the cricket XI of 1858 shows nine boys and two masters. The boys wear their ordinary Sunday best, and Thring, then in his late thirties, sits in the middle, wearing his favourite black wide-

---

[1] Gym was an 'extra' subject from 1860. It was cheaper than many other activities. 25% of pupils opted for it by 1865. Thring held that gymnastics skills helped develop reading: another link between body and intellect.

awake hat. Next to him, the captain wears a long tail-coat.[1] It proclaims his refusal to give high status to cricket or any other single game, because 'no good school will be without many different appliances for securing the interest [of] *all* the boys… Training means *everybody* learning how to use time well'.

All through the 1850s and early 1860s the games programme was informal and homespun, with boys expected to play a minimum of just one game of football per week. There were plenty of pick-up teams such as Tall versus Short or Cambridge versus The World. Cricket apart, many of the games were still largely based on local rules. Housemasters played in house matches, and an Old Boys match began in 1865, though only a few turned up. Thring disliked slackers, shirkers, and teams which played without spirit but he was equally sorry if a team won too easily. He did not want sporting success to become an obsession and he spoke frequently against the 'donkey worship' of mindlessly turning games champions into heroes.

Thring's philosophy can be seen as more in keeping with the all-round, creative mixture of aesthetics and athletics of Athens than the narrower, more physically-focused tradition of Sparta which would come to dominate many schools later in the century. He may justifiably claim to have developed a pioneering physical education curriculum: a programme whose five constituent parts spanned country pursuits (essentially recreational, for freedom and communion with nature, including paper-chasing, running with hounds and skating); gymnastics (for organic development); athletics (for personal challenge); ball games (for social mixing, healthy competition and moral training), and swimming (to prevent drowning).

Above all there should be no separation of boys into athletes and aesthetes, and he strove for a balance between manliness and learning: 'If bread strengthens man's heart, the oil and wine of games make him a cheerful countenance'. It was a balance which at times annoyed both the devotees and opponents of games, and it risked giving prospective parents the idea that outstanding games players – like high-flying scholars – might do better elsewhere.

By the 1870s Thring would be increasingly out of step with the muscular Christianity prevalent in many other schools. For the moment,

---

[1] See the photograph in the first plate section. C E Green (on Thring's right) was the captain: see chapter 13. Three of the boys are wearing the black cloth student cap which Marie Thring had introduced from Germany to replace the old-fashioned mortar-boards. Later, cricketers wore the blue caps which featured in Thring's poem 'The Rockingham Match'.

however, games-playing masters were encouraged to involve themselves in other activities to show their breadth of interest, and boys would balance the pleasures of games with those of climbing trees, afternoon reading in the countryside, and games of hop-scotch, peg-top and marbles outside the boarding houses. He was especially gratified when the winners of the athletics races asked him if they might attend that evening's concert as a reward.

****

By 1860, educational reforms in the wake of Arnold had not yet embraced school music. If Thring's vision for games was distinctive, his ambitions for music were extraordinarily enlightened. His enthusiasm for it owed much to another of Plato's beliefs: that the whole life of man stands in need of grace and harmony. This was hardly a fashionable view in late-Victorian boarding schools, where music tended still to be seen as an essentially feminine accomplishment.[1]

Music appears to have impinged little on his life before Uppingham, probably because he was tone deaf: his family believed that the only tune he could recognize was the National Anthem, contrasting with his ability to identify every bird by its sound without seeing it. While he found the *Letters of Mendelssohn* 'a noble book which has done me much good', he could have had little appreciation of the composer's music because he admitted to being 'an ignorant, careless savage, and know[ing] nothing about it, although I support music zealously from a sincere belief in it'. In contrast, Marie and her sister Anna Koch (who lived with them) shared a passion for it, and both participated in concerts in the boarding house.

Thring appointed his first music master within two years of his arrival: another German (Herr Schäfer), who taught the piano and was in charge of a small choir. By 1861 there was a singing class practising sacred music every Sunday evening. Four years later, with nearly 300 boys and a newly-opened school chapel, it was time to find 'not only a first-rate musician who has made music his profession and is a master in it, but a man of personal power and go who can inspirit the boys, and breathe some enthusiasm into them'.

---

[1] Arnold himself was un-musical. Harrow had recently introduced house singing, but piano and organ playing were seen as unmanly there. When one new boy brought a violin to Winchester in 1853, it was confiscated on the grounds that 'he had come to work and not to idle'. There was choral activity in (e.g.) Woodard schools such as Lancing and Hurstpierpoint. Chapel services at Eton and Winchester were sung by professional choirs.

Through advice from a composer friend, William Sterndale Bennett, Thring recruited Paul David from Leipzig.[1] David was only twenty-five, but already steeped in music: his friends included Liszt, Schumann and Brahms. Accustomed to music's high status in German schools, David was disappointed that at Uppingham it had to be learned outside the timetable, but he was heartened by the pupils' enthusiasm and he saw how Thring recognized 'the power of vocal music to enhance and emphasise the meaning of words'. Their admiration quickly became mutual.

Thring thought David was 'of all the men here, [the one] who seems to me to work in the most purely unselfish, noble way'. David loved Handel and Mendelssohn oratorios (and thoroughly disliked Wagner's work). He was musically ambitious: too much for some, causing the new *Uppingham School Magazine* to note of the Beethoven violin concerto that 'its length as well as its character prevented a large proportion of the audience from fully appreciating it', but he employed less highbrow methods to woo boys into the choir, including a Whit Monday picnic. Within three years, concerts also featured works by Haydn, Chopin and Gounod. Sterndale Bennett himself visited the school twice a year and was especially impressed by the strings and piano teaching. 'I can account for their chorus-singing', he once said, 'but to learn an instrument is a different thing'.

David allowed boys to watch the orchestra rehearsing on Sunday evenings, later recalling that 'when we were preparing Beethoven's C minor symphony, our audience grew larger from week to week; sometimes a hundred boys, [and] you began to hear the symphony whistled on the cricket-field, and in the quads of school houses'. Thring was thrilled by David's success, seeing him as 'one of God's many little springs of comfort. When I recollected my own school life, to sit and listen to our boys singing beautiful music of the best kind, with the rest applauding... I could have cried for joy'.

David gave boys another memorable experience: visits by professional musicians, usually from continental Europe. They included the greatest violinist of his age, his friend Joseph Joachim, who came every spring to the end-of-term concert and marked David's ten years at the school in

---

[1] Sterndale Bennett was one of few Englishmen in touch with the vibrant musical world in Germany. In Leipzig, he stayed with the violinist Ferdinand David, a close contact of Mendelssohn (who had written a concerto for him in 1844) who was conductor at the Gewandhaus. Bennett asked David (who had been a notable encouragement to Brahms, Schumann and Schubert) if he knew anyone who might go to Uppingham 'to make music take a proper place in English education'. David replied: 'Perhaps my boy might suit'.

1875 by playing one of Bach's sonatas for unaccompanied violin. He returned repeatedly over three decades, once playing to such an enthusiastic audience that he broke his rule of a professional lifetime by giving them an encore,[1] and after his third performance Thring (perhaps uniquely amongst headmasters of the time) was moved to talk to the boys about opportunities awaiting them at the Royal College of Music.

Not everyone shared Thring's enthusiasm for music for all, feeling that it was given too much favour compared with academic subjects. He dismissed this as 'simply a bit of the old-fashioned Spartan brutality theory versus true education'. One of his many disputes with Mathias concerned the balance between the latter's preference for choir anthems and Thring's own wish to promote congregational singing in chapel. Pupils too could be sceptical. One boy, later a notable composer, took several 'lickings' (beatings) from contemporaries after music manuscripts were found in his study. David overheard one concert described as 'the usual rot: fiddles', and another boy's diary merely noted that 'Dr. Josef Joachim played violin, very nice, went on till about 10.15'. The *Magazine* published a letter in 1863 complaining that all the time spent in practising for the annual concert could be better devoted to 'getting up some good play', and alleging that Thring disapproved of drama on the grounds of its expense. Another writer asked if anyone knew 'of any great public school where the breaking-up is accompanied by a stupid concert, to which visitors are compelled to listen for two hours [to] bad shouting?'[2]

Despite his own musical limitations, Thring collaborated with David on the first collection of his *School Songs*,[3] writing most of the words and adding a new translation of the German Christmas carol *Stille Nacht*. Many of the songs had a sporting theme, designed to reinforce the idea of wholehearted but fair play and healthy exercise. They were undoubtedly

---

[1] Joachim always refused encores to London audiences. He gave another encore in 1885, the year of his last meeting with Thring, who wrote: 'Joachim really likes coming here. He is astonished at David's success'. Joachim continued to visit the school after Thring's death: in 1896 he led the school orchestra at both the rehearsals and the performance, and in 1905 he played the Beethoven Concerto, as it turned out, for the last time.

[2] The writer believed that such goings-on were more suited to a small private school, and pointed out how plenty of 'great schools' put on inexpensive plays. When Thring arranged a concert for the local townspeople, the idea of singing in French struck them as so comic that they burst into laughter. The concert ended in chaos.

[3] These may have been the first vernacular school songs - over a decade before the much more famous Harrow songs appeared. They were published at Thring's own expense by Macmillan.

popular in their time, and they boys cheered them to the echo at their first public performance, although nowadays their sentiments seem quaint: 'Cricketers all, if wickets fall, as fall full well they may, give honour due, good hearts and true, to those who win the day'.

In the *Football Song*:

'Shrieks of triumph, shrieks of woe, heads like nuts together go.
Cowards staring, cracking shins, rubbing hands and no one wins.
Heels are flying into air, heads and shoulders anywhere'.

At least one of them has chivalric overtones:

'Ho, boys, ho! Ho, boys, ho!
Gather round, together stand, raise a watchword in the land;
Stand, my merry craftsmen bold, brothers of the crown of gold,
Wrought in stirring days of old, England's crown....'

In 1876 music became a timetabled subject, and by the time Thring died there were no fewer than seven full-time music staff. A third of the boys (108) were learning an instrument, of whom at least 35 were string players; the instrumental teachers played chamber music to the boys on Thursday afternoons, and the chapel choir numbered more than 100, half of them trebles. By then, Sunday evenings were given over to choral rehearsals of the many oratorios, cantatas and songs which boys performed.

David's motto was uncompromising, for music specialist and enthusiastic chorus-member alike: 'For the young, the best is just good enough', and Thring himself had gone out on a limb to assign a real educational value to music: 'It is the only thing which all nations, all ages, all ranks and both sexes do equally well ... and that is why, though pitifully unmusical, I set such store on it'. He explained his enthusiasm in his introduction to the *Songs*, emphasising that in music (unlike team games) pupils of all ages could join together:

'<u>Any</u> genial solvent is valuable... Music supplies self-respect for young and old, a boon to the ignorant, a refinement to the intellectual, the little boy's hope, the elder's pleasure, a family tie including ladies, an all-pervading influence which takes little heed of differences of age or knowledge'.

****

Two decades of swelling pupil numbers and a burgeoning curriculum were exhilarating for Thring, but they created problems with his employers. His evident success and his radical ideas perplexed – and at times alarmed – them, becoming a major factor in his dysfunctional relationship with them throughout his career.

Archdeacon Johnson's Trust for his two schools gave their oversight to a board of governors. There would be a hereditary patron from the Johnson family, and several senior churchmen could vote by proxy at the appointment of a new headmaster. In practice, however, control lay with a self-selected body of local figures – mostly worthy squires and clergymen.[1] Sixteen held office during Thring's early years: thirteen of them living within 25 miles. Five had been High Sheriff of Rutland, and three had been Tory MPs. Their average age was just over sixty-five. Few had academic learning or knowledge of educational developments nationally; even fewer had sent their sons to the school.

In character they were similar to Thring's father, though less able intellectually, and just as baffled by Thring's vision, restless spirit and impatience. They quickly came to see him as high-handed and unpredictable, partly because he handled them poorly. He clashed particularly with Lord Aveland, whom he described (mostly in his diary, but occasionally more publicly) as a man of 'sordid character... [who] showed his usual narrow bigotry' in what he said at meetings: 'a great conceited baby' and 'a running sore in the body'. When Aveland spoke, 'anything more ignorant I never heard'.[2] As a body, he was apt to describe the governors in epithets such as 'mean spirited consequential dignitaries', feeling that 'I spend my days in leading jackasses up Parnassus'. He complained bitterly after five years that apart from the chairman/patron, General Johnson, they had done nothing to support his school – nor, although they met within it, ever properly looked around it.

Unfortunately for Thring, Oakham was the county town, and the governors had recently decided to build a new school house there. After long delays this had cost nearly £7,000 by 1858 – by which time Uppingham's expansion was well under way. Aveland, who had responsibility for the Oakham buildings, thought Thring's expansionist plans irresponsible. The Trust had other interests, too: it was committed to buying up farm houses next to lands that it owned in Lincolnshire. Its

---

[1] The Bishops of London and Peterborough, the Deans of Westminster and Peterborough, the Archdeacon of Northampton, and the Masters of two Cambridge Colleges, Trinity and St John's, were governors, though rarely active.

[2] Gilbert John Heathcote, 1st Baron Aveland (1795-1867). He lived locally in Normanton.

income of a few thousand pounds per year and its reserves were under pressure.

Thring made an early tactical mistake. In 1856 he drew up a scheme which he presented to the governors on behalf of himself and his Oakham counterpart, Dr. Wood, a surprisingly meek ally – if indeed Wood really acquiesced. The proposal was for the two schools to become complementary. It argued that recently improved roads and railways made it inevitable that they would come into greater competition against each other unless one of them became a preparatory school for the other, or turned into a 'middle school' offering low-cost boarding places to boys 'of a class inferior', and with a curriculum more centred on commercial than academic skills. Uppingham having already expanded so successfully, it was suggested that Oakham should be the school to make this change.[1]

Logic was not everything, and General Johnson wisely warned Thring that he would never be able to get the governors to agree to the idea. Not only would it have reversed the policy of favouring the county town, but 'you are not aware of the very strong local feeling, not only of the governors but of the two towns of Oakham and Uppingham and of the jealousy which has always existed between them'.[2] Johnson was right: the proposal was coldly ignored. Thring took it as a clear but negative message from a body which showed little interest in either opposing or supporting his expansion plans.

By now he faced an urgent need for new teaching buildings. Numbers had far outgrown the Elizabethan schoolroom, and he and other housemasters were holding their own classes in house dining halls. He was also determined to build a chapel. On Sundays at the parish church the boarders were crammed into narrow pews in the gallery, where they could see and hear very little of the service. He produced plans in 1858 for the chapel on land owned by the Trust next to his boarding house. He and the masters would provide the first £500 (later raised to £1,000): he hoped the governors would at least match it. However they were already facing large outgoings for their Oakham project, and he was kept waiting outside

---

[1] John Barber: *The Story of Oakham School* (1983) p.82 suggests that Thring may well have misrepresented Wood when he claimed the latter's support. Such suggestions were not unique though. Dr. Collis of Bromsgrove proposed an amalgamation with King Edward's, Birmingham: Bromsgrove to be a boarding school and King Edward's a day school.

[2] The expansion of Thring's Uppingham had little to do with the decline of Oakham. The fees charged by each school show that they were drawing their boys from different income groups.

'dangling all day like a servant', while they discussed his proposal. In the end, they made no decision at all.

The issue assumed much larger significance a few months later with the unexpected opportunity to acquire a large strip of land stretching from Thring's garden almost to the High Street. The site offered long-term strategic possibilities for other buildings too. Boarding numbers were growing fast; the new gymnasium was about to open and the housemasters' confidence was buoyant. They clubbed together to buy the land, contributing over £1,100 in all, in addition to the £1,000 already pledged towards the chapel. Thring praised their commitment: 'This sudden event gives us the mastery of the ground we want, besides putting it out of the power of the townspeople to screw us... Laus Deo'. Yet even this initiative failed to sway the governors to relax the purse strings.

In his desperation he even suggested temporarily giving up the salary they paid him (and living off just his boarding income) if only they would match the masters' contribution towards the chapel. He also wrote them an upbeat *Statement,* summarising his principles and his achievements to date. He had expanded the school from only 25 (or so he claimed, again ignoring the day-boys he had inherited) to nearly 150, but in reality it had dormitory capacity for 200. Its growing number of houses all contained individual studies where a boy could work undisturbed 'in what is in fact a private sitting room... without being at the mercy of uncongenial companions', while also being part of a small community.

Soon afterwards at a governors' meeting he explained the chapel project for 45 minutes. However, he again made a tactical mistake, linking the chapel development to the idea of a second major building which he now proposed should be built next to it: a new schoolroom-cum-assembly-hall. Each would be large enough for 400 people: far more than the pupil numbers at that time.

This revealed the full extent of his long-term plans and seriously frightened the governors. Thring was especially riled by Lord Aveland's 'usual narrow bigotry [and] obstinate repeating' in asking why they needed buildings for 400. He countered that only five years earlier they would have thought it an absurd idea that the school would reach even its current size. He dismissed Aveland's concerns about the chapel's cost by stating that he and the masters had already committed £10,000 to the school. The governors should show similar faith in it, 'but of course he did not change, a man so sordid in character as he is'. After a long discussion, and despite Johnson's best efforts, they refused their support.

Johnson suggested to him privately that he should resubmit the request. Thring thanked him, but said that with so much momentum already generated he could not risk further uncertainty: he and the masters would never apply to the governors again to fund any major building, but would 'leave the country to judge'. Even so, after a time he did revive the issue, and (when even Aveland seemed more positive) he commissioned GE Street, a notable architect and leading proponent of the Victorian Gothic style, to produce designs and costings for the chapel. This persuaded the governors to pass a motion endorsing the school's progress, though not pledging any funding to the project.

Now resolved on an independent path, Thring reissued his *Statement*, adding a pointed announcement of the governors' decision and a further sentence: 'NOTE (sic): The buildings will certainly be proceeded with in about a year, when the proposed site is free'. The *impasse* dragged on. To hammer home the point, he ended Sunday attendance at the parish church and started his own services in the existing schoolroom – although he was careful to assure Rector Wales that the school's financial support for the church would continue.[1] His relationship with the governors deteriorated still further after a rumour that they wanted to cut their contribution to the school's exhibitions (scholarships) as an economy measure.[2] He described them in his diary as 'a set of dotards and narrow minded breeches pockets' and began discreetly to lobby local supporters against them.

They were equally unconvinced about his ambitious plan for a new schoolroom. Despite his explanation that he needed a spacious building for assemblies, concerts and other major events, some governors, prompted by Old Boys, suggested that the Elizabethan building with its ink-stained and much-carved-on desks was quite good enough, and they added a claim that the proposed chapel/schoolroom site had insufficient access to the High Street. Thring was furious: 'They have no business to reject our plans. But they are a set of heavy snobs barring one or two'. He quickly persuaded Holden, who still owned one of the run-down properties restricting the access, to sell it for demolition. When this failed to satisfy the governors, Hodgkinson bought up the entire row of cottages within a week, and Thring started negotiating with a local landowner for an extra piece of land adjoining them.

The governors saw all this very negatively as another attempt to pressurise them. They continued to vacillate, briefly offering to buy Holden's property themselves (and even to make a small contribution to the schoolroom) but then losing their nerve and deferring *any* contribution

---

[1] Shortly after Thring's arrival in 1853 the masters had given £500 towards the restoration of the parish church.

[2] Equivalent to a bursary or means-tested scholarship in modern parlance, and mostly awarded to day boys. They had existed over a long period. Not to be confused with the boarding scholarships that Thring initiated.

for eight years, during which time Thring and his colleagues would have to bear the capital cost *and* the interest charges. The masters felt in no position to resist. They desperately needed the project to go forward.

Worse still, the governors now took against Street's designs for the chapel, preferring George Gilbert Scott who had designed Keble College, Oxford. To their chagrin and Thring's amusement, when Scott heard of Street's earlier involvement he declined the commission, criticising the governors for having any doubts about Street, his friend and fellow-architect, and telling them that it was essential to chooose someone favoured by Thring. Keen to disguise the results of their own poor judgement, the governors then put it about that they had found Scott's estimate too high.[1]

Late in 1861, despite Street's sound tendering process, they once more questioned the plans and Thring was again furious: 'Lord Aveland prominent, anything more ignorant I never heard... they talk of these plans quite ignoring that in the main it is *our* money, and certainly our risk entirely, as we are to be responsible for the building'. As the year ended he bombarded them with circulars and letters, but they refused to call a special meeting, leaving everything in limbo for weeks. He thought of giving them an ultimatum: 'We have eaten dirt enough. I for one [will] eat no more'.

By now he realised that the fates of the two projects (chapel and schoolroom) had become closely intertwined, and that it would be especially difficult for the governors to ignore the growing enthusiasm for the chapel, because he had already launched a successful public appeal for funds. Instrumental in this was his old friend from Eton and Cambridge days, William Witts, who had joined the staff that year and who donated the whole £1,000 sum that the governors had refused. Other donations quickly followed.[2]

Despite resenting this latest attempt to circumvent them, in May 1862 the governors finally approved both buildings. Even now Aveland described them as 'a mere money speculation' and Thring rounded on him, telling him that they stemmed from 'an anxious desire to serve God':

---

[1] Ideally they would have preferred a classical Greek design. They further proposed Butterfield (who had designed the chapel at Rugby) as a reserve choice in case Scott proved too busy.

[2] Both Thring's former Eton tutors contributed. He thought the most important local contribution was £50 from the Earl of Gainsborough: '*That* will tell on the tuft-hunting rank worshipping Rutland mind: governors and all'. Lord Lyttelton (see ch. 8) declined, but John Keate, son of the Eton Head Master, agreed to serve on the fundraising committee; his contacts would be useful and would 'stop a good deal of jaw in Eton quarters'.

if money-making had been his motive, he could have found safer methods.

Only General Johnson was an unfailing supporter. He had great faith that under Thring 'a few years will make this school rank among the best of England', and he came to meetings whatever the weather, despite being in his mid-80s. Thring had long recognised that although, as the hereditary voice of the Founder, Johnson's words carried some weight, he could not over-rule the rest of the Board, and he often spoke of the general as 'a great trump, sparing no personal trouble in the cause'. Johnson lived just long enough to see the opening of the new schoolroom in June 1863, marked by a prize-giving, concert and Latin recitations followed by a supper and speeches.

Thring reminded the assembled company that day of the previous decade's achievements: 'You see today what honest work and patience can do with scarcely any external aid, and none of the glitter that usually dazzles mankind...' The *Uppingham Magazine*, whose text he must have approved (and possibly wrote himself) was 'glad to see some of the governors there, and we hope *they* saw the unfinished state of the chapel, and witnessed what the masters have done for the school'.[1] The chapel opened two years later (1865), with Dean Goodwin of Ely preaching at its first service. Nearly £6,000 had been provided by masters and subscribers, but further work remained to be done, and on completion in 1872 the total cost had run to nearly £10,000.[2]

The struggle with 'those rich, stupid squires, giving nothing themselves' had consumed well over a decade of Thring's time and energy. It created a lasting distrust between him and his employers, showing him all too clearly the governors' limited ambition. Fundamentally they wanted to keep the school as it had always been. He recalled with irony how he had once privately vowed not to ask them for money until he had proved himself, expecting then 'how they would meet me in funds and gladly help us on!!' When they were especially obstructive, he observed that 'the crows gather round the sick sheep, but the crows are not shepherds'. Even in public he did little to hide his

---

[1] It praised Thring's ten-year struggle and pointed to dramatic improvements in music, 'in consequence of which, may the next report of the audit be wanting in those pregnant words: "the governors declined to move"'.

[2] More work was needed on the exterior, and on seating, choir stalls, a reredos and an organ. Thring often gave thanks for both buildings: in 1871 at a rehearsal for Handel's *Samson*, 'my heart felt deep and strong as I listened... a full quarter of the school was there rendering that glorious music with disciplined, willing zeal'.

frustration with them: 'It has always seemed to me very wrong, when people have deliberately, for years, set themselves against a thing, then at last, when, in spite of their efforts, it succeeds, to let them go off with a flourish of trumpets, and wipe their dirty hands on the back of success'.

The governors' attitude also determined that the future development of the school (as well as the houses) would be funded largely by Thring and his colleagues, with only a small proportion coming from the Trust. There was, however, a second reason for this. With pupil numbers increasing so rapidly after the impact of the Fowler and Jackson affairs had died down (200 in 1863; 300 in 1865), the housemasters, of whom Thring was one, were making significant boarding profits, some of which they were prepared to plough back into whole-school projects beyond their own houses, recognising that if the school was visibly prospering, their houses would, too.[1]

These profits, combined with their private means, gave them greater financial resources than those which the governors could call upon via the Trust's limited income. It enabled Thring and his colleagues to challenge the governing body, but it also resulted in their personal finances – and especially Thring's own – becoming inextricably bound up with those of the school.

For the moment Uppingham was prospering, but if times changed, they had everything to lose. Meanwhile, with the schoolroom and chapel successfully built, Thring felt 'a strong sense of, I trust, righteous triumph in Him who has enabled me... my heart is full of gratitude and my hands feel strong for the future'.

---

[1] The school's finances, and Thring's own, are discussed in ch. 13. It is hard to know the precise scale of Uppingham housemasters' profits, but the Clarendon Commission was told in the early 1860s that their counterparts at Rugby might expect to make a profit of between £12 and £14 per boy per year (£17 in the case of the Head Master, whose house was larger). See Hinchliff, Peter: *Frederick Temple, Archbishop of Canterbury: A Life* (1998) pp.105-6.

CHAPTER SIX

'HAPPY HOME: CONSTANT STRUGGLE'

IN April 1854, four months after his marriage, Thring began a diary. Early on in it he included a description of himself: 'A most happy husband... somewhat settled after the bustle of furnishing and the still greater annoyances of a disorganised household. Engaged in honourable work and prospering. May God give us strength to do his will gallantly, with a happy home. What a great work education is!'

A year later his assessment was somewhat more sober in all respects but one: 'My dear wife's birthday. The only earthly thing that has not brought me disappointment is my marriage'. Marie, whom he met so unexpectedly on his European travels, was a few months older than he, and although unobtrusive she had great strength of character. She was a deep source of strength to Thring throughout his life, quickly learning how to deal with his extremes of mood. He in turn learned to rely on her, valuing her judgement and recognising their complementary qualities.

In 1861 she left him alone for the first time as she went to visit some old friends in Boston, Lincolnshire: 'I miss Marie uncommonly. I don't know what I could do with this guiding life without her'. Even through middle age, nothing changed: 'I can only say I have found my marriage the most perfect earthly blessing, and worth all'. One of his greatest pleasures was buying presents for her and even in his final decade, when their respective frailties became increasingly apparent, they sustained each other. However, Thring always exerted the ultimate authority within the family, as in the boarding house which was an extension of their home.

During the first six years of their marriage they had four children in rapid succession: two sons, Gale (born in 1854) and Herbert ('Bertie', 1859), and two daughters, Sarah (1856) and Margaret (1858). A third daughter, (Mary) Grace, known by the family as 'Little Buzz', was born in 1866. The household also included Marie's sister Anna Koch, fifteen years her junior, who had accompanied her to England and who became Thring's secretary and personal assistant. Universally popular, and known by everyone as 'Aunt Anna', she was a good intermediary with parents and Thring relied heavily on her organising skills and powerful memory.

She more than anyone made suggestions for his speeches and sermons. He once declared publicly that she ministered to him with 'a sister's love'.[1]

The house offered them little privacy. Downstairs there was Thring's study, a small family dining room and a 'dark' sitting room. These were sandwiched between the communal kitchen and matron's sitting room on one side, and on the other the boys' dining room, a pantry, the sixth form room/library, a small study/sickroom, the music room and a wash room. Above, much of the space was given over to six boys' dormitories (for 33 boys: each with four to nine partitions) and the matron's bedroom.[2] When the new schoolroom was built, the sixth form room moved elsewhere and the Thrings gained a guest room, with the re-sited matron's room becoming a boundary between the private side and the boys' side.

Thring felt that their limited accommodation close to the boys exemplified the community ideal and that his family's presence at the heart of the house lessened any risk of an excessively male ethos. He was instinctively against bachelor housemasters, preferring to show the boys 'the *power* of a good marriage [where] the helpmeet for man is found'. He had a particular scorn for the 'insanity' of monastic schools: places where 'the springing fountains of young life are entrusted to those who have no living experience of the widest field of human life at all'.[3]

He and Marie took great pleasure in their greenhouse and garden. Early in each school year as the fruit trees ripened, he summoned the boys outside and gleefully shook the trees, bringing down showers of plums for them to pick up. Each pupil had a small garden rectangle (nine feet by three, bordered by a box hedge), which Thring and Marie inspected on summer Sunday evenings, handing out supplies of small bedding plants to encourage the boys' gardening skills and more exotic specimens as prizes for the best-kept plots.

Beyond occasionally showing a new servant girl how to lay a fire, Thring left the domestic arrangements to Marie. She oversaw the matron and under-nurse, footman and four maids. She revolutionised the house catering, providing plated forks, ivory-handled knives and smart table

---

[1] Anna appears to have been the only person to call Thring 'Eddy'. His *Poems and Translations* (published posthumously) was dedicated to her. Marie's widowed mother continued to live in Bonn, but recent political upheavals there had impoverished her family and Thring assumed financial responsibility for her, too.

[2] There were 23 boys' studies nearby, but not actually in the house.

[3] The idea of woman as 'helpmeet' became significant later – see ch. 21. One former pupil stated that 'the [family] life of the masters was made to touch the whole school. [Thring's] daughters moved like sisters amongst us [in] the atmosphere of purity as one finds it in a good home'.

cloths, as well as cups, teaspoons and the white sugar which she was certain made tea taste better.

On some winter evenings all work was cancelled and the boys put on their Sunday-best. At 7.30pm Thring, Marie and Anna hosted them in the family drawing room for musical evenings. The whole house attended, some as singers and the rest as audience. Other staff, wives and friends joined them in quartets, part-songs, Victorian ballads and other works sung by a choir gathered around the piano. The programme often included items from Germany, reflecting the growing number of masters from that country now working in the school. Afterwards there was a substantial tea, which included Marie's famed plum cake. Family, staff and pupils played charades at parties at the start and end of each term.

As the school grew, Marie extended her influence beyond their own boarding house. The annual gymnastics competition was held each year on her birthday and she presented the prizes. The sixth form farewell dinner, to honour those leaving for university in October, was originally cooked in a run-down shop next to the school, but to improve its quality she brought it in-house. She oversaw the catering for the termly praepostors' supper, the prizegiving, the opening of new buildings, and for an ever-increasing number of visitors. The supper during what became a two-day cricket match against the Old Boys assumed the scale of a civic banquet with toasts and speeches.

She was also *prima inter pares* among the housemasters' wives, however much her sister-in-law Lydia might dislike it. In all, the houses employed over 100 living-in servants, and it is likely that Marie gave advice about them to other wives, as well as being involved in a range of social activities in the town.[1] Her relatives caused the school one significant difficulty, when the husband of her other sister (Louisa) faced bankruptcy and asked Thring for a job (1860). He briefly considered it, but the request coincided with his difficulties with Charles and Lydia, and he resolved to take on no more family members – even though Marie, like him prone to worry, suffered great anxiety over the decision.

Even before their first son Gale was born, Thring had strong views on how to bring up children:

'Anything is better than one parent dealing with children through the other. Let all be honest and open affection, and the end will be

---

[1] One housemaster's wife kept a diary, giving details about running the domestic and catering side of the house; sending out and accepting dinner invitations from other houses; corresponding with parents; walking the dogs; attending chapel and watching cricket matches or athletics races.

happiness... Separate relations and differences [between] father and mother will keep them from ever knowing their children... whilst the children will mistrust and suspect an intercourse which they can never reach the exact truth about... [and] will in consequence gradually cease to open their hearts unreservedly at all'.

With childhood memories of his overbearing father, he was concerned to be sympathetic and loving to his own family. When they were quite young he warned himself of the dangers of still treating them as children long after they had grown up: 'They will be wiser in many things in their generation'. He was keen to play his part in their upbringing, and he had a child-like sense of fun. Gale's fifth birthday party found him relaxed and crawling around on the floor of the house dining hall pretending to be a horse with noisy, excited boys and girls clambering all over him. Two years later, on Gale's seventh birthday: 'Had great fun this afternoon, races and leaping in the garden with the children'. He took Gale to help him lay the foundation stone of one of the new boarding houses. Family cooking sessions led to Marie's book of his favourite recipes, including carrot soup, cider cup, sheep's head pie and summer pudding.

Gale and Bertie passed through Uppingham as pupils and eventually went on to university. Meanwhile the three daughters had a succession of living-in governesses from abroad, and cared for a succession of dogs, cats and tame birds. In term-time, the girls went tricycling in summer and skating in winter: they were allowed to use slides made by the boys – but only while the latter were safely away from the house at lessons. They were expected to go to chapel with Marie and Anna and could sometimes attend sporting events, but there too they had to keep a strict sense of distance and decorum. They joined in with musical events in house and school, partly because their greatest friend was Paul David's daughter Lottie: it was with her that they spent a happy afternoon decorating the violinist Joachim's music-stand with wall-flowers (his favourites) to surprise him.

With five children and many other calls on his income, Thring took his family abroad only occasionally, usually to relatives in Germany.[1] Summer holidays were spent in a variety of coastal resorts, including Llandudno, where Thring spent several days with the children 'busy in marine zoology and aquariums'. There were visits to Alford, to Derbyshire when Theodore lived there, to Henry's house in London, or occasionally to former governesses in Switzerland. Later the family discovered the Lake District and eventually Scotland.

---

[1] He had meant to learn German properly, but never found the time. Many masters went abroad far more often.

Christmas and New Year were a special family time – unsurprisingly, given Marie's German background. Even after his daughters were grown up, Thring helped them to make illustrated cards: he provided the words, Sarah pressed some flowers and Margaret did the drawings around them. The girls and their friends decorated the chapel, and there were celebrations on Christmas Eve with drinks and cake in the hall, candles lit on the Christmas tree and the excited exchange of presents. December gave way to January with family skating parties with friends, theatricals 'for the trades-people the first night and for our friends the second', and a party with large quantities of food, games and presents around the tree for the children from the town's National School. All these occasions, and Thring's love of hectic activity in the company of the young, did much to fortify him for the more difficult times, and to cement the sense of community in those around him.

****

A very different side of Thring is apparent in the term-time diary that he kept for most of his career. His view of life as a constant battle between good and evil paralleled the struggles which went on within his own character – with its contrasts of extreme highs and lows and of public confidence and private anxiety. He was sensitive and vulnerable, yet with a tendency to be domineering, and his conviction that he was right was tinged with honesty about his faults. Equally paradoxically, he was sociable but with a need for private thoughts and space. It is small wonder that he sometimes exhibited the psychological and physical symptoms of acute stress and depression.

Although half expecting that the diary might eventually be published, he wanted it to be a genuine rather than cosmetic record of his true feelings, however transitory. It should give his children an account of 'the vicissitudes and daily wear and tear, [so] that no fellow-worker may ever quote me as *gliding* on to success'. If they knew that his achievements had not come easily, it might one day encourage them in their own lives. Writing up the diary in the privacy of his study each night was also a safety valve for his frustrations: he could give vent to his true feelings about people and events. With vigorous underlinings and exclamation marks, his unpunctuated, rambling sentences pour out his pent-up emotions, rapid changes of mood and unpredictable streams of consciousness.

After some brief entries for 1854, the first surviving volume spans four years (1859-62): a time when his family was growing and the numbers of pupils and staff were starting to increase.[1] Its introduction is a typical mixture of gratitude and exhilaration, gloom and self-doubt. Believing firmly that he is doing work for God, he is quick to find biblical analogies. On the sixth anniversary of his arrival in Uppingham, he spends the day reflecting on how 'with my staff I came over the Jordan':

'I believe I am successful here [but] every personal hope of joy in the work has withered. With much to encourage [me] there is [also] so much of doubt that all the feelings have to be kept in hand and sternly closed up, whilst the eye and heart uplifted to heaven alone brings comfort. I think I could heartily welcome a poorer quieter lot. There is no compensation excepting in God's blessing for the toils of this anxious but responsible, noble and therefore happy life. Six years. Deo gratias'.

The anxiety which first revealed itself in Gloucester is never far away, and in this respect too he shows classic symptoms of depression. In November 1859: 'Words cannot tell how sick at heart, how hollow, how weary I feel sometimes, how hopeless almost... tied to a stake to fight out the incessant worrying'. A year later: 'The place is emptied of delight and nothing left but a feeling of duty done and the recompense of the grave'. He recalls his first weeks in post: 'Lonely and not yet married; suffering acutely from boils; with sleepless nights, stomach cramps and loss of appetite because of anxiety'.

To relieve the tension he plays games; picks strawberries in the garden; takes a weekend walk to nearby Rockingham and returns for tea with some of the boys, feeling 'fresh and pleasant in mind'. He is fiercely protective of Marie, who worries about life even more than he. Whilst out walking, he loses her betrothal ring: 'A very black day'. He frets about her workload and what will happen to her if he dies. He is furious when a housemaster (Stokoe) asks *her* whether he is diverting prospective parents towards other houses, and he worries when she is so anxious about his dispute with Stokoe over references. He records her 'great strain' over a sick boy or her children's measles, or the forthcoming catering for the Old Boys' match. At one point he fears she may have 'paralysis or brain affection'. In both 1860 and 1861 they worry together about reputational

---

[1] The only other volume which has survived covers the final year of his life, and is discussed in chs. 20 and 21. The others were all destroyed after his death, once Parkin had been through them, on Marie's orders: see ch. 22. We do not know whether Thring kept any diary before 1853.

damage when two housemaids become pregnant by school servants: 'We don't know what to do, such scandal is frightful'.[1]

He struggles to find private space. Mathias wants an evening discussion about the curriculum. Thring refuses because it is 'the only night I shall sit quietly with my family'. He thinks that the masters have no idea about the cumulative pressures on him: their bright ideas are 'pleasing excitement to them, but death to me, the aggregate of worries, of which each [of them] gets only a small fraction'. He is noticeably revived by holidays: at New Year in 1860 'we begin in good style: all the masters very pleasant'. However, the time between terms also gives him more time to worry, when 'troubles and anxieties have more power'.

He frequently wonders whether it is all worth it: 'Would that I could now hide my head in peace [from] the grinding power and yoke that has been riveted round my neck... the work and pain and pain and work; boys and masters, and masters and boys'. Too many 'vexations' disrupt his teaching: money pressures, government cares, inadequate masters and foolish parents. He regrets feeling reactive rather than proactive: 'Simply banged about [like] the wool which is flung in at one end of a machine, carded, torn, worried, washed, entangled, disentangled, pulled, squeezed, thumped in the darkness, and come out cloth at the other end'. He sees the risk in being 'the slave of work, not its master', and he rues his inexperience: 'I had not the *remotest* notion beforehand of a school master's real trials'.

He strives for greater self-awareness, deeming himself 'far more concerned and thoughtful for others when heavy hearted', yet 'there is less time for thought and self examination than there used to be, and I am certainly less <u>consciously</u> devout, but I am far more patient and enduring in spirit, less irritable [and] proud, I hope'. As a difficult meeting with the governors approaches, he realises that 'when light-hearted I am too apt to let out an incautious expression or two which is remembered... the very tone of my voice must be tutored to bear and answer their strictures'. He learns that 'little cares when the heart is weary and the body faint, coming incessantly have a very absurdly disproportionate effect. When strong and well and fresh, things look and feel very differently'.

---

[1] 1861: 'A most trying day. At a little before seven this morning there was a faint knock at our door and our Matron came in crying and told us that her niece who was our kitchen maid had had a baby in the night. The father was a little lad of 17, our page: the girl only 17. It was an awful blow. The lad we sent off by the next train; the unhappy girl we got into the workhouse in the course of the day. My heart does bleed for her... Of course this has been a great affliction and blow to my wife, we took the girl out of charity... She was so quiet and stupid she was not suspected, and nothing was actually known until the baby was already born'.

Small incidents affect him too much. He becomes deeply upset when the governors make him pay for gravel for the house drive. He is thin-skinned about local rumours that Earle's new house is to become a breakaway preparatory school. He hears that Holden is criticising the choir and alleging from afar that old honours boards have been taken down, so he fumes that it all stems from his predecessor's jealousy, and that 'no Honour List has ever <u>been up at all</u>'(sic). By contrast, he seizes joyfully on small signs of progress: the gift of a new communion set; the fledgling debating club; crystals from Iceland brought back by Benguerel; persuading older boys to roll the cricket field rather than leaving it to the fags. He rejoices in unexpected triumphs – as when he scores 53 in a cricket match in which 'I hit tremendously and astonished the parents looking on'. His child-like delight reveals itself in a 'capital' game of fives or a lively evening of charades, or when, on a snowy morning, a fox leaps up at his study window and bangs its nose on the glass.

When he falls out with staff, he is extremely forthright. Mathias' ideas for science teaching are 'conceited and absurd', and his sermons are 'conceited drawing room talk' – yet he baptises the Mathias' baby, illustrating the complex relationship between the headmaster-clergyman and his difficult housemaster. He is unsettled when Stokoe sits 'for half an hour this morning at the masters' meeting, without moving a muscle or opening his lips'. He picks remorselessly over issues with Charles and Lydia, and the drip-feed of the negative gossip they send back to Alford.

Even those masters who mostly support him are a source of irritation: Earle is variously 'a firm and conscientious ally', and 'always itching for a little intrigue'; Hodgkinson is 'a tower of strength' but 'too ready to be made a cat's paw'. Collectively, masters' behaviour prompts a torrent of words such as treason, conspiracy, rebellion, insolence, conceit, insanity, fools, poison, blindness. His colleagues 'embitter my existence' and 'suck the zest and spirit out of one's life'.

Trivial issues quickly become direct challenges to his authority. When a town solicitor asks for his son to become a private pupil at a reduced fee, it is 'a very serious and awkward question. The town give us no help and then, when we succeed, pick our pockets if they can by exorbitant prices'. He resents farmers' opposition to boys running over their land and he believes that Lord Berners, who complains about boys walking in his woods, suffers from 'the curse of the English squirearchy, the pheasant mania'.

He takes all town-school setbacks very hard, whether they involve confrontation at the bathing pool, assaults by 'beastly local women', a drunken wedding party, or town boys ambushing pupils and stealing their books. He is outraged when an 'impudent' local girl joins the procession of boys walking back from the parish church, or when his dog is attacked by others in the town: 'What a lawless blackguard place we live in!' He regularly seeks help from the police or magistrates. Local tradesmen who let the boys run up debts or sell cider to them are summarily threatened with the loss of school patronage.

Unsurprisingly, the diary pulls no punches over his governors. They are 'our demagogue autocrats' and they include 'an Oakham party always refusing to see change'. He dreads each meeting, 'so identified is it in my mind with meanness, insult and injustice... internal difficulties and money plagues'. He has special contempt for Rector Wales who, although he has the means, declines to buy the old Elizabethan schoolroom at a time when Thring needs to relieve his debts, and who refuses to put pressure on his farmer-tenants to lease the school their land for games. He believes that the town is full of 'fools, knaves and beasts from the Rector downwards'.

The diary reveals the full extent of how he is worn down by his prolonged battles with the Fowlers and Jacksons. He recognises what a shock the Fowler family has suffered, but the boy's version of events is 'vile... a flimsy, lying, scurrilous absurdity', and his uncle is 'an old madman, full of rabid abuse'. It is the same with the 'insolent and meddling' Mr. Jackson, whose actions demonstrate 'the recklessness, the conceit, the ingratitude, the abject folly of men'. He worries that the school may not survive such publicity: 'Mr. Jackson has mixed a most bitter potion for me (with other parents)'.[1] He despairs that 'the more I see of the middle classes, the more their self indulgent, presumptuous folly fills me with fears for the future of this country'.

Underlying this invective is a continuous concern about pupil numbers. The diaries refer regularly to 'loomers' (prospective parents) coming and going, and his hope that leavers' successes at Oxford and Cambridge will help recruitment. He tenses up in the days before the examiners' visits are due, and takes their criticisms very hard. Conversely, he is deeply relieved when he gets 'a glorious letter from the Rector of Edinburgh Academy giving us the highest praise for the way we have got on (improved) his boy'.

Boy-numbers link in turn to worries about his own finances. When Mathias disputes the funding proposals for the new gymnasium, 'I told him I pay five times as much as most of the rest'. He worries about debt and complains that the masters are 'splitting pennies... quite forgetful of the pounds I have sacrificed'. In February 1861: 'Today my heart has

---

[1] It all creates extra work, too: after 'a longish paragraph in the *Stamford Mercury* on the subject, not very bad but still nagging', he writes to 40 parents: 'I am occupied every day for hours in correspondence about this'.

been weighed down utterly by money cares. I am one year's income behind my work and needs, utterly crippled and ever pained by it'. He worries about whether Macmillan will pay him properly for a forthcoming grammar book. Money concerns haunt him and Marie: 'Would to God our debt was wiped off: [it] is very bitter. Have been talking to my wife about it. She thinks of the children'.

He sees pupil behaviour as a litmus test of the school's health, and takes it very personally when he is let down. Early confrontations with the praepostors are described in great detail; cheating, lying, drinking, smoking, betting, billiards playing and 'indecency' all grieve him – although support from his school captains buoys him up. He records a 'mean trick' run-out during Stamford cricket match, and he catches 'two young scamps in Rowe's house pea-shooting in the street at his door'. He has to 'speak very severely to that great cad Burrows laughing and talking and making a mock of the prayers', and he canes three boys (including Fitzgerald, his nephew) for breaking windows, along with others who have forged permission to miss call-over. When boys in his house complain about the food, he tells them 'of their shameful luxury in refusing some of our puddings', and threatens to provide no more of such food for a year unless they apologise.

When under particular pressure, he makes worst-case assumptions. Watching athletics is soured by suspicion because 'the blackguards of the school not there, taken the opportunity to go smoking or drinking, no doubt'. Occasionally he goes in search of troublemakers himself: 'Heard again that two of our blackguards frequent Bisbrooke (a local village) and follow two girls who live there. Took a walk with Earle and Hodgkinson; saw our suspected Bisbrookers... but they were too quick for us... now we must catch them [red-handed]'.[1] He expels a boy named Lister who stands up to him after a long series of disciplinary run-ins: 'I never met a more hardened fellow. He returned to say defiantly that he'd been going to be confirmed next month, but had now thought better of it... May God have mercy on us all!'

Contrasting with these tales of woe is his pleasure at sharing his life with his pupils. Their common endeavour sustains him and redirects him towards his more positive characteristics. He regularly records details of prize-winners, exam successes and athletics results, along with glowing accounts of school events. On 26 March 1860: 'Races on Saturday: 60

---

[1] 'Past Hawthorn's shop... though we started on their track, came home and went out to command the Bisbrooke path about the time they had to be in. Sure enough by the luckiest chance we came on them from behind and let them go home without knowing that we had seen them'.

started in 8 heats. Very good fun. I promised the winners a good supper'. As a new term begins: 'Boys back. We had a capital party last night, all the ladies and masters and boys charade acting etc. I am in the thick of it. Everybody pleased'. A fortnight later: 'Benguerel gave a lecture on chemistry in the evening, very effective, made some appalling stinks, which delighted the boys. One infernal compound of ammonia which I innocently put my nose to, nearly knocked the roof of my head off: I spilt it, the boys delighted, of course, great fun and general enlivenment of us all'. He picnics in Wardley wood, and plays croquet and cricket with the boys: 'It is a great thing sharing everything with them'. When he prepares two sixth formers for the Cambridge scholarship exam: 'The terms one is on with the older boys are simply delightful. I am so gratified by the way they always bring me any little bit of literary news etc, if they think it will interest me'.

Despite all his setbacks, when he looks back on events from a distance he remembers a strong feeling of Providence: 'My trust was in God, and that it was his work'. In the middle of an argument about money, he tells himself to stay calm: 'Care, care. If I have sought God in this work, may He bless it and make it stand. If not, may He punish and save me and bless my fellow-workers here'. As he wrestles with threats from the Fowlers, he prays that God will not spare him if he has been wicked, and on his 39th birthday in November 1860: 'Every year more brings the deep conviction of My Lord and Saviour working and redeeming'.

Always affected by his mood of the moment and temporarily forgetting all his troubles at Christmas in 1860, he is again optimistic as he contemplates New Year visits to Henry in London and his parents in Alford:

> '1861 opens with the brightest prospects I have yet had. May God be with us whatever comes. On looking back a full year I can hardly believe this is the same place, so great has been the onward stride. O God Thou hast indeed been with us, but I feel the incessant battle very severe. But are we not told life is a battle? ...O hear my prayer this night, and give me strength and courage... Faith – give us Faith. Amen'.

CHAPTER SEVEN

EDUCATION AND SCHOOL

WITHIN a few years of joining Uppingham, Thring resumed his writing. After King's, his commonplace book had grown to several volumes as he regularly added new snippets: quotations; notes on his reading; books he might one day read, or ideas for future speeches or sermons.[1] Frustrated by the lack of suitable teaching material for boys whom he tutored privately at Bisham, he persuaded Macmillan to publish two small compilations, *The Elements of Grammar taught in English* (1851) and *The Child's Grammar* (1852). Both books drew on his experience in Gloucester.[2]

Thanks to its innovative approach, *Elements* went through seven editions during the next three decades. Its central idea was that grammar consisted merely of common sense applied to language: it should be taught inductively and analytically through example sentences. Even very young pupils should be taught to order and express their thoughts clearly, but adult methods and examples were not appropriate for them.

Expounding what would later become one of the cardinal principles of child-centred learning, he demonstrated how young minds must be guided gradually from the familiar to the unfamiliar by starting from a child's first-hand experience, and progressing gradually from the concrete to the abstract.[3] To support this process he included sections on each part of speech (including interjection, participle and clause) with graduated passages of prose and poetry to illustrate them, carefully chosen as suitable for young minds.

---

[1] Proverbs; axioms; snatches of poetry; a brief exposition on Cain and Abel; quotations from Milton on the nature of God; Advent poems in German and English; a chorale from Bach's *Christmas Oratorio*; ideas from Ruskin's *The Seven Lamps of Architecture* (see p.16).

[2] He was praised by Benjamin Kennedy, author of the famous *Primer*. Macmillan thought his *Child's Grammar* 'the only book in existence on the subject which is the result of profound knowledge, and yet a clear and simple statement of the laws of speech'. *Elements* spawned a variety of spin-offs and shortened and junior versions – see bibliography.

[3] 'Learning is an exploring expedition with or without a guide; lessons, like explorers, ought to start from home already trained and equipped amongst known and familiar scenes, before they try unknown and unfamiliar.'

In Uppingham he used the town bookseller, John Hawthorn, to publish his sermons and pamphlets, whilst working mostly with Macmillan (and later the Cambridge University Press) on his books, and he published articles in journals at home and abroad. His belief in 'sentence anatomy' led to a succession of classics textbooks. *A Latin Gradual: A first Latin construing book for beginners* (1863) deployed what he claimed to be an 'intelligent system' of declensions and conjugations. It too went through several editions, and he followed it up with *A Manual of Mood Constructions* (1867): examples from Latin, Greek and English literature of the four moods (imperative, indicative, conjunctive and infinitive).

He also produced a translation of the complex lyrical verse of *The Agamemnon of Aeschylus.* Rival headmaster-writers criticised his methods as poor preparation for university,[1] perhaps fearing that their own publications might be under threat, or that Thring's approach could feed growing doubts about the dominance of classics in the curriculum.

He had an impulsive, quirky style of writing and he frequently included examples from his own teaching experience. In the *Latin Gradual,* he diverted from an explanation of sentence construction to pass on some 'Uppingham Hints':

'How to learn: First, see. Then examine what you see. Lastly answer, or write. Live with the scenes. Make no attempt to remember anything you can put before your eye, or can picture to your mind's eye. Memory is not sight.

Picture an apple. Note its size, shape, colour, inside, texture, parts, pips, core etc; skin, juice. Compare with other fruits.

The untrained boy begins to try and remember what he knows about an apple and flounders hopelessly for ever... Think in shape.

Why we learn:

1) Skill is the object of all good work

2) Skill means the power of doing exactly what is wanted to be done, at the right time

3) Skill is produced by thought and practice

4) Anyone without skill is so far without education

5) Memory is not skill, and may be a hindrance to skill

6) Skill does not mean being full, but being master of strength, and trained movement

7) The trained mind is worth all the knowledge in the world.

---

[1] There were strong rivalries between headmasters who produced textbooks and primers. *Agamemnon* resulted from of his evening extra classes held in the poorly lit hall of his boarding house. It was repeatedly re-published after his death.

Why we do not learn:
1) Because we suppose knowledge is all in all
2) Because we only half believe in knowledge
3) Because we don't think we shall quite get it
4) Because if we get it, we don't quite see the use of it
5) Because the gain, if a gain, is very far off
6) Because the present process [of learning] is very unpleasant'.

He defined a fool as 'a person who does not use the sense he has got', believing that everyone could acquire at least some academic skills if they received 'proper' teaching. This should include instilling in boys some precepts: 'Do what you are told; never guess; sense first, then think, then write or speak; never change the order of classes, terms or even words without reason'.[1] He was well-known for his pithy axioms, many of which were printed as memorial cards after his death:

'If you don't do small things well, you will never do great things at all'.
'Great minds think nothing beneath them'.
'Any fool can find fault'.
'Never do doing nothing *(sic)*; either work, or play, or sleep. Never combine two of these'.
'Mind is Life; and Life is what has to be dealt with, not lessons.
The Teacher's subject is Mind: but the dropping in of dry knowledge, instead of calling out and strengthening living power is no training of mind'.[2]
'Great fools are sometimes full of knowledge and great fools still',
'A dull boy is a wise man's problem'.
'Leisure hours most affect the character and are the hinges on which true education turns. There is no such thing as making up for lost time'.
'No man can do for another what that other ought to do for himself'.

Through the 1850s he was gathering wider educational ideas. His 1859 *Statement* for the governors reiterated his disgust at the unsupervised lawlessness of the so-called 'great' schools. A collection of nine essays, *School Delusions* (1860), claimed to be written by his senior boys ('scarcely a word has been altered') although his own ideas run unmistakably right through it, showing how deeply his ideas were influencing his pupils. One contributor described the 'true life' principle almost in Thring's words; another used a Thringian metaphor in

---

[1] 'Grinding at words and thinking of thoughts are different: if you don't do small things, you will never do great things'.
[2] There is a strong resonance with the often-used maxim: 'Education is about lighting fires, not filling buckets'.

describing a school as 'a safe harbour'. Three proclaimed sport as a central feature of school life, and others provided remarkably faithful expositions of his views on trust, discipline and good teaching.

Letters and Axioms on Education (1858) began as an article in the *English Journal of Education.*[1] It was an early venture into territory to which he would often return later: how governments ought to value education *per se*, not as 'an engine of political power... looking only to results through the inspectors'. Teaching was a 'great science: let no man think, because a quick boy acquires knowledge under him that he is [therefore] a teacher'. He challenged the notion that a full-blown traditional curriculum was suitable for all: 'Convinced as I am of the merits of a classical education, there are many who... never get beyond the grinding labour of the attempt. [They] are thrown aside to rot... No school which does not deal effectually with them can be a good society'. This led him to 'the difference between a school capable of turning out a few first-rate men, and a first-rate school'. The former was exemplified for him by Arnold's Rugby.

Recalling how Eton had taught him that 'boys cannot be dealt with in masses, without a fearful waste and individual loss', he was at pains to emphasise that anyone can teach the gifted, whereas those attending to less talented pupils require the professional skills which comprise 'real' teaching. He made a distinction between the mere teacher and the true educator in another series of axioms which harked back to his days in Gloucester:

'The educator deals with latent powers. The teacher puts in a given task.
The educator considers, the worse the material, the greater the skill in working it. The teacher does his task, and charges the material with the result.
The educator knows his subject to be infinite, and is always learning himself to put old things in a new form. The teacher thinks he knows his subject and that the pupil ought to know it, too.
The educator loves his work, and every day finds fresh reason to love it. The teacher goes through his work and finds it more irksome every day.
The educator encourages. The teacher punishes.
The educator is a boy amongst boys in heart. The teacher has the hardness of a man, and with the want of thought of a boy.
The educator meets the young on their own ground, and from their own point of view. The teacher stands above them and makes laws'.

---

[1] A published discussion with the Revd. William Grignon, Headmaster of Felsted, reprinted as a pamphlet (1866).

He added that teachers must be punctual, must earn respect and not be petty in their criticisms. *Truth in Schools* (1862) quickly followed: a short pamphlet-diatribe, similar in tone to those written in his undergraduate days, against allowing tradition to become ossification. He believed that education was peculiarly prone to maintaining traditions that were little more than a series of 'social despotisms' propped up by memory, custom, affection and ignorance.

With ten years' of school experience behind him, it was now time for a much longer book.

****

Education and School was published by Macmillan in 1864. It encapsulated Thring's broad thinking about education over time, and it later proved highly influential, despite its complex analogies and meanings convoluted by compression. His arguments could be repetitive or occasionally contradictory; his terminology vivid, though often eccentric.[1]

Despite all this, his ideas poured out.[2] He reiterated how his generation lived in a time of change caused by population growth and the industrial revolution. This would place new demands on education, which must help the population to use its time constructively and to pass intellectual capital on to future generations. He saw the second ten years of a young person's life as crucially formative: a time when 'strong' minds must not merely be stuffed or crammed, but instilled with 'life power'. Real education was 'nothing less than bringing [together] everything that men have learnt from God, or from experience'. Schools must not exist merely to provide advancement or good connections, or to allow parents to pay someone else to bring up their children. They must be

---

[1] Stansky, Peter: 'Lyttelton and Thring: a study in Nineteenth Century Education', *Victorian Studies* (V) March 1962 p.222: 'Thring's principles were never concretely defined: to him they were a matter of feeling, not of logic, and he was intolerant of anyone who would not agree with him'.
We do not know whether Thring ever read Lewis Carroll's *Through the Looking-Glass* (1872), but his style of argument has overtones of one passage in it: '"When *I* use a word", Humpty Dumpty said, in rather a scornful tone, "it means just what I choose it to mean—neither more nor less". "The question is", said Alice, "whether you *can* make words mean so many different things". "The question is", said Humpty Dumpty, "which is to be master - that's all"'.
[2] 'I have done shipwright's work and gathered some knowledge of construction in doing it. If not, it matters little provided the conviction that there is shipwright's work to be done becomes a definite and fixed idea'.

well-ordered communities offering many opportunities. Knowledge alone was not enough, because to live only for the intellect 'is to be a devil, not a man'.[1]

This call for new thinking contrasted with his distinctly orthodox defence of the classics. Here he focused on the idea that minds needed reasoning powers, imagination and endurance: the 'universal consent of many ages' was that these skills were best developed by studying Greek and Latin literature. These texts also taught the lessons of history, the powers of intellectual thought and accurate speech, and how God worked through human events.[2] Living languages were less useful than classical ones as analytical tools because of their imperfect structure and their emphasis on conversational skills.

He explained how innovation and conservatism could be reconciled if a school's curriculum was varied enough to suit every boy. Schools sending pupils to universities or the Indian civil service must teach classics and mathematics in significant quantities: high-flying boys enjoyed them, and making other subjects compulsory for this group would be counter-productive. However, the high-flyers needed less exhausting pursuits too: there was a limit to the amount of 'severe' work that could be done in a single day.

By contrast, it was pointless to make weaker boys struggle with huge amounts of Latin and Greek, especially after the age of 13 or 14:

> 'If they are merely set in a treadmill; if all their intellectual work is one long dull punishment where they get nothing but discredit, and are hopeless of excelling... they must fatally injure their school-life. They can never hope to sail in the great language-ship and see the world... never get beyond sawing the planks... How can they have any feeling of the school being a place for them when they are no better than outcasts there? When self-respect is lost, all power for good is lost with it'.

---

[1] John (Lord) Wolfenden (headmaster of Uppingham, 1934-44) gave a lecture on the centenary of Thring's arrival (1953), asserting 'the revolutionary nature of his theories and the profound effect, on the whole development of English education, of his practice'. Wolfenden had created a 'non-Latin' form at Uppingham in the early 1940s to increase boys' self-confidence – e.g. through studying geography.

[2] 'They are the perfection of mere humanity, as distinct from that living power [of] Christianity. No one can know the true progress of human life and thought who does not know what has been... Above all, the New Testament is written in Greek. No religious nation can give up Greek [for the New Testament reveals how] the human agencies of intellectual and physical power are transformed by a new fountain of life from God'.

A boarding school must therefore offer time outside formal lessons for other occupations: 'There [boys] can find something to interest them... something in which they can attain distinction [and] self-respect... Healthy moral life depends very much on it'. He listed all the options that his own school offered, suggesting that there should be only a few compulsory subjects. Parents and boys should choose the others, although he conceded that a system based on choice would be expensive to deliver.[1]

He was especially insistent that boys of lower ability needed – and deserved – as much attention as the brilliant, both as individuals and to ensure the health of the community: 'The worse the material, the more power is required, and the greater skill in those who work it'. Every boy must receive full and equal attention: 'It is dangerous to do anything that breaks a school up into parties. The beneficial power of the place will be diminished in proportion to the schism'.

He insisted that a school must have good 'machinery', defined as 'everything pertaining to the intellectual, moral, religious and physical life [for] work and play, the two great divisions of boy-life'. In administrative terms, machinery created order and harmony. It must be provided in all its aspects: nothing must be left to chance, so that a school would continue to function well, however temporarily adverse its circumstances. Machinery's constituent parts were many and varied:[2] good buildings and playgrounds and (not surprisingly) a large schoolroom/assembly hall and a chapel. Boarding houses must have gardens, giving boys space to explore. Other desirable features included a library, museum, workshop, gymnasium, swimming baths and fives courts.

Machinery's administrative features included a clearly defined role for each master so that no school relied unduly on the power of the headmaster's personality. Staffing levels must be generous with enough classes to ensure easy upward movement through the school: 'If a school professes to teach, then every boy must have his [proper] share of teaching'.

If classes were too large, masters would be reduced to lecturing rather than teaching, passing on dry facts while the weakest struggled to keep

---

[1] 'A mixture of hard and supplementary subjects benefits the mind; difference of occupation rather than idleness benefits the more able, and this choice of easier work is of infinitely greater importance to the backward and stupid boy than to his better-trained companion'.

[2] See Adonis, Andrew: *Education, Education, Education* (2012) p.186 for an interesting modern parallel with Thring's 'machinery' in the view of Greg Martin, headteacher of the Durand Academy for 24 years. Adonis quotes a *Times* journalist, Helen Rumbelow, as recounting her visit: 'As Martin starts his tour, I notice that he repeats a single word nearly every other breath: "Structure"'.

up: 'There is very little want of *ability* in boys naturally, [but] there is a great want of *willingness*... It is very painful sometimes to see the hopeless despair with which boys have got to look on tasks which require only a little explanation and time. All can learn, but the clever boys learn more quickly'. Teaching the less gifted must never be seen as a chore, allocated only to junior masters. It was a matter of professional pride, because 'a good teacher ought to rejoice in a stupid boy as an interesting problem and when good and willing, a delight and a reward... To teach an upper form requires more knowledge, [but] a lower one more skill in a teacher'. The less able and even the indolent had just as much right to good teaching as the rest: 'As infinite as the human mind is in its variety, [so] ought the resources of the teachers to be. The more stupid the pupils, the more skill required to make them learn'.

Moreover, the masters must want to learn how to teach better, because those freshly arrived from university would have enthusiasm and 'lumps of knowledge', but not the accumulated experience to impart them effectively. The best teacher never stopped observing the reactions of his classes, and he reviewed his lessons after delivering them, devising new questions and illustrations and finding new ways to create that 'electric communion' of minds between himself and his pupils. Teaching also involved stamina and staying power: there would be bad days as well as good ones and a master had to be continuously engaged and enthusiastic. School should broaden boys' horizons, helping them to acquire the skill of independent learning without masters always standing over them.

The masters must be 'educated gentlemen'. He believed that too many schools relied on short-term peripatetics, thrown into crowded classrooms with no training and neither skill nor interest in their work. Others paid a pittance to well-meaning young clergymen, committed only to preaching *at* boys and oblivious to the idea that teaching was a skilled science. This mind-set was fundamentally wrong, because teaching was 'interesting, holy, great, and good, but no afternoon's by-play... [it] cannot find place in the heart of a man who has just pitched his tent, and will be off again to-morrow. He can pour out knowledge, but he will be no teacher'.

Schools which recruited unsuitable men were often run by headmasters who enlarged their own houses purely to increase their profits, and who taught too few pupils themselves. However, Thring also poured scorn on the idea that schoolmasters should give no thought to their earnings. They had families to support, and teaching was a profession, not a philanthropic pastime. If society wanted first-class teachers, it must pay for them. Otherwise, ambitious men would head off into better paid careers, while idealists would reject teaching in favour of work as clergymen in difficult parishes.

Permanent staff could also promote what would now be termed pastoral care. A master had to become 'a friend with his boys... with time to know them'. Pupils would then accept even his severer side: 'Boys like justice, even severity, if [it is] just, and not capricious. [He] will not lose them as friends even when earnestness means punishing wrongdoing'.

Boys were sent to boarding school to teach them how to live with people whom they did not know: 'How bad it would be if there were no corrective for the different failings of different homes, nothing to take a boy out of the pod in which he found himself, nothing to prevent his thinking that the pod rules the world'.[1] Good boarding houses provided 'domestic management and discipline; training boys to be honourable free men', but boys would thrive only in a school with a high-quality house system. This must provide something akin to home comforts, with good accommodation and food, and no corners cut. Otherwise, 'untruth will make itself felt'.

Young boys needed good surroundings, food, teaching and care just as much as older ones. Despite recent press criticism, he stuck to his view that individual studies should not be a privilege of seniority. Every house must have an individual study for every boy: 'a sanctum of his own... [where] the boys shall be trusted, and free to do anything that a wise father should wish his son to do'.[2] It was quite wrong to put a boy into a room with four or five others and then to expect concentrated work from him.

He was at pains to emphasise the needs of younger pupils: 'The little boys most of all require a place by themselves, for they are most unprotected, most exposed to temptation, and most in need of a refuge'. Moreover 'a boy's study is his castle. Any interference with a boy's study will be heavily punished':

'How needful it is for the little exile from home, with strange new life amongst strangers round about him for the first time, to have a spot, however small, which shall be his own, where he shall be safe, with his books, and his letters; where he can think, and weep if need be, or rejoice unmolested, and escape... out of the press of life... into a world of his own, a quasi-home, to find breathing-space, and gather a strength before he comes out again. Nowhere on earth is six or eight feet square more valuable than at school, the little bit which is a boy's own'.

---

[1] The 'pod' illustration was no accident or coincidence: see ch. 19.

[2] A 'study' was a small room, with enough space for a desk, two chairs, books and a few other possessions.

93

Open dormitories were an anathema, and partitioned cubicles an essential. To support this idea he cited the celebrated description of young George Arthur's first night at Rugby from *Tom Brown's Schooldays*: 'The idea of sleeping in the room with strange boys had clearly never crossed his mind before, and was as painful as it was strange to him'. Thring added: 'Do not suppose, whatever novels may assert, that little Christian confessors say their prayers, and kneel, and at last win the respect of their more hardened companions by doing so. Is this an ordeal that a boy ought to pass through?'[1] However, he was not in favour of study-bedrooms: it was not good for a boy to live in the same room day and night, and his room would either be permanently untidy or needing constant rearrangement for different uses. It would also be too small to have proper ventilation – but large enough to give boys the opportunity to crowd together indoors, thus making bullying more likely.

He emphasised the virtues of dispersed houses rather than the central quadrangles being developed in some of the new boarding schools. These quads might look impressive to prospective parents but they offered boys little difference between their school life and their house one, and they reduced house membership to little more than an administrative convenience. His own model, far from compromising loyalty to the school as a whole, made the houses integral to the school's success and the boys' happiness:

> 'A small number of boys are knit together in a little common-wealth. The house-master and his wife have the entire management subject to the main school laws ... They can, and do, become very intimate with their boys, and their boys with them. In fact, it is to both parties a home... [The boys] love their own house and uphold it. They rejoice at it being distinguished in school; in its triumphs out of school. It has a character which they are jealous about'.

---

[1] '[Prayer] is not done, for the coming and going, and talking and stir, of a number of boys makes it impossible'. The study-and-dormitory arrangement gave the best of both worlds. Health experts who disliked small stuffy bedrooms, and puritans who feared the mischief of private bedrooms liked the dormitories, while studies satisfied Thring's insistence on privacy. The idea that *all* boys needed their own sanctum was not widely shared: the *Contemporary Review* stated that privacy was a 'lawful luxury' only for older boys. There are overtones on Thring's ideas in the statement of Education Secretary Michael Gove (reported in the *Daily Mail,* 6 September 2013) that every child needs a 'room of one's own', providing space to learn and read.

The quality of housemasters was equally important, and prospective parents could choose a housemaster and a style of house which they particularly liked. He repeated his preference for married housemasters, telling sceptics to sneer if they wished: 'The influence of the ladies and their care [is] very appreciable. The home feeling becomes real... and both in sickness and in health the boy-life is gentler and more civilized'. He firmly believed in the 'for-profit' system: it gave housemasters an incentive and ensured high standards, making it less likely that parents would vote with their feet.

No housemaster should teach only his own boys. Such a system would make him little more than a private tutor with no direct interest in the school's academic success, and his classes would be too dependent on the skill of a single teacher. It would also create excessive competition between houses as well as academic isolation for high-flyers within their small house group. Thus it was much better if housemasters taught a form, spreading their talents and influence amongst boys from every house, and enabling their form to bring together boys of similar ages and abilities. Some masters would provide continuity by taking their class through several consecutive years; others would change classes each year, specialising in a particular age-group. There should be as many classes as there were year-groups, and not too wide a span of ages and attainments. 10-19 was a school's possible age span, but 13-19 would be better.

He was emphatic that no form or house should be too big. Ideally there would be 10-12 houses (each of about 30) [1] and classes of under 25 – large enough to have lively interaction but small enough to avoid being impersonal. As for total school numbers, 'there is no hard and fast line, but each boy added to the numbers over about 330 or 340 begins to act as a drag... whereas every boy [up to that number] adds to the efficiency of the school, by securing a sufficient graduation of classes and a sufficient number for the training of the outdoor life'. He was at pains to explain that taking in boarders enabled the funds of a school trust to be augmented.

He highlighted the characteristics of a great school in another set of aphorisms which expanded his thoughts on the nature of a school community. There must be a sense of common purpose uniting the young and the old. Teachers must 'help the young in all things, imposing no unnecessary rules, thinking energetic power'. Trust was all-important, and there could be no half-measures: 'It is safer to trust much than to trust little, and there must either be complete prison rule or a wise trust. One of the strongest motives for good is the consciousness of having a character

---

[1] In Uppingham there were usually 32 or 33 in his house: c30 in the others.

to lose'. 'Prison rule' demeaned everyone: it weighed heavily on those who *did* keep the rules, and merely forced those who did not to go further afield in order to break them.

In developing character, 'plenty of occupation is the one secret of a good and healthy moral life... everybody learning to use time well'. Masters had to be involved in far more than merely teaching lessons or they would become 'ill-tempered machines, always turning on one rusty handle. The pleasure of seeing the boys enjoy themselves, of sharing in and promoting their joys, of meeting them in their walks, of hearing the last new discovery, of playing their games, of oiling the hinges of old bones with a little of the freshness of young hearts, all would be gone'.

Different age-groups had different needs. Older boys needed longer lessons to learn thoroughly, whereas younger ones had a strong curiosity but a shorter concentration span; good memories but poorly developed logical skills. He told his readers: 'Look at the restless activity of the puppy when it is not asleep, but observe every half minute or so it has little rests and pauses. Look at the young child at play, it is the same'. As boys grew they needed more time to work independently rather than having everything explained to them. There should be examinations at the end of every term, dealing uncompromisingly with mistakes but testing mental skills as well as the mere accumulation of facts. These exams must be 'just, certain and not liable to shift by change of examiners'.

He had equally strong and reasoned views on punishment. Shame could sometimes be produced by a teacher's gentle but piercing glance, because 'all schoolmasters have eyes of forty angel-power'. If punishment had to be given, it must be proportionate: designed for training rather than vengeance; consistently and speedily applied. Punishment tasks should not take up the masters' valuable time and they should never be pointless. Writing lines only made handwriting worse, whereas learning by heart was more useful – but only if the boy was capable of it. Thring warned that 'all work-punishments with an obstinate boy soon accumulate, until everything comes to a deadlock; the victim cannot do the accumulated heap'. Depriving a boy of playtime must not be overdone, or it would prejudice health. Taking away privileges could become too protracted, but was effective if used sparingly. All kinds of public disgrace merely eroded self-respect, 'making criminals, not mending them'.

Thring briskly rejected the idea that caning was a degrading punishment. Such an argument was used only by misguided 'theorisers of a mature age' rather than by boys themselves. However, corporal punishment should never be administered in haste or in private. It was useful in teaching boys to submit to lawful authority or as a short, sharp shock for 'wilful faults' such as repeated lateness, impertinence and idleness. Some people wanted to reserve the cane for 'grave moral offences' to emphasise their seriousness, but this was incompatible with appealing to a boy's conscience. It was better to seek repentance in such cases through a more discreet and protracted punishment. Only when all other options had been exhausted or when the pupil-school relationship had irretrievably broken down should a headmaster expel a boy, because expulsion wasted the education already given, and over-use devalued it as a sanction in the eyes of other boys.

Praepostors should promote responsible self-government by the entire pupil-body, because without this the masters had to become 'despots'. Furthermore, they must uphold the trusting 'free life' within in a school. He explained the limits which he put on praepostors' power, and that boys who gave them information should not be regarded as sneaks. Conceding that fagging had its critics, he thought it little different from the hierarchy which existed in many families, where routine tasks rarely fell on the eldest and strongest. Fagging must not allow small boys to become perpetual servants, but when working well it prevented the rule of brute force by 'a certain number of big stupid boys'. He accepted that bullying would occur periodically but he thought it less likely in 'a school that was conducted on the basis of trust and fairness, treating all boys carefully and truly'.

The book concluded with some sober reflections on the extent to which a school's success depended on parental support. A master's job was so demanding that he should not have to waste time and energy in standing up to parental pressure – especially in respect of allegations about unfair punishments. He warned against giving in to parents: 'The mere exhaustion of hard work makes a man inclined to give way, if only to escape the trouble of resisting', but taking the line of least resistance was ultimately counter-productive because it made parents unrealistic about their son's academic performance and behaviour. He was especially critical of parents who saw schools as merely providing a service which the client paid for, and he ended with a side-swipe at 'ignorant and hostile' governors.

****

Education and School provoked criticism as well as praise. In *The Contemporary Review* John Mitchinson, headmaster of The King's School, Canterbury, wrote an anonymous critique. He acknowledged Uppingham's achievements but questioned Thring's naive optimism that an atmosphere of truth would guarantee pupils' cooperation: 'It is curious to observe how *half-virtuous* boys can be'. Mitchinson believed that in his pursuit of individuality Thring underestimated the need for team games. He rejected Thring's notion of individual studies, on the grounds that small boys were naturally gregarious.

Perhaps prophetically, he suggested that although Thring claimed that a school succeeded through 'machinery', Uppingham's success might eventually prove too dependent on Thring himself: 'The great schools can tide over an interregnum of incompetency on the part of their Head. Not so the grammar schools'. He concluded that 'no one who reads Mr. Thring's book can doubt that he possesses vigour and vivacity, high animal spirits and an indomitable sense of fun. In fact he has evidently carried a large slice of the boy in him through to middle life'.

Three years later a more hostile review appeared in connection with Thring's defence of a classical education. This was part of a wider controversy, centring on the divisive politician, Robert Lowe: after their unsuccessful opposition to extension of the franchise through the 1867 Reform Act, Lowe and his Liberal allies were determined to ensure that the new electorate was properly educated. It was an aim which in turn raised questions about the still-dominant position of classics in the school curriculum.

One keen reformer was the Cambridge philosopher Henry Sidgwick, who contributed an essay in F W Farrar's *Essays on Liberal Education* (1867).[1] Sidgwick was at one with Thring that classics could train good academic minds in schools, although he wanted less time devoted to them. However, as a merciless sceptic and a man of rigorous intellect,[2] he believed that all loose thinking should be challenged, and Thring's dogmatic arguments in defence of classics profoundly irritated him.

Sidgwick went into battle declaring that, despite its prestige, classical literature had 'very little attraction for the masses of cultivated persons at the present day'. Asserting that even the highest-flying boys suffered from the narrowness of the existing system, he was particularly caustic about writers who derided science as being of merely utilitarian value, or who made exaggerated claims about the perfection of classical studies, or who promoted the idea that the ancient languages somehow acquired additional worth simply by being use-less. The sway that the classics gained over the minds of such claimants and 'the indiscriminate and unreserved adulation' of the ancient authors *en masse* warped their champions' critical faculties.

---

[1] Farrar then taught at Harrow. A well-known author, he was Master of Marlborough 1871-6. See also ch. 12.

[2] Harrod, R F: *The Life of John Maynard Keynes* (1951) p.135: Sidgwick was once described as a man who 'never did anything but wonder whether Christianity was true, and prove that it wasn't, and hope that it was'.

He ridiculed Thring's 'sweeping statements'. How could Thring possibly claim that all these authors displayed 'perfect standards of criticism'? How could he maintain that 'there is no "false ornament" in Aeschylus, no "tinsel" in Ovid, no "ungracefulness" in Thucidides?' Sidgwick held that even the best classical writers exemplified only certain kinds of perfection, while others showed none at all or exemplified 'the precise imperfections that *the enthusiast, Mr. Thring,* enumerates'. Thring's claim that it was scarcely possible to speak precise English without a knowledge of Latin and Greek amounted to 'the words of a vigorous writer [illustrating] the ignorance of the real nature of language', and Thring showed 'pedantic frivolity' in regretting the loss of the original meaning of words such as 'edify' and 'tribulation'.[1]

Perhaps Sidgwick need not have worried so much, because *Education and School* sold few copies in the 1860s. In some respects it was ahead of its time and Thring was not yet sufficiently well-known, although later the book would help to confirm his reputation.[2] For the moment, however, it proved more useful as a pre-emptive strike as he faced a new, external challenge: the forthcoming enquiry into the state of the endowed grammar schools. He feared that it would deal only with processes rather than educational ideals, but as he prepared to face the Endowed Schools Commissioners he hoped to make them see the error of their ways.

Meanwhile he remained unrepentant about his vision: 'I don't want stars or rockets: I want every boy here to have a chance of showing his little light to help the world'.

---

[1] Tribulation: derived from the ancient Latin word *tribulum:* a device used for threshing grain.

[2] For further details on Sidgwick, Thring and the Greek question, see Goldhill, S: *Who Needs Greek? Contests in the Cultural History of Hellenism* (2002) p.208: 'Thring's exemplary conservative defence [in *Education and School*] of classics as the only possible school subject, had already been overtaken by... political trendies and their pamphlets'; also p.212: 'The extreme assaults on classics had the effect of making total support for the status quo seem quickly out of date. Headmaster Thring could only seem a dinosaur...'

CHAPTER EIGHT

COMMISSION AND CONFERENCE

IN November 1865, having never addressed much more than a medium-sized school audience, Thring suddenly found himself thrust on to a wider stage. Mid-Victorian governments were increasingly interventionist in many areas of life (notably public health) and had become conscious of the educational advances being made abroad. At the same time, the aspiring middle classes were questioning whether the long-established schools and universities really prepared young men for the challenges of modern Britain and its expanding empire.

It was against this background that government inquiries took place into the state of Oxford and Cambridge universities (1850-2), elementary schools (the Newcastle Commission of 1858-61) and the nine 'great' public schools (the Clarendon Commission of 1861-4).[1] Clarendon criticised the narrow curriculum of these elite schools and their tendency to produce too many 'men of idle habits and empty and uncultivated minds', but the politicians hoped that reform of them would come about through pressure from powerful parents rather than by legislation.

Clarendon's logical successor was the commission chaired by Lord Taunton (1864-7) which inquired into the state of the several hundred endowed grammar schools – of which Uppingham was still legally one, despite its changed size and nature under Thring.[2] Only a few dozen of these schools were found to be giving an effective education to pupils other than their most able. Some had few children at all while others, despite their still strongly classical curriculum, were sending few leavers on to the universities. Government viewed them as trapped in a 'chaos' of private charity. This could only be remedied by redefining and redistributing their endowments.

---

[1] 'The Nine' had become objects of criticism for their perceived immorality and their anachronistic curricula: 7 boarding schools (Eton, Winchester, Westminster, Charterhouse, Harrow, Rugby, and Shrewsbury) and 2 predominantly day schools (St Paul's and Merchant Taylors'). The Commission used 5 other schools for comparison (Marlborough, Wellington, Cheltenham, King's College School and City of London).

[2] Also known as the Endowed Schools Commission. It looked at nearly 3,000 schools, including 800 secondary schools. The Argyll Commission looked into Scottish schools at the same time.

Lord Taunton himself had little educational experience and Lord Lyttelton,[1] four years ahead of Thring at Eton and also a member of the Clarendon Commission, was an academic elitist. For him, education should 'develop the best youthful minds, for the service of the state'. One commissioner however, Dr. Frederick Temple, [2] headmaster of Rugby, shared Thring's philosophy of a broad education. This prompted Thring's brother, Henry, a man long experienced in government,[3] to believe that that the Commission would help to strengthen Uppingham's reputation'.

Thring himself was unconvinced. He resented the fact that the Clarendon Commission's existence had singled out the nine 'great' schools for special attention: it would strengthen their social exclusivity and it gave 'the greatest criminals a badge of honour'. He deeply mistrusted intervention by politicians with little experience of education and he regarded Robert Lowe's recent Education Code (1860-2) as an alarming sign of things to come. Drawn up in the wake of the Newcastle Commission's enquiry into elementary schools, the code proposed that the payment of grants to schools should depend on examinations (even for very young children) according to six standards in reading, writing and arithmetic. The system introduced payment by results.

Thring and many other teachers were deeply concerned that the examination standards were based not on experimental enquiry into what children of a given age actually knew, but on what men with little or no teaching experience thought they *ought* to know. Greater numbers of pupils in the schools would surely mean larger class sizes, leading to mass cramming rather than the encouragement of individual talents.[4] Furthermore, schools would all be structured on the basis of annual promotion through classes whose names would reflect these standards (I to VI: roughly corresponding to ages 7 to 12). This smacked of an

---

[1] George William, fourth Baron Lyttelton, (1817-76), Principal of Queen's College, Birmingham from 1845. He keenly supported working men's institutes, teacher training and the Oxford and Cambridge local examinations.

[2] Temple strengthened Rugby's classical reputation but also instituted science scholarships and built a laboratory.

[3] See ch. 13.

[4] Lowe played a leading role in education in Lord Palmerston's government from 1859. He was by instinct a decentraliser, wanting to pay teachers through school managers rather through the Post Office. Later there was some relaxation in the arrangements for testing, and state schools were able to include (e.g.) geography, history and needlework for girls. Payment by results gave way in 1897 to 'surprise visits' by inspectors. Thring was wary of Lowe's curriculum emphasis on physical science as opposed to classical studies.

alarming degree of government direction, confirmed by ministers' growing enthusiasm for inspection.

Notwithstanding his concerns Thring went to London on 14 November 1865 to give evidence to the Taunton Commission. The meeting that he hoped might bring wider recognition of his work proved to be a long and wide-ranging skirmish.

Lord Taunton began by reminding Thring that he was headmaster of Uppingham *Grammar* School before plunging straight into questions about its endowments, and the opportunities and fees charged in respect of local day boys. He asked whether its new identity had departed too far from its original charitable purposes.[1] Thring explained the school's key features, asserting that the governors had approved them, whereupon the Commissioners quickly turned to questions about boarders. Thring argued that the school's income and 'educational power' depended entirely on its boarding numbers (296 in ten houses). He explained his philosophy of giving boys spaces to call their own: 'We give each boy a study and a compartment... what for convenience I may call a horse box in a moderately sized room'. He repeated many of the arguments in *Education and School* for distinctive house identity, cohesive class groups and extra subjects to give opportunities for every boy. Housemasters would lose heavily if the number of boarders was reduced, whereupon he explained the financial contribution of the masters in building the houses and the chapel – and the governors' obstructiveness over the latter.

The Commissioners pressed him closely on the scholarships financed by the housemasters: were they open only to boarders, and what proportion of the fees did they represent? Did the boarding fee preclude all but the most affluent families? Thring accepted that it might, whereupon they returned to the day boys: 'From what class of society do [they] come?' Thring countered: 'Uppingham is a very small town, and we have never had many but the tradesmen's sons. I have at the present moment the ironmonger's son'. They asked: 'Any farmers' sons?' Thring explained that most farmers lived well outside the town, and that lessons which began at 7am tended to deter their boys. He brushed aside a suggestion of establishing cheaper houses for less affluent pupils: it would create a social barrier within the school. Yes, there were some day boys

---

[1] Thring appears to have stopped calling Uppingham a 'grammar' school in c1863. He explained that the Trust provided for day boys' fees in the form of scholarships for 'grammar scholars' born and bred in Oakham and Uppingham, regardless of their means. It also funded three annual exhibitions of £40 to Oxford or Cambridge, and the salaries of the headmaster (£150) and the usher (£120). He claimed to know nothing about the Trust's other activities.

whose parents could not have afforded boarding fees, and one of his best pupils was a farmer's son who spent his morning reaping, before travelling fourteen miles to school to play cricket in the afternoon and to take part in evening tutorials. The Commissioners suggested that the £10 extra fee charged for these evening sessions was a further disincentive to day boy parents.

Taunton himself asked whether tradesmen's sons were given exactly the same education as 'those of gentlemen and clergymen, and those destined to go to the University afterwards'. Thring confirmed that they were, adding that local parents were content and that the ironmonger regretted that he had not sent his elder son to the school too. Pressed as to whether his curriculum really helped the sons of tradesmen and the lower middle classes, he cited the benefits of learning to draw well, and the strong demand for French. He defended classics and mathematics as 'a first-rate education for any young shopkeeper' and he affirmed the merits of English grammar studied through poetry. When asked whether Greek might be dropped from grammar schools, he suggested that in some schools (but not in his own) even Latin might merely be 'tacked on to other work' for weaker forms.

He enthused about the benefits of all his extra subjects, but stated that they should not be compulsory because conscripts were a drag on interested volunteers. The contrast between Uppingham's breadth and Lowe's curriculum for government schools (restricted very largely to the '3Rs'), greatly interested the Commissioners, and they asked Thring to list all the subjects on offer. He reeled them off in full,[1] adding that he had tried hard to encourage botany: a lecturer had been found, and 'I went out myself a good deal with the one or two I got to join, but nobody else would come' because other subjects had proved more attractive.

They pressed him on this, too: 'They like their games better?' He conceded that games and extra subjects sometimes clashed, because even a boarding-school day could not be of infinite length. They were surprised that he counted outdoor activities as part of education, and even more by his response to their question: 'You play [games] with them yourself?' 'Very much indeed', Thring replied, 'I have even played at football'.

---

[1] 'Drawing, painting, English lectures, German, chemistry, and physics, natural science (i.e. biology), French, music, wood and metal turning, carpentry, gymnastics and fencing. There are a fair number for drawing and German, a moderate chemical class, a large number for French (80); a large number for music, a large number for the gymnasium and fencing, and a large number for the carpentry... a third of the school learns carpentry, at all events they go into the room'. He asked for time to check the figures for instrumental music.

As the exchanges became more animated he again denied that the fees charged for extra subjects were a barrier to poorer pupils. He emphasised that his clientele came from all over the world,[1] claiming that he could attract enough pupils for any number of houses, but that he did not want the school to get too big. This prompted the Commissioners to ask about housemasters. Were they expected to build and own their houses? What happened if they retired or died? Thring replied unapologetically that a new housemaster was expected to pay the market price to his predecessor if still alive, or to his family or executors if not. They were still unsatisfied: 'If he would or could not [pay]?' Thring pointed out that the school commanded the market and could divert parents to other houses, leaving any new housemaster who dragged his feet over such payment saddled with a house which had little rental value for other uses.

After questions about Uppingham's relationship with Oakham, Thring confirmed that there were seven *ex-officio* Uppingham governors, and that the Board's role in day-to-day affairs was 'almost nil', as long as the day boy provision conformed to the Archdeacon Johnson Trust's statutes.

The Commissioners moved on to wider issues. Thring reaffirmed the importance of good teaching, and of schools as unified communities of teachers and taught, ideally with good governors involved too. He objected to any proposal for national or district boards to reallocate endowments, because their officials would have little concern for individual schools: it would be better for each school to have a visitor to oversee its governors. If forced to choose, he would prefer national oversight rather than supervision by any 'ignorant and interfering' local body. He would never teach in a proprietor-school, where teachers would always be at the mercy of shareholders demanding rapid results.

If school inspectors were either agents of Lowe or fledgling dons, he would have none of them: 'I object exceedingly to [them] setting my school an examination totally irrespective of our ways of working, and then giving an *ex officio* decision on it; [they] being... not half so well qualified to judge the state of the school as we are'. However, if their role was merely to check that endowments were not being abused, he would accept them. The recently-devised Cambridge local examinations were 'exceedingly beneficial'[2] but the Indian Civil Service examinations were merely an inducement to cram: parents seemed indifferent to them and he wanted nothing to do with them.

---

[1] 'Australia, Canada, India, Bermuda, Mauritius, and from everywhere'.
[2] The University of Cambridge had begun a new 'Local Examinations Syndicate' in the late 1850s to administer examinations for people who were not members of the University. It also inspected schools.

Asked whether the Uppingham model could be replicated elsewhere, he warned against siting boarding schools in large towns: it would be better to use the endowments of urban schools to provide 'the very best day education that money could buy'. He would enlarge the smaller grammar schools to make them able to teach more subjects, and he suggested re-creating some of them as boarding schools for the children of tenant farmers and other families living too far away to travel to school each day. Schools thus reorganised might be placed in one of three tiers: pre-university, preparatory and lower, with various categories of exhibitions (scholarships) ranging from entry to Oxford and Cambridge to apprenticeships for 'giving boys a start in life in any honest way'.

After reminding them again at some length of exactly how Uppingham had been transformed, he departed. 'We have had a longish day', wrote one bemused commissioner, 'that good little man Thring of Uppingham giving us a most interesting picture of his work'.[1]

Once home, he was initially optimistic that Uppingham really might become a blueprint for others.[2] He had been allowed almost a whole day to give his evidence; he had been a confident witness and the Commissioners had complimented him as he left. He may, however, have misjudged his impact on men who found him interesting rather than convincing, and it is likely that he overestimated Temple's support or underestimated Lyttelton's strong belief in intellectual (as opposed to moral or other) training.

His euphoria did not survive the publication of the Commission's report in February 1868: indeed, he found its twenty-one volumes a 'most unexpected reverse [to] true work'. The report proposed a complete overhaul of English secondary education, backed by greatly increased central government oversight.[3] Each school's charitable endowments would be reviewed, with some being re-assigned to create new schools. The report supported Thring's idea of three tiers of school, suggesting that

---

[1] (Sir) Thomas Dyke Acland.

[2] 'A feeling of a new world rolling into sight for schools, and of our work being blessed beyond my dreams'.

[3] The Commission had examined reports from Matthew Arnold and others on English schools, along with comparative evidence from abroad, notably Prussia and North America; it considered girls' education as well as boys'. Of the secondary schools looked at, it deemed 218 to be 'first grade' – i.e. providing a proper classical education, but 101 of them were no longer sending pupils to university. 183 were 'second grade' offering a semi-classical curriculum up to the age of 16 or 17, and the remaining 340 were 'third grade', offering education only to 14 or 15. There was no education above elementary level in two-thirds of all English towns and cities.

the government should take account of an area's overall educational provision when determining the future of any individual school.

There would be a national system of boarding and day schools, distributed according to population within eleven administrative districts.[1] The concept of a 'free grammar school' would be replaced by a scale of fees according to the grade of the school, with scholarships to enable bright children to rise through the system. These would be awarded by open competition (any form of means-testing being seen as an invasion of parents' privacy).

Thus all endowed schools would be permanently supervised by an enlarged Charity Commission, and answerable to a Minister of Education whose officials would visit schools, produce re-organisation schemes for parliament's approval, appoint inspectors and audit school accounts. Science would be given a greater share of curriculum time. There would be a central council for pupil examinations and only state-certificated teachers would be employed. Headmasters would be deprived of their rights of freehold, making it easier for governors to dismiss them, but they would also be given greater powers to dismiss inefficient assistant masters.

If carried through in full, the Commission's recommendations would greatly increase central government power and erode or remove the independence of those who ran schools. The first three Commissioners appointed to oversee the legislation necessary to make the proposals a reality were Lyttelton, Canon Hugh George Robinson and, ironically, Arthur Hobhouse, Thring's Somerset cousin.[2] Among their very first actions was the despatch of one of their assistants to Uppingham. He would give Thring a foretaste of how the Commissioners' new powers might be enforced.

---

[1] Jones, D K: *The Making of the Education System 1851-81* (1977) p.37: 'The first grade, including the public schools, proprietary schools like Clifton and Haileybury, and grammar schools with a national intake of pupils such as Oundle and Uppingham, would provide a mainly classical education to the age of eighteen for the children of the aristocracy and gentry, the higher professional classes and wealthy industrialists. Second-grade schools would serve the smaller professional and businessmen's children... up to the age of 16 in Latin, English literature, political economy, mathematics and science, while schools of the third grade would serve the lower-middle and upper-working classes up to the age of 14 with a curriculum comprising the elements of Latin or a foreign language, English history, elementary mathematics, geography and science'.

[2] Robinson was Canon of York and Principal of its Diocesan training College. Hobhouse had given up his barrister's practice because of ill-health. He believed strongly in the reforming of endowments.

****

Despite its ambitious and laudable aims, the report and subsequent Bill aroused great hostility. Some saw any reorganising of endowments as an attack on property. Many headmasters were outraged that the Bill excluded the nine Clarendon schools *and* newly-founded public schools such as Marlborough, Wellington and Cheltenham. Hugo Harper of Sherborne was one objector. His school was not directly affected by the Bill but he feared it as a precedent, complaining of a 'lack of fair play' and believing that it resulted from the large number of MPs and peers who were Old Boys of the exempted Clarendon schools.[1]

In January 1869 Thring wrote gloomily to Harper that the Bill was 'the heaviest blow education could have received'. He believed that Uppingham would be 'in perfect working order' if only the governors and local neighbours were more friendly; it needed none of the measures proposed in a Bill which had come about only because the Clarendon Commissioners had been star-struck by schools with famous names. Moreover Taunton and his colleagues had apparently been incapable of asking themselves what constituted a 'good' school.

He believed too that exemption for the nine Clarendon schools from the legislation not only implied approval of them but would hinder reform in the rest. Four aspects of their protected status deeply incensed him.

One concerned a proposal in the Bill for teachers to be compulsorily certificated. This mirrored his own belief that teaching method needed to be studied more seriously, but the Nine would be free to recruit men directly from the universities, causing all other teachers to be perceived as second-class and lacking the ability or ambition to teach in the 'best' schools. Another was their freedom to appoint uncertificated teachers as headmasters.

---

[1] Newsome: *Wellington* (p.138): 'To [the objecting headmasters] it smacked of a political compromise to appease the many MPs who had links with those schools. Benson of Wellington was especially forthright, drawing from Dr. Temple an admission of regret that the Bill did not cover all secondary schools, but also the observation: "Of course a guerrilla chief like you does not like putting his men into line. But if the Great War is to be won it is the only way... Wellington has less claim [for exemption] than most other places". Benson continued to rage against the fact that "Half our boys are brothers of Eton, Harrow, Winchester, Rugby boys — and they will mind it, and their parents will ... We shall lose clientele, connection, resources". So powerful was the pressure of Lord Derby and other Wellington trustees that the Bill had to be withdrawn, and a revised version drafted which would exempt not only the Clarendon schools but also any endowments less than fifty years old'.

Worse still (Thring believed), endowed school headmasterships could now be held by laymen as well as clergymen, which appeared to put schools such as Uppingham potentially at risk of being 'de-churched'. However, his biggest fear was that independence would be smothered by bureaucracy, the final insult being a demand for a payment of five per cent of tuition fees, equivalent to the salary of one master, towards the expenses of the new administrative districts.

He foresaw that the proposals as a whole would hand control of schools over to men like his own governors, removing it from practising teachers:

'You cannot conceive how galling it is... to meet a set of irresponsible, clever, ignorant men armed with absolute power and see them dissect your own heart-strings in a clumsy omniscient way, and use their *fiat* on the one great work of your life [which] you understand and they don't... How ridiculous it will seem in years to come appointing a lot of squires and a stray lord or two to gather promiscuous evidence on an intricate professional question, and to pronounce infallible judgement on it'.

He and a few others now began the tentative moves which led to the foundation of the Headmasters' Conference. They had no ambition to become like the socially 'fashionable' Clarendon schools (as Thring termed the Nine): they preferred to keep their distance, lining up with what he called 'smaller schools which one may hope to see doing honest work', in a coalition against a government determined to control them and to make all schools adopt the worst characteristics of the Nine without consulting the 'working man' (i.e. the teacher) about his future.

Harper suggested a circular letter to seek a consensus on the best way forward, whereupon John Mitchinson (King's, Canterbury) organised a meeting of some fellow-headmasters at the Freemasons' Tavern in London in the first week of March 1869 to discuss the Bill. Thring was not especially keen to get involved and initially declined to attend, knowing that his opposite numbers disagreed with him on many other issues, and recognising that concerted action flew in the face of his instinctive belief in independence.[1] Mitchinson, however, could see that if

---

[1] 'I have written to say I cannot go. Like Mitchinson, but much as I disapprove of the government move, my objections do not belong so much to the Bill itself as to the muddle they have made in glorifying the [Clarendon] schools; and in not [even] raising the question of what is a *good* school... As Uppingham stands alone I must either lead or be in a false position (by joining in), and as I am sure that I should not lead... I can at least avoid being in a false position'.

schools merely protested individually, they had little chance of opposing the legislation.

He made a strong appeal to Thring to think again, finally convincing him that if the 'non-workers' (i.e. government) insisted on acting as a body, the 'workers' (headmasters) must do so too. Thring sensed that his sixteen years of isolated work at Uppingham were ending and his public life was beginning:

> 'Perhaps I launch out into a sea, and this is the last night of unmolested work' I may pass for years... I feel a solemn dread mixed with the excitement of change. Tonight I am here quiet, tomorrow the one step forward on a possible new life in many ways is taken. I hate, too, the thought of this external battle, and yet I do not see how a man can shirk it'.[1]

He was pleasantly surprised that the London meeting was so 'well and influentially' attended. Just over two dozen headmasters were present and he was 'very much struck with the general appearance and behaviour', feeling that he had never seen 'so little time wasted... or good sense shown: much pleased at having gone... I feel a sense of support from having met'. He wrote next day to Mitchinson, 'suggesting that we should combine and have an annual meeting at Christmas, taking each time one of our schools as the place of rendezvous, I receiving them at Uppingham this year. I hope this will be approved, as we [need] more communion and intercourse'. He sensed that it would be 'the beginning of a great work... more beneficent than any Act of Parliament'.

The group sent a deputation to W E Forster (the minister responsible for the Bill) who received them courteously and promised to consider Thring's views on the classification of schools. It duly reported back to a second meeting of the headmasters at the Westminster Palace Hotel on 12 March. Thring again commented on the meeting's usefulness and congeniality as evidence of the need for an annual gathering, and publicly invited them all to Uppingham in December.

One dissenting voice suggested that the meeting should again be in London, but a formal London meeting was not at all what he intended. He wanted to reduce the isolation of headmasters by giving them an opportunity to visit each others' schools. Typically for him it was to be all or nothing: if others insisted on London, he wanted nothing to do with

---

[1] He was also persuaded by John Walter MP, an Eton contemporary, who asked him for guidance on what he should say in the House about the Bill's proposals for examinations and inspections.

110

them.[1] He won the day, and in doing so assumed the leading role. In his letters of invitation he spoke of a log-jam of educational legislation and the risky silence if the headmasters failed to combine. They could also learn so much from each others' schools:

'The reasons ... are not far to seek. The pressure of continuous heavy work, and the wide area over which schools are scattered, are the two most obvious. The first obstacle must remain; but the second can at least be mitigated, if not entirely removed, by choosing alternately a school north and south of London as a place of meeting. The plan also gives year by year, new interest and practical knowledge of what is being done in different parts of England'.[2]

Some of the replies were sceptical, some downright disdainful. One felt that 'no federal action is needed'; another 'did not find any great difficulty in ascertaining what others are doing', and a third doubted 'whether I shall ever be able to attend the proposed meetings, so strongly do I value the perfect rest of the holidays, and the privilege of complete independence in dealing with... such educational difficulties as may arise'. A fourth had 'not much stomach for councils'.

Thring was acutely aware of the possibility of failure: 'I wonder how the schools will answer. I am not thin-skinned about it. If they won't combine, they won't. If they will, my position as the leading school [affected by] this Bill makes me the fittest person to send out such a summons'. Yet by now he was increasingly enthusiastic about the idea. Keen to scotch any notion that the Conference was intended to impose unified standards or interfere in how individual schools were run, he circulated an agenda before the meeting with a list of questions about eligibility and election for membership, and some suggested ways of governing schools and administering endowments. He repeated his hope:

'That year by year, the seeing different schools, learning each others' difficulties, hearing the views of thoughtful, educated men, making acquaintance with one another and enjoying a little intercourse, may tend

---

[1] 'It would frustrate the whole object. I wrote to say that if this was the general opinion, I would drop the project at once.' He told Harper and Mitchinson that if they backed the idea of gatherings only in London, they must go it alone.

[2] According to Percival: *Very Superior Men* p.190: 'Until the Conference became established, headmasters often did not know what other Heads and their schools were like'. This wish for more meetings within the profession had long been an issue for the Eton group of reformers; eight years earlier Thring's old rival, there and at King's, William Johnson, had suggested 'a conference of schoolmasters'.

in time to bring about, if not common consent on the main points, at least a kindly feeling and readiness to give help and counsel'.

Of the 37 headmasters invited, twelve finally came to Uppingham on 21 December 1869.[1] Mitchinson travelled up from Kent to Uppingham, just over 100 miles north of London, with Welldon of Tonbridge who observed repeatedly 'as we traversed the dreary, sodden, mist-clad country, that Thring must be a wonderful man to have made a school like this in the midst of such a howling wilderness'.[2]

The headmasters shared information and many ideas about buildings and governance.[3] Thring saw it all in glowing terms: 'On Wednesday morning I felt a unit; on Thursday a power – so completely has even this meeting altered things ... Make us a brotherhood to be a light in England; lift us not up, O God, as beacons, but as a saving clear light'. The metaphor echoed Harper who, in seconding Thring's opening address, declared that headmasters were like scattered stars: if they were to meet and work together their light could be brought into focus and would achieve a much more powerful effect.

By now Thring had come to see the gathering in Uppingham as much more than a declaration of war with Forster and the government over the Bill.[4] Despite rivalries between individual schools, it must be a communion of working men [with] a common spirit of earnestness... and common action'. His main speech was an appeal to set aside former school snobberies and exclusivity and to create a unity of purpose within the profession. He looked for a great expanding of contacts and a willingness to learn from one another: 'If we are going to work for the

---

[1] The headmasters of Bromsgrove, Bury St Edmunds, King's Canterbury, Felsted, Lancing, Liverpool College, Norwich, Oakham, Repton, Richmond (Stokoe), Sherborne and Tonbridge. Another five had accepted, but were prevented from coming at the last minute: Highgate, Dulwich, Ipswich, City of London, and York. Four more were prevented by previous engagements: Christ's Hospital, Durham, Magdalen College School, and Marlborough. Invitations for Rugby and Rossall were kept back, their headships being vacant.

[2] Parkin recorded Mitchinson's claim that Welldon said this over and over again as the two men headed out of the Home Counties and into the Midlands.

[3] E.g. Wratislaw of Bury St Edmund's, who was able to tell his governors in 1876 about the buildings of the host schools, with obvious implications. Butler of Liverpool tried the same tactic.

[4] Forster's 1870 Education Act brought the teaching of children in elementary schools (done hitherto on a voluntary basis) under the auspices of the state. It also provided women with opportunities in teaching, in turn providing a major impetus for education for girls. Forster was Arnold's son-in-law.

good of education, wherever we find good educational work we should recognise it, and invite it to co-operate with us, and not exclude any man doing such work'. If they proceeded on the basis of 'common progress, common life, and common desire to do our best', many other benefits would follow.

The headmasters discussed the Bill and passed resolutions designed to uphold the integrity of the teaching profession. They debated the new Latin pronunciation. They affirmed that governing bodies should include representatives of masters' interests,[1] and that 'in cases of variance' between governors and headmasters there should be an easy and inexpensive process of arbitration. They agreed that they should retain the right to expel boys, but should not themselves be subject to dismissal from their schools without appeal.

They also approved an expanded list of sixty-six headmasters to be invited to a second gathering at Sherborne a year later, with Thring signing the invitations. However, the absence of the 'great' schools had already become an issue. Pears of Repton was anxious to support Eton's inclusion - even proposing that its Head Master be appointed president of the Conference. Thring's old friend, Butler of Harrow, agreed but Mitchinson objected to being associated with the Clarendon schools and Thring's intervention in support of him was decisive: 'I laid down plainly that I thought it was simple death to do so; we rested on our vitality and work, they on their prestige and false glory. If they would meet us on common ground, well and good; if not, not'.

It is easy to see why some headmasters looked longingly at Eton's longstanding fame and its recent exemption from state interference. However, Thring's first-hand knowledge of Eton made him wary. Making overtures to the Clarendon schools might give them even more public recognition at a time when, despite Eton's reforms under Hawtrey, the Nine still appeared to be prisoners of their past:

'If they come in on the basis of working power and life, we shall be glad, but we can acknowledge no other common basis. Eton I hold to be one of the most difficult and insoluble problems of the present day, not because the men who are working at Eton want zeal, or energy, or earnestness, but because they are hemmed in on every side by an unpleasant glory that belongs to the past, trammelled by a blind affection.

---

[1] Although masters themselves could not be governors. They also discussed whether future conferences might be partly open to masters, but came to no firm conclusion.

Our schools depend entirely on the vitality of progressive work... If we put ourselves in any attitude but that of simply inviting co-operation, we must be slaves... To me Eton seems the perfection of a school in external advantages, a fairyland (I speak with no comparison or disrespect to others). It has wonderful powers of a certain kind and earnest men using that power; but [in] progressive work, we stand better than they; more alive to the necessity of it; comparatively unfettered in carrying out our discoveries, and we do carry them out more effectively'.

As it turned out, delay was wise. By the time the second meeting took place at Sherborne at the end of 1870, the Clarendon group had loosened, and Eton had made its own decision to join the Conference. Others of the Nine gradually followed during the next decade.

Thring's advice was sought again by the Commissioners in 1872 over a wide variety of matters about curriculum and boarding costs, reasonable class sizes in each subject, and which subjects best trained young minds. In considering whether new boarding schools might realistically charge lower fees than the well-established ones, they wanted to draw on his experience. He provided them with plenty of financial and other guidance but hectored them rather too much on some of his familiar themes: how every boy was unique; the virtues of small classes and houses, and the right of teachers to be well paid – especially in boarding schools, where they 'undertake much more than tuition, and demand far severer work, and quite a different and higher average work than day schools'. His twin assertions that parents could only appreciate the true cost of education if they had to pay full fees, and that any fee-subsidy by government would cause the public to undervalue teachers, effectively ended the prospect of further dialogue.

Even so, as a result of the Uppingham conference Thring had become a well-known figure amongst his peers – and more widely. Looking back on it all Mitchinson famously claimed: 'I think that if I may fairly claim to have laid the egg which developed into the present Headmasters' Conference, Thring did all the clucking necessary'. A century later, the historian of HMC pointed to the irony in the fact that the action for which Thring is best known is the calling of that first gathering:

'Not only did he *not* call the first meeting of headmasters (i.e. at the Freemasons' Tavern), but he nearly did not go to it at all. Even when, at the second meeting, he offered an invitation to Heads already gathered (and later sent it out to others) to meet at his school in the Christmas holidays, it is doubtful whether he was sure that a permanent body could be established. Equally ironic and untrue is the common notion that a conference was held by the Heads of the great public schools with the

114

idea of deciding who should be admitted to their group and who should be excluded; had it been so, Thring would not have been there... As by definition the schools affected [by the Commission] were the endowed schools – grammar schools like Uppingham – those conferring were the Heads of schools *not* then generally regarded as public schools. The Clarendon Nine were by this fact excluded. No headmaster had been asked from Eton or Rugby, nor even from the newly-founded schools such as Cheltenham and Clifton... None of these were at the first gathering, and many did not join the Conference for two or three years after Thring's venture started'.

However, she added:

'Though Thring did not call the first gathering, popular opinion is right to associate the Conference with his name... Mitchinson and Harper, the men who, one by his initiative and the other by his organisation, had made the first gathering possible, without hesitation yielded first place to Thring. Looking at the variety and individuality of the Heads who had attended the first meetings of the group, it must have been very clear to them that only a very exceptional man would be able to get and hold them all together. It could only be Thring'.[1]

---

[1] Percival: *Very Superior Men* p.197-8.

CHAPTER NINE

UPPINGHAM'S NEW SCHEME

WELL before the headmasters' inaugural conference in Uppingham in December 1869, Thring had gained first-hand experience of the workings of the recently-passed Endowed Schools Act.[1] In February that year, a youthful assistant commissioner arrived in Uppingham to investigate the state of its endowments. His visit (one of the first of its type) was no act of vindictiveness by the Commissioners, who thought that Thring's school had less to fear than many far less efficient ones. As one of them explained: 'We dealt with Uppingham, which is an admirable school which we cannot improve, because Mr. Thring gave us no rest until we took the case in hand'.

Thring was determined that his school should be a test case, and if necessary a warning to others. H W Eve, the investigator, had been a boy at Rugby and subsequently a junior master at Wellington: Thring conceded that he was a pleasant, agreeable fellow', but also thought him 'a man who had just attained the sort of distinction that I had twenty-five years ago, and others of the masters since. What regard was due to his opinion, trained as he was in an antagonistic system,[2] and lacking our experience?' Eve was permitted under protest to examine the sixth form and one of the middle forms in classics, but Thring insisted on adding a footnote to Eve's report:

> 'In the name of myself and my colleagues I beg to protest against any examination of the school classes by a stranger: such flying examinations are utterly unreal as any test of average proficiency, though the results stated in a report look real. Therefore we believe such examinations to be full of danger, and, if constant, sure to introduce strong disturbing influences into good steady school work'.

Eve was in fact an able young man, regarded by Benson (Master of Wellington) as the most talented member of his staff. Eve amassed statistical material – on pupil numbers, fathers' occupation, fees and extra

---

[1] The Act had proved less radical than the Commission's proposals: see the final section of this chapter.

[2] Probably a reference to the fact that Eve had attended Rugby, which was a Clarendon school.

charges, buildings, fields and play areas, periods per week in each subject, syllabuses and texts used in every class, and prizes and punishments.

The report which resulted from his researches was very favourable. The domestic arrangements were judged to be 'perfect', and he praised the masters' investment in houses and other buildings.[1] He noted that the statutes 'do not interfere with the internal arrangements of the school', but that 'the governors seem to have dreaded not only the expenditure of money on [the] school but even the cost of repairs'. He praised the 'thoroughly friendly relations between masters and boys, and the Old Boys' appreciation of how much Thring trusted pupils.

He found no evidence that the school failed to stretch its academically ablest pupils, but he recorded the concern of some people (possibly masters) that it was not attracting more of them: 'The school may have suffered from the reputation it has gained for bringing on dull and idle boys'. He also noted the contrasting paths taken by Uppingham and Oakham since Thring's arrival: Oakham had fewer buildings, and 18 day scholars compared with only 7 at Uppingham, but a mere 34 boarders, compared with Uppingham's 261.

Apart from some reservations about the mathematics teaching, Eve criticised only one significant aspect: few town boys attended the school and he 'could not find any strong desire to recruit them'. Possibly as a result of being lobbied by local people he echoed the Commissioners' earlier suspicion that charges for extra tuition deterred applications from local tradesmen.

Despite all the praise, Thring was alarmed at the zeal with which Eve collected his information and statistics. It seemed to confirm his own worst fears about the bureaucratic world to come, with the Commission focusing merely on legal and administrative matters rather than a school's teaching standards. He thought that Eve had failed to appreciate Uppingham's distinctiveness and (like his superiors) had tacitly assumed that the Clarendon schools should be models for others. Thring still resented the exemption of the Nine from the Act, and the fact that Taunton's terms of reference had excluded the recently-founded boarding schools. Their religious identities would remain protected while the endowed grammar schools had to resist the march of secular government.

For Uppingham which despite all its boarders was legally still an endowed school, Thring was determined to win similar protection.

---

[1] Eve pointed out (cf the *Contemporary Review's* opinion in ch. 7) that studies did not prevent boys from congregating in the halls and elsewhere – and only they provided a sanctum. He noted that mathematics was examined by Mr. Barnard Smith (Rector of nearby Glaston): see ch. 14.

However, some months after Eve departed and a week after the first headmasters' conference, the Commissioners notified him that there were no grounds for Uppingham to be exempt from the legislation which permitted laymen to become headmasters.

Describing himself as trapped between indifferent and supine school governors and a government with a lust for power, Thring conceded that the letter was kindly in tone but he saw it as a sign that 'again war has begun'. He described the legislation as being designed to 'un-church' schools, portraying the Commission as part of a wider move to dilute the religious nature of endowed schools, ignoring their history. For him, it revealed the alarming likelihood that the Church of England itself might eventually be disestablished.

He was sure that Uppingham's ethos was a Christian one whatever its constitutional arrangements and he would fight fiercely to stop this being watered down: 'My sole motive was to do a work for Christ. The school as it now works is entirely the result of this belief'. If the Commissioners ignored the fact that the school had been founded by an archdeacon, they ought to reimburse him and the masters for all their investment in its facilities, leaving them free to start their own school based on the boarding houses that they owned. He added an unequivocal threat to resign if they failed to satisfy him.

The Commissioners respected his conviction but, believing that they were doing good work themselves, gave him assurances that his fears were groundless. Lyttelton even wrote personally, gently chiding Thring for seeing the Commissioners as natural enemies and inviting his confidence. Thring replied twice, repeating all his concerns and denying that he was reacting out of cussedness. He felt 'the best part of [my life] gone, absolutely at the mercy of parliament and this Bill'.

Eve's inquiry and the drafting of Uppingham's new scheme of government eventually took three years. When the scheme finally appeared in December 1872 it gave wide-ranging powers over all aspects of the school to a reformed board of governors, now to be known as 'trustees'. It was a logical development, but one which confirmed Thring's worst fears that the Commissioners had 'truckled to the squires and left them in possession', leaving professional men (schoolmasters) to be controlled by amateurs (governors/trustees).

As so often, Marie was his rock: 'For the first time in my life I believe, care kept me awake a great part of the night. Then when I came out of school my gallant-hearted wife said she had been very down, but suddenly it came across her that God had given me a resolute heart to fight for Him, and fight for Him I must'. Heavy-hearted and short of sleep, he got up to read the psalm next morning in chapel, and 'out flashed

on my soul the first verse, "Lord, remember David and all his trouble"...
How my heart rose as I read it. God will not forget'.

He wrote protestingly to Lyttelton yet again: 'Every great profession
is full of complicated knowledge. I claim that the skilled workers shall be
well represented in the management of the trade, and not interfered with
by external unintelligent power'.[1] He hoped and expected that 'you and
your colleagues will do us justice' and he deployed new arguments: the
masters too would be affected by the Commission's proposals, because
many of them had invested money in a venture which was now legally
given over to the new trustees despite the fact that the Trust had financed
only a tiny percentage of the school's capital costs.[2]

He hoped this argument would strengthen the housemasters' resolve
to support him, but he feared that they might take the line of least
resistance, submitting to the Commissioners and then letting the school
embrace values which had become all too fashionable in other schools.
When they held a meeting to which he was not invited, he feared their
capitulation – but he need not have worried. On 16 December 1872 they
signed a remarkable document, listing six considerations:

'1. That Mr. Thring has been Head Master for nearly twenty years:
2. That when he came the school consisted of about twenty five boys,
and that it now consists of four hundred:[3]
3. That from the first the school has been worked at great risk and
expense upon definite principles, considered by Mr. Thring and by all of
us to be of vital importance, and that to the working of these principles
the success of the school is due:
4. That of the present school buildings, the Trust has contributed 8 ¼ per
cent, & Mr. Thring and his masters 91 ¼ per cent:
5. That the school is thus virtually a new foundation, and Mr. Thring the
founder:
6. That 'the efficiency of a system depends for the most part upon the
living power that sets and keeps it in motion'[4] — and that this living

---

[1] 'No governor or council, short of the highest in the kingdom, should have
absolute power to alter at will the structure and character of a school'. Although
he wanted teaching more widely recognised as a profession, he could not accept
the idea that schools should be regulated or teachers certificated by government,
whose leaders had no specific educational expertise. He never completely
admitted or resolved this contradiction.

[2] This time he estimated it at 3%.

[3] This 400 figure was surely an exaggeration.

[4] They were citing a description of the school by one of Thring's allies, James
Fraser, Bishop of Manchester.

power cannot be created but may easily be destroyed, by a scheme imposed as extra'.

They asserted that Thring and Uppingham should be treated as a special case and promised that they would back him to the hilt. Demonstrating that freedom for the school to choose its own pupils came before any concern to bolster the school's academic reputation, they were especially forthright in rejecting any externally imposed system of competitive scholarships, because 'a good ordinary boy properly qualified to enter, and duly entered, has as much right to a "public" education as the cleverest'. For Thring, this was a 'precious document', and his mistake in doubting them prompted him to make them a rare apology.

Support came from another source too: the large concentration of parents which had formed in the major cities of the North-West. A Birkenhead parent, Wensley Jacob, came to see Thring, bringing another from Liverpool (across the River Mersey) and supported by a third, Thomas Birley from Manchester.[1] Jacob told Thring that Uppingham families in their area were completely behind him: if he felt forced to resign, they would help him to found a new school elsewhere, leaving the bureaucrats only with empty buildings. Meanwhile they were petitioning the Commissioners themselves: Jacob would meet them in London the next day, and would lobby several north-west MPs who had already indicated their support. Within a month, the parents of 260 boys had signed a petition.

Thring saw this as a vote of confidence beyond his wildest dreams: 'How bright the past looks, when I see what fathers, men of such sense and power, think of it, and how much they support the work!' He was careful to spell out that it was the ethos of the school that was at risk from the Commissioners rather than its existence, and his parent-advisers urged him to fight his case on the grounds that his school was a church foundation. Even though Uppingham was legally subject to the Endowed Schools Act, the tiny proportion of its growth financed by the Trust compared with the masters' contribution made this status wholly inequitable. He should also parade the school's vulnerability as a warning to others, claiming that if the Church of England were ever to be dis-established Uppingham might become the precedent by which any church-affiliated institution would have its property seized by the state.

On 7 May 1873, Thring returned to present his case to the Commissioners. This was a much stormier encounter than Thring's description of it as 'slightly gladiatorial', especially with the academically

---

[1] Thring's association with Jacob and Birley would be a long one: see later chs.

elitist Lyttelton, who began by stating that although the Commissioners wished Uppingham no harm, they could not make it an exception. Thring countered that he and the masters had 'an irresistible claim in equity' and would fight to defend it step by step. When he added his warning about church precedent, Lyttelton predictably broke in: 'That is speculative and a great jump':

> 'I answered: "Perhaps; but these are days of jumping: we are getting familiar with great jumps, and it is necessary to provide for jumps in these jumping days". He said, "Do you mean to say you will go on [fighting], even if you are not one of the exceptions provided for in the Bill?" I answered, "Certainly we should." He said, "That is running your head against a wall". I answered that that was exactly what we meant to do; we were going to run our heads against a wall if necessary"'.

After the furious Lyttelton left, the other Commissioners continued the discussion for another two hours in a much more relaxed atmosphere, with Thring continuing to defend Uppingham's uniqueness. Three draft documents followed. Negotiation continued over nearly two more years before the agreed 'New Scheme for Uppingham' was published on 18 January 1875. Essentially, Thring agreed to drop his opposition in principle to the Commissioners' work, and they agreed to make Uppingham a special case. It would remain a church school in ethos, and its internal management, including its control of its admissions, would be left in Thring's hands.[1] The masters were to have two elected representatives on the reformed trustee body. The trustees were given a formal right to oversee the curriculum, but not to prescribe it. The headmaster must still be a member of the Church of England. Unusually, and to the dismay of some of his colleagues, Thring kept his right to dismiss masters without appeal.

His victory was widely recognised, but the Commission was wise to treat him as an exception, rather than risk a national pressure group against a perceived attack on property.[2] Even his church argument was

---

[1] The distinction between oversight and prescription is similar to practice in most independent schools today. The elected representatives were not to be mandated delegates, and could not be current masters. Protection against arbitrary dismissal was campaigned for by one of Thring's staff, Rowe (see ch. 11) in an anonymous pamphlet – but was not won until the Endowed Schools (Masters) Act of 1908.

[2] The Oakham scheme was less accommodating. Its trustees gained powers over the curriculum and term dates; parents could opt out of religious instruction (unlike Uppingham); there was no requirement for its headmaster to be a Church of England member, and the masters gained rights of appeal against dismissal.

more tactical than real: he admitted that he cared little about the legal status of the endowment, but he was determined to run his school in his own way and to be exempt from any clause in the Act which might give the town Rector rights of control over the school chapel. Independence and freedom from outside interference were the central issues:

> 'On the most important parts of school management, all the great schools had already given way and quietly accepted the dead hand of ignorant external power. Now I can breathe again. Uppingham furnished the backbone: no other school could or would hold out on any distinct principle... If we had given way, all would have been lost'.

****

It is possible to see Thring's battles with the Commissioners in two ways. The critical view states that the Commission went on to produce improved new schemes of management for hundreds of schools, reallocating some endowments to provide much-needed new schools for girls in the process: therefore if Thring really believed in education as much as he claimed, he should have supported its work. His resistance, for example, to the use of ancient endowments to fund state-sponsored scholarships, was reactionary and selfish. Moreover the 1870 Education Act which followed the Commission was an essential measure in securing the universal education system that Britain needed to remain competitive in the world. The opposition to the Act can thus be seen as narrowly ideological (like Thring's), or rooted in self-interest, jealousy of the power of the new School Boards, concern about the loss of local or church influence, or even fears that children would no longer be able to work at harvest time.[1]

The supportive view of Thring's stance recognises that there was no-one else to take up the battle to protect his school – certainly not his supine governors. His opposition to Lyttelton's narrow concern for the academic elite was genuine and consistent, and so was his vision for a united profession to resist the combined pressures of exam-fixated officials and parents wanting only a limited, utilitarian education for their sons. He challenged those who would have rushed into wholesale control of education by the state to think again, thus fighting a battle for schools

---

[1] Sir Joshua Fitch: *Educational Aims and Methods* (1900) p.282-3: Thring wrongly thought that 'he could secure for himself all the prestige and influence of a great public institution, and all the freedom and independence of a private schoolmaster carrying on a commercial venture of his own... [He was] wholly out of sympathy with the [provision] of secondary education and the examination and inspection of schools by public authority'.

well beyond the independent sector. He was also fighting for the principle of independent schools being *independent,* for example in curriculum innovation and in appointing staff beyond those with formal teaching qualifications.[1]

Whichever view one takes, his victory was at best a pyrrhic one. While the Act's new schemes helped to stabilise or improve many endowed schools, education in many of them came to focus more narrowly on the intellect than he would ever have wished. Few schools took the opportunity to adopt his broad curriculum or the other reforms outlined in *Education and School.* His system would not, after all, become a national blueprint.

Some of the Commission's more radical suggestions were dropped or shelved, and Disraeli abolished it in 1874 after mounting opposition, transferring its powers to the Charity Commission.[2] Hobhouse believed that its proposals had been ahead of their time and far too extreme for the unprepared public, but Education Acts over succeeding decades ensured that successive governments became ever more involved in national education. Moreover the Charity Commission would henceforth scrutinise the accounts of every endowed school in the land far more actively than had previously been the case.

In local terms, Thring won some constitutional victories. However, the Scheme also held hidden dangers for him. It was a highly detailed document of well over 150 clauses, including provisions about his stipend and other emoluments; scholarship and curriculum arrangements; reporting procedures and much more. Significantly, it included a template of how the Trust's annual accounts should in future be presented.

---

[1] Leese, J: *Personalities and Power in English Education* (1950) p.201: 'The Commissioners realised - how could they fail to, after the evidence of Thring? - that private schools would always be the natural field for the energies of enthusiastic teachers who hold peculiar views, and cannot work in the trammels of the recognised system of the day... These are the men who most often make improvements, and discover new methods. The private schools offer a field for their experiments which [other] schools can hardly do'.

[2] Measures which were dropped included regional organisations of schools with a Charity Commission district official and parent representatives on each governing body. The school Boards created by the 1870 Education Act were only for elementary schools. For now, there was no central council for examinations, and no registration tests for endowed-school teachers. In practice the re-launched grammar schools became dominated by the middle class. The Charity Commission's new powers were transferred again in 1899 - to the Board of Education.

Overall it gave the trustee body – previously so distant but now reformed – a checklist of aspects of the school about which it might usefully inform itself. Many of the Scheme's individual clauses bear a striking similarity to those which appear in any model contract for independent school Heads in the twenty-first century. Its carefully crafted text described theoretically the respective powers of governors/trustees and headmaster, but in practice their relationship would ultimately depend on an unwritten understanding about where the lines should be drawn between governance and management.

If the Scheme had been in place fifteen years earlier, it would have been far more difficult for Thring to develop Uppingham as he did – but it could also have saved him from the difficulties he faced for the rest of his career as a result of the school's finances and his own now being inextricably and dangerously mixed up.

For the moment, however, he rejoiced in his victory. At the supper after the Old Boys' match in 1873 he reflected on the fact that he had been in post for only ten days short of two decades. He had never expected to be 'thrown into a government cauldron to be stewed, and it was no light thing to be turned out of what was one's life'. He also praised the Merseyside parents for their support, declaring that what he was really proud of about Uppingham was that 'here each boy has his chance'.

CHAPTER TEN

PRIME OF LIFE

AS Uppingham grew, some of his colleagues thought that Thring held on to too much teaching for too long. He loved the classroom, as an escape from the other demands on him and an outlet for his nervous energy: long after the school reached its steady state of 300 he continued to be form master of the sixth form, responsible for the whole of its work.

In his heyday he cut a formidable figure through his teaching: highly enthusiastic, with an ability to paint vivid mental pictures through his powerful way with words and dramatic gestures. Accounts of it were mostly written by pupils who were taught by him in the 1860s and who subsequently returned as staff: men who (as boys) had undoubtedly been amongst his more academically-minded pupils, so it is hard to know just how typical their reactions were. That said, one thing is not in doubt: his teaching style was never for the faint-hearted, and even those who admired his energy felt that he could never appreciate how much some pupils were over-awed – even terrified – by his dominant presence. They had difficulties in following his unpredictable train of thought, lateral thinking and butterfly mind, especially during lessons involving progressive language skills when he suddenly digressed to describe a historical situation or another aspect of *True Life*.[1]

Junior boys encountered him in groups each week for a test of their progress: 'an hour of undiluted terror to be lived through as best [we] could and then put out of [our] minds until it came round again... the square, gown-clad figure would sweep into the room; the steel-blue eyes took in the whole company at a glance'. With the class still trying to assess his mood, he often plunged straight in, questioning them on the Latin grammar which they had been set to learn. Sometimes he took them by surprise, as when he jabbed a finger towards one victim asking: 'How do you make a plum-pudding?' When he got no reply, the question was passed down the line: 'Next?... next?... next?'. He reached a very small new boy, who blurted out 'Please, sir – I don't know' and was greeted with a grin and the reply 'Of course you don't know! How should any of you know? Only sensible answer!'

---

[1] Much of this chapter comes from books by three former pupils, John Skrine and the brothers Willingham and Hardie Rawnsley, together with letters to Parkin after Thring's death, and Rigby's interviews with elderly OUs in the 1960s.

A revealing description survives of an oral construing exercise based on a passage from Cicero's *De Senectute*:[1] After a sweeping glance around the entire class:

'[Thring] says, "Construe – Jones minor." Jones... rises to confront his fate, in stony dread. Parts of speech swim before him; his voice sounds hollow to his ear, like noises to a drowning man, but he proceeds unscathed'. (Several other boys then take over from Jones in turn). 'But then, just at the point where Cato the Elder was commenting to Scipio and Laelius on the grumblings of his companions, the construe is stopped: "Jones minor – quod voluptatibus carerent – why <u>carerent</u>?" Jones minor cannot say. Brown major is no wiser. Robinson, a boy of assurance, repeats a rule from [his Latin] primer: he is extinguished by a request to explain his explanation.

White tries a rule from Thring's *Latin Gradual*: it would have been a capital answer last week, but this week [it] is a section too late. Then Grey seeks to conjure with that word of all work, "indefinite". "Yaas – very much so – you!" is the sarcastic welcome. Green, a novice, falters "indirect question", unconscious that this is a "certain draw". But Green is new, and the presence (i.e. Thring) restrains itself, and looks on, long-sufferingly, to the next: the lightning does not fall. Black, a reclusive student, hesitates an answer [to which Thring replies]:

"My – good! – fellow! Do you generally stand on your heels or on your head?" And before Black has seized the relevance of the rejoinder, the question is going down the class with a rapid "Next – next – next?"'.[2]

Right at the bottom of the class sits the stoical Grubbe minor, who is thinking – or hoping – that Thring can't possibly cane them all for their ignorance. However, they are all saved by the fresh-faced Wilson minor, recently arrived in the school, whose precocious Latin has been gleaned from his learned clergyman father:

'[Wilson] lisps out an inspired something. A flash, not of lightning, comes into [Thring's] eyes, and the deep-trenched lines of the mouth relax: "Yas, – excellent, excellent, Wilson." And then, though it immediately appears that Wilson, like many a creative artist, has uttered things deeper than he knew himself, the work is done. The gathering storm melts in a benign effusion of syntactical exposition'.

---

[1] 'Construing' is the analysis of the syntax of a text, sentence or word. Thring conducted it as oral work.

[2] The question about 'carerent' relates to subjunctives and indirect speech; it would have been hard for a schoolboy. Not knowing Black's hesitant reply, we have no context for Thring's curious question about standing on one's heels or one's head – but the incident confirms his idiosyncratic teaching style.

Even Grubbe understands some of what follows, as Thring takes over the construing himself and the boys listen to his voice, full of 'rich and strenuous English sounds':

> 'We would be content to hear him construe the whole three-quarters of an hour. But he is harking back to "carerent" when a clock strikes, and a stern "You may go," judicially and massively spoken like a sentence of acquittal, empties the room. Whew! to breathe the blessed air again! Purgatory over for a week!'

Once boys were old enough to escape this group interrogation, they had to take a weekly exercise to him, facing 'the terror of his corrections in the school-house hall, the torrent of papers flying to the floor scored with the hatchet strokes of the huge carpenter's pencil, the grain of the oaken desk reproduced on the back of the paper as in a brass-rubbing'. Many pieces of work were dismissed as nonsense and some were torn up.

Higher up the school he took the fourth and fifth forms for Latin translation. Even then he could be disconcerting, punishing them quixotically (depending on his mood) and sometimes disproportionately for their grammar mistakes. An entire class lost its half-holiday after one member got his Greek verbs wrong, and when Thring briefly left the room afterwards, the others held the unfortunate cause of their punishment down while one boy gave him 'a sound thrashing'. When Thring returned he fixed his eye on the chief perpetrator (his godson) with a quizzical '*Well*, Master Rawnsley!' but the lesson then resumed without further comment.[1]

He was determined that boys should develop thinking and observational skills for themselves, making them write down their impressions as poems in Latin or English. One of his favourite essay topics was *Today*, but he would not settle for half-hearted descriptions: if they merely told him that the sky was blue, the birds were singing and the grass was green, he countered: 'No! To-day the sky was grey with thunder-cloud in the east, with flashes of bright sun. I heard a thrush sing, a chiff-chaff warble'. Then he would add that the grass was green all over England – so what about the violets and the sheltered celandine and the colt's foot seeds at the side of the lane? Sometimes he then told them to take their poems back and make

---

[1] Hardie Drummond Rawnsley, who later wrote a book about about Thring as teacher and poet. See next chapter, and subsequently.

better use of their eyes and ears next time. When at his most cheerful, he followed up the lesson by walking pupils round his garden or nearby fields, explaining features of the natural world and asking them to describe the differences between the trees in detail. If they caught him on a bad day, however, he ripped their exercise in half.

Even the cleverest boys found some of his tasks very demanding. If they were told to write Latin verse based on a piece of Tennyson *'Risest thou thus, dim dawn, again'*, he added: 'There's your model. Now don't go and write me any stuff about "the sun shines bright", or "snow covers the earth". Notice what to-day is like, and what makes it different from other days'. According to one boy: 'Off we went to gather straw for our bricks; to find something to say, and some Latin to say it in...'.[1] Thring saw it all very differently: 'It will interest them in their work and open their eyes exceedingly to the genius of the different languages'.[2]

Older pupils came to appreciate this insistence on using language correctly and the range of examples that he used in his teaching: 'It was quite clear even to our boyish minds, that the drudgery of turning Napier's *Peninsular War*, Scott's novels, Ruskin's *Modern Painters*, or portions of them, into Greek or Latin prose, was so that we might realise the simple beauty of Napier's description, and Sir Walter's colloquies, and Ruskin's English... We were taught to read English aloud, prose and poetry'. In later life many of them came to appreciate Thring's love of poetry and of the works of Shakespeare, Spenser and especially Wordsworth.[3]

Each day began with a divinity lesson with his sixth form: the occasion on which he was arguably at his best. Always a believer in Socratic questioning methods, he would read aloud about some Old Testament hero and then slam the book shut with a question such as: 'What great law of the spirit world does that illustrate?' Other probing questions followed, along with references to ancient and modern authors;

---

[1] Tennyson: *In Memoriam* LXXII: 'Risest thou thus, dim dawn, again, And howlest, issuing out of night, With blasts that blow the poplar white, And lash with storm the streaming pane?'

[2] Diary (1862): 'Have today required my division to bring a short translation into English poetry with the *Lyrics* weekly, not to exceed 14 lines nor be less than 8. They may choose any passage or any metre they like...'

[3] Thring had strong likes and dislikes in his class texts. Favourites included Spenser's *Fairie Queen,* Shakespeare's *Macbeth* and *Hamlet;* works of Chaucer, Milton and Johnson. Younger boys worked through Keble's *Christian Year.* History texts were chosen for their moral worth. English grammar had to be thoroughly taught to junior pupils: it provided a good grounding for other work and 'you might just as well feed and clothe an Indian like an Esquimaux (eskimo) as generalise rules for English from Latin and Greek'.

current and school events. Sometimes, however, the question was even more elusive than the answer:

'He looked straight at the form captain with the words; "And Moses?" If he got no reply he tried others: "Next-next-next?" One suggested: "Went out of Egypt?" to which he retorted, "Of course he did! And Moses? Next-next? How did he go out? Next-next?" "With a mighty arm?" suggested another. "I never said he didn't," [Thring] replied, "But how did he go out? Next-next?" "With children, and wives, and much cattle," whispered one. "Next-next?" "In haste," muttered another, "with camels and horses". "Bosh! Next-next? He walked, you fools. Moses walked"'.

Boys thought that he used his divinity lessons as an alternative pulpit, as he took them through sections of the Old Testament in English and the New Testament in Greek on alternate weeks. Examiners complained periodically that the boys did not know enough of the 'peculiarities of Hellenistic Greek', but he was far less concerned to teach boys theological or classical theory than to give them personal and civic lessons for their later lives, drawn from biblical or ancient experience and linking points from the Bible to the ideas of Plato and Aristotle or *vice versa*.

One of his favourite themes was the wanderings of the Old Testament Israelites. He could provide memorable verbal portraits of men such as Abraham or Moses, the latter 'heir-apparent to the greatest throne in the world'. His pupils remembered how he laid down huge ground-plans of world history or drew lessons from the Bible for some topical disciplinary issue. Some felt that they had only understood his best ideas once they became adults, but others had less happy memories: of how the same few pupils answered his questions (and got credit for it) because only they understood how his mind worked. The rest were likely to be silent unless the favoured ones were away,[1] and all too often the reticent majority made him frustrated and cross. On those occasions he indignantly slammed his Bible shut with a staccato: 'Take your

---

[1] 'I still recall our dismay, as we faced the prospect of the divinity lesson when our protagonist was away, engaged in winning the Balliol. [But] nothing wholesomer for us could have happened. We screwed ourselves up, and came prepared, rank and file, for a soldier's battle. The first question asked, our deuteragonist (i.e. second string), mustering all his resources, and delivering himself of he knew not what, answered with such effect ("A very good answer; I didn't think you would have seen that") as to be scared by his own success. Spent with his effort, he found himself supported staunchly by all the reserves in the form, and a halcyon week followed, in which our master's ideal of a dialectic between teacher and taught came nigh to being realised'.

Thucydides, then', before punishing them with a few more Greek particles.

Thus he walked the tightrope which faces all big classroom personalities: how to inspire pupils without allowing one's showmanship to obstruct what they are trying to learn. His eccentricity can be seen as exaggerated, contrived, self-indulgent or born of an insecurity that needed to overawe the impressionable young. One of his closest proteges (J H Skrine) conceded that despite Thring's innovative ideas about teaching method his technique was flawed, making little allowance for the limitations of younger boys: 'It is a teachers' art to make answer possible: to deal out truth in morsels which can be swallowed; not, like a child at a nursery window, to toss a whole crust at a sparrow'. Yet he could be greatly touched when a struggling boy asked him for help: 'After I had showed him how to do [his Greek prose], his face glowed, and he said I opened a new world to him... One such speech as that from a boy makes up for a great deal of criticism. He really felt it'.

Skrine also criticised the fact that although Thring gave boys skills for general essay-writing, his eccentric approach resulted in too little technical knowledge of the Latin verse required by the examiners and university admissions tutors. Although he might see his divinity lessons as a dialogue in which he was the questioning Socrates, in reality they were an expression of his own dominance: 'An initiation; a mystery of which he was the priest'. Yet Skrine also wrote of how Thring's remorseless pressure helped to develop boys' minds, describing him as a genuine sower of seeds which would ripen later.

Thring won unstinting praise too from arguably his most intellectually able pupil, Lewis Nettleship:[1] 'He sometimes rode rough-shod over those who required their intellectual food to be carefully prepared for them... but to those who came to understand [them his] ideas were an education in themselves... the effect of which lasted through life'.

****

If any boy arrived late for the early morning lesson, Thring would already be there, 'his stern eyes fixed on the schoolroom door'. Folklore said that he had only ever been late once himself, and that on that day he let all the other latecomers off. After breakfast, he took the 10am roll-call, springing up the steps from his study in the early days when school assemblies were still held in his house's dining hall. He could be indignant and scornful for effect, or when feeling under pressure, especially over issues such as

---

[1] Skrine and Nettleship are described further in ch. 11.

walkers damaging a farmer's fences or crops, and above all over bullying. He fiercely denounced 'the selfish louts who push a little boy [away] from the fire', and after pupils threw some town boys into the bathing pond, 'no terms of abuse were too bad to describe the cowardly meanness and insensate folly of our conduct', as he punished the culprits and compensated the victims.[1]

Whilst too convoluted to be an eloquent public speaker, he had a good line in repartee. After telling off the members of his house he once walked down the hall to the sound of hissing, turning back at the door to say: 'There are two things that make that noise, gentlemen: geese and snakes. You can take your choice'. Then he departed, to relieved (and perhaps sycophantic) applause.

Morning lessons ended at noon: the time for his daily business session which after 1863 took place in his classroom under the new schoolroom. Senior boys were sent to him with good work, from which he kept the best examples after giving them a signed ticket for a half holiday. Large breaches of discipline or serious idleness led to boys being caned, and he let their friends peer through the windows while he administered it, feeling that such punishment should be open for scrutiny, and that witnessing it might deter others.[2] If there was no business, he played fives instead.

Lunch at 1.30pm was taken with his boys at long oak tables in the house dining hall.[3] After intoning grace he carved beef or mutton with more vigour than skill, eating plenty himself but forgoing most sweet food for fear of putting on weight. However, he had little time for dieting: 'Fasting? Why, for a man who is trying to do his work in the best way, life is a perpetual fast' (a remark which baffled the boys). He reserved special contempt for weak tea: 'If you have it at all, have it strong'.

He never took the 2.30pm lesson. This was often cancelled anyway, because he found almost any excuse to give half-holidays: for skating in

---

[1] When pupils ran off after a snowball fight with some town boys, one junior pupil ran full-tilt into Thring coming round the corner 'and looking up at his "Hulloa! Hulloa!" found himself in Thring's embrace' - but Thring thought him small game, thrust him aside and pursued the older miscreants up the hill.

[2] It could frighten new boys. Thring's diary records that 'this afternoon a gentleman came suddenly to remove a boy who had lately come, an only child, because he had written home in alarm having seen some boys caned! The boy proved not quite so great a fool as his mother, and has written again to prevent it. She was going to put him into a second rate private school as an improvement!!! (sic) on this'.

[3] In the early years the dining hall in School House was a major social centre even outside meal times for all members of the school, day boys or boarders.

cold weather on the quad; when boys won university scholarships; when new governors were elected; to mark the births of masters' children, and once when his own father visited him and asked for one. It was John Gale's only visit: he arrived on horseback accompanied by a mounted servant and stayed two days. Walking around Thring's house on his own, he came across one junior boy sitting alone in his small study. Having been informed that the boy was missing the holiday as a punishment, John Gale gave the boy no less than five shillings.[1]

Thring joined in the afternoon games until age and increasing infirmity caught up with him. He loved them and felt quite bereft if the weather or some other reason forced them to be cancelled. After his notable cricketing success on his very first day in post, he and Earle (the Usher) played in the XI for some years, Thring cutting a memorable figure in formal dress as he stood low in front of the wicket with his bat held horizontally, waiting for the delivery of the ball. He was a good slip fielder; no mean bowler of 'twisters' which came out of a 'curious fast under-hand', and 'a rustic batsman not afraid to step out to hit balls crisply through the on-side'.[2] In an exhibition cricket match to mark the opening of the Middle field (1865), he scored the first run. Later that year: 'To-day the masters played the school. I got a 0, and 37 was our whole score, but we rather collared them after, and got them all out for 87. It was good fun'. He took five wickets too that day, and continued playing until in a house match in 1871 he was allowed a pupil as runner who let him down after 'a short merry innings'. Thereafter as a coach he tried to persuade small boys to imitate his batting, to the horror of his more expert colleagues.

In the early days he took part in athletics, once recording 4' 5" (1.35m) in the high jump and 16' 1" (5m) in the long jump. After a game of Uppingham's arcane brand of football between the sixth form and the rest (1862): 'I could not help thinking with some pride what Head Master of a great school ever played a match at football before. Would either dignity or shins suffer it? I think not'. He took part again the following week, but rarely managed to resist dictating the tactics – usually with poor results.

He played fives, usually in hat and grey flannels, coat off and braces showing and, as at Eton, always playing to win and hitting the ball with tremendous force. He once smashed it into the back of Witts' (his regular partner's) head and merely complained that Witts had got in the way. The

---

[1] c£25 at 2014 prices.
[2] In a Thring v.Witts double-innings house match, Thring top-scored both times, and took 7 and then 5 wickets.

two men were undefeated in their annual challenge match against the school's best pair until Thring was nearly fifty. Thereafter as he got older, and work and age took their toll on him, he went on vigorous walks, took up croquet (devising his own rules) and was a frequent spectator at cricket matches.

The later part of his afternoons was taken up with looking over boys' compositions and the dreaded weekly examination with each junior class. The boys' supper (which he did not attend) was followed by what he thought to be the two 'most dangerous' hours, between tea and prayers (7-9pm): a time that ought to be used to prepare the next day's work but which was too often wasted or used to break the rules. Each evening he went round the studies, sharing jokes or discussing the events of the day. It gave boys the chance to talk to him without having to go to see him in his study, but for them: 'Your door suddenly unlatched disclosed a keen face framed against the night: it came and vanished like a phantom, with just a moment's pause, either for a curt official glance of inspection or a beaming grin'. His hatred of smoking, coupled with his strong sense of smell, was widely-known. After he caught two smokers asleep, latches were fitted to each door with a peg so that he could enter without knocking. He once found two boys frying a cockchafer (beetle)[1] to whom he commented: '*Bene olet qui nihil olet*' before quietly shutting the door, and later he encountered another skinning a hedgehog.

At house evening prayers and call-over (9pm) he read a psalm with typical force, the boys recalling how 'one verse we always looked out for, on the third evening of the month: "The foundations of the round world were discovered at thy chiding, O Lord: at the blasting of the breath of thy displeasure"'. They imitated phrases too from the prayers that he used regularly, such as 'for the whole state of Christ's church, militant here in earth' and 'more especially for this Thy school'. After prayers they could visit friends in other studies or (on evenings when Thring held no extra classes in Hall) they were allowed to practise jumps and vaulting over the dining tables. Meanwhile he remained on the private (family) side of the house, believing this was a time of day to trust their behaviour, or visited the sickroom to chat to the invalids - but also to check whether boys were

---

[1] 'The best smell of all is no smell at all'. In another version, Thring gave this response to a boy after a daddy-longlegs burnt itself on the boy's candle. However, his distaste for smoking was such that a famous musician-smoker who once stayed with the Thrings was reduced to having to eat his cigar in bed.

feigning illness to get off the next day's lessons.[1] Finally he went round the dormitories, turning out the gas-lights with a firm 'Goodnight to you'.

His daily engagement with boys in so many ways ensured that his empathy with them extended well into his middle age. He was also fascinated by how young minds worked in leisure as well as in the classroom. In imagery which harked back to Ilminster days he held it 'better to let children find experience in their own little world and roam in it with them, than to lift them up into your castle even though it be a castle of truth and enclose them in its stone walls'.

This fascination was fed by the powerful, sometimes over-powering 'paternals' (one-to-one meetings) that he held with boys, especially those in his own house. To some: 'He spoke to you as a father appealing to your better nature and your love for those at home'. Others remembered how when saying farewell to a leaver, '*The Old Man* could make... even the most hardened boy "blub", and none could ever forget the few solemn, kind words that went straight to the heart'. He had a special ability to make unconfident boys believe in themselves: 'A few score words, broad and plain, and gentle without a touch of sentiment, and the heavy-witted, leaden-natured boy had looked and seen himself in an enchanted mirror'. He always tried to reassure boys going off to try for university scholarships: 'Never mind whether you win or lose; in one sense I don't care: it will not alter my judgment of your work'. Character was more important than competitive success. He described how a boy came to see him in 1861, abjectly apologetic:

> 'He had been told by physicians in the holidays that it was as much as his life was worth to work hard at present, and he had so set his heart on trying to win distinction (at university) for the school, and the worst was he should be obliged to leave Uppingham this year in consequence. I comforted him about it and told him all I cared for was that my men should bear themselves with truth and honour. He had thanked his uncle with all his heart for having sent him here, that it had been everything to him'.

He could be deeply moved when boys came to own up, especially in the early years when trust was a precarious commodity, not yet to be taken for granted. It took courage: 'Two boys came in and told me that they were very sorry that a day or two before they had thoughtlessly thrown in a nut through an open window in the town and the man was very angry;

---

[1] Rawnsley, W F: 'Always ready to quote Horatius or Ivry... real kindness never forgotten'. Extreme cold at night, occasional bouts of rats and rudimentary sanitation in the house meant that few boys avoided the sickroom altogether.

they were very sorry for having done it and thought they had better come and tell me'. Almost simultaneously, one boy 'told me yesterday that he had brought his verses late [and] that he had been very idle with them. It is very cheering, finding truth'. In 1863 a boy had been helped by others with his Latin, and said 'with many tears that he could not bear to go on doing wrong in this way any longer. I had some nice talk with him and comforted him about the future, and after a very short prayer sent him away much relieved in heart ... Thank God, they do think this of me, [that] those who are in need can come to me for sympathy'.[1]

Like his teaching, these encounters were an antidote to his own insecurity because they validated his work. Once he was well established, he was even prepared to confide his own vulnerability to boys, if it would encourage them:

'Went to comfort my [school] captain, who has broken down from overwork. I gave him sound advice through my own sufferings and weaknesses, but still more to make him feel, I think, quite differently when he found out how much I had had of the same kind. He said, "I always thought you had an iron constitution". I answered, "Indeed no, for 17 years here I never had a day of perfect health, and I owe, under God, my sitting here alive by you to-day to the care in diet and exercise I have taken ever since I went to Cambridge". I think I left him much comforted as well as wiser about self-training. I feel very thankful for being able to do it, and for all the painful experience that has opened my heart, and made me able to give comfort'.

Even when he had to cane and expel two boys:

'I was deeply touched after their caning by their coming up to me, and one said, "But won't you forgive us, sir? Do forgive us!" I assured them I would, and that I never would recollect it against them if they went on well [elsewhere], and that I thought they had slipped into their evil without being aware of what it really meant. Indeed, I could have cried myself, so much did I feel the trust and honour that these two poor fellows showed for me'.

In the 1960s some of the last survivors (then aged well over 80) remembered him for his 'deep voice and strict discipline'; his end of term addresses about duty and individual responsibility, and his disapproval of obsessive competition at games. They still held a conviction of his

---

[1] Diary 1863: He marvelled 'to think of a little boy, voluntarily, in no row, deciding of his own accord to go to the headmaster to get the painful burden of secret dishonesty... off his mind and to be comforted and seek help'.

'wonderful knowledge of each boy: [he could] 'meet any boy in the street and show him that he knew all about him, his character and his work'. Some stated that they had copied his maxims into their bibles.

****

Unlike their counterparts in secondary boarding schools nowadays, Victorian headmasters were often housemasters too.[1] At first Thring had this dual role in respect of every Uppingham boarder, but as the number of houses and the administrative demands on him grew, his direct influence inevitably became more concentrated on boys in his own house. Even then he was determined not to be remote to the rest; he must know them all if he was to discuss them on equal terms with his colleagues and to be the dominant figure in boys' lives.[2] To a new arrival in his house, he created a powerful first impression, because his vice-like hand-shake and strong greeting compensated for his lack of commanding height.

Thring's dealings with one young pupil show his pleasure in the minutiae of housemastering, even after the school became 300-strong. Being the eldest son of Thring's clergyman-mentor in his days at Bisham,[3] the young Edgar Powell was not wholly typical – but he was struggling with many aspects of his new life, especially the communal washing arrangements. Thring faced the classic dilemma of how to keep a boy happy through being busy, but without his extra activities putting more pressure on his poor classroom performance. Edgar's work had become 'a tropical wilderness of false concords and grammar monsters' at the time when Thring wrote to the boy's father:

> 'I have put Edgar in the choir, the expense is £4 4s a year. The washing objection was (as you imagined) founded on the feelings of some antediluvian mammoth and does not pertain to the facts of our period. I don't think he looks very well, but he says he is all right, [but] if he is, his school work is not, at present. We hardly know how to deal with it... One does not like to punish a fellow who may be trying. We shall give him a little time'.

---

[1] Most Heads gave up running houses during the twentieth century (e.g. Charterhouse in 1925), as headship demands grew. Uppingham made the change in 1972.

[2] Thring: 'If a headmaster does not know his boys, the assistant master who does is the boys' headmaster and the headmaster's headmaster too'. It was a source of friction with housemasters: see ch. 4.

[3] Edgar arrived at Uppingham in 1865. The youngest of the Powell brothers left in the year of Thring's death, 1887.

Consultations with the masters resulted in a second letter a few days later. Thring had consulted Edgar's form-master and they both felt the boy needed time to adjust:

'I had a talk with Edgar... though it ended well [it] was in some respects very unsatisfactory. I never met a boy who quibbled over words more and endeavoured to evade facing his fault with more twisting: half our talk was a settling what words we would use and what meaning we would attach to them. I did succeed... in making him admit he was wrong, and he wept and promised to do better. He is very anxious not to be turned out of the class, which I hinted at, [unless] the work really was oppressive to him. He evidently did not feel it so. I have no doubt we shall pull him through. He is perfectly up to a public school; out of school he is the most cheeky boy in the place... and in school evidently quite self possessed.

The difficulty is he is dreamy to the last degree and easily frightened [by failure]... His powers of application require to be formed, they are almost non-existent, this is difficult but not impossible, all boys like being idle, and all dream more or less... I think matters are all right on the whole'.

Thring's optimism about Edgar was well-placed. Over the following year, despite having his finger badly squashed in his study door, the boy's letters home described 'awfully jolly' visits to Thring's garden; 'practising away rigorously' in the choir for Handel's *Judas Maccabeus;* cadging a lift in the coach of a local gentrywoman back to school from one country walk, and (after another) being offered a glass of stout by a master which almost made him late for afternoon lessons.

Thring wrote during the summer holidays, telling father Powell that Edgar's temporary difficulties had reminded him of his own experience as a parent. Gale, his twelve-year-old son, had started poorly at his first school but (he assured Powell) Gale had later improved. Edgar had been caught using Latin cribs, which Thring did not condone, but boys did such things, and it was far from the greatest crime that he had dealt with that year: 'As bigger evils are strangled and lie out, lesser ones crop up. The stone of Sisyphus is a fit emblem of a school master's life... one stands beneath a load of untruth and evil which is perpetually rolling back again'.

Edgar's timid younger brother George ('Georgy') arrived four years later. 'Ever with much love, your affectionate son, G H Powell minimus' (as George described himself in his letters to his mother) was timid at first, but not without a sense of mischief: 'Had some fun last night in the Quad, Mr. Thring did not come round, and we expected him every minute'.[1] Later George wrote again. 'Our form went to Mr. Thring this morning. He seemed in a very good humour'. Shortly afterwards he was summoned as an individual: 'I had to go to Mr. Thring this morning in his class-room for not being at call-over at 20 minutes to nine last night, when we had come home from a lecture. I was not licked (caned)'.

By June 1870, George (whom Edgar had once scorned for crying at dinner because there were no radishes) was much more confident: 'We were all sitting out before our study doors reading books before prayers, it is frightfully hot still. Old Thring will be round soon I expect'. Brave enough even to mimic Marie Thring's German accent, he answered a request from home to bring back his jam pots: he couldn't, because 'Mrs. Thring bags them all and uses them for her jam, *so you shee hit ish ha himposhibility*'.

Thring's dealings with the Powells demonstrate that alongside his big visions for Uppingham he retained strong pastoral instincts. For all his magisterial qualities, in the right circumstances he could unbend and treat boys as if they were equals: an ability which he showed in June 1872 when he wrote to Edgar, a year after the boy had left:

> 'Dear Edgar, I send you a testimonial with pleasure and am glad to hear you are better. I suppose your brother keeps you posted up in school news. We have nearly finished the chapel spire and are going to have three bells'.

The same empathy was evident four years later, when the fifty-five-year-old Thring wrote to a fourteen-year-old boy (not in his own house):

> 'My dear Roughton, Thank you very much for the ground ivy which arrived in beautiful order on Saturday afternoon. I rushed to [the garden] with Grace, and planted it on the bank by the water with my own fair hands; and was late for lock-up in consequence. It seems to be growing well, and will be a great ornament. Believe me, your affectionate friend, Edward Thring'.

---

[1] G H Powell to Mrs. T E Powell, 3 April 1869: 'I was going about the Quad and it was immensely dark, I saw Allington (sic: 'Alington' wrongly spelt) sitting in his study and I blew out his candle... My study is almost furnished. I have not finished one pot of jam yet. Mind you write to me on my birthday and send me a parcel too, and please don't forget to send me the *Aunt Judy* for this month (Aunt Judy's magazine: a popular journal for children, written by Mrs. Ewing: see ch. 19). Allington minor is very jolly. I walked about seven miles with him the other day. Tell me when Papa comes home to Oakhurst. I must go and have some of Allington's cocoa now, so I must say Good Bye. I like the Chapel very much it is so beautiful. I am in the Regular Choir'.

CHAPTER ELEVEN

COLLEAGUE AND MENTOR

IN the fifteen years after *Education and School* (1864) Thring arguably reached the height of his powers. His school was firmly established after the reputational damage of the Fowler and Jackson cases, and his dealings with the Commissioners and his fellow-headmasters had given him a growing public profile. In this period he also forged some working alliances and friendships which he would keep for the rest of his life.

By the early 1870s his full-time staff had grown to over 20[1] and there were a dozen houses.[2] The housemasters' average length of service had risen to nearly 14 years, giving parents a picture of reassuring stability. Some would remain in post for three decades or more, and having seen off early housemasters such as Stokoe, who had made him 'sick of Oxford men with their flimsy, pretty ways, like weedy racehorses at best', he found the next generation of (mostly Cambridge) housemasters more responsive – and less inclined to make conditions on their arrival.[3]

He was also getting strong support from the old-stagers. Hodgkinson was one: he not only sold his existing small house and started a lower (junior) school in a lavish new property costing £12,000,[4] but he was also instrumental in persuading Earle to turn an old High Street grocer's shop into boarding accommodation. After only three years (1861) Earle then built a much larger house (Brooklands), the first of a quartet which would spring up on the hill to the south along the London Road. Thring was elated, noting that Earle's wife seemed 'radiant with satisfaction'.

Three new appointments in 1861 furthered this improved atmosphere. One was a mathematician, Howard Candler. 'Tolly'[5] was appointed in

---

[1] Thring and 13 masters taught classics/mathematics; 1 was a specialist in mathematics; 1 in German; 2 in French; 2 in music; 1 in science.

[2] Four new houses were built in 1856-62; other buildings were converted. Three more came into being 1866-72. The two appendices give details.

[3] William Campbell (Lorne House) was a Cambridge man who immediately impressed Thring. Six of the 1873 housemasters in place were still in post at the time of his death.

[4] Hodgkinson's new house is now The Lodge.

[5] 'Tolly': another word for 'tallow': used to make candles before wax became available. One Old Boy described Candler as 'the only man who could walk with one leg and run with the other' – but he had a First from Cambridge.

haste to cover for another man's illness, but Thring quickly came to value his enthusiasm for teaching the gifted and his knack of cajoling the strugglers with ploys such as counting 'nine, ten, onety-one'.[1] Candler was a Londoner who found Uppingham (where the daily papers did not arrive until mid-day) very isolated. He once remarked that 'as masters, we are admirable, but as men we vegetate' - yet once he settled, he became just the man-of-many-parts whom Thring needed: housemaster, timetabler, overseer of the library, passionate in debates and fearless in football, and the author of a long essay on botany for the *Victoria County History*.

Candler brought a mathematician's logic and practicality to some of Thring's wilder visionary ideas: colleagues spoke admiringly of his taking on 'the role of His Majesty's Opposition to Thring's government' because he spoke his mind – yet even when the two men disagreed strongly (as when Candler suggested more, shorter lessons) neither took it personally: Thring admired Candler's honesty, thinking him 'a gem of a fellow'.

William Witts ('Daddy') had been Thring's near-contemporary at Eton and King's and was now godfather to his second son Bertie. During many of Witts' selfless years of educational and social work in a run-down part of Cambridge, Thring had wooed him for his gifts and his willingness to be a team-player. Witts eventually arrived at just the right psychological moment to propel Thring out of his despair over Mathias' diphtheria outbreak: 'I get the best working man I have ever known... he will build a house at once. It is wonderful – a miracle'. Parents warmed to Witts: his well-connected friends helped recruitment and his generosity made the chapel possible. The boys admired his travel lectures and sporting skills, even if they occasionally took advantage of his innate tendency to believe what they told him.

However, Witts' story also reveals that Thring's less attractive traits had not been entirely banished by better times. At great inconvenience he moved quickly into his new house for the imminent school year, only to be strongly reprimanded by Thring (another sign of the latter's remorseless anxiety) because the new plaster which was still drying out might put the boys' health at risk.[2]

---

[1] Candler gave a medal each year for the best arithmetic papers from boys below the sixth form. His book *Help to Arithmetic* (1868) was commended in the *Museum* magazine for understanding boys' struggles with mathematics. The son of a wine merchant, a public-spirited benefactor to both school and town and a supporter of women's education, one of his daughters married Hodgkinson's son.

[2] Thring shared a widespread fear of the risks of damp, and was still sensitive about Mathias' diphtheria outbreak. Overlooking all that Witts had brought to the school, he told him to be thankful for his 'merciful deliverance' from having his new house 'a focus of disease and death'. The phrases bit deep.

After twelve years (1873) there was a much deeper disagreement. Concerned at the financial pressures which even a full school were placing on Thring, Witts suggested raising the fees, only to be accused of treacherous interference. He left shortly afterwards to work in the London slums, and a letter which Thring subsequently wrote to Godfrey does him little credit: 'I was sorry old Witts left, for I liked him much as an old friend and an estimable man, but as a master I have without doubt got a better in his successor. He is now at North Woolwich, a place he is utterly unfitted for'.[1]

Candler and Witts were both men of means, but Theophilus Rowe had entered Cambridge only after three friends lent him the money to go there.[2] He achieved a Double First in classics and mathematics and was seen by many as Thring's 'ablest coadjutor' (or right-hand man). Rowe's letter to his wife on being offered the appointment includes an interesting echo of Candler's concerns about Uppingham's isolation as well as some misgivings about Thring himself:

'The school's prospects seem sound, but the school buildings and Thring hardly come up to my expectations. He is evidently a shrewd man and a good administrator: but by no means impressive in presence and manner. If he and I were to disagree, my position here would be untenable. The town is small and intensely dull. Our happiness would have to lie in the school'.

Thring's letter of appointment was equally revealing. He recognised Rowe's potential but, determined to learn from his earlier mistakes with appointments, he spelled out his expectations about their future relationship very clearly:

'You are able to be a valuable colleague [but] has your experience shown you that a great school must be... a body without schism? Ability is a positive injury when working apart instead of co-operating. I have had some painful experiences of young men who have forgotten that older men have proved [themselves]; and though I am not an exacting despot, I [must] be sure that in taking you I should be finding a fellow worker instead of a touchy critic. Without... standing in the way of your promotion, I require an assurance, if you come, that you intend at present to make this your permanent home'.

---

[1] For the significance of North Woolwich, see ch. 16.
[2] Rowe was a Durham School scholarship boy with John Mitchinson. His reading ranged from Bishop Jeremy Taylor to Charles Darwin.

As things turned out, having inherited thirty boys in Stokoe's house Rowe stayed for fourteen years. He impressed school and town alike as a memorable teacher, benefactor and supporter of good local causes, and a forward-thinking preacher and lecturer on scientific and many other topics. His exposition of Darwinian theory to the town's Mutual Improvement Society provoked fury from Rector Wales.[1]

It was inevitable that Rowe's exceptional ability would sometimes cause friction with Thring. Rowe disliked Thring's frequent use of military metaphors:[2] Thring was irritated by Rowe's pedantry. They held diametrically opposite views about the purpose of the weekly masters' meetings which Thring began in 1860 (Tuesdays at 9.30am) and which were often tense affairs. Thring saw them as briefing sessions rather than democratic debates: voting must be rare, and then only on narrow administrative issues. He was determined to remain *primus inter pares* and when he claimed that 'I am in the habit of hearing and consulting much, but not one hair's breadth will I give way when [consultation] is claimed as a right', the second half of the assertion was surely more accurate than the first. He felt the housemasters were fortunate to have him to look after their common interests, and he found chairing their meetings a tiresome ordeal. His fuse was short and he could be very heavy-handed. 'You spoke to me of your claim [to be listened to] because you built [a house]', he told one housemaster. 'You have no claims'. To another he declared 'I am not a constitutional monarch... You cannot share the main responsibility of the school... My position is far more that of a military commander who must act on his own responsibility, however much he may listen to advice'.

Rowe saw the meetings very differently: as 'the proper outlet for opinion, an educating [of] all to a common purpose, and as securing finally for common action the assent and the co-operation of all'.[3] Perhaps because he aspired to run a similar school himself, he understood Thring's strengths and weaknesses better than other housemasters – especially Thring's intrinsic difficulty with such gatherings: 'They were a trial to him. He was commander-in-chief, and over [our] actions absolute. But he

---

[1] When a shop, house and cottages in School Lane came on the market in 1872, Rowe paid £750 for them and held on to them for the school's use long after he had left Uppingham. Wales boycotted all future lectures: it deepened his suspicion of Thring. The masters rallied behind Rowe.

[2] Rowe 1875: 'I have before expressed my objection to the misleading metaphors of soldiers led into battle. Soldiers are not called upon to judge and we are'.

[3] Rowe remembered these meetings vividly: 'The strong initiative of Mr. Thring; the generous devotion [and] straightness of Mr. Hodgkinson; the sweet reasonableness of Mr. Baverstock, the *Mitis Sapientia* of Mr. Witts'.

hungered for our convictions, and no man however loyally obeyed, can always carry with him the convictions of others. This he realised well enough, and yet it was a grief to him'.

Like Candler, Rowe was a good foil to Thring. His colleagues thought that 'Thring might go up the Mount and hear the Voices and come down with a shining countenance, but he needed the help of Rowe to interpret them into practical use'. However, whereas Candler played the role of sceptical inquisitor of Thring's plans, Rowe became more the shop-steward: a role in which he could be extremely direct, once telling Thring in connection with a contentious parental issue: 'Opinion depends on knowledge; and on some parts of the school life you are by necessity extremely ignorant... Do you know how often any one of us may have helped to stop a conflagration? You don't'.[1] Thring's reply that day was surprisingly meek, accepting Rowe's integrity of motive and stating about the masters' meetings: 'I do not deny your right to oppose me. I only demand that when you do, you should admit [that this is] your intention and that you should cease talking of helping me by your opposition. This is no great demand'.

Thring puzzled more over Rowe than any of his other colleagues: 'A wonderful fellow, [but for] all his cleverness the most puzzle headed when he gets off the track, always spinning nets for himself'. He listened to Rowe because he recognised that Rowe's mind was 'finer and more delicate' than his own, but he felt that Rowe's extreme insistence on 'mathematical justice' sometimes obscured his understanding of the wider issue. He wished that Rowe poured less cold water on his ideas and he was wary of Rowe's support for campaigns in and beyond Uppingham to give assistant masters greater protection against dismissal.

Despite all this, in calmer moods he saw Rowe as one of his most valuable colleagues, writing to him as 'Your sincere friend'. When Rowe started applying for headships, Thring's testimonial was unstinting: 'He is popular with the boys in a right way... He loves education, and believes in it as a thing worth spending life on'.

Rowe left Uppingham in 1875 to be headmaster of Tonbridge. Many years later he wrote a highly perceptive retrospect on his former mentor:

'The difficulty began when Thring took his stand on something more than [as] a leader, [but] as a divinely inspired prophet of God... He was a man of prayer [but] it seemed to him from time to time that he was divinely lifted into new worlds of power... and a spirit breathed into him

---

[1] 'If by "helping you" we mean helping the school, then we do help you. And I shall always say so'. Candler described Rowe as 'just, judicial, a firm friend, a most trustworthy counsellor'.

that gave him [authority] to speak... [and that] he received "daily messages" from God, and, like St Paul, he was not disobedient to the heavenly vision.

Such men must be measured as we measure a Savonarola, a St Francis, a General Gordon, a St John of the Apocalypse... Their function is to keep the blood warm round the heart of humanity. Can we expect that they should be without the defects of their qualities, if defects they are? The prophet sees only two sorts of men — the inner circle of the faithful who ask no questions, and the outer circle of the faithless "trying to destroy the work of his life": bitter words and hard to bear for men of real loyalty. Some marring of the best results no doubt there was; some pain, some quite needless self torture of a spirit so sensitive, so keen, so introspective'.[1]

****

During this decade Thring also forged close ties with two former pupils, Lewis Nettleship and John Skrine. Nettleship's father was a Kettering solicitor who sent his six sons to several different schools.[2] Thring quickly marked out fifteen-year-old Lewis (1846-92) as special: 'A beautiful English verse translation; he will indeed be a star if he goes on, and a steadier, nicer fellow never breathed, or more trustworthy'. A year later he remarked on the boy's 'constantly questioning, [with] a rather donnish sense of fun... I had the nicest talk with him on art and literature that I have had with any boy for a long time, when we went into the drawing room for tea'.

As school captain (1863-5), the seventeen-year-old Nettleship's appeal to other boys' sense of honour persuaded an offender to own up: 'Uppingham is a little place, and I daresay, you fellows think it doesn't

---

[1] Rowe had been a candidate for Shrewsbury as early as 1866, and later for Wellington (vacated by Benson), to which he sent a copy of Thring's *Statement* to show the type of school he wished to run. Thring wrote to him: 'I will do my very best for you... You have in my judgment ripened wonderfully in the last few years... I also have very strong feelings for you of personal regard and trust. I will... give you a testimonial whenever you want. Your sincere friend...' The *Magazine* wrote of Rowe: 'He knew something about nearly everything... the configuration of the moon's surface, the marks on a snail-shell, life on a lighthouse, the approaching end of the solar system. Troglodytes, the North Pole – he could make all equally clear, equally amusing'. Rowe did not have an easy time at Tonbridge – for reasons not entirely of his own making.

[2] Henry Nettleship became Professor of Latin at Oxford; John was a painter and critic; Edward a surgeon.

146

very much matter how we treat either our masters or one another; but at least it shall never be said, if I can help it, that Uppingham boys are either liars or cowards'. The whole school rose and gave him three cheers.

Thring's teaching methods, with their tendency to dwell on lessons for life rather than linguistic technique, did not hamper Nettleship. He was the first Uppingham boy to win the top Balliol scholarship (in 1864), later adding to it a string of university prizes and exhibitions. By 1866 Thring was writing that the impression made by his young protégé at Oxford seemed extraordinary: it certainly helped to cement Uppingham's reputation.

Surprisingly however, Nettleship failed to gain a First. He wrote abjectly to Thring, confessing to working too little and rowing too much. The result did not matter to him, but he was very sorry for the school and for Thring himself: 'I will try to blot out any stain it may leave'. Thring replied by return: 'You know very little of me yet if you think I care for your second class. I do think that other [activities], rowing even included, have given you better things than a First... I care little for honour. Humble true work... with or without honour, is sure to do what God means it to do. Never think your [second] class raises or depresses you a hair's-breadth with me. As for what people think, I am not afraid for the school, and you have no reason to feel on that score'.

He visited Nettleship in his Oxford rooms, relaxing with a cigar and a large drink and talking animatedly about runners in the forthcoming Derby and how much money he (Thring) had lost on the outcome of that year's Boat Race. The two men kept up an intense correspondence for nearly a decade, exchanging ideas not only on classics and philosophy but also on art, music and religion and the beauty of the Lake District. They shared thoughts on whether Nettleship should spend time working with the poor in a London parish, which Thring regarded as 'the best possible supplement to the purely intellectual atmosphere of the university, and the best preparation for high and true thinking on life subjects'. Always at his most eloquent when writing about Providence, Thring emphasised that 'in God's work there is no hurry, no, not even when He employs men, and if He blesses you with the seeing heart and eye, He will sooner or later bring out the harvest in the best way'.

He continued to hope that Nettleship would go on 'to play a great part in upholding God's truth' but the younger man's religious doubts persisted and grew. Thring admired his honest lack of certainty, and offered him a post at Uppingham if teaching were to be his destiny: Nettleship gratefully acknowledged the offer, but knew that his future lay in Oxford. Despite his degree result, Balliol elected him as a Fellow in 1869, where his acquaintances included Arnold Toynbee and Henry Scott

Holland; he became a close friend of T H Green and generations of undergraduates discussed social liberalism with them.[1]

Although they went their separate philosophical ways, Nettleship's friendship and respect for Thring remained. He wrote again in May 1872 admitting that his views had moved a long distance from Thring's own, but acknowledging that the religious ideas that he had been imbued with at Uppingham would never fully leave him: 'It seems such a miserable mockery to talk about differences of opinion ... I suppose it will be made clear some time; and one must be content to feel one's heart beat true at times to the old simple war-cries'. He added: 'God fulfills Himself in many ways, and if the spirit which you stirred in me has grown into something which you could not acknowledge as your own, I can only say that what is vital in it is still the same and will always be so, however different the forms in which it appears'.[2]

Like his old mentor, Nettleship revelled in the grandeur of nature, viewing mountains especially with an intense love, tinged perhaps by fear. The boy who wrote in an essay for his headmaster that 'Communion with Nature should be one of the great restorative powers for Man's fallen being, seeing that it is a communion with God's truth' grew into the man who wrote to Thring in 1870: 'Mont Blanc stood as if cut out of ethereal marble against an azure sky, and flushed from white to gold and from gold to rose every evening'. It was a prophetic remark. Perhaps the greatest scholar that Thring's Uppingham produced and the most academically gifted member of staff it never had, he remained a stalwart Old Boy until Thring died. Five years later (1892) he perished in a fierce summer snowstorm – on Mont Blanc.

At Nettleship's memorial service in Balliol, the Master, Benjamin Jowett, paid tribute to how Nettleship had 'found out that the greatest gift of the teacher is sympathy. He knew how to talk to one of his pupils alone, which is perhaps the higher part of teaching, as well as how to address an audience'. Had Thring still been alive to hear it, he would surely have been proud.

****

[1] One of Nettleship's tutees was (Sir) Frank Fletcher, later Master of Marlborough and headmaster of Charterhouse: see Witheridge, John: *Frank Fletcher 1870-1954: A Formidable Headmaster* (2005) pp.55-6; 61; 92.
[2] Nettleship's ODNB biographer refers to his 'difficult and self-questioning temperament', but he spoke often at Old Boys' gatherings of his debt to Thring. He helped to found the Uppingham School Society in 1879 (see ch. 16).

John Huntley Skrine (1848-1923) entered Thring's house three years behind Nettleship.[1] His family in Somerset knew the Thrings well. At school he was in Thring's house for seven years and he later developed an idealised view of his time there, harking back to his arrival as a twelve-year-old in February 1861 after the longest journey he had ever undertaken 'across England to my *big school*. It is not a very big one, nor very well known yet. But it will be, some day, says my tutor (at home), for the headmaster is a great man'.

Skrine claimed that the recently published *Tom Brown's Schooldays* had been in his head all through that journey. On his arrival, 'a short, firm, angular figure, with a keen eye, strides up to the door and welcomes me. It is the great man...' In the dormitory that evening, 'lying in bed, I hear a quick, strong step at the door, and the light is turned out to a succinct, military "Good-night". ...My heart seemed to say to itself: "My headmaster!" – meaning it as a soldier might say: "My general!" Then I was gathered into dreamland'.[2] Unknown to him, this first encounter greatly impressed Thring too: he wrote in his diary next day that 'little Skrine came last night – such a bright innocent looking little fellow. I quite loved him as I looked on him'.

As captain of the school from 1865-7, Skrine (like Nettleship before him) strove hard to propagate the ideal of trust. He too eventually confirmed Mr. Eve's view that Thring did not sell intelligent boys short: after winning an Oxford scholarship he went on to gain two Firsts and a poetry prize. Then, having taken holy orders, he returned to Uppingham in 1873 to teach, becoming a housemaster five years later. Like so many of his colleagues he was a gifted all-rounder: teacher, literary critic, preacher, travel lecturer and sportsman – although possibly a man old before his time, and one whom the more divergent pupils found hard to take. One member of his house described him as 'a *pompous sneak*: he used to crawl about in noiseless felt slippers in order to catch us doing what we ought not to be doing'.[3]

---

[1] Pronounced 'Screen'. He and his elder brother were among 23 new boys: the largest winter entry thus far.

[2] 'He ought to be bigger, but it is something else than this want of size which makes me not afraid of him.... he was unlike all the other people whom we knew... Why did we say to ourselves: "No-one speaks like him?"'

[3] Skrine became master of the Lower Sixth in 1875, after Rowe. He wrote two hymns to mark the beginnings and ends of term, and poems for other major events. The critic was Norman Douglas: see *Looking Back: an Autobiographical Excursion* (1933) p.59.

Even as a junior member of staff Skrine formed (or resumed) a special relationship with Thring, becoming his employer's close confidant and valued adviser. He was offered a headship in Liverpool as early as 1874 but Thring advised him that he was not yet ready and that he should gain further experience at Uppingham for a few more years: 'It was good that he should have my experience'. Within a year, he was referring to Skrine as 'my disciple'.

Marie and her daughters had a deep affection for Skrine too – though perhaps respectful rather than close on the part of the girls – and Skrine's wife was a great favourite. Marie thought her 'charming and gifted'. She was widely-read and was described by young Grace as 'the wandering story book'.[1]

Despite their closeness, Thring and Skrine had a complex relationship. Skrine was shocked by how much the school had changed during his six years away from it (1867-73): he thought its pioneering ideal had given way to complacency, slack discipline and a depressingly conventional spirit. The boys wanted merely to be like their contemporaries in other schools, and the staff included too many selfish individuals. Worse still, he felt privately that Thring (tired and jaded) was in danger of losing his personal magnetism – and that Thring himself knew it.[2]

Skrine's tendency to sanctimoniousness, his nostalgia and the inclination of many former-pupils-turned-teachers to remember their youth as a golden age do not necessarily mean that he was wrong about the school or Thring himself at that time. His years as Thring's pupil had coincided with those when the school's spirit of adventure and experiment was at its height, but since then Thring's struggles with the Commission had partially distracted him from its everyday affairs. Between 1867 and 1874 the *Magazine* included a string of complaints about untidiness in the sixth form room and the studies; low usage of the library; poor behaviour at games; small and badly behaved audiences at concerts. Skrine came to believe that Thring's mission to every boy did indeed militate against the needs of the ablest, and caused the school difficulty in recruiting them: 'Water finds its own level, and the currents of academic mediocrity [were]

---

[1] A strong supporter of the Mothers' Union, she later became a prolific author as Mary Jessie Hammond Skrine.

[2] See ch. 13. Skrine claims that Thring discussed it with him, seeing it as an example of how the spirit of a pioneering generation is not always passed on to its successors. Characteristically, Thring had expressed the phenomenon with an Old Testament quotation: 'There arose up a new king, which knew not Joseph'.

set towards Uppingham, those of genius in other directions'.[1] He could be very caustic about Thring's bouts of dejection.

Thring had parallel reservations about Skrine: 'He is in many ways most zealous for good, and always at work, but an unhappy trick of somewhat hairsplitting and considering a good sentence as powerful as a good fact will always somewhat impair his power'. However, in his later years he would come to rely increasingly on Skrine as his eyes and ears. To others observing them taking walks together once Thring could no longer play games in the afternoons, Skrine was 'Mr. Thring's intimate and trusted friend, his chief minister... his counsellor'. Skrine unwisely told colleagues that he enjoyed 'ties of nearest intimacy' with Thring, which inevitably aroused jealousy because it was evidently true.

Despite his concerns about the school, as an aspiring headmaster himself Skrine deeply admired Thring's stand against the Commissioners, and in the late 1870s he would be the one to write a book describing in glowing terms how Thring faced his next, quite different, crisis. Ultimately though, he came too much to see himself as Thring's natural successor. Their friendship was as much professional as personal, and it was largely confined to Uppingham and term-time. With the Skrines (unlike the Thrings) able to afford frequent trips into Europe, in the holidays the two men went their separate ways.

****

Meanwhile a young man with no Uppingham connections became Skrine's rival as Thring's *confidant*. George Parkin (1846-1922), a young Canadian headmaster, was based at Oxford University for a year in 1873-4, studying well-known English schools. At Balliol Lewis Nettleship shyly introduced himself and invited Parkin to breakfast to tell him more about Uppingham. Later Parkin visited Eton and Rugby and was invited to attend the annual Headmasters' Conference. There, whilst talking to – and perhaps wanting to detach himself from – the earnest transatlantic visitor, Dr. George Ridding (headmaster of Winchester, the host school that year), saw Thring approaching. Ridding introduced Parkin to Thring with the words: 'Here is the man who can tell you more about education than anyone else in England'.

Despite a 25-year age gap Thring and Parkin struck up an immediate rapport and a regular correspondence began that was broken only by

---

[1] Even Skrine felt that Thring was playing with fire when he chose to preach to the boys on the dangers of over-intellectualism. 'Boys, indeed, are rarely tempted to sins of intellectuality'.

Thring's death. Thring recognized much of his own youth in Parkin. They had both suffered nervous breakdowns (Parkin's amid a crisis of religious belief) and Thring constantly told him not to overtax himself and to take good holidays. Parkin was just the impressionable protégé whom Thring needed psychologically: someone with whom to exchange ideas but who lived well away from the internal politics of Uppingham – yet Parkin was able to appreciate the professional pressures that Thring faced.

Their friendship also gave Thring another psychological safety valve. His early letters described family illnesses and the sorrow of his father's death. He poured out his frustrations when the local hunt allowed its hounds to rampage across Witts' garden, sending Parkin snippets from local newspapers to show how he had to endure local hostility so different from the appreciation shown by neighbours of similar schools: 'The Uppingham people break down our cricket fences, and [have] bodily smashed our turnstile into the field'.

The two men discussed the gulf between teachers and government; the need for a general teaching council; the role being assumed by universities in public examinations. Thring bombarded Parkin with his views on interfering governors and on the need for school inspections only every ten years. He described how the Conference had fostered friendships amongst schools. He felt that 'the lower middle class in England is exceedingly effeminate' and he scorned payment by results. He envied Canadian headmasters their freedom and 'the space of the New World. I feel like a bird in a cage beating against the bars, longing to be free [but] I see clearly it is God's will'.

During the 1870s and 80s Parkin was the headmaster of Fredericton Collegiate High School in New Brunswick. It was a difficult assignment and he drew heavily on Thring's boarding experience, studying Thring's *Statement,* the ground plans of Uppingham's boarding houses and a commentary on them which Thring sent him. This stated that studies should ideally be situated around a square, opening on to a common area; that servants must have easy access to the dormitories and the dining hall without going near the boys; that houses needed a library as well as a hall and that 30 boys in each house was a good number.

Like Skrine, Parkin would be a family friend of the Thrings for half a century. He (and later his wife) exchanged letters not only with Thring himself but with Marie, her sister Anna, all three of Thring's daughters, and occasionally with his sons and brothers. Even the five-year-old Grace wrote to Parkin, her lined paper and copperplate script describing a recent visit to Furnace (Furness) Abbey in the South Lakes and signing herself 'M. G. Thring, your affectionate little friend' as he became something of an additional older brother to her. Godfrey became another regular correspondent after Parkin praised his new book of hymns.[1]

Parkin visited Thring in March 1874 three months after their Winchester introduction, spending his first evening in Uppingham with Skrine who was only two years his junior.[2] For Thring the visit was a tonic: '[Parkin's] hearty enthusiasm and hope to do something good out there (i.e. in Canada) has cheered me very much. The New World is opening [up]. I feel in talking to him the difference between talking to the blind and to the one who sees'.[3] Parkin stayed for five days, meeting staff and taking notes on every aspect of the school's ethos and workings. His notebooks show how he even adopted Thring's phrases, praising 'Mr. Thring's idea of the new creation of the world in modern times, by crushing it as it were into a smaller compass through the operation of railways and telegraphs etc'. By the time he bade Thring farewell, Parkin saw him as 'an educational and moral dynamo... unquestionably the most original and striking figure in the schoolmaster world of his time in England'.

Their friendship also shows how far Thring's horizons were starting to reach beyond Uppingham. Meanwhile he had bestowed on Parkin an accolade usually reserved for old friends or former pupils: an invitation to join the Thring family that summer at Ben Place.

---

[1] Thring wrote to Parkin of Godfrey: 'He is rather inclined to brooding over himself too much in his quiet country village and a little sunshine from outside does him good'.

[2] Skrine planned to visit Parkin in Canada in 1876, but events prevented it – see ch. 14.

[3] 'It is like a fresh breeze let into a sickroom to have had him here... giving an outside, enthusiastic, thoughtful view'. Parkin was too modest to include the remark in his collection.

CHAPTER TWELVE

BEN PLACE

DURING the fifteen summers from 1863 the Thrings spent some of their happiest times in the Lake District. From 1867 they rented Ben Place, a house overlooking Grasmere in an area which Thring regarded as having 'some of the loveliest scenery in the world'.[1] These expeditions began with a stately progress northwards by private railway carriage and were a time to unwind; read poetry and Romantic novels; find stimulating conversation in an area filled with artists, writers and intellectuals;[2] visit Wordsworth's grave or his favourite waterfall at Tongue Ghyll, and go on ambitious walks in Easedale or on the Langdale Pikes.

Thring responded to Nature as a mystical experience because 'what consoles me is the sight of *Life* everywhere: the rush of life in the tree and the grass'. Beauty was 'the expression of the mind of God seen through a material medium' and he preached at Grasmere church in 1874 on God's natural world 'that speaks a new language to all men'. His sons were still too young to go off on the cricket tours (Gale) or fishing expeditions (Bertie) that would occupy them during later summers, and the family made the most of their holidays together - with long walks, bird-watching, painting and botany projects. They often visited nearby Ambleside to meet or bid farewell to a continuous procession of friends, favoured colleagues and Old Boys, up to twenty of whom visited them at a time.

Marie and Anna were lively correspondents on holiday. Anna wrote to Parkin of 'bright, pleasant delightful days at dear Ben Place'. Their visitors' book had been filling up rapidly, and some of the guests had been sketching. Seventeen of them had been to Keswick in a party of wagonettes, where they went out on two boats on the lake, only to be caught in what Thring called a 'laker' (heavy rain-shower). When they sought refuge in a local hotel, some of the men had to seek privacy in the bedrooms while the amused landlord dried out their clothes, and the muddy and crumpled party eventually returned home in high spirits. Marie described a similar-sized party, led by Thring and including several of his children along with ponies and guides, successfully ascending Scafell in three and a half hours. On their way up they were applauded 'for their British pluck by various parties of gentlemen, and the ladies

---

[1] He had always tended to judge things in extremes: see his time in Italy in ch. 2.

[2] It was much loved by Ruskin, Wordsworth, Coleridge and other *literati*.

were complimented as bricks';[1] on the way back they stopped for a substantial tea. She also wrote of a musical evening with the Ben Place choral society, culminating in a rendering of *Auld Lang Syne* that could be heard right across the valley.

A neighbouring family of holiday makers noted how completely Thring shed his headmasterly *persona* and became a schoolboy once again as he planned each day's expedition and picnic. It was the same during the evening cricket match: no professional at Lords ever sent down the (rubber) ball with more determination than he, and no batsman got more pleasure from punishing a loose ball outside his off-stump. When the next-door families visited each other at dusk for games of hide-and-seek, Thring buttoned up his coat tight around his throat so that his white tie no longer showed up in the twilight, entering completely into the spirit of the game and crouching in the bushes around the rocks while the children shouted across the garden to each other that he was not there. Then triumphantly stretching out an arm to make them shriek, he gripped them by the ankle. The game over, he gleefully recounted it all to anyone who had stayed indoors.

Until their final year there (1877) the family was able to arrive by the time of the longest day (21 June), but thereafter the New Scheme decreed a three-term school year which pushed holidays back to later in the summer. Marie welcomed the prospect of more frequent (if shorter) breaks, but Anna regretted the change. Holidays in July or even August would mean evenings spent indoors instead of playing games and climbing up on to the rocks to watch dusk falling across the lake.[2]

****

Thring found Ben Place a creative place in which to write poetry, which he saw as an extension of nature and an 'unveiling of Truth'. His sonnets often had overtones of Wordsworth, dominated by images from the natural world which he saw as a mirror of the mind of God. One of his

---

[1] Scafell is one of the highest peaks in the Lake District. They again got caught in rain and had to change clothes on the way back.

[2] Previously the Uppingham year had consisted of two halves of 18 or 19 weeks, with long holidays of 7 weeks from mid-June and at Christmas. Marie wrote to Parkin that each term would last for 12 weeks, with 5 weeks of holidays at Christmas, 3 at Easter and 8 in the summer. By contrast, Anna told Parkin that 'the new pattern ... shows what a creature of habit one really is...changing [it] seems almost to change one's whole life. We cannot get at all accustomed to the thought that we shall not be at Grasmere in the summer any more. No more little cricket on the lawn in the evening after tea...'

favourite themes was the pilgrim's journey through this earthly life towards God's judgement:

'Mortal breath of death in life, dreamlike shadows of a dream,
Sparks from chance flints in the night, that by chance hoofs smitten
    gleam.

Gleam and pass away as pass iron footfalls down the street,
And the darkness closes in, on the smiting of the feet.

Smitten so ye live, O men, ye who dreamlike shadows seem
Come to us, you shadows leave, be for ever what ye dream.

All of glory, all of good, passes through our mystic gate;
Fear not, the lost battle wins, dreamland infinite and great'.

Dreams were one of his recurrent themes. *Dreamland* expresses 'the conviction that noble dreams are great realities'. It is a place where 'toil and strife, all the seeming life, stricken heart and stumbling blind, over, over, [are] left behind'. Other poems related to specific Lakeland places: Loughrigg spoke of 'a little tarn beneath the hill, a jewel in the grass, a little cup, where clouds and sun in gleams and shadows pass'. In the Langdales he saw 'a leaden-coloured ocean, a mighty wand'ring plain that breaks in rifts and gathers, and breaks in rifts again'. High up in the hills by Easedale Beck, he observed how 'the sundew dreams its scarlet, tiny elves weave moss, and run along the river shelves'.

In *The Fountain of Youth,* he reflected on how the qualities of childhood are lost in adolescence, yet sought again later in adult life:

'The sun out of the children's hearts is gone,
Their own clear sun is lost, which from them shone,
And turned to gold whate'er they looked upon...
Youth starts at dawn, and oft again returning, thinks
To find the merry little fool he left in days past long behind'.

He was influenced by *The Song of Roland,* an anonymous eleventh-century poem drawn from a Scandinavian legend. Well-known in France at the time of the Crusades, it was revived in the nineteenth century by (amongst others) Robert Browning in his complex poem *Childe Roland to the Dark Tower Came* (1855).[1] Roland died a hero's death in the face of overwhelming odds in a battle against a Saracen army 400,000-strong, but

---

[1] It was the inspiration for a well-known painting by Thomas Moran four years later.

his final act was to order the sounding of the horn which summoned the arrival of Charlemagne's army and ultimate victory. The poem's theme of 'the battle lost but the victory ultimately won' fascinated Thring all through his life: he referred to it in his correspondence with Nettleship and it became a symbol of hope in many of his own struggles. In his poem Childe Roland wanders through woods: 'The summer through his heart did run, and all the world was summer gold'. Roland observes the tumbling to earth by a ladybird as 'dropped from the sun; sycamore trees amidst whitewashed cottages, tarns in sunlight, rivers, birds'.

Thus the imagery of the Lake District came to signify the pilgrimage of Thring's own spirit. The theme of water featured prominently in his poetry too, and *The Waterfall* was surely another description of his own variable temperament, with its contrasts between light and dark, strife and exultation:

'His young life
Drawn from the deep heart of the inner world,
Came clear and sparkling from the eternal hills,
Flowed through a boyhood gemmed with flowers and grass,
Song-visited, whilst o'er it gentle wings
Dropped little happy shadows on the pools,
Sweet memories of life that might not stay.
And so he grew to manhood, and was dashed
Tossed to and fro betwixt the hard, smooth hate,
In the wild tumult of the torrent fall,
His soul, laid bare and stricken, showed the life
Churned into spray of noble thought, and sheet
Of whiteness. All the glory, all the strength,
By busy hatred shattered in and out,
Leapt with a rush of light and onward power,
Snow-pure; and o'er the misty tumbled deep
God laid his sunbow, and His peace came down,
And made the troubled waters breathe of peace'.

Thring's character always had a strongly whimsical side. 'You will laugh at the idea of my writing children's stories', he told Alexander Macmillan (1863) as he submitted a curious 22-page fairy story entitled *The Enchanted Wood*. After Macmillan turned it down, he published it as an extra edition of the *Magazine* for his Old Boys at Christmas 1871. It was a tale in the style of Hans Christian Andersen and its sub-title was 'The true history of Phlup, and how he won Lingula, the Fairy Lady of the English language, and became Lord of the Enchanted Wood, the glorious empire of speechland and of thought'.

In it he explored the chivalric ideals of manliness and Christian bravery. The central character, little Phlup, inhabited a rural world similar to that of Thring's own childhood at Alford, with hills, rivers and trout-streams. Phlup knew every inch of his terrain: he tumbled into hedges and rabbit holes; he encountered characters with names such as Knubs and Tummles, and a dog called Corker. Visiting the enchanted wood was a requirement for status in his world, but Phlup was fearful: things were not what they seemed in a place in which rabbits could turn into wolves, and trees suddenly cried out with frightening questions like 'What's my name?' However, he was befriended by a 'maid-of-all-work', whom he came to call 'My dear Lingula' (Latin for 'little tongue') and who persuaded him to venture further and further into this forbidding area towards the place where the king lived. There the scales fell from his eyes as he realised that Lingula was in fact a princess adorned with jewels and other trappings so wondrous that they seemed reminiscent of some of the early chapters in the Book of Revelation. She told him: 'Humble, kindly hearts who love me in my rags, and do true things as children, are taken to my throne and loved by me as men. I am the Princess'.

Thring rounded it off: 'Then all the happy creatures with one accord made a joyous melody of wings and voices as Phlup took his seat on the throne to reign with Lingula, as he still does'. The story confirms his lifelong wish to empathise with the child's world of imagination, although it is hard to imagine quite what his Old Boys must have made of it.

****

During one of these summers Thring also wrote another full-length book. *Thoughts on Life-Science* (1869) was intended to show that there was no contradiction between science and religion: he dashed it off in a few weeks with little previous research and no access to notes or books, and its first edition appeared under the pseudonym, *Benjamin Place*.

In the atmosphere of fevered public debate about scientific discovery at that time it was a risky subject for him to tackle, and quite why he did so is unclear.[1] While some of his wider intellectual circle such as Maurice and Kingsley could accept the scientific evidence for evolution, Thring

---

[1] Frederick Temple (Rugby's headmaster: later Archbishop of Canterbury) contributed a chapter to Parker, J W (ed): *Essays and Reviews* (1860), which came to be seen as a challenge to biblical history by scientists working in the new fields of geology and biology. It caused a huge controversy and got Temple into some difficulty at a time when the Bishop of Oxford, 'Soapy' Sam Wilberforce, was leading the assault on Darwin's views on evolution.

found it much harder, describing the controversy as 'nursery babble' and dismissing one of evolution's chief protagonists, Herbert Spencer, as 'a most consummate donkey'. A letter which he wrote a decade later (1880) contains the clearest summary of his own position: 'Science is making great and good discoveries, but many of its theories are in direct contradiction to the facts of the human world and human reason'.

Life-Science was directed against science's moral pretensions and the book reflected his growing interest in powers of observation applied to the natural world. He had become a keen student of Ruskin, and Darwin had recently declared that 'all observation must be for or against some view if it is to be of service'.[1] Possibly the book was also meant as a rallying call to friends and colleagues (although it is far from easy reading): he was concerned that some of his former pupils were straying from conventional belief. They included Nettleship, a lover of Ben Place but a young man plagued by deep religious doubts as he awaited the award of his Balliol fellowship. The challenge of a writing project which was much longer than his poetry may also have offered Thring a mental break at a time of exceptional pressure, when he was simultaneously struggling with a rising tide of philathleticism (an excessive pre-occupation with sport) inside the school[2] and the Endowed Schools Commissioners beyond it.

The book typifies the Victorian love-hate relationship with a world of change, and he began from his familiar premise that the times were exceptional. They constituted 'a new creation', comparable in scale only to the transformations brought about by a trio of historical forces: ancient Rome; Jerusalem at the time of Christ, and the rise of slavery 'with its narrow contempt for the brotherhood of mankind'. The modern agents of change were again cited as railways, telegraphs and other new methods of communication. However, discovery and change brought with them risks of confusion and turmoil, making men no longer content with their existing world and its thought-forms. Society needed to pause and take stock of what was of lasting value and what was merely transitory; it must define 'True Life-Science'.

All worthwhile activity proceeded through the medium of language, and men must be secure in their use of language before they turned to questions of science because, if used loosely, language caused ambiguity and conflict. Even when well-deployed, language could not always break down walls of prejudice, and science could learn from the limitations of language as it strived for its own measurable certainties. Above all, no words were adequate to describe the infinite scientific complexities that

---

[1] Darwin to H Fawcett, 18 September 1861.
[2] See next chapter.

Victorian minds were struggling to understand: 'Man is but a speck in creation'.

Science had its limitations, too. It was restricted to describing things literally, whereas 'Reason tells us that words are more than mere air: that human life and feeling is in the air, and passes into other lives and feelings by this means'. This was something which he alleged 'baffled' science. The existence of Spirit was the proof of intelligent life: 'The worlds and all the things on the globe, each made in accordance with an intelligent plan, are a language. Intelligent life speaks in them... a speech of God, a language by which he declares Himself to things incapable of seeing Him in other ways'.

Ultimately, Life-Science could be nothing but the study of the higher kind of life: the life of feeling and thought peculiar to man as expressed in man's ability to love and to contemplate the Infinite. Its key component was 'true knowledge': anything short of that was merely the science of matter or animation. Moreover man had to be aware of the limitations of human intellect; to admit that he was a fallen being and needing the guidance of revelation and the scriptures to live a true life. He must be careful to avoid idolatry and must always be aware that there was 'a higher and better power on earth than intellectual knowledge'.

Through 320 pages he laboured to expose the claims that science made for itself, in a succession of vivid but sometimes enigmatic or tendentious arguments. His terminology was often unorthodox (as in *Education and School*); his definitions and historical examples carefully selected to support his case. Despite its limitations the book sold well at a time when national interest in its theme was very high, and he revised it over a second summer two years later.[1]

One reviewer suggested that forceful writing was no substitute for strong argument and that Thring's sarcasm and innuendo about the views of others was unfair: 'He really seems to hate intellect, and there is hardly any mode of argument too invidious for him to employ [to show] that power and intellect are subordinate to morality'. The reviewer challenged Thring's assertion that history showed a link between high intellect and

---

[1] This was the same year in which Charles Darwin produced his second great book on evolutionary theory *The Descent of Man, and Selection in Relation to Sex*, twelve years after *On The Origin of Species*. Fierce debates about Darwin's writings would rage for over forty years: see Moore, James R: *The Post-Darwinian Controversies: A Study Of The Protestant Struggle To Come To Terms With Darwin In Great Britain And America, 1870-1900* (1979) pp.8 and 10. Moore also refers (p.109) to Sidgwick's long 'interior debate' between irrepressible religious sentiments and the irresistible demands for a 'scientific study of human nature'.

low morality and suggested that in assuming the existence of God and the correctness of conventional religious doctrine whilst triumphantly opposing reason, Thring's views made for 'a very comfortable faith'. The book should be seen merely as 'a protest of the spiritual element against being hastily ignored or crushed out of existence by an encroaching empiricism'.

Thring was far from the only headmaster of his time to venture into religious writing, but *Thoughts on Life-Science* provides yet more evidence that his strengths were intuitive rather than logical,[1] even allowing for the fact that he probably suffered frequent interruptions whilst writing the book. It turned out to be more a disguised religious tract than an objective treatise on science and religion because deep philosophical argument was never his strength. He read and wrote selectively and unsystematically because for him, as the *Uppingham Magazine* acknowledged after his death: 'From God Life began, on Him it centred, unto Him it returned. Words... were to him of little account, save they were expressions of eternal life'.[2]

He needed convictions and certainties. A C Benson recalled a visit that Thring made to Lincoln, when Benson's father (later Archbishop of Canterbury) was a prebendary at the cathedral: 'I have a very clear memory of how the little, fresh-coloured man stumped into the drawing room with a book in his hand, of which my father relieved him and,

---

[1] See Goldhill, Simon: *Victorian Classical Antiquity: art, opera, fiction, and the proclamation of modernity* (2011), pp.153-4, 262-4. F W Farrar, Master of Marlborough, published his *Life of Christ* (1874). His prolific writings provoked outrage from liberals and evangelicals alike, and although criticised by reviewers for pandering to a popular readership, it sold over 100,000 copies and did nothing to stop Farrar from eventually becoming Dean of Canterbury. Thring admired Farrar as 'not a mere knowledge-box with the lid open, but a true guide and teacher, able and willing to help, inspirit and lead the way'. Farrar's children 'recalled the large book-box filled with German theology that always accompanied them on holiday', but it is very unlikely that Thring's children had similar memories of their father, who wrote much more from the heart.

[2] Sidgwick, who had been so scathing about Thring's defence of the classics in *Education and School,* would later write in *The Method of Ethics* (1874) that 'the predominance in the minds of moralists to edify has impeded the real progress of ethical science: this would be benefited by the application to it of the same disinterested curiosity to which we chiefly owe the great discoveries of Physics'. He could easily have had Thring in mind. See Grayling, A C: *Cultural Olympians: Rugby School's Intellectual and Spiritual leaders* (2013) p.98.

glancing at the title of the book, he said "Don't you find it rather dry?" "Dry?" said Thring, "why, brickdust is as butter to it".[1]

****

Parkin travelled up with the Thrings in the family railway carriage in 1874 and stayed at Ben Place for a week, rowing and swimming in the nearby lake and exploring the surrounding area. He found Thring 'eager to talk at length about any aspect of school life' and totally convinced that he was doing God's work. Eventually Parkin returned home to Canada, to find a letter waiting which was addressed to 'My friend over the sea' and which contained Thring's poem about Loughrigg Tarn as a memento.

They had discussed whether Thring might visit Canada, but once he got back to Uppingham Thring wrote again describing how, whilst visiting his brother Theodore in Liverpool on his own way home, he had realised how much he disliked sea travel. He would visit Parkin if he ever had the time, but if not 'the dream, like many dreams, is a pleasant reality in one's heart and sings its own song there like a bird in a cage, happy though imprisoned'. He added that 'the busy monotony of school life, with its changings and frettings, like a river always in the same place, but always changing, goes on as usual'.

Meanwhile at least one other future life was shaped by an invitation to Ben Place. Hardwicke (known as Hardie, or H D) Rawnsley, was one of five sons of a Thring family friend, all of whom who went through Uppingham.[2] As well as being the boy's godfather, Thring was also his housemaster for eight years. Rawnsley became a star pupil in Thring's lessons and was rewarded by being introduced to the writings of Wordsworth and winning the school prize for English verse.

Rawnsley fell in love with the Lake District when he visited Ben Place whilst still at school. At Oxford (where he was tutored at Balliol by Nettleship) he met John Ruskin at a college breakfast. Ruskin, delighted to meet a fellow Lakeland devotee, put the young man in touch with Octavia Hill, the prominent housing reformer. Through her, and after obtaining a disappointing degree result, Rawnsley went to work in a London hostel for the destitute. Like Thring in Gloucester, this experience

---

[1] A C Benson taught at Eton and later became Master of Magdalene College, Cambridge.

[2] Sometimes also known as Drummond Rawnsley. He was also the pupil who took it out on his neighbour in class, whose mistake with Greek verbs cost the form a half-holiday (see ch. 10). His brother, Willingham (W F), became a housemaster: both men wrote books about Thring after his death.

resulted in a nervous breakdown and it was thanks to Hill that Rawnsley convalesced in the Lakes.

There he met the Things again at Grasmere. Just as he had consoled Nettleship, Thring sensitively guided Rawnsley, telling him that God would shape his life if he was patient: 'Don't get into the habit of thinking God cuts out the world with a pair of scissors and that you hold the handle of them, as so many [young men] do... His judgements are like the great deep. Your whole inside may feel like a scraped wall before whitewashing, so bare and empty and hopeless, yet something must be produced'.

Thring had once taught the schoolboy Rawnsley that 'Wordsworth was pre-eminent as the poet of true life', and now Rawnsley noticed that wherever Thring was, up on the mountain tops or walking along the lakes themselves, he 'saw in the fair pavilion of the clouds God's power and love enshrined; he never tired of translating the life of man into the life of nature, and of making the trees and rocks and streams and waterfalls speak with human language'.[1] After social work in London and Bristol, Rawnsley was ordained in Carlisle cathedral in 1877 (by Thring's old friend Harvey Goodwin, now Bishop of Carlisle) and during a ministry of nearly four decades in that area he developed a passion for protecting its landscape. His Lake District Defence Society soon had 600 members including Ruskin, Hill and scores of well-known poets and artists. With Hill in 1895 he became one of the founders of the National Trust.[2]

Near the end of his own life Thring visited Rawnsley in the Lakes at Easter. The two men reminisced about the happy Sunday evenings in Uppingham many years earlier which Rawnsley and other boys had spent with Thring in the boarding house garden. Afterwards, they strolled out with their field-glasses along the Lakeland lanes, seeing how many different bird-sounds they could identify. As Rawnsley himself acknowledged, 'I should never have learned that spring-tide pleasure but for Thring'.

---

[1] '[He let me], as a lad, come up to the Lakes and stand with him at Wordsworth's grave, and walk with him in Wordsworth's Easedale... Most of his pupils went away from Uppingham with the belief that if they did not regard Wordsworth as the poet of common life, they ought so to do, and might one day find him their companion and solace'.

[2] See Thompson, Ian: *The English Lakes: A History* (2010) pp.245-251. Rawnsley also encouraged Beatrix Potter to publish *The Tale of Peter Rabbit* (1902). Despite Thring's view of railways as 'a great connecter', Rawnsley shot to prominence in the 1880s as a result of his passionate opposition to the Braithwaite to Buttermere railway through the heart of the Lake District.

CHAPTER THIRTEEN

PROBLEMS OF SUCCESS

THRING returned home from Ben Place each year to face a pair of increasingly intractable problems, both generated by Uppingham's growth and success. One was the rising tide of philathleticism – the extreme preoccupation with sporting success – which he felt was now blighting many schools. Some headmasters embraced it enthusiastically, believing in muscular Christianity themselves or sensing that sport (especially football and cricket) could be used as a unifying tactic or to divert pupil-energy away from bullying,[1] but Thring was concerned that games should not become an obsession. With so many calls on his time he might have appointed a master to oversee games for him, but he feared that doing so might raise their growing status even further.

In the 1860s and 70s as former pupils started to win university and national recognition in major team sports,[2] philathleticism in Uppingham began to grow. Local rules gave way to more widely-accepted versions in order to make inter-school matches possible. Internal competitions proliferated; trophies and cups became more numerous; the number of grounds, pavilions and fives courts grew. There were new team strips and caps; house jerseys; colours (a scarf or band tied around the recipient's waist); honours boards; demands for sporting scrapbooks in the library. Previously voluntary contributions to funds for each sport now became compulsory. The Committee of Games rulebook grew to 31 pages with an elaborate system of privileges about who was allowed to watch matches from each side of the pitch. The committee, which was made up of senior boys, ruled that its members 'attend house football matches with a whip, to keep the ground and mark their authority'.

---

[1] *Tom Brown's Schooldays* (1857) was both a symptom and a cause of philathleticism's growth. George Cotton, once a master at Rugby and the model for the 'grave young master' in Hughes' novel, found Marlborough in anarchy when he went there as Master (1852-8), and promoted games to break up the domination of the bullies.

[2] Thring's time as headmaster saw great sporting success for OUs in the new international matches: 3 in cricket, 8 in rugby union and one in Association football. In the same period there were 27 Blues.

Younger boys were strongly encouraged to act as fielders at cricket nets and coaching sessions and to man the new heavy-roller.[1]

Increasing moral pressure was put on 'shirkers'. By 1870 games were being played every day except Sunday, and non-attendance was punished by fines. Thring wanted to protect the status of gymnastics, but the boys were keen to introduce boxing and to phase out what they saw as 'non public school sports' such as hop-scotch, marbles, quoits, rounders and bowls. Even hockey was thought to belong 'to private schools and to street boys... it ought not to rank as an established game in a school like this'. A fierce debate began about the relative merits of cricket and swimming.

Thring managed to head off demands for a rifle corps by introducing drilling classes in 1864,[2] but an additional cause of friction with his housemaster-brother was Charles' enthusiasm for codifying the rules of football and making Uppingham a member of the new London-based Football Association: something which Thring feared would inevitably accentuate the games-cult.[3]

Cricket became the most emotive issue. With the leading XIs now playing fashionable schools some distance away as well as the prestigious MCC,[4] the masters withdrew from teams, although Thring always insisted on a master going to away matches to ensure that the boys attended chapel at the host school. After a four-day expedition to Rossall in 1863, victory by ten wickets resulted in united school-town celebrations on the players' return. Five years later the entire school watched the two-day match against the Old Boys: an event which

---

[1] Thring thought that rolling wickets benefited all, whereas fielding benefited only the batsman and bowler – but he was prepared to make compromises, given the pressure he was experiencing on this issue.

[2] The rifle corps would have been similar to later OTCs or today's CCF. Boxing was tried, but only briefly. Hockey all but vanished by 1870. Even fives was questioned for a time. Swimming suffered temporarily too, with comparatively few pupils learning to swim, but it picked up again later and by the mid 1870s half the school watched the swimming races - although cricket still came first. The rifle corps idea was revived in the 1870s, when the *Magazine* believed the boys' physique was poor.

[3] See *The History of the Football Association 1863 to 1953,* p.24 for details of Charles' draft laws, known as 'The Simplest Game' He expanded them a year later, adding the rules of the Cambridge University Committee and London Association itself.

[4] Rugby School rejected the first request for a school match, offering to send a house team, which was declined. MCC is the famous Marylebone Cricket Club, based at Lord's, which sends teams to play many leading schools.

became linked to a Founder's Supper with toasts and speeches. The new Uppingham Rovers Club for invited Old Boys quickly became successful on the field and socially significant off it, with its own regalia and its first London dinner in 1871 during the Eton and Harrow match.[1]

The *Magazine* published editorials praising the character-training aspect of sport along with cricketers' averages; tips on technique; player-profiles; match reports; letters from university correspondents and news of national sporting developments. Similar publications began arriving from rival schools so that results and statistics could be compared. A school shop was set up to supply games equipment, its proceeds being used to augment the sports funds. By 1873 expenditure on games had risen by 250% in a decade.

Not everyone approved of this worship of athletic activity. The April Fools' Day edition of the *Magazine* in 1873 included an elaborate satire suggesting that each boy should be measured and weighed (including his girth), so that it could publish their respective vital statistics. One correspondent suggested house matches in reading, prompting a letter from *A Cricketer* complaining about the reduced coverage of sport and the excessive number of articles about plants.

However, the games lobby amongst Old Boys was strong and vocal – something of which the editors (surely overseen by Thring) were all too aware. They mostly gave short shrift to complaints about excessive sports coverage and were especially critical of one correspondent whom they described as *A Very Old Boy* who had cancelled his subscription because he had no interest in reading cricket statistics (1872): 'He forgets that sixteen years ago there were few here to make the scores and win the marks... [and] two-thirds of our subscribers *do* take an interest'. A year later, new editors changed tack, apologising for the magazine's previous sporting emphasis and stating that they would henceforth put the Rovers' results and match reports into a supplement – but this prompted the Club to produce its own publication which sold more copies than the *Magazine* itself, forcing the editors to back down.

Even Thring could not swim against a tide in full flow and it surged with particular force over the long-running, emotive question of a cricket professional. He agreed reluctantly to appoint one in 1864, but only for

---

[1] They played matches in the holidays: one of the founding members was C E Green (see next page), hero of the Rossall game. There were 48 members, chosen by ballot – and a lengthy rulebook. An Old Boys' football club began five years later, with protracted discussion over possibly adopting one of the new national codes. Players had flannels, ribbons, coats and caps; there was a dinner sash for the players and a club ribbon for wives.

2-3 weeks at the start of the season. Thereafter, pleading a shortage of funds, he made it an alternate-year-only appointment to deny post-holders any power through continuity, but the question did not go away. Some enthusiasts wanted *two* appointments (one for each ground): it was pointed out that Marlborough had three. He initially stood firm, believing that 'cricket ought not to be turned into a science', but the ground was cut from under his feet in 1872 when a wealthy Old Boy, C E Green, offered to pay for the well-known H H Stephenson as professional for the entire term.[1]

Thring accepted the offer, despite fearing that the appointment of *any* professional represented 'the setting up of a rival power in the school'. It seemed better to agree than to have his hand publicly forced, and holding out would risk damaging both his relationship with the boys and Uppingham's reputation as a school. His fears appeared all too prescient when six leading players were discovered celebrating their successes by sharing a secret claret cup. He thought their action 'a deliberate, lying betrayal', although he was gratified that other praepostors had reported the incident and that Stephenson had not been involved in it. After much agonising he decided to risk outrage by banning the miscreants from the Old Boys' match supper. There was no alternative if 'school honour' was to be upheld.

Stephenson returned in subsequent summers and cricketing standards steadily improved. In 1875 the boys won a huge victory against Haileybury, which Thring feared would go to the team's heads: 'They are a nice set of fellows and it will spoil [them]. I don't want the cricket to get too powerful in the school and to be worshipped and made the end of life'. Worse still, it led to demands for Stephenson's appointment to be made permanent and Green offered to continue paying his salary. Thus Thring's dilemma increased: Green had a huge following amongst pupils and Old Boys; Thring liked Stephenson personally and knew that he was a hero to the boys. Parents very much liked the social *cachet* of sporting success, but he could see the side effects and he wanted to decline offers of yet more matches in London.

---

[1] Stephenson was a Surrey player who had captained the first team to visit Australia. He settled in the town and opened a sports shop, its walls lined with souvenirs of his success. A trustworthy man, his success took pressure off Thring to appoint more Blues to the staff.

In 1875 as Uppingham appeared at Lord's for the first time (against the MCC) the sporting mania seemed still to be growing.[1] It was a far cry from the ethos of manliness which Thring had promoted in his early years and it was little comfort that philathleticism was even more pronounced in other schools. In the new *Public School Magazine* founded to promote 'a spirit of healthful rivalry between the youthful athletes of our several schools', Uppingham was conspicuous by its absence. As the year ended Percival (headmaster of Clifton) mounted a brave attack on athletic mania at the Headmasters' Conference, but otherwise Thring resisted the tide almost alone.

****

Thring's financial problems had been accumulating for two decades. He had always been disappointed by his relatives' view that he was throwing himself away on 'a miserable little country grammar school'. They visited him rarely and criticised him frequently, prompting him to complain that they were 'always going on about money [with] imperfect knowledge of facts'. He yearned for his parents' approval and he was greatly upset by his mother's suggestion of 'schoolmaster dogmatism' at the time of the Fowler case.[2]

Of Thring's siblings his sister Theresa, who had married the Archdeacon of Wells, sent her second and third sons to him (1859).[3] Theodore was called to the Bar in 1843 but seems to have struggled there, his career and his bank balance rescued by going to work in the Liverpool bankruptcy courts in 1862. Although never completely won over to Thring's work and never very close to him, Theodore helped to publicise Uppingham to wealthy parents on Merseyside. Thring and his family visited him there, and later in Alford after he returned to inherit the estate on the death of his father in 1874.[4] Henry, whose successful legal career

---

[1] Cricket and football now prevailed over all other sports. There was continuing debate over whether to play Uppingham, Association or Rugby football rules. The formation of the RFU in 1875 added to the debate.

[2] He recognised her grief over the death of his sister Elizabeth, but had no idea how to build bridges to them.

[3] Augustus Fitzgerald, a Balliol man from Somerset, who became Archdeacon of Wells in 1863. Their eldest son, Gerald, went to Sherborne, but Maurice and James were both sent to Uppingham.

[4] Theodore graduated from Trinity, Cambridge. With legal, as well as estate management knowledge, he was Registrar in Liverpool (1862) and Commissioner (1869). Thring felt these posts were 'an important and lucrative office which just comes in time to solve [his] difficulties'.

was crowned by becoming a parliamentary law commissioner in 1869 and receiving a knighthood four years later,[1] remained as unconvinced as his father. Thring felt that Henry more than anyone seemed to 'understand nothing and only saw ruin possible', although he was a generous London host to his Uppingham relatives.

Thring's daughter Margaret always believed that of his four brothers only Godfrey really understood her father. 'Goo' was gentle and sensitive: a country clergyman whose hymn-writing skills were widely admired. Whereas Theodore and Henry used words only with legalistic precision, Thring and Godfrey shared a love of poetry. They were always close and mutually supportive friends. It was Godfrey who encouraged Thring in his struggles with his governing body; Godfrey who persuaded Henry and his father to moderate their criticisms in the early 1860s and who poured oil on the troubled waters stirred up by Charles and Lydia.[2] Yet his efforts within the family on Thring's behalf were never wholly successful, and only in John Gale's final years would the father start to appreciate his third son's achievements.

Even if they had not been so sceptical, Thring's family had comparatively few available funds with which to help him. John Thring (John Gale's father) had left very substantial assets on paper when he died in 1830, but decided to prevent future generations from having uncontrolled access to them. The estate was entailed to prevent its lands being sold off piecemeal, and aside from some individual legacies to his widow and female relatives he put his personal wealth into a trust fund. This effectively barred disbursements without the agreement of all the male members of the family *and* two other trustees.[3] It may also explain why Thring often spoke of 'Alford' collectively as resistant to his work.

---

[1] Henry Thring had long legal experience of drafting government bills, notably the Second Reform Bill (1867). When the new Office of the Parliamentary Counsel was set up in 1869, he became its head. His DNB entry described him as 'a keen, vivacious little man, with a sharp tongue, often outspoken in its criticism of those whom he loyally and efficiently served'. 'Now, Thring,' said Edward Cardwell one day at the outset of a cabinet committee, 'let us begin by assuming that we are all d----d fools, and then get to business'. Created a peer by Gladstone, he died on 4 February 1907.

[2] Charles was ordained in 1849. After working for Thring, he returned to help his father at Alford, later becoming chaplain of the Avoncliff workhouse near Bradford-on-Avon. Lydia's father was a naval officer.

[3] After legacies etc, the Trust Fund stood at £47,536 in 1844. The capital had been built up mostly from John Thring's legal work. The external trustees were Sir Henry Hobhouse and Revd. John Wyndham. The fund may have included monies set aside as dowries.

Both John Gale and later Theodore saw maintaining the estate as their priority and both feared the recurring agricultural depressions which threatened its future – especially in the mid 1870s. Henry took a substantial drop in salary on leaving his London law practice to work for parliament. Godfrey and Charles both married well-to-do wives; it is possible that Godfrey and Lilla (his wife) helped Thring, but after their earlier disputes with him and with a very large family of their own to support, it seems unlikely that Charles and Lydia did so.

As the third son in a family of seven children, who had launched himself on a career unknown in his family and in a place far removed from Somerset, Thring had little claim on the family inheritance. The family trustees gave him occasional sums during his father's life-time: just under £7,000 in total, mostly as loans or to recognise his coming-of-age and his marriage,[1] but during Uppingham's early expansion he spent way beyond his means to attract and appease the early housemasters.

Blakiston (1854) was guaranteed a minimum salary, however many boarders he attracted. Through mismanagement he had only 14 pupils by December 1855, which not only affected Thring directly but also diminished the school's income from fees. In that year Hodgkinson's willingness to start the third boarding house created some economies of scale, but there had been guarantees to him too – and to Baverstock. Thring helped other housemasters with subsidies or loans: he promised to buy their houses when they left – and did so in Stokoe's case, reimbursing him in full 'to get rid of that disagreeable fellow'. He bought out Mathias from his house *and* refunded Mathias' investment in the land purchased for the chapel, taking out bridging finance to do so and praying that his decision might be 'blessed, and not be a stone round my neck'.

By 1857 Thring was over £2,500 in the red, near despair and wracked by doubt about his own judgement, but he raised yet further sums as guarantees to new housemasters by borrowing nearly £2,000 repayable over fourteen years from the Wellingborough Building Society, backed by life insurance to protect his family. While masters and boys were enjoying a special holiday to celebrate a former pupil's first-class degree at Oxford in 1860, Thring was poring over his accounts, deciding that the family might have to give up its summer holiday and railing against 'the perpetual little sniggling' of some masters on money matters: 'Oh that no debt remained!' However, only a year later he and other masters took out

---

[1] E.g. £5,000 in family shares in 1844, to mark his coming of age, and after his marriage the promise of a further £2,000 – but this payment would materialise only on John Gale's death (1874). Thring was also granted a £1,600 loan in the late 1850s. There was a small, unexpected legacy from a distant relative in 1862.

a further mortgage of £1,600 to buy the cottages which cleared the way for the chapel.[1]

Thanks to growing numbers after the Jackson furore died down he cleared most of his debts in 1865, but only for a short time. He would do so again in 1875 after receiving family trust money on his father's death amounting to a further £3,200, only for subsequent events to engulf him.[2] Financial worry never left him.

****

It might seem surprising that a school which had expanded so successfully still needed significant financial support from its headmaster. However, with no corporate backing and (as yet) only a small number of Old Boys to approach for donations, there was little alternative to masters funding capital projects out of house profits or private income. The school needed to be put on a much sounder structural footing, but the trustees were unwilling (and legally unable) to do it alone, and Thring insisted that they oversee only what legally belonged to the Trust.

Finance was never his major interest and he had many other calls on his time. Right up to 1875 he may have hoped that somehow a solution would emerge through the New Scheme. He did make one strategic approach to the trustees in 1872, presenting them with a *Statement of Capital Invested and Comparative Annual Expenditure of Trust and Masters 1853-1872,* but it was more a venting of frustration and a description of a problem than a solution.

In it he repeated the claim that over £80,000 had been invested in the school since his arrival, of which the Trust had contributed a mere 8.75% while the masters had provided the rest. The figure included the gymnasium; extra fives courts and the covered playground; the sanatorium; cricket fields; rent for various bathing places owned by local landowners, and furniture in all the main school buildings including the chapel.

The *Statement* was deliberately provocative and in some of its details exaggerated. It conveniently ignored the fact that the Trust's assets and income were small, and that Thring had set out on a path which the then governors had done nothing to encourage (nor, admittedly, to stop). Predictably the document achieved little – other than showing that the

---

[1] This event made him decide to set up a Domus Fund for future projects.
[2] For the events referred to, see ch. 14.

masters had a grievance.[1] The trustees merely noted the situation, which was soon overtaken by the pressing issues raised through the New Scheme.

Thus by 1875 there was still no consolidated termly fee and no centralised means to collect the various components of any unconsolidated one. Everything continued to grow on an *ad* hoc basis. Uppingham was far from unique in being a school with a system of multiple accounts, subscriptions and internal transfers of funds, and there were others where housemasters ran their houses as for-profit enterprises, yet in few schools of Uppingham's size did so much of the financial responsibility fall directly on the masters, and especially on the headmaster himself.

In the decade after 1865 boarder numbers climbed well above Thring's ideal 300, peaking at nearly 340 in 1873 with the extra boys being admitted to offset escalating costs: Witts had rightly been concerned that Thring refused to raise boarding fees. Thring also told Parkin that annual *school* costs (masters' salaries for the compulsory subjects; equipment; maintenance of school buildings etc) totalled around £25,000.

Income came from several sources. The trustees were legally required to provide salaries for the headmaster and usher, leavers' exhibitions and *tuition fees* for day boys: a total sum of nearly £2,000 p.a. The housemasters collected these tuition fees for the boarders (around £10,000). Legally these were the Trust's property but in practice they were handed straight over to the school.[2] Housemasters kept boarding fees for house running costs and their own profit (so these must be left out of any calculations about the school's finances) but they also collected certain *extra charges* on parents for centralised services such as the sanatorium and *required payments* which they had to make to the school.

---

[1] The £80,000 total did not include the houses, or subscriptions to the chapel building. Some items listed were counted twice if they had multiple uses – e.g. house dining halls used for teaching. It also claimed that the masters' share of the recurring costs was even higher than their share of the capital costs: no less than 97.75%, including various improvements and repairs and the provision of scholarships. This too was a dubious claim, as it included boarders' tuition fees, collected by housemasters on behalf of the Trust.

[2] Accurate estimates are hard to make throughout this section. Figures are incomplete, and Thring explained them in a variety of ways over the years. There were also changes under the New Scheme and (later) to the tuition fee. The Trust itself had an annual income (mostly from land rents and investments) of only c£4,300, of which 4/7 was spent roughly equally on the schools in Uppingham and Oakham, while the remaining 3/7 was mostly designated for the almshouses and other properties. It recouped some day boy tuition fees from parents.

The Masters' Guidebook for 1870 gives a flavour of this vast and arcane array of small sums. The *extra charges* paid by parents included payments to 'the General School Fund' overseen by Rowe on Thring's behalf (entrance fees, use of library and chapel); the cricket club overseen by Earle (along with a 'voluntary subscription') and funds for other sports. There were also payments for 'concerts, lectures, or incidental charges'. *Required payments* from housemasters included contributions to a fund for liquidating the loan on the chapel; prizes for the cattle show and a grant to the 'agricultural fund'; the Decayed School Masters' Annuitant Fund[1] and the new school Mission in London. Housemasters also contributed their share of school lighting expenses, fees for a visiting lecturer in public speaking, and a capitation levy on any day boys attached to their houses.

The total sum raised through these 'extras' is likely to have been around £7,000. Overall the evidence points towards a total annual *school* income of around £19,000. Even allowing very generous margins of error, the shortfall between expenditure and income appears significant: possibly up to 35%.

There was, however, one other large category of transfers: the charges made by the school for all the optional subjects. Variable (or even nil) uptake from year to year made them hard to budget for – and the small size of each group made them expensive to run. The difference in the charges made for each subject adds to the difficulty of estimating the total sum that these options brought in: possibly around £25,000. In addition, an absence of information about what each option cost to provide (including a salary or fee for whoever taught it) makes it impossible to calculate whether overall the options programme made a surplus or a loss. If it was profitable, some of that surplus may well have been used to subsidise other school costs. Ultimately, surplus or loss, the entire system relied on housemasters collecting and passing on all the various payments efficiently and honestly, and the school processing them efficiently – yet Thring had no bursar and Anna had to serve as his book-keeper as well as his secretary.

There is greater certainty that Thring used his own funds to make good the shortfalls in school income and to finance some capital developments. The combination of the trust stipend, house profits, capitation fees and other sums due to him suggests that he enjoyed a total income from his work by 1875 of between £3,000 and £4,000, possibly

---

[1] An early charitable pension scheme.

rising to nearer £4,500 during his final decade.[1] This was far from negligible, even for a man with a wife, sister-in-law/secretary, five children and a governess, who gave periodic support to his German relatives and paid full boarding fees for his sons. Thring probably had no accommodation or food costs for himself or his family; their lifestyle was unextravagant and (unlike other housemasters) their house was maintained by the Trust. He also gained income from his books, especially in his final years.[2]

All this enabled him to contribute to school projects whenever he saw a need. His contribution towards renting the Upper cricket ground in 1863 was up to forty times that given by any of his colleagues. When the fledgling *Magazine* suffered a financial crisis (1872) he subscribed one of the largest payments in advance. An ally in the town recalled that he would fund any beneficial project with no regard for its cost to him personally, and that when he was once warned about his lavish spending he replied laughingly: 'Well, it has got to be done!' He contributed to a large range of charitable projects undertaken by Old Boys.[3]

The *Guidebook* also gives insights into his style of managing his housemasters. Detailed rules were laid down about the provision of extra meat and milk at some meals; the supplying of wine; the charging for boys on long-term absence. Many of these made practical sense and ensured that housemasters did not become too greedy for profit or too competitive against each other – yet they suggest too that he was more of a micro-manager than a strategist. Year on year his own finances had become inextricably mixed up with those of the school, but he remained determined to maintain the standards of boarding outlined in *Education and School*. Whilst complaining about the trustees' emotional distance from the school, he resisted all their attempts to extend their financial influence beyond funds relating strictly to the Trust.

---

[1] His salary as headmaster was only £152 in the mid 1860s, rising to £250 under the New Scheme by 1880. Then his capitation fees rose too (see ch. 20). He told the Commissioners that while most housemasters made a profit of £1,000 per year, he managed £2,000: he expected it to rise by about £500, if the school remained in a steady state and the rate of new building slowed down. These figures seem broadly consistent with the housemasters' income at Rugby, described in the final footnote of ch. 5. In real terms Thring's income represents far more than modern, salaried Heads earn – and he had little tax to pay on it.

[2] See ch. 20 for his success with his final major book.

[3] The warning was against buying expensive land (Fairfield) as boys' garden plots and for his aviary. He confounded the doubters in one respect: the plots were in great demand. For finance, see also chs. 17, 19 and 22.

Rejecting advice from Witts and others to raise boarding fees, by the 1870s he had finally been forced to expand the roll to well beyond 300. His financial system, devised piecemeal for a small school in the 1850s, had long become an anachronism, contradicting his belief in 'machinery' because it was a system that he alone could oversee. As the years passed, he had developed a certain tunnel vision: the school must continue to develop whatever the cost, and with luck someone, somehow, would provide for him and his family in the end. However, if numbers dropped or the system failed for some unexpected reason, disaster beckoned.

****

In other respects the early 1870s was a time of great success for Thring and his colleagues as Uppingham's reputation grew. Recognition of this came in a letter from a barrister/banker, Mr. William Whiteford, to Rowe in 1875. Whiteford had been determined to get his son into Rowe's house because he knew of many other boys 'the usefulness of whose lives is probably due to you', especially one who had arrived at Uppingham as 'an idle dullard whom everybody despaired of. But you and Mr. Thring decided to [persevere with] him for yet another year – with notable results'. His letter concluded: 'Having long looked on English public schools as exercising a most important influence on the national life and character, I have watched with especial interest the marvellous work done at Uppingham under Mr. Thring's regime, which has transformed a small foundation into one of the most vigorous institutions in England'.

If Thring ever saw the letter he no doubt welcomed it, but by early 1875 the effect of two decades of remorseless work was taking its toll on him. He was approaching his middle fifties and had played his last cricket match four years earlier. He was near exhaustion and perhaps sensed that Skrine's criticisms of declining standards had some validity. He may also have been aware of a nagging rumour that he would soon retire.[1]

Even a comparatively quiet winter had done little to restore him. He wrote to Parkin in frustration that 'some of the masters are on their hind legs again'. Under the New Scheme they and he could together nominate two trustees. To him, Birley and Jacob, the parents who had helped him to fight the Scheme's initial draft, seemed ideal. The trustees respected (and perhaps feared) them; they were men of local influence in the North-West who could raise money for the school there, and if needed they could rally their local MPs to speak on Uppingham's behalf in parliament. However

---

[1] Skrine described him as 'worn down with work, ill-health and gloom'. This was when he was so open about his health to his school captain – described in ch. 10.

his colleagues complained about lack of consultation and concluded that the two businessmen would be too close to Thring. He told the masters: 'I am supreme here, and I will brook no interference', and in his fury he wrote to Parkin that they were ignorant fools because of their small-mindedness and inability to suggest alternative names. He would crush their rebellion, because:

'They have given me infinite trouble and done their best to smash up my plans. It is almost incredible the amount of incapacity and blind self-complacency to which they worked their foolish doings. What do you think of Rowe and Candler at the election of our two trustees quietly getting up in my study and proclaiming with superior blandings that they were helping me by opposing the men I wanted to work with, and getting nearly half the masters to aid and abet them? I only carried my men by a single vote. We were bound to [Birley and Jacob] by the strongest tie of gratitude for having stood out and done battle for us with the Commissioners, and won our cause.[1]

They were the only men who could raise money for us; they were known to our old body of governors as very powerful, they were friends, and accustomed to work together, and they were men of influence with the government, and able to turn on parliamentary power if needed... yet for all this our wiseacres opposed, and nearly succeeded in flooring me by their ridiculous help, though they had no policy of their own, and no candidate whom they had secured to hand. However, that danger is happily over'.

When he wrote again in July 1875 the summer at Ben Place was restoring him physically, but he would willingly leave Uppingham if God gave him a clear sign of what he should do next. In September his next letter declared (as he returned to work) that he felt completely rested. He looked back on good holiday memories of walking his dogs and watching his children playing tennis: 'God has given me back some of the old elastic work power. I feel so full of life and spirits that I hardly know myself. I can do ten times as much as I have been able to do for years'. The trustees seemed more co-operative and the election of Birley and Jacob had gone through. He even suggested that the New Scheme's innovations were a great relief.

As autumn turned to winter, however, a further letter to Parkin in November showed that this optimism had been short-lived. Again he said that he longed to live in a young country like Canada where new

---

[1] Despite the narrowness of the vote, events in the next two chapters show that he was far-sighted on this issue.

institutions did not have to battle with stifling tradition. Government interference was making all schools in England depressingly alike, turning them into crammers of 'superficial knowledge'. Ministers were constantly demanding the teaching of new subjects, or old ones taught in a different way, or new examinations. It all amounted to 'putting the government stamp of approval on a rotten system... it is not a nice lookout. God protect Canada from such a mess!' Nevertheless he remained 'determined enough in my ultimate convictions'.

Even by his standards, recent months had seen dramatic swings of mood – and there was another reason for his gloom. This letter made brief mention of trouble with Liverpool parents over an outbreak of typhoid. He had a 'heavy, heavy dread of fresh cases' and he was being forced to end term prematurely. He was about to face the greatest challenge of his career.

CHAPTER FOURTEEN

TYPHOID

BY 1875 Uppingham's population – only 1,400 at the start of the century – had increased to nearly 3,000 in term-time. The town had grown as well as the school and new housing was crammed into yards and gardens putting severe pressure on its cesspit sewerage. The school's success had provided local employment in the town's shops and work for a small army of local builders, gardeners, tailors and furniture makers; other townspeople worked in its boarding houses, along with over 100 living-in staff from further afield. Thus town and school were interdependent.

Despite the town's growth its streets remained dirty and poorly-drained. Its water supply, still drawn from wells supplied by local springs, often ran near to leaky sewerage piping. Over the previous two decades a cycle of events had developed in the wake of periodic small outbreaks of fever in the town, their source usually undiscovered. Inspectors from London made visits and wrote reports recommending piecemeal sewerage improvements. Applications were made by the town's Rural Sanitary Authority (RSA)[1] to central government for loans to carry them out. These were followed by the plans being cut back to keep them within budget.

The Uppingham RSA, like many of its time, struggled to reconcile its income from local rates with the escalating costs of improvement and the public's expectation that improvements would be made, but without large rate increases. It had already spent – and borrowed – more in the previous decade than nearly all other comparable authorities. Yet even with some recent additions the town's sewerage system was still incomplete,[2] especially in streets near the school houses where cesspits were still the norm. The RSA's members were elected volunteers: well-intentioned, but facing technical, legal and financial challenges which they were unprepared and under-qualified to meet. Many were farmers and professional people who had recently been hit by economic and agricultural downturn.

---

[1] The RSA was effectively the same body as the Poor Law guardians: an elected, amateur body responsible for questions of drainage and water supply. Members were elected for 3-year terms. County Councils began a decade later under the Local Government Act of 1888, resulting in paid, more expert, sanitary oversight.
[2] Two sewer extensions and an outfall works had been added since 1857 but the work had again been cut back to save expense.

179

A succession of public health Acts had left RSAs unsure about their powers to enforce improvement through bye-laws and they relied for expertise on Medical Officers of Health (MOHs). These officials, appointed to each rural area as health improvement caught the imagination of both the government and the public, faced strong resistance from those who saw them as interfering busybodies.[1]

Uppingham RSA members left day-to-day affairs to their chairman, the Revd. Barnard Smith, Rector of the nearby village of Glaston,[2] and his ally, William Wales, Rector of Uppingham. Barnard Smith had arrived in the area only two years after Wales (in 1861); not only had he taught mathematics at Cambridge, but he was a former senior bursar of Peterhouse. His logical mind and financial rigour brought out similarly negative feelings in Thring to those stirred over fifteen years by Wales' austere high-churchmanship: temperamentally and in his priorities Thring was poles apart from both men. However, the two Rectors had plenty of allies amongst other RSA members, many of whom had long resented the school's high-handedness in failing to consult them about its expansion and Thring's apparent indifference to providing places for local day boys.

The situation was further complicated by limited medical knowledge. Typhoid was thought to affect 100,000 people each year in England and Wales and to result in 10-12,000 deaths, but its cause was unknown. Both the RSA and the school were aware of the risks of water-borne disease but it was assumed that the main danger lay in germs, miasma (polluted air) or contagion. Major breakthroughs in bacteriology were still some years away and medicines were ineffective in countering most epidemic diseases.

Nineteenth century boarding schools were highly vulnerable to infection. With crowded and poorly-ventilated dormitories and rudimentary water supplies and drainage systems, many schools suffered recurring outbreaks of diphtheria, typhoid, cholera, measles and scarlet fever. Periodic deaths of pupils were an accepted fact of life.[3] Thring had been haunted by the possibility of epidemic illness ever since the

---

[1] The first MOHs were appointed in big cities in mid-century. Thring was one of those who saw government officials as interferers: 'an Englishman's home is his castle' was the prevailing idea. The police experienced it too, as in Kate Summerscale's: *The Suspicions of Mr. Whicher* (2008).

[2] He had resigned his fellowship on marrying.

[3] See Richardson, N: *Typhoid in Uppingham: Analysis of a Victorian Town and School in Crisis* (2008) for much more detail on the events of this chapter and the next. Other frequent diseases included smallpox, influenza, ringworm, mumps, pneumonia, meningitis and acute rheumatism.

diphtheria at Mathias' house fifteen years earlier and Uppingham had been one of the first schools to build a sanatorium (1869-70).

In February 1875 word reached him of four deaths in the town from scarlet fever and multiple cases of measles.[1] Worried that cesspits and animals might be fouling the water sources, he asked the local authority to commission expert analysis. This took five months, and confirmed both the natural hardness of the water and some pollution of the supply, but no action was taken.

It was a year of extreme weather. Early in the year sharp frosts cracked many of the drains, but the warmest and driest spring for half a century hid the extent of the damage. Then, extreme cold and eight times the normal rainfall in June mercilessly revealed the cracks as the town became a sea of mud. The mud dried out in a six-week heat-wave in August and early September – the month when Thring wrote to Parkin that his summer holiday had restored his health[2] – only for the autumn rains to arrive with a vengeance, followed by bitter winds in late November. The tiredness that Thring had described in his next letter to Parkin was compounded by frustration at being unable to secure further improvements to the town's drainage.

On 28 June a nine-year-old boy (Hawke) had died at the Lower School[3] (now run by Hodgkinson) after three weeks of fever and sore throat. Thomas Bell, the school doctor, certified typhoid as the cause of death. The boy's parents questioned why it had not been diagnosed earlier[4] but took things no further and over the summer Thring and Hodgkinson kept news of the fatality to themselves. They had no legal obligation to inform anyone[5] and the school could do little if the source of the problem lay outside school property.

Thring's critics would claim later that his reticence showed too much concern to protect the school's reputation and that Bell, as an Old Boy and parent, was too loyal to go against him as well as being complacent and poor in his diagnoses. Bell was certainly concerned to protect his well-paid position as school doctor, and as there was an over-provision of GPs

---

[1] Probably originating in the town's infants' school. An anonymous letter urged Thring to raise the issue.

[2] See the end of chapter 13.

[3] A separate legal entity from Thring's school, but closely linked to it. It is now The Lodge. Hodgkinson had opened the Lower School there in 1869.

[4] Parents had been told there was no cause to worry, but when Lady Hawke visited her son, she immediately summoned a specialist from Peterborough. Hodgkinson was himself ill over that summer, with no known cause.

[5] This was fourteen years before the Infectious Diseases Notification Act 1889.

for a town of Uppingham's size, Thring could have found a replacement without difficulty.

The two men hoped the disease might simply vanish over the summer. However, autumn was typically the time for typhoid to emerge and in 1875 it brought classic typhoid conditions: heavy rain and mud. On 2 September just before the new term began a local plumber (Mr. Chapman) was called to investigate a blocked drain between the Lower School cellar and its cesspit. He lit a candle, whereupon 'a tremendous explosion took place, the sewer gases igniting, passing up to the ceiling like a streak of lightning, burning [his] whiskers, eyebrows and hair'. Nevertheless the boys were allowed to return. Bell diagnosed typhoid in a thirteen-year-old within two weeks and there were three more cases by the end of the month. During October thirty other boys – spread among several houses – showed similar symptoms and there were some mild cases affecting staff families.

On Saturday 9 October a football match took place in torrential rain and deep mud between the pupils and a masters' invitation XV. Spectators noticed a pungent smell coming up into the town from the churchyard. Thring was deeply worried: he had heard the church bell tolling that morning, although he later discovered that it was for a man who had died in the workhouse. Even so, he feared that the school would 'not escape death'. That same evening a seventeen-year-old boy arrived by coach from Southampton to become a servant in the Lower School. Thring later claimed that the school warned him of the illness there and offered to pay his fare home, but he chose to stay, only to die three weeks later.

Next day the Sunday chapel service briefly raised Thring's spirits and in mid-week he found time for a long afternoon walk with nine-year-old Grace. Bell decided belatedly that all sick boys should be sent to the sanatorium rather than being cared for in the Lower School.[1] By now there were new cases right across the school, including Stephen Nash, aged 14, of Redgate – a house on London Road nearly half a mile from the Lower School. Thring met Nash's parents and found them 'kind and sensible' but panic was spreading as some parents descended on the school and others began to call their sons home. Doctor parents in Uppingham's recruiting

---

[1] 13 boys were in the sanatorium that weekend. It was arguably better to keep the victims in their houses than to send them to a building visited daily by older pupils from the other houses, thus risking further spread of the infection. This geographical spread of cases made it far harder for all parties to determine whether they should be looking for germ (i.e. water-borne), miasma or contagion causes.

heartland on Merseyside contacted Thring. They had heard a rumour that there were over 40 cases and they demanded that he summon the MOH.

Thring faced a major dilemma. If he sent all the pupils home, infection might spread still more and the school might never reopen. However, if he failed to do so he might be accused of self-interest and complacency – which could prove just as damaging. He decided on balance to keep the term going, but over the next few days typhoid claimed the lives of Nash, two other pupils and a housemaster's baby son. Somehow he had to stem the panic, stop parents besieging Bell with enquiries and shore up staff and pupil morale whilst also comforting the bereaved and attending the funerals.[1]

He also needed to balance assertiveness and respect in his demeanour towards the RSA and MOH with whom he must now work. Many of the first-generation rural MOHs were of low calibre but Dr. Thomas Haviland of the Northamptonshire Districts was a highly qualified exception. Unfortunately for Thring Haviland was also extremely contentious, suffering no fool gladly and letting few obstacles get in his way. With a promising career in surgery cruelly cut short by a surgical accident, his disappointment and love of controversy made him an unusually zealous crusader for better public health standards.

Thring approached Haviland for help on Tuesday 12 October, asking him to examine the drainage and water supply of all the houses. He needed 'an inspection by a man whose name will carry respect and conviction' with parents all over the country. The RSA, keen to be seen as proactive, sent a similar request. Haviland duly arrived in Uppingham three days later, although not before Thring and a lower-grade local sanitary official had traded accusations of secrecy and inertia. By now he had received a further shoal of telegrams from Liverpool: 'When will it end?' he wrote in his diary, 'I am myself very tired and done up... all one's feelings of joy in doing one's best, and the happy sense of... one's [life's] work is so utterly destroyed'. He feared that all his previous achievements might 'melt like the snow of spring'.

He met Haviland on the Saturday morning, an hour after attending the burial of the housemaster's baby. Their meeting coincided with a gathering of angry parents at the nearby Falcon hotel discussing whether to take their sons home, away from the hands of these 'murderers'. Thring's anger on hearing of it ('Nice for poor old Hodgkinson, whose whole life has been bound up in the house and boys; nice for me too, for I

---

[1] Three parents were at boys' bedsides. Bell claimed that there were only 12 cases. Thring told the masters that it would look very bad if he sent the boys home.

am murderer number one') was compounded by discovering that Haviland felt that he could dictate to the school as he briskly told Thring that it must remain in session. Thring confessed that 'my blood boiled when I heard this man deliver an *ex cathedra* statement, as if all he said was gospel on a question where there was so much to be considered. [But] had he decided otherwise, I don't know what I could have done'. Haviland then pointedly inspected Thring's house and after having its water supply analysed he declared it pure. As yet he had offered no judgement about the source of the problem, and he would later vacillate about keeping the school open.

Thring urged parents not to panic and to trust him, but in order to show that he was not complacent he recruited Dr. Christopher Childs, a recently qualified Old Boy doctor, as science master and sanitary officer.[1] Even this failed to dissuade the trustees from suddenly 'recommending' him to end the term at once. They refused to commission their own sanitary expert and ordered him to work closely with the RSA and Haviland. He could hardly ignore them, and swallowing 'most bitter disappointment' he announced that term would end on 2 November so that all the houses could be inspected and if necessary improved. Painfully aware that this might prompt more parents to consider alternative schools, he assured them that he hoped to re-open immediately after Christmas.

He also tried to rally the housemasters. Costly though it might be, their houses must be put into a faultless condition. On the last night of term he confided in his diary: 'It is strange though, the childish relief I feel at not having to get up for school tomorrow... [and] the lifting of that fearful weight of the possibility of fresh fever'.[2]

****

The RSA now commissioned a notable sanitary engineer, Rogers Field of Westminster, to report on the drainage of the town's properties and streets, but its prime and predictable concern was to make the school the scapegoat. On 27 October it served notice publicly on four housemasters to 'remove nuisances arising from their cesspits' and declared that 'serious blame' attached to them and to Dr. Bell. Thring was furious at the contrast between what he saw as its years of inactivity and this sudden new energy. On discovering that the RSA intended to write to every

---

[1] Childs had first class honours in science from Oxford: he could reassure parents, and take pressure off Dr. Bell.
[2] This outbreak had run its course: 46 pupils, including 17 from the Lower School. Bell knew of 12 in the town.

parent,[1] he felt that he could not trust Haviland to see through its tactic of shifting blame. He would have to go higher up, seeking help from central government authority in the form of the Local Government Board (LGB) in London.

The LGB oversaw the nationwide network of urban and rural sanitary authorities: a huge and difficult task.[2] It stayed above the local fray wherever possible, but it could not escape involvement in this epidemic. All through the winter Thring, Drs. Bell and Childs, Barnard Smith, Haviland and their various local allies lobbied and visited its officials, right up to its president. This resulted in a stream of conflicting allegations: not only about possible causes and remedies but in connection with a bitter territorial dispute between Bell and Haviland over the latter's powers to visit the homes of Bell's patients.

In mid-November after pressure from Sir Henry Thring the LGB agreed that its chief inspector, Robert Rawlinson, would produce a report in addition to those already planned by Haviland and Field. The furious RSA protested against Thring's use of his powerful contacts in this way, but to no avail. He then sought to seize the initiative by persuading the masters to engage Alfred Tarbotton, a Nottingham engineer, to draw up plans to streamline the drainage in every house and to take the first steps towards setting up a private water company to supply both school and town.

What had started as a local issue was now attracting much wider interest through a prolonged series of (often anonymous) attacks on the school in the national and medical press. In *The Lancet, Medicus* made allegations about Bell's incompetence and Thring's obstructiveness,[3] prompting a hostile editorial about the school's poor boarding house facilities and contrasting it with a town allegedly free from typhoid.[4] The journal encouraged Haviland to investigate the school minutely. Remembering the press fall-out during the Fowler and Jackson affairs, Thring insisted that no master should write to the press without his

---

[1] 'The most wonderful bit of Jack-in-officism. The Sanitary [Authority] and town generally have resisted all improvement [for] twenty years... and ignored fever in the town for the last six months... it is astonishing'.

[2] The LGB had a reputation for ineffectiveness and bureaucracy because of its huge workload. An amalgamation of medical and political agencies, its leaders were divided over how much to intervene directly in local issues.

[3] 'Studiously shutting their eyes to the real nature of the disease, and keeping boys in mere pest-houses...'

[4] *Medicus* was probably supplied with information by discontented parents whose sons had been taken home before the school broke up: 'The dormitories are supplied with water from the cisterns which supply the water-closets'.

consent. *The Times* criticised the school's initial complacency, whereupon *The Lancet* returned to the attack. It praised the RSA, insinuated that Thring had ordered Bell to be uncooperative, and urged the trustees to consider Thring's future as he was little more than 'a bigoted old-fashioned hater of pure air and water'. Critical articles appeared right across the North-West, with the *Liverpool Daily News* thundering:

> 'Even the autocratic will of the Headmaster of an English public school is inefficient against the laws of nature... perhaps the Local Government Board will send a teacher of elementary physiology into Rutlandshire. It would be a good investment of time... even if the... study of classics were intermitted for a month or two'.

Worse was to follow. In December Bell finally admitted the extent of the shortcomings in the sanatorium, prompting the sudden resignation of its matron. After an encouraging but short-lived rumour that the LGB might impose its own improvement plan on the town, Thring received a message from a Northampton parent that Haviland was spreading doom and despondency there: 'He said quite enough to deter any father from sending his son to Uppingham'.

The reports of the four experts came out in rapid succession over New Year 1875/6. Three of them were largely predictable. Tarbotton's was the first: commissioned by Thring and the housemasters, he conceded that there had been some defects in the houses, but only those 'too often found in the most modern houses and mansions'. The masters were sparing no expense to remedy them, but they were hampered by the deficiencies in the town's sewerage and water supply. Despite the report's cautious optimism, the trustees postponed the start of the January term, pending publication of the other reports.

Rogers Field's findings were technical and comprehensive. Although the RSA was his client he pulled no punches about the deficiencies and poor maintenance of the town sewerage system. He was also adamant that mains water was needed – both for drinking purposes and to assist with sewage disposal. However, whilst conceding the good intentions of the housemasters he was much less optimistic than Tarbotton about the state of the houses.

Rawlinson's brief report to the LGB cited plenty of past history about the actions and inactions of both town and school. He too criticised street maintenance – and the small-minded meanness of local people in failing to improve their properties and in resisting rate rises for improvements. He felt that the RSA should have been more assertive, and he was mostly supportive of the school. This impressed the trustees, who agreed that the new term could begin on 28 January – despite protests from Rector Wales, a man with conflicting interests as both a trustee *and* an RSA member. It was the two masters' trustees, Birley and Jacob, who thwarted Wales but it was a close-run thing.

Thring later claimed that he would have resigned if this decision had gone against him but his temporary victory did little to ease his fears about the possibility of collapsing pupil numbers. By late January there were alarming rumours that advance copies of Haviland's report were circulating privately in London. Although deeply worried about the masters' low morale and the school's future prospects, even Thring could not have foreseen how critical Haviland would be of the school.

The MOH's report spared no detail in its long narrative of events. The school was accused of taking inadequate precautions, subsequent complacency and prevarication, and failure to keep parents informed. Haviland criticised Bell for territorial defensiveness and Thring for supporting him, and he listed in remorseless detail the alleged shortcomings in each house, especially of their cesspits. He seized on many other aspects of house management (including catering and mealtimes) and the treatment of individual cases in the sanatorium. Studies were said to be overcrowded and ill-ventilated. The *coup de grace* was a lurid picture of the stream which flowed out of the Lower School garden and fed the school's bathing place nearly a mile downstream:

'It flows along the south of the town, receiving first an effluent which may be traced to the overflow of the town spring. It is contaminated by the oozings from the site of the old gas works... after this it receives the drainings from manure heaps, of a cowshed, a pigstye, a stable, and other accumulation of filth... and before passing under the bridge it becomes still further polluted by the small overflow of a cesspit in the neighbourhood of the National School. After this the stream skirts the cemetery, and receives its drainage; it then flows on beyond the town and becomes the feeder of the bathing place and swimming pond! There the water becomes so filthy, that from the information of men who were old Uppingham boys, many wisely declined to enter its befouled waters... [It] then passes to the south of Bisbrook, where I am informed it is used for brewing purposes'.[1]

---

[1] Locally it was known as 'piss brook'. Haviland believed at least one boy had contracted the disease there. The mis-spelling of Bisbrooke suggests a report written in haste.

187

Finally Haviland used the report pointedly to thank the RSA for its support, prompting Barnard Smith to distribute copies locally with a long memorandum of his own version of events and his criticisms of Dr. Bell.[1]

Why Haviland had turned so decisively against the school is unclear. He had a duty to people well beyond it, and although he must surely have had a notion of the damage he was doing to its standing he did not see it as his duty to protect it in any way. He certainly resented its lobbying of the LGB, and there was a personal dimension to his battle of wills with Thring and Bell. In criticising Thring's failure to restrict boys' movements he showed little idea of the school's geography or the practicalities of its day-to-day workings.[2] By contrast he made only mild criticisms of the state of the town, thus ensuring that any possibility of collaboration between school and town now disappeared.

****

The boys returned on 28 January. 'Pray God keep us this term', wrote Thring in his diary: 'Masters' meeting this morning. 'Had to speak to them strongly about tittle-tattle'. Bell and Haviland were still trading accusations, with *The Lancet* supporting Haviland and its rival, the *British Medical Journal,* mostly favouring the school.

Even so Thring was reasonably cheerful. Parliamentary processes and trial borings were under way for the waterworks.[3] Despite all the drama he claimed that there were 30 new boys, preferring to overlook the fact that 50 boys had left the school since October.[4] He had 'proper work again',

---

[1] Suggestions of both infection and contagion were mixed with references to poor ventilation and sewer gases. It contrasted with Mr. Eve's praise in 1869 for domestic arrangements as 'perfect' – but public health expectations had risen rapidly even within a few years.

[2] Haviland showed little concern for the difficulties facing housemasters. With the days drawing in, pupils' morale would have been increasingly tested. Moreover, rules for boys about where they might go were hard to enforce. Housemasters taught classes and could not watch boys all the time. Many lessons still took place in house dining halls; boys needed to move around the town to go to them.

[3] The RSA was now threatening to produce its own scheme. It did not wish to be seen to obstruct the public good, but it was unlikely to be enthusiastic about endorsing a private company outside its control.

[4] 'So we have not suffered any appreciable check: 305 on the school books'. In fact, numbers were 20 down. Another 16 would leave in March. 30+ of the leavers were from the North-West or London, suggesting a strong parental grapevine. Several boys transferred to Tonbridge when Rowe became headmaster

and with it returned his complex mixture of fatalism and belief in Providence: 'As we often said in the old days: "If this thing is of God, it will stand; if not, let it go"'.

A week after term began he felt that the worst might be over, but during an afternoon walk with Skrine he could not refrain from sharing fears for the future, which proved well founded. On 20 February: 'I have entered once again the valley of the shadow of death'. Cobb, a housemaster whose property had not previously been infected, now had the first case of a second wave of the epidemic. This time parents were told at once, and Cobb's boys were immediately sent home. Tarbotton made new checks of the houses. Thring braced himself for a rapid general exodus, but the parents initially proved 'wonderfully steady'. He again went to the LGB, and a housemaster deputation met the RSA and found them 'frightened at the gathering storm... today the sewers have been examined and found foul enough to account for any fever. The Rector was hauled to see it, and has heard some plain truths too, I understand'.[1] Any sense of vindication was quickly snuffed out by new cases in three other houses and another hostile volley from *The Lancet*. On 3 March he felt 'quite sure this is the beginning of the end. The school will slip away like a wreath of snow'.

Large numbers of boys began to visit Bell's surgery, afraid that they were developing typhoid symptoms. Telegrams arrived from worried parents and there were new rumours of mis-diagnosis. Tempers rose when Cobb flatly refused to admit Haviland to inspect his house, whereupon Haviland reported him to the LGB.[2] This presented Thring with another delicate balancing act to perform in supporting his beleaguered housemaster whilst not alienating the government agency whose support he needed so much. He tried to play the incident down as a misunderstanding.

He was acutely aware of how vulnerable Uppingham was compared with better-known schools like Marlborough and Winchester: 'We cannot

---

there. Houses most affected by typhoid were the largest losers. It was just as well that numbers had been allowed to rise above 300.

[1] The navvies were so disgusted that they refused to raise all the drain covers. The new outbreak might have been carried by a returning pupil or town visitor; possibly the disease lay dormant in the drains or water.

[2] Haviland: 'Mr. James (the local inspector) called [and] delivered my message to which Mr. Cobb replied that "he would meet Mr. Haviland either in the street or at the Falcon [hotel] but he would not see him at his house" (in School Lane). I declined to meet him in the street or at the Falcon and said I would only meet him at his house, where the enquiry must be made. Mr. Cobb's reply was: "His compliments and he had nothing to say"'.

hold the school together much longer; [The boys] are melting away. This is ruin'. He was now convinced that it would have to break up early a second time. Suddenly the housemasters' desperation gave rise to the idea that the school might temporarily leave Uppingham – at least for a time. William Campbell's house was part of the new outbreak, little more than a hundred yards from Cobb's. Campbell's terse question, voiced at a housemasters' meeting: 'Don't you think we ought to flit?' caught the imagination of most of the housemaster body.

Thring met Birley and Jacob in Manchester on 7 March and was shown newspapers filled with advertisements from parents searching for private tutors or alternative schools. His first instinct was to find a property in the Lake District, but Birley knew a hotel keeper in Wales who was interested in meeting them. Running ahead of the true state of affairs, Thring assured both men that the housemasters were unanimous in supporting Campbell's idea and that Johnson, the trustees' chairman, had already given him a free hand in principle to take any necessary action. He then proposed that the school should break up early for Easter, reassembling three weeks' later in some healthier place.

Within a few days the press was reporting that Borth near Aberystwyth seemed the most likely choice, although the trustees as a body had yet to consider the idea. When they did, a minority were very hostile – notably Wales, who took it on himself to argue for the interests of the small number of day boys.[1] Thring told Birley that the Rector 'might just as well try to stop a train with his finger' and, despite Wales' delaying tactics and their collective resentment at having been presented with a *fait accompli* through the press, the trustees agreed to the plan. In doing so, however, they effectively washed their hands of the school while it was elsewhere:

> '[Wales] spoke of the... buildings as burdensome to the Trust, and endeavoured to saddle [the masters] with the burden of any deficit... Then he brought forward the day boys and the necessity of having a master here. I (Thring) simply said I should not leave any one of my staff, but if necessary a man might be got to do it. But that [the day boys] could come with us, and the trustees could pay a fair proportion of their board and lodging. Then he threatened that the trustees would have to cut down the masters' salaries. I quietly pointed out... that the scheme appointed that the tuition fees must first go to paying the masters'.

---

[1] Some trustees resented hearing the news via rumour. Wales, living locally, understood the implications for the town better than others. Thring failed to mention that some housemasters had strong doubts about the move.

On the following weekend Thring sat in chapel wondering if he would ever again spend another Sunday there but sensing that 'a great shaping power is round about me'. He was buoyed up by increasing support from the masters and by a letter from Thomas Jex-Blake, the recently-appointed headmaster of Rugby, promising that his school would not capitalise on Uppingham's misfortune by trying to recruit its boys.[1]

Soon after the first typhoid case in his own house a few days later, he preached at the end of term service. Skrine described it as a day of 'wild winds and pitiless snows' as Thring told those boys who still remained that 'difficulties become tests of willingness and strength; all hardship, everything that tries life, when overcome, strengthens life'.[2] As so often, adversity energised him. He felt sure that 'some strange, good and marvellous divine purpose will come out of it all. On Tuesday I start out for Borth and other places in North Wales. Borth seems likely to suit'. The reference to 'North Wales' suggests that at this stage he had only a vague idea about where Borth was, and that evening as the boys packed up to go home neither they nor their parents nor most of the masters had any idea about when and where the school would reassemble – if at all.

****

Thring was soon in central Wales at Llandrindod Wells. Cobb, whose boys had gone home two weeks before the rest, had been sent on ahead to prospect possible locations but the two men quickly decided that accommodation there was too limited. They travelled on to Borth, a sprawling village sandwiched between a two-mile coastal strip of shingle and sand and a mountain range, with Aberystwyth a few miles to the south and the huge estuary of the River Dovey a mile to the north. Summer tourism had slowly developed there since the railway had arrived a decade earlier giving rise to the over-ambitious Cambrian Hotel, with its 120 rooms dwarfing the guest houses along nearby Cambrian Terrace but virtually empty at that time of year.[3]

---

[1] The *Times* published *Pater Alumni's* letter, contrasting the 'plague-stricken' town with the resolute school.

[2] Skrine: 'The Old Testament lesson recounted the wanderings of Jacob in the wilderness [including] the promise: "I will keep thee in all places whither thou goest and will bring thee again into this land"'. Some wondered whether the lesson had been specially chosen, but it was in fact the one appointed for the day.

[3] Skrine: 'A maritime semi-circular plain with a sea-front of five miles, and a depth inland of two to three miles. This plain, part still in marsh, is surrounded by a ring of hills [between] the summits of Cader Idris and Plinlimmon... straggling dwellings, from primitive mud-cabins to the stately hotel'.

The village comprised around 150 people mostly employed in farming or fishing, although some families took in holiday makers. The two prospectors arrived during a howling gale but Thring would have clutched at almost any straw. He quickly struck a deal with the hotel owner for accommodation for his family, two masters and 160 boys: the rest would live in the Cambrian Terrace houses and in two dozen cottages spread along the main street. After summoning Bell on a flying visit to confirm the location as medically satisfactory, he searched inconclusively for cricket fields. The trio then headed straight back to Uppingham by train.

Somewhat optimistically he reported to Birley that Borth's water and drainage were exceptionally good and that a fortnight's hard work there would be enough to create 'Uppingham by the Sea'. Had he looked more closely he would have discovered that Borth was far less developed than Uppingham: it boasted a post office/general stores and some small shops and inns but little else. Its church was still being built. A limited water supply had been installed when the railway was built, but its pipes tended to fur up and the drains smelt powerfully in summer. Moreover, despite the bracing Atlantic climate Borth had long been prone to cholera and tuberculosis and it had no doctor. The school's presence there might well create similar sanitary pressures to those which had already overwhelmed Uppingham. The recent growth of Aberystwyth, which provided Borth with many essentials, had stretched its public services to the limit too.[1] There would also be a significant language difficulty: Borth was predominantly Welsh-speaking.

On arriving home Thring found the cautious RSA resolved to move things forward only in accordance with proper legal process. Barnard Smith and Wales may perhaps have seen a letter from the anonymous *One of the Townsfolk* to a Manchester newspaper questioning whether Borth would be any safer than Uppingham. They and their RSA fellow-members had weighed up the challenges facing Thring and hoped that eventually he would have to make a humiliating return.

The trustees remained unhelpful, too. At their meeting on 24 March they seemed much more concerned to assert their authority over Thring than to support him in his hour of need. When told what he had arranged at Borth, they offered just £50 towards the day boys' travel, board and lodging, but declined to grant travel costs to the masters, threatening even to withhold the boarders' tuition fees. They would be trustees of the

---

[1] Aberystwyth still had only a dozen hospital beds, patchy sewerage and refuse collection and a hopelessly inadequate water supply. Water could be obtained for only about 2 hours per day at the height of the season.

school *at Uppingham* in the most literal sense, leaving Thring and the housemasters to bear any other costs.[1]

Despite all this adversity, Thring felt a sense of liberation. Although he had seen Borth so fleetingly he had revelled in its views and sense of space: it was like 'an escape out of prison. Things may be hard... but it is the hardness of liberty'. As he let parents know the place and starting date for the new term he had no idea what it would cost to take the school to Borth or how long it would be there. He hoped it might be just for the summer term.

Three weeks after the first suggestion to 'flit' and after only minimal time to pack up their possessions, arrange for their houses to be looked after and organise further tests to be carried out on water supplies while they were away, Thring and his advance guard of staff families left Uppingham. Others followed, but Dr. Bell would remain in the town as protector of the school's interests and Thring's main source of local intelligence.[2]

****

Meanwhile the local *Cambrian News* reported that there was to be a 'spring invasion of Borth', predicting local disruption but also some welcome opportunities for money to be made. Thring arrived, buoyed up by anticipation that 'tomorrow begins real hard work, but liberty'. Next day he directed the setting-up like a military operation: 'Everybody is so kind and helpful – such a contrast to Uppingham – I have really enjoyed

---

[1] Initially they ignored the main question, limiting housemasters to 30 boarders and stating that boys from infected houses could return only with Thring's permission. The fee implications would have been legally problematic. Yet despite claiming to be responsible only for the school *at Uppingham,* they were responsible to the Charity Commissioners for its administration. Their social standing locally would suffer from the school's absence too.

[2] Bell could not leave his town patients without risking his practice being eroded by rival doctors. With Childs now to be school doctor at Borth, Bell regularly demanded assurances from Thring about his own long-term position. He worked tirelessly and ferociously for the school during its absence, perhaps with this in mind.

The Lower School pupils remained in Uppingham. Possibly Hodgkinson thought leaving was wrong, or that his boys were too young to go; possibly Thring told him there were no beds for them at Borth. Medically it seems a strange decision, given the Lower School's history, and vulnerability of younger boys to typhoid.

my day although I was kept at it incessantly from 8am till 6'.[1] He haggled with local women over rents for their cottages and allocated lists of boys to properties while Dr. Childs (the sanitary officer) and the new sanatorium matron devised rudimentary washing facilities. Orders were sent to the Potteries for chamber pots and china wash-basins. Local workmen, augmented by others hired in Aberystwyth, were surprised at the masters' willingness to roll up their sleeves to help. Together they removed hotel carpets and fittings, spring-cleaning every room. Trestle tables to feed 300 were set up in the larger rooms and corridors. Stables became workshops and outhouses provided a rudimentary gymnasium, music practice rooms and a sick-room. A large but rather basic wooden schoolroom/assembly hall – 83 feet by 20 – was hastily built on ground behind the hotel.

A specially chartered goods train arrived. 'If anyone wishes for a new experience', Thring wrote later in *The Times*, 'let him try unloading eighteen railway trucks and distributing their contents among twelve or fourteen houses in a fierce march against time'. Marie and her girls helped to reassemble beds and the heaviest item, the school cricket roller, was sent further on down the railway line to Bow Street. Sir Pryse Pryse of nearby Gogerddan House, an eccentric but generous local landowner, had offered six acres of grass there on what had once been a race-course for just £1 (which he later waived because regular rolling work by the boys had improved it so much). Thring immediately warmed to this fellow Old Etonian who also offered to allow the boys to follow his hounds and fish in his estate's lakes and streams.[2]

---

[1] 'I inspected all the houses... Then I secured three more small houses'. He was involved in all the detail: a list survives of rooms and numbers for Cambrian Terrace houses, scribbled by Thring on a piece of hotel notepaper.

[2] Pryse was a former officer in the Royal Horse Guards and a keen huntsman: generous to his tenants, but keeping his children so short of money that they had to sell fruit in Aberystwyth market. Gogerddan, his country house, had stuffed peacocks on the staircase, birds, animals and fish in glass cases in the entrance hall and a notable collection of van Dyck paintings and family portraits. He did much to support the building and upkeep of local churches including St Matthew's, Borth. His enthusiasm for cricket was eccentric too: before one match he walked through the neighbouring village in his cricket whites, to the consternation of some distant locals who thought that he was stark naked: 'There was a general stampede into the houses: blinds were hastily pulled down and the doors were locked. "Indeed", said an excited villager, "if it had been anyone but Sir Pryse Pryse, we would have killed him for coming out like that without his clothes"'. When the school returned to Uppingham Thring gave him 1,000 salmon for his streams.

Thring wrote later to his brother Henry that things were falling into place much better and more quickly than he had anticipated and that he knew from memory the price of every room in every house that they had commandeered. However, it still remained to be seen whether parents would keep faith with the school and just how many of the boys would actually turn up. Meanwhile the *Cambrian News* reported on the unfolding events: 'Excitement in Borth and neighbourhood is great. The main body of immigrants has not yet arrived, but evidence is not wanting of their speedy advent'.

CHAPTER FIFTEEN

BORTH

BARELY a week after returning to Borth Thring joined his colleagues on its small station platform to greet a series of afternoon trains. Skrine (whose subsequent small book *Uppingham by the Sea* chronicled events there) reckoned that the mass of heads hanging out of windows as the trains approached made the carriages look like poultry wagons, and he likened the excited mass of boys released after their long, slow journey to biblical scenes around the Tower of Babel. Masters sent them off for tea and then free time on the beach. Trunks, hampers and book-boxes were sorted and delivered around the village until nearly midnight.

To Thring's immense relief the parents had backed him in the most emphatic way: only a handful of those boys who had been expected to turn up failed to appear.[1] Next day he addressed the entire pupil body about the great experiment on which they had all embarked: they were making history and they had a responsibility to make life harmonious for themselves and local people. Because they would enjoy great freedom of movement they must 'show to all England that boys can be trusted, and need not have prison walls and bars and bolts to prevent them from going wrong, but can be self-governed, trustworthy, genial companions'. Many last-minute arrangements were still being made, so there were no lessons. To prevent homesickness the boys were kept busy exploring the area; fishing; swimming; looking for snakes; starting an aquarium.

For a man always so preoccupied with *machinery* it was a huge exercise in improvisation – and the ultimate testing-ground for his belief in collective responsibility and trust, although a few teething problems were inevitable. Up to six boys shared a room with one fireplace and one table: there was minimal privacy and a cacophony of noise from violins and pianos at music practice time.[2] One group ignored a ban on lighting fires in their cottage: Thring summoned them for a fierce dressing down, ordering them to return two days later. According to one: 'It was an awful interval, we did not know what was in store for us, but when we came into his presence a second time, he was so gentle and appealed to our sense of

---

[1] Pupils included 17 new boys: further evidence of parents having regained confidence in Thring after their criticisms during the first epidemic.

[2] One elderly landlady cherished the 'pianass' she was asked to house. Possibly she had never seen one.

the influence for good that we might exercise [so much that his] words went right to our hearts [and] I believe we cried'.

Everyone had to get used to rapid changes of Atlantic weather. With accommodation so spread out, lessons tended to begin late. It was hard to get members of school societies together. Thring had to waive his strict no-smoking rule for the elderly man who swept out the hotel. Local ladies were reduced to tears by the volume of hotel laundry, after which it was despatched to Aberystwyth. Yet there were compensations too, and as spring turned to summer Thring described their new life in a long article for *The Times*: 'Tea is over, and all the school is flocking to watch the rising tide. They are doing what boys always do on the sea-shore: dodging the waves, hurling pebbles at them as they come in, burrowing in the sand for shells'.

At first there was an element of alien tribes learning to live together, as the newcomers came under watchful local eyes. Thring's pupils dressed and spoke very differently from the local boys who had little formal education.[1] He noted at a football match 'the unintelligible cries of the Welsh rustic children' and how they tried to imitate the Uppingham boys' athletic achievements, 'scrambling down the street in corduroys as in a footrace, jerking their awkward little limbs'. Skrine wrote that 'our boys looked on [in the same way] as men look at monkeys, half-amused, half-indignant at the antics'. Elderly women 'cast a glance under their bonnets at the boys and exchanged muttered comments'. There were occasional misunderstandings over language and after one old lady complained about 'those very wicked boys who foolished me', the teacher from the Borth school was engaged to teach basic Welsh to two housemasters' wives who then acted as mediators.

Thring wisely supplied the *Cambrian News* and the *Aberystwyth Observer* with news items under the pseudonym of *A Correspondent*: positive messages such as 'most of the boys confess that Borth is the best place they have ever visited' and the unlikely claim that 'they keep away from public houses that are in the place: not one boy has yet been seen entering any of them'. *A Local Inhabitant* praised the boys' behaviour, pointing out how much they could learn in Borth about the natural world.

Boy-writers were not always so enthusiastic, however: a serial satire appeared in the *Magazine* which poked fun at Borth's remoteness and insularity. Pupils missed the school library and their individual studies, prompting one wit to suggest hiring a fleet of bathing machines which could be converted into bed-sits and eventually driven back in convoy to Uppingham. *Grumbler* and *Cheerful* protested in an editorial about a

---

[1] Fulltime education in Cardiganshire was compulsory up to the age of 11.

shortage of butter, green vegetables and any meat other than Welsh mutton. There were calls for one of the Uppingham bakers to come down to make hot rolls in the morning, because the Borth bread supplies came from five miles away and only twice a week.

Wherever possible, school events carried on as before: house football matches left over from the previous term (with spectators travelling by train down to Bow Street); athletics; cricket against local teams or traditional school rivals from within a reasonable distance.[1] In May the choir performed Bach's *Christmas Oratorio,* five months later than planned and hampered by the poor acoustics in the wooden schoolroom. For the annual chapel commemoration a flagstaff was put up in front of the hotel – after which flags became the means to call pupils to lessons.[2] The choir sang at the opening of the new Borth church in June, and Thring's Trinity Sunday sermon showed him at his most eloquent: '[This] house of prayer stands today, fresh out of your hands, between the mountains and the sea: the mountains, those earthly thrones of God; the sea, that eternity'. Thereafter the school used the church twice each Sunday.

Science and archaeology expeditions went off to Cader Idris or Devil's Bridge. Shooting took place on friendly neighbours' land and stuffed sea-fowl were collected into a museum. The aquarium acquired an octopus (which soon died) and one boy had to be stopped from shooting at a seal while out on a fishing trip. One summer night search parties of masters and police combed the area for a missing new boy. Homesick, he slept rough but turned up again next day.

Thring took long, energetic walks as he revelled in his new surroundings. He remained deeply angry that 'Uppingham has turned us out of house and home amidst a torrent of lies and abuse', reserving special venom for Rector Wales: a man of such 'plausible evil'. However, after a clever poem in the *Magazine* poked fun at the Rector's name, ending with the line 'Since Wales won't come to you then go to Wales',

---

[1] E.g. Shrewsbury and Repton. Pryse raised a cricket team. Matches v. the Old Boys took place too: as big an occasion as usual, with speeches expressing sympathy for the school's plight, and Thring replying that from the calamity 'the school would issue with quickened vigour and life'. The choir gave an impromptu concert.

[2] Three flags were made, and used throughout the school's time in Borth. They came back to Uppingham with the school, and were hung, first in the chapel and later in Thring's schoolroom, for over a century.

he reluctantly sent his old foe a tactical apology, feeling that he still needed to conciliate as well as confront the RSA.[1]

Some weeks earlier, as the masters prepared to leave Uppingham the RSA's leaders had faced a stormy meeting of local ratepayers who had begun to realise what the economic impact of the school's absence might be. Thring had briefly hoped that they would exert enough pressure to get drainage improvements moving, but he had been disappointed.[2] In May, however, there was a chance to test local opinion through the annual RSA elections – and to get new blood into its membership.

Voting slips had to be returned within a strict time limit, so the RSA sent them out at the last possible moment, making it hard for the absent housemasters to vote. Undeterred, friends of the school took up the challenge, quickly collecting up the slips from the empty boarding houses and passing them to Charles White (a local ironmonger) who was rushed to Rugby station to catch the evening train. On arrival at Borth early next morning he found Thring and the masters on the station platform with voting tables. Marie served White with breakfast while the train carried on down the line to Aberystwyth and back, and within minutes he was on his way home, handing in the votes with fifteen minutes to spare and ousting several opponents of the school in favour of (amongst others) Dr. Bell.

Despite this victory as the weeks went by Thring's bouts of gloom returned, especially about his rising debts. The arrival of his bank books was 'a heavy weight', although some Liverpool parents had started a fighting fund which raised £200 in the first week. He was glad not still to be in Uppingham 'sitting like Job, scraping boils on a dunghill', but it was deeply frustrating to be 'sitting here waiting quietly for one's doom, and at such hands'.

The hands were not only those of the RSA but also of the trustees. They were still legally Thring's employers and their attitude to these

---

[1] *Uppingham Magazine* (May 1876): *How I came to Borth:* 'Leave bickerings and cesspools far behind, Take thy stern future with a quiet mind. Better are herbs and peace, be well assured, Than all the Local Sanitary Board. Weigh dilute sewage 'gainst pure mountain springs, Weigh unflushed drains 'gainst air the salt sea brings, Weigh all the chances well with equal scales, Since Wales won't come to you then go to Wales…'

[2] Protesters were mostly housemasters and professional people who supported the school. For tradesmen and shopkeepers, despite having plenty to lose from the school's absence, the prospect of rate increases to pay for improvements was still the greatest concern. The meeting supported the idea of a private water company and rejected any idea of a cheap, surface alternative to pipes. It insisted that the LGB be informed. Fearing possible ratepayer anger, the RSA decided after this to moderate its opposition to the Water Bill.

unfolding events was still highly uncertain. There had been almost no communication with them since leaving Uppingham: only Birley and Jacob (who had sons in the school) had visited the school at Borth. Now, where staff and boys would reassemble in the autumn was becoming an urgent issue. When Thring received news of a special trustees' meeting to take place on 17 June he told Birley that he would ignore any order for a rapid, unconditional return, adding that most of the masters would support him. Privately though he had doubts: they had initially been deeply opposed to a second term in Borth until he reminded them that to go back to Uppingham before sanitary improvements had been made would represent complete surrender.[1]

Whether or not they knew of these tensions, the trustees confirmed Thring's worst suspicions by ordering him back to Uppingham for September without any assurances about the future from the RSA. He knew that defying the Board would give it grounds to dismiss him even if it had to face parental wrath afterwards, but two things came to his rescue. The trustees' stance backfired spectacularly by rallying the housemasters behind him. Then a few days later Bell sent news of fresh typhoid cases in the town: 'I cannot see how you can come back'. Faced with this the trustees declared that while they had no cause to change their minds, they would 'graciously' accede to Thring's wish to return to Borth in September.[2] They also agreed to advance £500 in advance of the following term's fees for the day boys.[3]

The term ended on a glorious summer day with Thring telling the boys 'to come back with the soldier spirit to face whatever remained'. He set off on his annual trip to Ben Place but even in his beloved Lakeland he remained pessimistic, raging at the RSA's 'blindness'. There was no shortage of advice: some Manchester parents and a few housemasters wanted him to set up permanently elsewhere,[4] although they had no idea of how the finance for it could be found. Bell kept up a war of attrition

---

[1] 'I had said it was running our heads into a rat-trap; this should have been the masters' opinion six weeks ago'.

[2] Thring: 'It is fun to see what a sour face they make over it, and are foolish enough to show [it]'.

[3] Given that there were only a handful of day boys, this sum suggests that the trustees were prepared to pay at least a proportion of the boarding fee as well as tuition fees for local boys who had gone to Borth.

[4] Birley: 'I find parents of boys here [in Manchester] very little inclined to lend any help – they argue that if Uppingham does not care for the school they need not have it – and that it would be much better if Mr. Thring would leave the place and set up his flag elsewhere'. Thring and some housemasters had similar thoughts.

against the RSA[1] and some of Thring's colleagues began to offer money for a legal fighting fund to put further pressure on it. There was more lobbying of the LGB and friendly MPs again asked parliamentary questions.

Meanwhile those who lived permanently in Borth and Aberystwyth had learned one important lesson from Thring's experiences. That summer they began to agitate for better water supplies of their own.

****

Summer progress back in Uppingham had been – and remained – painfully slow. When the LGB's inspector arrived to check the state of the town's drains on a hot day in early July, he was overwhelmed by the stench and told RSA officials that they were presiding over a scandal.[2] To Thring's amazement and frustration, although townspeople spoke well to the inspector about the school and its contribution to the town, the ratepayers still seemed hesitant to assert themselves. The RSA was still determined not to be hurried, and it was deeply suspicious of any private water company – especially if Thring were behind it. The LGB decided to support this scheme but trial borings proved problematic and Haviland returned to argue powerfully that the proposed waterworks site was too close to sewage outfalls.[3]

Local tradesmen and others finally changed their attitude in August, as it became clear that the school would be away until at least Christmas and possibly longer. Seventy five residents raised a petition which forced Barnard Smith and Wales to meet them once again. It was a stormy encounter at which Wales lost his temper, but it finally broke the deadlock: the RSA hastily dropped opposition to the Water Bill. Three days later tenders for sewerage improvements were opened. On 15 September as sewerage work began in Uppingham, the autumn term began at Borth.

Thring continued to see Rector Wales as the real villain of the piece: 'Just like a naughty little boy crying "I don't care, I don't care!" when put in a corner. I am sick of his cant'. He was again under pressure as he

---

[1] He began a new dispute with Haviland over the MOH's demand to visit any of Bell's patients who had been affected by typhoid.

[2] The inspector said 'his duties took him to many queer places, but he had never been in one so foul' - but the LGB invariably favoured local decision-making if possible, and it still hoped local opinion would assert itself.

[3] The Water Bill received its royal assent on 13 July. It gave Thring and his four fellow-directors the power to raise capital through shares, make borrowings and levy charges. Its powers would last for only one year.

began to realise just how hard a coastal December might be, and the *Magazine* was alleging that the boys 'looked forward to wintering in Wales as much as they would to hibernating in Greenland'.

He still hoped to be back in Uppingham by Christmas, but over the summer he had not been idle. Even before the decision had been made to remain in Borth for a second term, Birley urged him to upgrade key buildings for winter (wisely adding that it was important that Rector Wales did not find out what he was up to).[1] Accommodation agreements were renegotiated. Exposed parts of the hotel were weather-boarded and a covered walkway was built between the hotel and the wooden schoolroom. 'Sanitary Tom', a local navvy, widened the drainage channels between the hotel and the beach to prevent flooding after storms.

The adults strengthened their local ties: Thring preached the sermon at the harvest festival, for which Marie and Anna decorated the church. Afternoon lessons were rescheduled into the early evening to make maximum use of the light for games and outdoor pursuits. There were new evening societies and a lecture programme but as the days shortened and the winds strengthened,[2] discipline began to fray. Halfway through the term Thring reminded the boys about 'the experiment in self-government which our special circumstances are affording'.

Suddenly in the last week of October there were seven cases of scarlet fever. With no hospital and no isolation facilities there was again talk of an early end to a term, but Thring rose to the challenge characteristically, finding a remote, half-built house big enough to become a makeshift sanatorium with 25 beds. Workmen put in doors and windows within hours; the matron scrubbed it out overnight and the first patients moved in next morning.[3] After so many dramas it was encouraging that the parents took this latest setback in their stride, one father writing to his new-boy son to 'stick to your work and don't mind such a trifle'. Thring continued to believe that all the difficulties of the previous year would eventually end in triumph, proving the truth of one of his favourite philosophies in life: 'The lost battle won'. His Advent Sunday sermon spoke of the

---

[1] Besides giving the trustees the pretext to dismiss him, it might have enabled Wales to dispute the costs. Skrine contributed £100 - a very large sum - on Thring's birthday in November towards his ever-increasing expenses.

[2] Rawnsley, W F: 'In our houses, when the street door was opened, the carpets blew up in every room'.

[3] Nurses were brought in from London. No source was ever discovered, and it was over within ten days. Large amounts of disinfectant and carbolic soap were applied to floors: cottage owners feared for their carpets.

opportunities which marked the start of the church year: they were 'a testimony that we are going to meet the coming Saviour'.

In contrast to all this activity, improvement work in Uppingham remained pedestrian. The drainage contractors pleaded for extra time: Bell was sure that their contract was full of loopholes and miscalculations and he began a campaign of embarrassment against the RSA over the appalling state of the drainage in the town's National School and the workhouse. Even when the water company site was agreed, local demand for shares was low amongst townspeople, some feeling the pinch of the school's absence and others still resenting any school-led enterprise.[1]

Thring was appalled that they seemed so negative. Worse still in early December reports began to reach him of yet more typhoid cases in the town: he decided to delay as long as possible any decision about where the school would be after Christmas. Term ended with a concert in the Assembly Rooms in Aberystwyth and Handel's *Messiah* at the Temperance Hall, after which the boys departed still not knowing (as in both the previous terms) where they would reassemble in January.[2]

Next day many of the masters headed back to Uppingham, determined to spend Christmas at home. Thring went back briefly himself to assess the situation with Oxford Professor Henry Acland, anticipating another round of arguments with the trustees and again resolved that if the 'Rutland clique' tried to force his hand, he would resign. This proved unnecessary: Acland quickly concluded that Uppingham was not yet safe and the trustees had no choice but to agree. They voted £300 towards the masters' salaries and £250 to Thring towards his expenses, asking him to provide them with a new *Statement* of the value of school properties which he and the masters claimed that they had paid for. Spurred on by increased engagement with the charity authorities since the New Scheme began, it was their first step in planning the school's long-term financial stability.[3]

Thring's relief at their decision was nullified by exhaustion. The masters had been fiercely disputing the sharing-out of the Borth costs with him: '[I am] so tired, and so worried... I shall want a secretary for the next three months and a lawyer at the end. My letters are such a heap... I write

---

[1] Thring subscribed £30 himself and other masters followed suit.

[2] Hodgkinson, whose recruitment to the Lower School was now feeling the effects of the school's prolonged absence, wrote that it was 'very disastrous to me that the school [is] not returning'.

[3] For Thring himself, it would prove to be a mixed blessing – see ch. 20.

from 10 to 1 daily without stopping'.[1] He and his family spent Christmas in Borth, and on Boxing Day he was back at work, writing to the parents that there would be no return to Uppingham yet.

The 1877 New Year brought the dramatic news that Barnard Smith, the RSA chairman, had himself died of typhoid on 29 December. Thring's reaction to this irony was unyielding: 'Poor fellow! He has fallen a victim to his own obstinacy and delusions. It is fearful to be suddenly taken away whilst doing wrong'. The shock of their loss stirred the other RSA members: during February all the existing drains were flushed and work on the additional sewers and the new water supply accelerated. Wales continued to protest, and after 'an astonishing exhibition that the Rector has made of himself' Thring was briefly tempted to agree to Bell's suggestion to stand against the Rector in the next RSA election – but he eventually thought better of it, deciding that it was a time for olive branches. In an acknowledgement of all that Bell had done for him, he also promised Bell that if the popular Dr. Childs tried to start his own practice in Uppingham, he would do nothing to support it.

****

Back at Borth from 19 January 1877, the boys quickly experienced the full force of the Atlantic winter, but Thring was determinedly cheerful. 'It is an unspeakable relief to me that we spend another term here', he wrote to an old friend, 'this year has been to me a year of wonderful deliverances'. He added an analogy which he would use many times in later years, the parallels between the school at Borth and the peripatetic existence of the Old Testament Israelites: 'I [now] understand the book of Exodus in a way I never did before'. In his diary, however, he contrasted all the boys' opportunities with his feeling that 'we (i.e. the staff) are the main sufferers'. Some wives and children had failed to return from Uppingham after Christmas (anticipating the eventual return), and others had moved to warmer accommodation in Aberystwyth.

It was becoming increasingly difficult to keep the adult community united, but the school community in Borth was again brought together by adversity. A three day storm which coincided with extreme spring tides caused widespread flooding and damage. Huge stones were flung up on to the main street; the railway embankment was breached and 150 sheep drowned. Boys' books and trays of food blew away as soon as the hotel doors were opened. Men in waders rescued people trapped in their homes,

---

[1] Thring, 20 December 1876: 'The inside of my head feels as if I was growing a fleece there...'

along with the matron and one lone patient in the isolation hospital. As roof tiles flew off around them one night, Thring joined some boys in the hotel attic, plying them with biscuits to prevent them being frightened. Next day 'it was a very fine sight to see the sea come in like a great wild beast, twisting and swirling and foaming under the fierce wind'. He acquired old railway sleepers as a makeshift path between hotel and schoolroom and 'I set all the school at work to help the people [clear up. It] was a grand thing for them to do'.[1]

In the spring, with mains water flowing in and new drains in place in Uppingham, it was agreed without dispute that the summer term would begin there on 6 May. Thring had mixed feelings about the prospect of leaving Borth. There had been so many uncertainties over the past year and now, determined to tighten their grip on him, the trustees had resumed their old habit of questioning his claims for expenses.[2] On a walk with Skrine he confided his fears about the debts he had run up, but he was emphatic that having learned so much from all the ups and downs of the past year, he believed he still had plenty of good work ahead of him.

On 28 March he gave a long lecture at the new University College of Wales in Aberystwyth. Unsurprisingly he took as his theme 'Education and True Life', drawing repeated cheers as he emphasised that 'inward power' was more valuable than cramming children with facts and pleasing governments. An early Easter meant that the school was still in session and his sermon reflected on its time in Borth as one of renewal, with the anticipation of 'new life that is to come [with its] fresher, greater power'. A week later, with the boys gathered at their final Sunday service in Borth church, he recalled the 'circle of death' from which they had escaped a year earlier and the deliverance which their experience represented. He wanted 'this last day [to] be also a day of birth to the truer life with our risen Lord'. There was a farewell concert in Aberystwyth, the boys returning by special train with 'a good deal of uproarious merriment', and performances of Mendelssohn's *A Midsummer Night's Dream*.

On the final day of term he wrote a long letter to Parkin. With farewell celebrations only a few hours away and his sixth form doing their English exam in front of him, he described his complex feelings:

---

[1] Mr. Lewis from the Post Office sent a letter praising the boys' work. A campaign began for a higher sea wall.

[2] Having postponed approval of the year's accounts until Thring sent them more details, the trustees now required that he 'state each term what sums be required for plant and apparatus, and that he make special application to the trustees before incurring any expenditure beyond the amount granted for this purpose'.

'Sorrow predominates, at going back to my prison at Uppingham...
leaving this free bright shore, these glorious hills, the hearty welcome
and the helping hand of the people here... [but we have] brought this
wonderful year to a successful close, and been permitted a great
deliverance ... I hope to hunt for shells on the beach with Mig (Margaret)
this afternoon; we have a beautiful spring day'.[1]

That evening, almost the entire village turned out for processions,
flag-waving, songs and speeches. One farmer recalled Borth's fear of the
'invasion' a year earlier; if disease ever struck Uppingham again the
school would be welcome to return. Others praised the clearing-up work
after the storm. Thring spoke about school-village co-operation as an
example of life-power: 'It is not the last time I hope to be in Borth
(applause)... I hope to come back next time, not as an exile, but to spend a
happy holiday among my friends here (loud cheers)'.

The boys left next morning[2] and he wrote in his diary of a 'grand page
of life turned, the glorious chapter come to an end'. Before departing
himself he wrote a second long article for *The Times*, recognising all the
kindnesses they had received and describing 'the shore [now] silent of boy
voices, a great stillness out on the sands, the campaign over and a strange
struggle closed'. Skrine recorded that some staff stayed on for a few more
days, somehow unwilling to let the place go, although its silence was now
broken only by the ever-present seagulls and the workmen's hammers
dismantling the wooden schoolroom: 'The village has returned to its old
solitary nothingness'.

Thring often said that Borth had been the happiest time of his 34-year
career: 'the only time in which there was any sense of free work'. He had
been so popular there that new mothers named their children after him.
The experience had confirmed much of his educational thinking,
especially his belief in the essential goodness of human nature and the
importance of trust.[3] His Old Boys and most parents had given him

---

[1] 'Many of the trustee questions have been settled...' Parkin later omitted the
second half of the sentence: 'and Mr. Wales with all his cunning has been
[re]buffed in his efforts to enslave the school or ruin it'.
[2] Skrine: 'By the end of the week the pupils were gone – to the sorrow of an old
colley (sic) dog named "Borth" which attached itself to a group of pupils and
followed them down to the station as they left to catch their train'.
[3] See Castle E B: *Moral Education in Christian Times* (1958) p.318: 'One of the
tests of a good school community is its capacity to respond sensitively to trial and
crisis. [Borth] was a remarkable testimony to the spirit which Thring and his staff
had developed in the school: there were few schools in England at that time
which could have survived such a test'.

unqualified support. He hoped Borth might spell an end to the school's previous drift towards philathleticism. Not only had it forced Uppingham's public health issues, but he saw it as a year that 'stands alone in the history of schools'.

Despite all the demands on him he returned from Borth in much better physical and mental shape than during his low-point in the early 1870s. Its restorative effect was confirmed in some of the *Borth Lyrics* (set to music by Paul David) which he wrote the following year, one of which described his impressions on arrival:

'Sweep, glorious wings, a-down the wind; fly, swallow, to the west
Before thee, life and liberty; behind, a ruined nest.
Blow, freshening breeze, sweep, rapid wing, for all the
Winds are thine. The nest is only clay'.

Notwithstanding the euphoria it had been a close-run thing. As a single term's exile extended to a year, pupil recruitment had been difficult: numbers dropped from their peak of 340 to 299. Morale had been perilously low at times and he had not always managed to carry his colleagues with him. Later Skrine confided to his own diary a view of events that is strikingly at odds with his upbeat account in *Uppingham by the Sea*: claiming that Thring had taken the masters for granted and failed to unite them into a team, seeing every disagreement as 'treason' and taking too much of the credit himself for what had been a collective achievement.[1] It is hard to know how to interpret this *volte-face*, although other masters confirmed that Borth had often been 'a horrid time'.

Even so, the epic dimensions of his two year battle against epidemic and extreme adversity further enhanced Thring's reputation. The experience stretched his psychological resources to the limit, bringing out the best in him. It also tested, and ultimately confirmed, his faith that God had given him 'a great deliverance' – though he had yet to face its full financial consequences.

****

---

[1] Skrine, 1883: 'Had he spoken to the masters as he spoke to the boys (whom he quite converted to endurance and cheerfulness), we should not look back [feeling] that a heroic enterprise had in truth a shabby lining of timidity, sulks, half-heartedness and even cross-purposes. "Treason" would have been its name at headquarters'. Cf. his book after Thring's death: 'Thring had to face an external danger which threatened to invade and overthrow his twenty years' work, and to face it almost alone, or with men, who, if they followed, followed him trembling'. Perhaps the diary reflects how in 1883 Skrine had career frustrations of his own.

Thring returned to Uppingham on 24 April 1877, with a mixture of cheerfulness and foreboding:

'Thankfulness to God for a page turned and closed; intense dislike of the place, mixed with a feeling of being home, and master once more in my own house; the old constriction of stomach and feeling of dread, mixed with a sense of no longer being at the mercy of others, and subject to the racket and disturbance of hotel life'.

Once term began, relieved townspeople celebrated the school's return by hanging streamers, bunting and evergreen arches across the streets, along with banners bearing messages such as 'Welcome Home' and 'Flourish School: Flourish Town'.[1] There were two more evenings of processions, bands and speeches. He was given an illuminated address - to which he responded with a speech emphasising that 'we are united now as we never have been before'. Only Rector Wales held back, initially declining to have the church bells rung. In Thring's diary it was 'a grand demonstration... a new start in life here'. Letters poured in from elsewhere – including one from a fellow-headmaster who thought he 'deserved to be hung all over with Victoria Crosses'.

He had to get down to work immediately. There were nearly 100 new boys (either joiners at Borth or new that term) to settle in, and still some sanitary concerns. Some householders were being slow to abandon their cesspits and link their properties to the new sewers. The water company's new supply proved fitful, sometimes providing only two hours' water per day in summer. There were minor outbreaks of scarlet fever, smallpox and even typhoid for another decade and the town struggled to pay off its huge new loan to the LGB. The RSA, which had warned so repeatedly that ratepayers would pick up a very substantial bill, was proved right – and as owners of large properties, the housemasters could not escape significant rate increases on top of all their Borth costs.

Having briefly been free of overdraft in 1874-5, Thring was again well over £3,500 in debt after Borth. As a result he now faced a dilemma over tactics with the trustees: if he was reticent about his money problems he would recoup little or nothing, but if he admitted them he would merely draw attention to his vulnerability. Despite feeling 'harassed out of all fitness for human society' by his employers' recent equivocation, he knew that he must try to work with them.

---

[1] It had been a hard winter for the town: at the annual spring fair in March, 'not much business was done'.

He finalised the new *Statement* which they had asked for. It was less confrontational than his 1872 version, and it assumed that the Trust would gradually assume responsibility for all properties used by the school (although not the boarding houses), refunding the masters for their earlier investment. However, he could not resist listing £22,000 of 'important and urgent' projects, including the purchase of strategically important land and property; the rebuilding of his own boarding house; better facilities for music; a new library, museum, swimming pool and a larger sanatorium; a fives court for joint town-school use; additional scholarships and accelerated repairs to all existing buildings. He proposed increasing fees and charges to pay for it all.

The trustees' reaction to his plan was distinctly cool. When they received the first version of it, the school was still at Borth and they had no guarantee that it would ever return. They had long resented Thring's tendency to plead poverty whilst proposing ever-more ambitious schemes. It was a time of economic downturn with uncertain future pupil numbers.

Now, with the school returned, they sensed Thring's vulnerability – and their opportunity to assert themselves.

Publicly they argued that never having formally sanctioned the move to Borth, they had no responsibility for its costs, which should be entirely borne by the masters. They also stated that all major financial financial decisions had now to be approved by the Charity Commission: a valid position given all the recent changes to the oversight of endowed schools. Privately, they resolved to concentrate Thring's mind. In June 1877 they postponed consideration of the main Borth costs, merely agreeing to refund any outstanding travel expenses for the day boys. In October they passed two motions of censure on Thring: for a failure of accounting procedures and for excessive spending on concerts and musical instruments. They also demanded a full inventory of property and equipment owned by the Trust and the disposal of any surplus items. In January 1878 they reminded him that they had no responsibility for any unapproved repairs or other work on buildings. In future there must be invoices to back up all claims, which a trustees' committee would examine, item by item.

They also took a fundamentally different stance from Thring on how to increase future income. He wanted the tuition fee raised from £30 to £40, whereas they preferred that the housemasters should take in extra boarders, at least until all the Borth costs had been defrayed. Thring felt he could not win either way: trying to expand boarding numbers during the late-1870s recession might be difficult, but if he succeeded it would further compromise his aim to keep school numbers around 300.

The masters had regularly lobbied Thring over the years to be allowed to increase their numbers (and their profits): it was this argument that had contributed to Witts' departure nearly fifteen years earlier. This time, led by Usher Earle, they solidly backed him, declaring that expansion would 'destroy the school'. They claimed that their houses were completely full and that, having carried out Tarbotton's recommended improvements and then helped to finance the move to Borth, they had no funds left to extend their properties.[1] They further suggested that a £10 (33%) increase in the tuition fee would allow for a contingency fund, not only to pay off outstanding debts but also to raise their salary levels at least a little towards the vastly higher ones allegedly paid to their counterparts at Rugby.[2]

The trustees, distinctly nettled, again prevaricated and hid behind the Charity Commission – whereupon Thring petitioned the Commissioners himself in April 1878, describing yet again how contributions from the masters over many years had made them effectively the school's second founders. He claimed that reduced fee income from recently lower numbers, together with the added costs of Borth, amounted to nearly £10,000. Furthermore, the amount so far reimbursed by the trustees was paltry: considerably less even than the proceeds of the Liverpool parents' fighting fund. He justified to the Commission all the proposed additional spending listed in his 1876 *Statement,* rejecting the idea of additional boarders and showing his clearest recognition yet of the fundamental problem that Borth had highlighted: the impossibility of carrying on the school without a major new or additional source of of funding.

He convinced the Commission, which agreed to the tuition fee increase – although not for day boys. It was in no doubt that although the trustees had not formally agreed to the Borth venture, their acceptance of it must be assumed, and it suggested that in the long term the trustees should buy up the boarding houses.

The trustees agreed to accept the fee rise, their initial reluctance now assuaged by the prospect of increased income, to be used at their discretion once the cost issues outstanding from Borth had been resolved.

---

[1] Although the school roll shows that 66 new boys joined during the year at Borth, given the downturn in numbers compared with the peak in the early 1870s, the claim that houses were all full seems hard to believe.

[2] March 1878. They alleged that both the actual sums paid and the differentials between the top and bottom of the salary scale dramatically disadvantaged them. The housemasters were also conscious that their counterparts at Rugby enjoyed much larger profits because Rugby houses averaged 45 boys, compared with Thring's insistence that at Uppingham the limit should be 30. See Hinchliff, *Temple* p.115.

In doing so, however, they failed to realise the extent to which Thring himself would also benefit through increased capitation fees.[1] In October they finally approved a final settlement of specific expenses for each individual master, well short of what had been claimed: barely 50% in Thring's case.

For a full eighteen months Thring's time and energy were sapped by this issue. In 1878, he was frantic with worry: 'Things are very bad now, but I have had that wonderful Borth miracle, that passing of the Red Sea, and am strengthened. Yet I fear stripes don't make an apostle, and St. Paul would have looked at my bank-book with calmer eyes, and better digestion than I can bring up to it'. Even in 1880 his bills appalled him and they brought back his old problem of stomach cramps and sickness.

As he struggled to balance his books, there was one particularly painful personal sacrifice: the family visit to Ben Place in 1877 was their last.[2] Several of their holidays thereafter would be spent in Borth but much as he loved it there, it was not the same. As he left Ben Place for the last time he contemplated the beauty of its surroundings in a farewell poem:

'What happy spirit breathed upon thy birth,
Thou youngest child of dreamland, foundling sweet,
In whom the charms of age and childhood meet,
 Thou little plot of grass, dear ring of earth?
Who gave thee thy twin lives? One full of mirth,
The voice and dance of ever prattling rills,[3]
One solemn with the silence of the hills;
Strange joy, strange peace within thy tiny girth...'

---

[1] Under the New Scheme he received a proportion of tuition fee as capitation income: see ch. 20.

[2] He told Parkin in 1878 that a letter from his local bank described him as £3,517 overdrawn: a 'large amount'.

[3] Streams.

CHAPTER SIXTEEN

CHILDREN OF GOD

THRING'S educational concern for pupils of all ages and abilities reflected a deep spiritual conviction that each of them was a child of God. However much his faith emerged through his lessons or his assemblies and evening prayers in the house, he saw his role in chapel as the defining focus of his work and he played the leading role in the worshipping life of the school community.

Chapel gave him much more than a sense of occasion or a chance to dominate: it strengthened his faith and confirmed his sense of destiny – even if he sometimes passed the time by memorising boys' names and faces when others were reading psalms or leading prayers. Skrine and Parkin both wrote of his certainty that by saving boys' souls he was doing God's work. He told Parkin that it was 'hopeless to think of a first-rate school in which the headmaster has not powerful religious influence'.

His book on Life-Science revealed a simple faith: one which was untroubled by contemporary scientific ideas, which he believed ran not against but parallel to spiritual truth. Preaching in 1884 he condemned those who tried to suppress new discoveries: if God counted nothing in His own creation as unclean it was not for man to rebuke Him. Thring's Bible contained a jotted-down reminder that 'God requires us to take His teaching, obey it, test it, thus find it true. Man a pupil, not a judge'.

His decision to enter teaching rather than parish work was prompted by the desire to lead a small community rather than becoming caught up in a much larger organization. It also reflected his impatience with theological niceties, which he defined as 'the religious etiquette which prescribes sixpences where pounds ought to be given'.[1] He believed that 'history knows no laws, human or divine': the undergraduate who had included Richard Hooker's pleas for religious moderation in his *Index Rerum* became the adult who refused to fast in Lent and who saw celibate communities of men as too cowardly to face the real world.

---

[1] According to a colleague: 'Of theological shibboleths, of pious phraseology... Thring spoke [with] profound contempt. Matters of ecclesiastical ceremony... were to him unimportant. But in essentials no man was more reverent... His attitude towards the doctrines and discipline of the Church of England was one of loyal devotion [but] religion was to him not a thing to be criticised, dissected, formulated'.

He declined to have the chapel consecrated for fear that the local diocese and Rector Wales would have more control over it, and although normally deferential to senior churchmen he could become very animated if any bishop dared suggest moving the annual confirmation service into the parish church. The chapel's unconsecrated status also allowed him freedom to stay aloof from church disputes about how worship should be conducted: his services contained minimal ritual and he resisted the introduction of the Athanasian Creed – not because he agonised himself over its explicit statements about the Trinity (as Arnold had done) but because he feared that they might prove divisive amongst his colleagues.[1] This in turn reflected his belief that 'more schism has come into the world from inside the Church… than from any difference of opinion outside'.

Masters had to attend chapel every day because chapel reinforced the boarding community's sense of identity. This aspect of monasticism attracted him greatly: it was another echo of the Old Testament Israelites whom he so much admired coming together to praise God. He told the boys that chapel was 'gathering into one for us the heart-life of the school, as the Temple did for them; it is the central point of our life, to which in after years your memories will go back most fondly, and cling to most enduringly'. Despite his tone-deafness he strongly believed in the uplifting power of hymn-singing: he and Hugo Harper, Sherborne's headmaster, compiled a hymn book for their two schools to which Thring's brother Godfrey contributed.

He read the lesson and the Commandments deliberately slowly and for maximum dramatic effect – greatly impressing visitors but enabling the boys to mimic his mannerisms and tone of voice later on. Believing strongly in the power of prayer, he expected the boys to kneel down and join in: it was '[just] *possible* to imagine a kind of common prayer from a congregation sitting, but not possible even to imagine common prayer from a congregation silent. Silence is a most fearful form of taking God's name in vain'. Prayer instilled conviction in people and it needed to be communal: 'We come to inspirit one another, to breathe fire into our fellow-worshippers, to receive fire from them'. However, prayer made for qualities in individuals as much as communities: 'When once any man has quietly tried daily with prayer, to live like Jesus Christ, he will soon begin

---

[1] The Athanasian Creed includes a declaration of the equality of the three persons of the Trinity. When the school chaplain expressed misgivings about this creed, Thring told him 'to let well alone. From the nature of my investigations into Life-Science I probably object to it far more strongly than you do; but as a matter of obedience to Church authority I see no difficulty whatever in accepting it'.

to catch some of the certainty of being like Him hereafter; a very different thing from believing in religion'.

As a strong believer in the sacraments himself he saw large numbers of confirmation candidates as a sign of the community's religious health.[1] Most boys who entered the school at 13 were confirmed in their second year, after a confirmation week in March or April which began with his inaugural Sunday sermon. He addressed separate year-groups each night, telling the youngest boys that in leaving childhood they were like the Israelites crossing the Red Sea: free from original sin and now walking at liberty as the sons of God. They must be pure and manly soldiers of Christ. He emphasised to confirmation candidates how God had fed the Israelites on their journey: the boys too must use their gifts well, showing 'true courage and true manliness'. Every group was warned that 'secret poisoners' would be expelled if they practiced indecency. Sex was not a curse, but lust was. Women should be treated with respect: 'It is manly in a man to be pure, as it is womanly in a woman'.

A visiting bishop (usually one of his many ecclesiastical friends) conducted the confirmation service on the third day of confirmation week. That evening Thring would address all the older boys at a communion service and the week was formally closed on the following Sunday when he again preached to the whole school, describing confirmation as the boundary between preparation for battle and eventual victory in their lives. He reminded boys confirmed in earlier years of their promises, again emphasising the need for purity and urging them to read their bibles every day and attend communion regularly. He also held a one-to-one interview with every confirmation candidate. These encounters could have a striking effect even on those with chequered disciplinary records. One boy, 'not of the finest type' according to his contemporaries, returned to the dormitory after his interview declaring that he would never say another word against 'Old Thring' as long as he lived.

Once confirmed, he expected boys to receive communion regularly, just as the Israelites had received manna from heaven. He was elated when over 75 participated voluntarily a week after the confirmation in 1859. Communion was to be given only at whole-school services. When the masters suggested a separate, voluntary one he vetoed the idea because it would create two tiers of pupils. He added caustically that the proposal seemed to suit the masters better than the boys.

---

[1] Notes found in the back of his three-volume bible state that 'Everyone must be a communicant'. The 1859 service was at Peterborough Cathedral, before the chapel was built. Thring had set out with boys at 7am.

In parallel with his view of classroom teaching as a graduated process which drew out talents whilst not forcing too many facts into a young mind too soon, a pupil's spiritual journey through life offered infinite possibilities from small beginnings. He was far more attracted by the idea of original righteousness than original sin because *True Life* consisted of a long succession of choices. If the schoolboy steadily developed a good judgment – doing in each moment what he felt to be right – he would carry the habit with him into the momentous decisions that he would have to make as an adult, especially about what God wanted him to do with his life. He emphasised that 'life is nothing by itself, only a quiet, daily, ceaseless, little progress, a steadfast belief in a good cause, a working every hour the work of that hour because it is right and good, knowing nothing of what will come of it'. All through life Truth was 'the doing what we know to be right each moment'.

The same idea appeared in a sermon on *The School and the Ship of Christ* (another often-used analogy): 'If but for ten years, this our ship, with its crew, could look on the lives of all as given into each other's hands, and stamp out school tricks and school iniquities, and make the cause of truth their own, it would alter the whole world'. This philosophy of accumulated goodness through small individual actions gave rise to another of the 'water' analogies so frequent in his poetry: 'Life touches life, and passes on in silence, invisible, into other lives, even as rain that falls gently on the earth, and seems to pass away until the harvest comes, and speaks of a hidden, wonderful spread of unseen goodness'.

He preached most chapel sermons himself, carrying each one up into the pulpit in his left hand in a purple embroidered sermon-case. Delivered with passion and directness and using powerful adjectives and variance of tone, these homilies – like his lessons and prayers – were shaped by his sense of theatre. Anna, who (as his secretary) perhaps heard or copied out more of his sermons than anyone, believed that there was no-one to match him: he embodied 'the peace that passeth all understanding'.[1]

Many of his sermons had conventional titles: 'Lost opportunities'; 'Noble dreams are true'; 'Half-heartedness'. Unsurprisingly, many of them centred around the word *Life*: 'Seeds of life'; 'Life the sculptor'. He

---

[1] One Old Boy met Thring at a wedding many years after leaving the school: 'He greeted me – "Well, Master James, have you forgotten the old place altogether?" "As it happens", I answered, "only yesterday at luncheon [two of us] were discussing a sermon of yours, which you have probably forgotten". "Which was that?" Thring asked. I told him: "A sermon about Christ before Pilate in the Judgment Hall." "I remember it perfectly," said Thring, "it was a grand sermon"'. Some sermons were reproduced as pamphlets.

preached about Christ as the light of the world no fewer than five times in the decade 1864-74, and there were repeated explanations of the Fall, Atonement and Incarnation.

Some sermons – 'A sower went forth to sow' or 'The kingdom of God is like unto a grain of mustard seed' – drew familiar and predictable conclusions. 'Maiden spirits waiting for a happy life' was an exposition of the parable of the wise and foolish virgins with a call for patience to wait for dreams to be realised. Others were more obscure: 'Balaam the son of Beor hath said' was a text drawn from an obscure narrative in the Book of Numbers, around which he preached on three successive Sundays. 'Who is this uncircumcised Philistine?' was a post-Borth retrospect about the faithful being rescued against all the odds. A few titles catch the eye: 'Public hangmen and scavengers' explained how, if ungodly men exercise power, they act as a sword of judgment on communities which deserve one.

Four hundred sermons survive in the Uppingham archives, painstakingly prepared beforehand and carefully stored afterwards. Only a few are from his early years but several were delivered more than once, a note being made on each one of its date so that no boy should hear the same sermon twice. He usually spoke for about ten minutes, keeping to time by writing out his thoughts in small booklets with a fixed number of pages. Because he meditated on his text for some time, only then writing what he would say in a great outpouring rush, he needed very few amendments other than to add vertical pencil-strokes to indicate pauses: usually one or two, but for the occasional moment of silent drama, three. There was often an acute congestion of ideas and words on the final page which must have made them difficult to read and even harder for his congregation to follow – especially smaller boys already struggling with his eclectic assortment of epigrams, analogies and definitions.

He had no time for preachers who lacked passion and he frequently appealed for an act of commitment. There was no sadder figure than 'the rich young man, whom Jesus loved as He looked on him, and gave a call to become one of His chosen apostles, but who went away sorrowful because he had great possessions and did not come'. Decisions which were evaded led to 'the hunger of a lost life: what I want the littlest boy here to see is that he and everyone creates the world he lives in'. He urged boys to 'put away any thoughts of having to wait for great events... in order to do great work'. Even the meanest man could let God shape his life. Unlike many evangelicals he declared that joy and gladness were marks of the true Christian: 'Everyone should take pleasure from small things, because God has scattered little pleasures in everybody's reach, [and] God's will is only another name for man's happiness'.

Periodically he preached about heaven: 'A state of the heart, the power of seeing God and loving Him', or about earth as preparation for it: 'The place where we men are being taught to love God'.[1] Occasionally he would focus boys' minds on hell: 'Perpetual banishment from His presence and His love, with the corroding curse of ceaseless crime in the heart. If this is not hell, I know not what is'. One sermon began with a graphic description of death - complete with bodies, worms and dust and culminating in the stark realities of Judgement and the weeping, wailing and gnashing of teeth.

More often he spoke of the gentlemanly virtues, because he worried that the fruits of a Christian life – chastity, obedience, kindness and bravery – had become devalued in the modern world. He therefore harked back to the Christ-like virtues as seen in the English tradition of the perfect gentle-knight, urging the boys: 'Be worthy of Christ's friendship, be His gentlemen, spotless and true'. He developed themes on manliness in all its aspects: 'Character, not thieving'; 'Fierce idlers, weak characters'; 'Half heartedness'; 'The cheerful bearing heat and cold, hunger and thirst, work and hardship, pain and weariness'. Boys' amusements should be 'manly, and hearty and honourable, that there shall be no cheating; neither the cheating that steals time and cheats God's working day of its work, nor the cheating which in the game itself takes more than is right'.

Defeat could be glorious because it implied 'the not worshipping [of] success'. He attacked philathleticism in a sermon entitled 'God's secret police': 'Can we not be champions of manly life in the world? I must think that to be known through England for true manliness is a better thing than to have a name for cricket'. Boys' daily lives must centre on the courage to resist temptation because 'St John the Baptist [showed] complete mastery over his body... true liberty... true manliness'. There was the manly joy in honest work; in the virtues of dogged persistence and 'the happiness of honest weariness'. The whole personality developed only through 'true and sound common habits' and the looking-back each night on a day well and honestly spent. Boys must master self, bear pain cheerfully and use their talents in pursuit of 'the honour and the power of being a Christian, [and] the true nobility of being enrolled in the army of Truth and of Christ'.

---

[1] On other occasions: 'Religion is nothing else than the art of making others happy... we must get rid of the idea of heaven being a mere place. For all we know we are in heaven this moment'.

His messages were mostly positive because, as he told the new boys in 1870, the gospels put far more emphasis on holiness than evil.[1] However, they must also shun 'mock manliness', temptation and sin: 'the dreadful insanity of loving wrong things'. Like good, evil too grew from small beginnings: the momentary temptations of one minute more in bed or a little more food.[2] If unchecked such lapses could lead to 'an endless line of death'.[3] In his later years he spoke fiercely about 'the devil work of impurity', drawing on a catalogue of symptoms and consequences of ill-defined 'secret acts' and 'hidden pleasures'. He spared the boys no detail: whether sexual incontinence took place at school or in early adult life 'the poisonous breath of sin' corrupted the soul; it spelt misery for a boy's parents. It might also lead to an early death: 'Who is that crawling along, pale and tottering, with his face full of pox and death even already claiming on his brow? Can this be he, the young, the handsome, the strong, who some eight years ago was the envied champion of his school or college?'

He contrasted this unfortunate man with the healthy and upright followers of Moses: 'Young, brave and strong, clear of sensual lust' with their eyes fixed on the future. The Old Testament heroes should be role models – for himself as well as his pupils – and he saw much of himself in David, whose lack of doubt he yearned to emulate. He admired Jacob: neither of high status nor well-known, introspective and complicated, yet a young man who, after some spectacular setbacks and mistakes responded to God's voice and was given new confidence. Jacob's story demonstrated the value of failure; that lost battles could be won and lessons learned from sorrow; that a patient spirit reflected God's peace.

He had little time for conventional heroes, because he saw history not as a succession of great men but as the chronicle of the people of God. From Abraham to the Apostles, many were humble and ordinary. Christ was the only proper object of hero-worship: giving that status to anyone else was a sign of a 'poisonous' view of life. The true hero's work went unsung: he was content to work in God's service without public

---

[1] 'It is not scriptural to dwell on vice... instead of proclaiming true and happy life'.

[2] 'You sell life for minutes; the price is so small you know not you have sold it. Beware of penny bribes'.

[3] Preaching to Godfrey's parishioners in Somerset (1884), he described: 'How fine a thing the strength of the healthy young man is, how his muscles and arms, and all his body hold together, hard, and active... but let him begin to drink, and idle, you can see at once the actual working of death; day by day the body begins to fall to pieces...There is no sermon like the face of a drunkard to anyone who cares to read it'.

recognition.[1] One of the few contemporary heroes whom he named was General Gordon, but even Gordon paled beside an unknown warrior of the Chinese war, a common English soldier taken prisoner (with some natives) and the next day brought before the local governor. They were promised their lives if they would fall down and prostrate themselves before him. The rest did so and lived but he, an ordinary man, refused as an Englishman to bow before so mean a power as that – and so he died. A similar episode in Afghanistan prompted a sermon on very similar lines. He urged the boys to remember that 'the martyr is the man, who in a good cause faced defeat, and was defeated'.

Otherwise he rarely spoke on current events except to extol the expanding British Empire as an example of faith in the future. There was no jingoism in this statement: England led the world in enterprise and colonising activity and the boys therefore had huge leadership opportunities. He challenged them: the best schools were 'the leading power in England', and they were fortunate enough to attend one. This gave 'each and every boy, be he clever or stupid' a privileged opportunity to make the most of his life: 'O leaders of the world, in what will you take the lead [in setting up] the standard of trust, honour, truth?'

At times he drew local analogies: when describing how Christ healed the sick he invited the boys to imagine what a similar scene would have looked like in their own era as crowds gathered to watch in the market square or one of the local villages.[2] He could also build sermons around mundane incidents even nearer home. When he estimated that his 300 boys were spending from £1,500 to £2,000 a year on tuck, he contrasted it with their average contribution to the chapel collection. This was about one penny and it too was unmanly. Esau had sold his inheritance for a small portion of soup, but Esau had thought he was dying of hunger: 'He did not lounge into a shop as you do, full-fed, and buy what destroys you'. When there was a bout of 'borrowing' other pupils' books he roundly

---

[1] 'The true hero is he who most succeeds in hiding... his inward pain, who [does] great things with the cheery ease of ordinary life... and who makes the service of God look, as well as be, a happy service...'

[2] Matthew IV, 24: *His fame went throughout all Syria: they brought unto him all sick people*: 'What a number there must have been! Every village, town, district, had some inhabitants who had been healed... here, so to say, in Uppingham, there would be two or three, Preston, Manton, Lyddington, all round would have their well-known figures of persons healed... The whole Midland counties would have had them...'

condemned it as stealing, telling his congregation that they deluded their consciences if they made light of it.[1]

Through Borth, he acquired an additional Old Testament analogy. A week after returning home he suggested that the school's flight from Uppingham had been like the Israelites fleeing Egypt and crossing the Red Sea. A year later, having initiated an annual commemoration service, he recalled the scene in chapel on a snowy afternoon two years before, as the spring term ended prematurely after the second typhoid outbreak:

> 'We went out, unknowing where [or] what might lie before us. But we had… a trust to keep, a heritage that might not be cast away, as long as there was any hope of saving it. A new school might have come in time, but it would have been new. THIS school would have perished. So we went out, carrying with us the resolve not to desert our posts as long as hope remained. We hold our thanksgiving today for a great deliverance'.

In subsequent years his commemoration sermons returned repeatedly to the idea of the chosen few, keeping the flame of truth alive. In 1880: 'The deep waters parted and [the school] was saved: the school died and is alive again. Do not betray that life'. In 1882: 'Those who have been saved by a great deliverance have been saved for a great purpose'.[2]

He preached regularly at other schools and, like many headmasters, he published his sermons as a prospectus. The first volume appeared as early as 1858, aimed at making boys into 'trustworthy soldiers of Christ', who in their adult lives would become 'the genuine products of a time and system [who] may shine as candles, though lacking the range and brilliancy of stars; humble but useful'. A two-volume edition followed in the last year of his life. In it he hoped that both the sermons and the chapel in which they had been preached would remain 'a kind of home in, and round, which the thoughts of the young have clustered, so that in after years the man may send a brightness into them from his own soul, because his boyish recollections are bright'.

****

---

[1] 'You cannot cheat yourselves here. You have not passed from death to life unless you are kind and helpful, especially to the weak, who are just those exposed to tricks of this kind'.

[2] 'The river parted, and the Israelites passed through… In one week's time this present school would have been no more… that year at Borth stands alone in the history of schools'.

Thring kept a bust in his study of Martin Luther, that champion of salvation through faith, yet he always believed that the true test of Christianity lay in good deeds. It was a conviction gained from his association with the Macmillans and the Black Dragoons in Cambridge and his subsequent experiences in Gloucester, coupled with a belief that doing God's work was the best antidote to doubt.[1] Life should be spent trying to improve the lot of others: in one sermon he defined Christianity as 'not a belief that may be intellectual [but] a life incarnate in the man who lives it, and only so far as he *lives* it is he truly a Christian'. He regularly told boys to use their time well. They must not be half-hearted, as the foolish virgins waiting to welcome Christ had been:[2] 'It is not a question whether you are fit to die: the question is, are you fit to live? Is anyone better in the least *because* you live?' The idea of a chosen people – a community-in-endeavour – was central to his thought.[3] Everyone, however junior, was a part of this: 'The quiet manliness of the humblest of us here is important. We want to feel not that the sea is large, but that every drop in the sea is a life, and a power. No drop is more important than another'. In His charge to the apostles, Christ had launched a historical chain of good examples: 'Life calling to life across the centuries, ever dropping fresh sparks of life into hearts that live'. His school congregation represented the latest link in that chain: 'Brethren, what might not be done if the Holy Spirit of God was welcomed here?'

This style of challenge produced tangible results. As a newcomer to Uppingham (and before Rector Wales' arrival) Thring organised collections amongst the boys for the parish church and the housemaster-body donated to its restoration. Subsequent collections were made for the Blind College in Worcester and a church rebuilding scheme in Leicester. When Old Boys began to enter the mission field abroad there was fundraising through the chapel for them or their church-building projects in India, Canada, Australia and New Zealand, Natal, Japan and Honolulu.[4] He invited visiting speakers to give Saturday evening lectures, sometimes

---

[1] 'No man who does faithfully what he knows he ought to do ever doubts the truth of God'.

[2] 'They fooled away their eternal joy... Fool not away your lives... be thorough, be earnest, be true... lest you too hear at the last the fearful words, too late, too late... When you are idling your time [away], it is not your own life that you are using up and wasting, it is your Father's life you are wasting'.

[3] Everyone having 'the pleasure of day by day getting on [with others], finding new power and hope'.

[4] £30 to Worcester; £24 to Uppingham church. St Leonard's Leicester had an OU vicar. After a lecture by the Bishop of Brisbane (1871), the school adopted a mission church in Queensland.

with lantern slides. One Old Boy working with the Universities' Mission to Central Africa came three times, resulting in one of his contemporaries funding a scholarship for native boys there. In the 1860s a Mr. Warren from the Home Mission Society in America came twice to give lectures on the problems of tightly-concentrated urban populations there.

From 1864 George Bell of the Boys' Home in Regents Park was an annual visitor, describing his work and admiring Thring's concern that Uppingham pupils should not take their privileged status in life for granted. The pair were friends for more than two decades. Bell's vision was to provide farm work for orphans (in Barnet, some miles from central London) and after work 'a humble little home which has the tone of a happy united family, the master, his wife and their family living with the boys who are taught to be gentle and forgiving with each other'. It had strong overtones of Thring's vision for Uppingham's boarding houses, and when he asked the boys to support Bell's work he again reminded them of how much they spent in the tuckshop.[1]

Five years after Bell's first visit, a lecture from Revd. John Foy, Travelling Secretary of the Additional Curates Society, was the catalyst for something more ambitious. The Society's Anglo-catholic churchmanship was far from Thring's own but Foy presented a vivid account of his missionary social work in the East End of London, after which several boys went to Thring with the idea of 'a small offshoot in the outer world'. He told them to develop their ideas more fully: thus the idea of a school mission came quickly to catch the collective imagination.

The date (1869) is significant because it was a year ahead of the decade in which harder economic times would stir social consciences in many places elsewhere. Thus Thring provided the prototype, bestowing on the mission concept a mystical quality: 'A visible embodiment of that invisible somewhere: England has never before had this fastening of a school on to real life work in the world outside'.

The masters collectively gave £40 to the project, seeing it as the ideal way to open the boys' eyes to the plight of the poor. Earle felt that 'many boys come from homes of ease and luxury where they would scarce ever hear of the heathenish way in which masses of Englishmen were living'.

---

[1] 'Youth is the time to give. A boy can spare a penny out of a shilling more easily than a clerk can spare £10 out of £100. God can do without our subscriptions, but not without our belt-denial'. The home had begun in 1858 as the 'Boys' Home for the Training and Maintenance by their Own Labour of Destitute Boys not Convicted of Crime', in London's Euston Road. Uppingham gave it £15 per year. Thring offered Bell a scholarship for his son, but the boy eventually went to Westminster.

He suggested that not only would giving small sums of money help boys to feel that they were helping a good cause, but 'it could not fail to lead some of them to become missionaries themselves'.

For three years there were special chapel collections to develop a partnership project with the Society. Foy and the Bishop of London advised on possible locations (including Bethnal Green) before it was decided to focus on the parish of St Mark's Victoria Docks out of which the school would establish a mission off-shoot in North Woolwich. The parish was a huge stretch of marsh country bounded by the Thames to the south and the railway into Fenchurch Street to the north: reminiscent of the backdrop to Dickens' *Great Expectations.* Its housing was acutely over-crowded: when one housemaster visited the area he found 'plenty of dirt, plenty of children, plenty of pigs: all three to be found in the astounding ruts of the main thoroughfare'. It was also a moral and physical no-man's land: a twilight zone between the old rural life and newer affluent districts only a few miles away enjoying modern amenities.

The vicar, Henry Boyd, was a man of remarkable energy and talents and Thring persuaded Wynford Alington, one of his earliest pupils, to be North Woolwich's first missioner.[1] After a glittering school career Alington had followed in Thring's footsteps as a curate in Gloucester: Thring saw him as the personification of the all-round manliness that he regularly praised in chapel and he referred to him as 'scholar, and gentleman, and captain of the XI... a Christian hero brought into the sanctuary of God'.

The venture began with a school-room (also serving as a church) and a mission-room. Each Sunday it offered mattins and evensong and a Sunday school for 240 children. Weekdays activities included men's evening classes and a mothers' meeting group and clothing club. The school soon had 400 pupils on its roll, taught in two shifts because of its limited buildings.

A new church (St John's) opened in 1872 with a whole day's holiday so that dozens of Uppingham staff, wives and pupils could travel down to the inaugural service and a cricket match. The Bishop of Rochester preached a stirring sermon and Paul David's large choir sang impressively, whilst also obeying Thring's instruction 'to be careful to follow the [local choir's] lead, as we came to help and not to show off'.

---

[1] Henry Boyd (1831-1922): perpetual curate at St Mark's, Victoria Docks 1862-1874; Fellow of Hertford College, Oxford 1872; Principal 1877-1922; Vice-Chancellor 1890-1894. The Alingtons were an eminent family: Wynford's uncle later became Head Master of Eton. Wynford came to Thring's house in 1854 and was captain of the XI and the school before going up to Oxford.

Thring was especially gratified by large numbers of pupil communicants and by the Old Boys who stayed on to hear him preach in the evening: 'Alington must have felt his loneliness swept away as he looked on the array of his school-fellows. I trust to see this mission a great central pivot of Uppingham life'. He also greatly admired Alington's common touch and his ability to go out and read with (or take the gospel to) local men during the factory dinner-hour.[1] It was Alington's achievements that inspired Witts to leave his boarding house a year later, succeeding Boyd as vicar and using his substantial private capital to provide larger school buildings and a clergy house in North Woolwich.

The Mission soon began to attract other financial backers, eventually resulting in three new churches and schools for 1,500 children. After eight years Alington moved to work abroad, but by then the Mission had transferred to Poplar where there was a large mission church with clubrooms on two floors. One of its off-shoots was a temperance society.[2] Thereafter a succession of speakers came to the school to report on progress and there was support from Uppingham for bazaars and other fundraising activities. Mutual visits continued and in 1884 the school gave a concert there. The performers (who included Anna and Grace) travelled down to King's Cross by train and Skrine led a procession of ladies and 70 tenors and basses into the refreshment room, onlookers describing the scene as reminiscent of a children's story book portraying Noah leading the procession into the ark.

---

[1] In 1870 Thring wondered whether one day he might 'try once or twice a week expounding the Bible as I do in class here, and also perhaps an evening of good English literature... I think I could get hold of some [people] in this way. We want, I think, not only more social intercourse but also more Christian talk as distinct from religious talk [to interest] people in good views of common things. But whether it will ever be my lot to do any work of this kind, God knows'.

[2] Thring: 'None but those who know North Woolwich can understand what [Alington's work] as curate there means'. In 1878 Bishop Goodwin persuaded Alington to work in Zululand, where he died of typhoid a year later. The reredos in the Uppingham chapel was erected in his memory, and the south window of the school-room became the memorial to the Woolwich Mission. St John's was destroyed in the Blitz (1940), including its stained glass memorial window to Alington. The Poplar mission was run by John Skrine's brother Vivian. In 1898 the Mission transferred to the Mersey Mission to Seamen in Liverpool, moving again in 1937 to a Boys' Club in the steel town of Corby, only a few miles from Uppingham. With the 1944 Education Act and the new Welfare State, the Mission idea seemed anachronistic: schools then turned their efforts towards voluntary service schemes at home or overseas.

In 1885 the Mission appealed for funds and help from Old Boys in running a club for '80 working lads needing instruction and control'. A year later it expanded into 'a large and growing Friendly Society for lads from 13 upwards' offering boxing and fencing; singing groups and a band; 'quiet games, long division and reading classes and a library, as well as a family room, full of babies and families'. There were further appeals for books and magazines, and Anna and housemasters' wives collected second-hand clothing and boots for a mission shop.

A second concert was held in Poplar on an evening in July 1887 to mark Queen Victoria's Golden Jubilee. Its varied programme included not only violin works by Beethoven and choruses from Handel's oratorios, but also one of the ladies singing the popular song 'Sally in our Alley'. By then feeling his age, Thring stayed at home pleading exhaustion and the heat, but the impressionable Grace described travelling with Gale to the East End after the university match at Lord's, 'the roads lined with troops saluting the Royalties as they drove past. The houses hung with bunting and flags, the corridors and balconies crowded with people'.

Support for other charities continued too. At Founder's Day in 1879 the Uppingham School Society was formed, aiming to raise a capital sum of £300 for grants to former pupils involved in public, social or mission work.[1] Thring told its supporters to have 'the readiest hand and the most open heart to assist each other'. There was an additional scheme to endow clergy placements in remote parts of North America, to which he offered £50 from chapel collections, along with £10 of his own.

How pioneering was Thring in his sense of mission? Uppingham was the first school to establish such a venture[2] but others soon followed, some of them under the leadership of Uppingham Old Boys. Six years after Woolwich began, Clifton College became involved in similar work in Bristol in an area very reminiscent of Thring's surroundings in Gloucester and with Hardie Rawnsley as its first curate. Another Old Boy, Herbert Lucas, took on a similar role with Wellington College.

---

[1] Also known as the 'School Mission Society'. Thring was its patron. £182 was subscribed by 300 members in 1881: it gave grants to schemes at home and abroad – e.g. to an OU clergyman needing a reading and coffee room for his church; a bagatelle board and piano for a Working Men's Club; evening classes; and a grant towards a curate's stipend. Other beneficiaries included the Oxford mission to Calcutta, and the Zanzibar mission. It should not be confused with the OU Association (1911) to keep OUs on touch with each other.

[2] Sir Joshua Fitch stated in Thring's DNB entry that Uppingham was the first – but its Mission was based at an existing church. Winchester was the first to set up a free-standing venture (1876: in Bromley and later Portsmouth). Others included Radley 1881; Marlborough 1882; Tonbridge (where Rowe was headmaster) 1883.

Thring told his chapel congregation that its foremost duty in adult life would be to 'make the life of Christ live in the miserable haunts of our great cities in pure and comforting power, wherever God calls you to work, unselfish, giving happiness'. He was careful to avoid a Victorian tendency to equate poverty with wickedness, one sermon asserting that 'our uneducated and ignorant poor are as capable of truth as we are'. His first priority was to improve the slums and to offer educational opportunity; only then, if the opportunity arose, to evangelise.

He frequently wrote supportive letters to former pupils involved in mission work elsewhere. Harry Mitchell, vicar of a Lancashire mining town, wrote to ask the dimensions of a fives court.[1] Thring considered fives an ideal source of fun for Mitchell's parishioners and invited him to preach at the school. Mitchell doubted his ability, but Thring retorted that Moses had been no natural speaker either: 'Don't worship talk, worship life!' He also sent Mitchell all the profits from the second edition of his book *Theory and Practice of Teaching*, declaring that every word of it had been a gift from God: 'The powers we have are nothing: talents which God gives or takes away... So, dear fellow-worker in the vineyard, take the money to help your people to the light. Use it as you please'.[2]

He urged Mitchell (as he had Parkin) to take proper holidays. When Mitchell later decided to move on, Thring revealed his pre-occupation with his own future: 'The best work requires to be tested by a new direction. Death does it in time if promotion doesn't'. He was harder on another young ordinand, telling him firmly that doubt was an idle luxury which could be dispelled by working in a good parish: 'Many a theoretical difficulty gets disposed of in good work by God's blessing'. He added that if only his school colleagues had done some parish work before entering teaching, they would have had a better understanding of human nature.

In 1885 he spoke with pride about how successive generations of pupils represented 'a special regiment in God's army'. This idea had first come to him well over two decades earlier (1861), during Mr. Warren's first lecture to the boys about the slum housing conditions in America.

---

[1] A note on the back of a photograph of quarter-mile runners in 1863 reads: 'Mitchell, leading, collapsed within 2 yards of the tape. A boy – Gordon – passed him and won the race but C Childs, running third, pushed him over the line in front of himself, thus giving him second prize. It shows Thring's sporting ideals in practice. For Childs, see also chs. 14, 15 and 20.

[2] 'You are indeed a big headmaster. I learnt my most valued lessons in teaching as a teacher in National Schools when I was a curate. I send some notes on teaching, which may be of some service to you'.

At the end of his lecture Warren described what he had seen and heard at a hotel in France during his recent travels there. A boy, 'full of life and spirits', had been asked by his companions to make a long journey on a Sunday. He repeatedly resisted, saying that his headmaster would have disapproved of starting out before church. The others laughed, telling him that his headmaster was a good five hundred miles away, but the boy stood firm.

Warren then turned away from his audience and addressed Thring himself: 'That boy was from Uppingham, and that headmaster was you, sir'. That night Thring wrote in his diary: 'I could have burst into tears, I was so touched. The school cheered vehemently, greatly pleased'.[1]

---

[1] 150 years later, headmasters have to rely more on sanctions than on moral or religious arguments in the war against temptation – e.g. Jonty Driver, former Master of Wellington, writing in the magazine *Conference & Common Room* (2013): 'When one of the boys told me that he had been offered a joint at a party and had declined it (he said) because his headmaster was such a bastard that I'd expel him if he were found out, I reckoned I'd won a kind of victory...'

CHAPTER SEVENTEEN

ELDER STATESMAN

IN 1881 Thring celebrated his sixtieth birthday. The school had grown out of all recognition since his arrival and his boarding house, once the only one that the school possessed, was now one of a dozen.

He cut a rather different figure from the energetic pioneer of the early days, admitting that after 28 years in post and now five times the age of his youngest pupils he became increasingly tired after long periods without rest. It was a decade since his last cricket match and he was no longer the keen mountain walker of earlier years owing to painfully rheumatic hips - although he could still perform 'furiously' in the gentler dances at the bachelor masters' Christmas Ball. Yet he was far from finished: on a November day's walk when he caught sight of a gang of workmen levelling a cricket field, 'I went up and took a turn of digging for half an hour, and the exercise did me good'.

At times he was serene, with 'a strange feeling of rest in the midst of cares... of blessing come on the work, of true progress'. Visiting Cambridge as the University's special preacher and sleeping again in his old rooms in King's after thirty years, he felt the years roll back as if nothing had changed. A few months later he wrote to Parkin that the prospects for internal peace and unity in the coming year seemed better than ever before.[1] At other times, however, he lurched back into depression. He still felt claustrophobic in Uppingham: within weeks of leaving Borth he was missing its wide open spaces. He looked forward keenly to summer at Ben Place in 1877 not yet knowing that it would be his final year there: 'Right glad am I to find myself near the end of this term. Every day off is like a fresh spadeful dug away from a man in a landslip'. A year later, he returned from holiday speaking again of a life of chains, prison and unsympathetic town authorities.

Unfortunately he tended to remember his colleagues' resistance to him over the years rather than their support as, after over two decades of comparative stability, the old guard of masters began to change. William Earle, the Usher since Holden's day, retired in 1881 - the year when Thring turned 60. Always the cautious pragmatist compared with Thring

---

[1] 'Most unexpectedly, all the ground between the schoolroom and the West Road along the brow of the hill has fallen into our hands, so the school is now secure... quite full again for the first time since the Borth troubles'.

the visionary, Earle had long been cast by Thring as a covert trouble-maker; now Thring's resentment was compounded by the handsome leaving present and pension given to him by the trustees and approved by the Charity Commission. It reminded him of his own uncertain future, and he contirued to run Earle down privately for some years.[1]

He also fell out with Hodgkinson, whose selfless generosity had arguably saved the school during the mid-1850s and subsequently, and who left the Lower School in 1882. The precise cause of their falling-out is unclear (possibly it was over the age at which boys should transfer from Hodgkinson to Thring), but Thring could never let go of the fact that the typhoid epidemic had begun in the Lower School. He pointedly heaped public praise on its new master-in-charge even before 'Hoddy' had moved on; a year later he declined to give a teaching post to his former colleague's son.[2]

Increasingly, small issues gnawed away at him. When the wife of an 'obnoxious' member of staff brought two uninvited guests to his end of term garden party he considered her bad manners 'stupendous'. He scorned a longstanding housemaster for his 'quasi-religion and his medieval ideas about women' and he ranted on about 'the Earles, the Rowes, the trustees and the little stagnant country town pond which naturally bred such creatures and fed them', declaring that 'as I enter my 29th year of headship, I am struck with astonishment at the infinite donkeyhood... of the men I have had to work with'.

Some staff remained in awe of him. When a housemaster praised his vision for the teaching profession as inspirational, 'I really felt a new life was coming to the place'. Yet there were also signs that collective standards were slipping, with masters beginning to go their own way. An examiner's report criticised the mathematics teaching: he rejected its findings publicly, but privately he fiercely berated the masters for the fact that Mr. Eve's criticisms back in 1869 had not been addressed. He used the confrontation:

---

[1] 1881: £270 was subscribed for Earle's leaving present and the trustees voted him a pension of £150 p.a. Thring thought him 'treacherous as ever [with] a certain number of flies always ready to walk into his parlour'.

[2] Possibly the Lower School boys not going to Borth still rankled. In 1883 (a year after Hodgkinson left) Thring wrote to him: 'You never made a greater mistake in your life than when you were led away in those disastrous days of malice and treason to think I was not supporting you'. His successor Bagshawe, like Hodgkinson, had private means: just as well, as scarlet fever in the Lower School (1885) cost him around £2,000.

'To condemn in very strong words the inaccuracy in reading, writing, and pronouncing words which I said was so widespread as to have become a school canker, and that it had grown worse and must be put an end to. I referred to the unpunctuality of masters themselves... deliberate lawbreaking and neglect of duty... masters leaving lessons to collect their newspapers'.

They heard him respectfully but later he was challenged in a masters' meeting as to 'why fellows were doing music when they should be doing mathematics'. It was a symptom of declining morale, prompting Skrine to ask in his diary: 'How can educated men be led by a chief who, after years of work with them, sums them all up as incapable from first to last? If it were true, it would be folly to say it. But how can he *dream* it to be true?'[1]

At one point Thring became concerned that a recurrence of boils had damaged his power to vary his voice in public speaking. With uncertain health and the need to pace himself, he confided to Parkin his fear that all his old problems – boils, sickness, nervous indigestion – were returning. He knew he needed to relax more and he sensed his mortality: 'I am old, and the long days' torture is near at an end. My own special work here is done – or failed; my only prayer is that the Lord will let his servant depart in peace. It cannot be very long now'.

****

There was a much happier new dimension to his life within the town. The Uppingham Mutual Improvement Society had been founded in the 1860s, quickly acquiring a hall and large library. Despite their differences, Thring and Wales had been the prime movers in it and after he returned from Borth Thring was elected as its chairman. Recognising the proportionately very large amount of local land now owned or rented by the school, he outlined a plan to provide 'a well organised system of public recreation to promote the welfare of the town as a whole'.[2]

---

[1] Skrine's diary 1883: 'Serious annoyance caused by an unguarded complaint [Thring] made about the teaching, [saying that] no master in the school, not one, did either "hard work" or "mind work"'. Thring recognised privately that Borth had been a distraction; in the tough economic times in the early 1880s, any criticism must be addressed.

[2] The headmaster and the Rector were ex-officio trustees. Debentures were issued: Thring purchased much the largest number, and Wales was also generous. No evidence survives about Wales' reaction to being displaced. Marie Thring designed banners for the Society. Thring provided a cricket ground and helped to level it.

The plan was a great success with cricket and football matches and sports days; plays and concerts; a choral society and evening classes in art, cookery, arithmetic, history, elocution, chess and draughts. Horticultural exhibitions, an expanded feast week and dance, and a Christmas exhibition of local skills were organised, along with architectural and archaeological visits for the ladies and a lawn tennis club run by masters' wives which attracted 130 members. After observing how they dressed, Grace was heard to suggest that members might be collectively termed 'the Bloomers'. One of Thring's very last pupils remembered him 'with a lawn tennis racquet before a row of daughters of Uppingham tradesmen, showing the motion and actions necessary for them to acquire'.

He gave literary lectures and presided over the Society's various festivities: 'At Christmas we have a gathering in the great Schoolroom, when I give them tea etc. A coffee tavern is just going to be started, and we have little boys' cricket, and football clubs for boys under fifteen'. In January 1879 he exulted: 'I am getting on capitally with the town now: we have some 200 persons attending classes... I wound up the year by inviting all the [Society's] members to a conversazione in the great Schoolroom last week. 777 out of 2,070 came, all in fact who would (i.e. wanted to) come; we had pictures and music and microscopes for the young people; plenty of cake and tea'.

He saw it all not only as providing enjoyment but also as an act of witness, consistent with his long-held view that deeds spoke louder than words. As in Woolwich, 'the great law of spiritual life and truth is simple: see and do it, and [in] doing thou shalt see more'. He enthused about it to his favourite brother: 'Godfrey! I have at last succeeded in getting a recreation ground for the town, comprising gardens, bowling green, croquet ground and cricket field in a ring fence, and I hope to begin planting at once. I am very pleased at this, as I believe the first thing in these days is to provide good amusement, the second to preach'.

There were two other reasons for him to celebrate. First, as enthusiasm for sport flourished in the town, so also its more extreme manifestations cooled within the school. The hope that he had expressed at Borth was realised: the rudimentary games facilities and many diversions there had given this generation of boys a more balanced view of how to spend their afternoons. Expenditure on games slowed down as cricket, the main symbol of philathleticism, entered a less obsessive phase than in the 1870s.[1] To the regret of its supporters the London matches were quietly abandoned; even home fixtures were more sparsely attended, although Thring's daughters continued to devise and sew on new colours.

When, in another spectacular example of generosity by a master, Candler paid £1,220 for the extensive 'Leicester' field in 1878, Thring was determined to use it for pupils as a whole rather than only the elite few.[2] He was able to go on dismissing any idea that Uppingham football might be replaced by rugby: 'A disgusting game [which] violates the first principle of every true game to make skill everything and to minimise brute force'.[3] Athletics training (now overseen by his son, Gale) declined. He regretted that there were only sixteen takers for gymnastics, but he was thrilled by the fulfilment of a twenty-year ambition to build an indoor heated swimming pool in 1883, one of the first of its type in an English school.[4] Still unwilling to make the school answerable to any outside authority and disliking the contemporary militaristic view of manliness, he again warded off demands from Old Boys for a rifle corps. Personally he remained as interested in sport as ever, following England-Australia Test matches avidly – but as much for their ability to promote ties of empire as for their actual results.

At the same time there was a second great cause for private celebration: in 1879 Rector Wales retired and left the town. As Thring returned from his Borth summer holiday that year, he 'never felt so clear, so hopeful as now [because of] a great gain in my life: when I get back, the Rector will be gone, who has guarded the place like an octopus these last 20 years. He was the cleverest dead man I ever knew; his touch was death and he touched everything he could touch'.

****

---

[1] Uppingham's defeat by Loretto – a school half its size – was a traumatic blow to the fanatics. Stephenson, still the cricket professional, complained at the slackness of the boys but publicly he remained loyal to Thring.

[2] Candler rented the Leicester to the school for 21 years by agreement with the masters: 23 of them pledged annual payments of several pounds each to the cricket fund. When the trustees bought it later for £1,280, Candler donated his £60 profit to the Committee of Games for turfing and the planting of trees.

[3] Old Boys were still divided on whether they preferred the association or rugby union codes. Uppingham was becoming unusual amongst schools of its type in not having a rifle corps.

[4] It allayed fears about unhealthy local rivers – and at the outdoor site a boy had dived in, dislocating his neck in mud. The swimming pool proved very popular: boys could go twice a week and all learned to swim, but it closed from December to February, when the demand for the limited supply of water was at its peak.

Despite his ailments and irascibility Thring's career now entered an Indian summer. He was proud that no fewer than eight Old Boys gained Oxbridge fellowships in 1879: it would contradict those who thought him anti-intellectual. A year earlier at Founder's Day the Oxford Old Boys had pledged to present him with a portrait, after Nettleship made a speech declaring that they all 'remembered Uppingham and remembered Mr. Thring as a school which made them better and nobler for having been there, and a man whom they had been the better for knowing'.

Over Christmas and New Year in 1880-1 he sat for a well known artist, Cyrus Johnson, and as the final touches were put to the portrait he gained valuable day-time rest between a series of hectic evening dancing parties. He thought Johnson captured 'my patient, genial power which so many years of pain did not wear down' and he felt relieved that the artist had painted his face from the left, which to him seemed his less care-worn side. Anna (his secretary as well as his relative), was horrified that the picture revealed the habitually disorganised state of his desk, and he was amused by her reaction: 'It was such fun when Miss Koch was admitted to the first view. She entirely disregarded my picture and flew at the table, rearranging this and that. General opinion in the family is that it has not enough of the ruler in it [and] that it is too earnest and not bright enough in expression'.

The portrait was unveiled in 1881[1] as planning began for celebrations to mark the three-hundredth anniversary of the school's foundation in 1584. During 1883 Thring confided to Parkin that he was increasingly anxious about the impending festivities: 'Once I should have rejoiced immensely in it... there is to be a great gathering, and fuss, and subscriptions and glorifications... I think abuse is easier to arrange than praise'. By the autumn he was coming round to the idea. New decorations and stained-glass windows in the schoolroom, three of them representing Faith, Hope and Charity, were progressing well. In April 1884 he was again dismayed: 'I hate it all'. He wanted no triumphalism: 'When I think of... how little has been done, and that [it] will probably all be swept away in a few years, I have no heart in me any more for tercentenaries. How I should have exulted in it fifteen years ago. I am wiser now'.

His fears were unnecessary: the day passed off flawlessly, with the town again lavishly decorated. The visitors included three bishops (one of them his Eton friend, Mackarness) and former staff including Witts. Even Thring's predecessor Holden made a rare appearance, receiving a warm

---

[1] 'Our great day was a complete healing of any doubts that have existed about my work at Uppingham'. Johnson was a well-known artist. See illustration on front cover.

welcome from his own Old Boys who had always supported him in rejecting Thring's claims about the poor state of the school in 1853.[1] Lord Carnarvon unveiled some striking new friezes around the schoolroom, the work of Charles Rossiter (the drawing master) which depicted many of Thring's classical, biblical and literary heroes.[2]

Thring's speech reminisced about past struggles and triumphs and repeated some of his key principles: 'Two words – three – will do it. *Every boy* and *tools*. There you have the whole thing. We have never knowingly neglected any boy – we have always tried... to get the means of dealing with each boy'. One onlooker observed 'how happy everyone looked... [a] host of loyal boys, and old boys... as the little man who created and saved the present Uppingham sat in state, surrounded by bishops and noblemen who paid homage to his marvellous work'. He gained his greatest pleasure from the concert: an event at which the attention was turned away from him and which included a cantata *Under Two Queens* with lyrics by Skrine and music by Paul David, Beethoven's second symphony and some of Thring's school songs.

The Tercentenary briefly revitalised him. In December 1884 it was 'astonishing how this term I have felt lifted up into a new world of power and feeling'. He told Godfrey that he was especially pleased that his mother had lived to appreciate how widely his work was recognised. Yet he was glad when the celebrations were over: 'Thankful that we have escaped the poisonous breath of false praise, of numbers and intellect worship, and all I have striven against all my life long'. To Parkin, he wrote that 'the dreaded day passed off excellently well. V. pleased with all the publicity', but that he shuddered when he recalled the early days: 'The meanness of the early services in the parish church... opposition... debt'.

He intended the three-hundred year milestone to be an opportunity for a fundraising appeal. After the rapid developments of his early years less building had taken place since 1870 and he was especially keen to create a

---

[1] Holden was now living locally in retirement: his Old Boys wrote to the *Stamford Mercury* about how under-recognised he had been. Witts died soon afterwards, and Thring preached fulsomely at his funeral. The 4th Earl of Carnarvon, (1831–1890), was Secretary of State for the Colonies and became Lord Lieutenant of Ireland. Ten years behind Thring at Eton, he was a keen supporter of Empire – including Canada (see ch. 19).

[2] Rossiter was drawing master from 1873. A keen pre-Raphaelite, the work took him a year. The figures included Dante, Chaucer, Spenser, Shakespeare, Milton, Corneille, Dr. Johnson, Goethe, Scott, Wordsworth, King David, St John, Homer, Aeschylus, Herodotus, Plato, Demosthenes, Euclid, Pindar, Cicero, Virgil, Horace and Livy. He also designed nine stained-glass windows for the schoolroom, depicting scenes from school history.

better sanatorium. The appeal brochure portrayed him as a second founder, true to Archdeacon Johnson's principles and reminding would-be donors of what the masters had already invested (now claimed to be £91,000) whilst reiterating that there could be no work without 'tools'.

The appeal was a great success. As a result the trustees, who had recently used the increased tuition fees to take over the existing sanatorium from the masters,[1] were able to buy back the original schoolroom, thus easing Thring's financial worries. Rather than letting it be sold he had acquired it from them in 1865 after the new one had been built, using it latterly as a carpentry shop and art studio.

They might have done still more, but despite this olive branch he persisted in limiting their role strictly to trust matters. He spelt out his reasons in a letter to Parkin:

> 'No governing body ought to have any power to control or change the school. They should be watchful authorities appointed to see that the school work is well done and all things carried on in order, and to protect the school in case of need... In fact the system of governing bodies in England has in my judgment worked very badly for these two reasons: they are men without knowledge of their subject, and always must be; and they are to a great degree irresponsible. An easy appeal to a higher tribunal is wanted. This alone gives the professional men who do the work a chance of being heard'.

Legally and constitutionally, an impasse had developed. Unless headmaster, masters and trustees united in embracing structural change, the Trust had no legal power over any buildings that Thring or the masters owned. Thring ignored all advice to open discussions with them, including the cautionary words of Bishop Fraser of Manchester who wrote to him after the Tercentenary.

After declaring that 'such a life as yours has been has a special richness of example, and it has been a privilege to me to witness it', Fraser added: 'The only element of regret... was that people told me, on all hands, that in carrying out this work you had thought of everything but yourself; and when a man has "given hostages to fortune", he ought not to leave that consideration wholly out of sight'.

The bishop was sadly prophetic: worry about his future would haunt Thring for the rest of his life. On the surface all looked healthy. After the 1870s setback in numbers the school was now full again. Accounts for the mid 1880s suggest that it had begun to generate a reasonable annual

---

[1] 1878: together with the half of its mortgage outstanding. It was a sign of their increasing involvement, post-Borth.

236

surplus which was being ploughed into a reserve fund for capital development. However, nothing had been done to address the complex system of internal transfers of funds or to untangle Thring's finances from those of the school.[1]

Over the next few years he struggled on financially, wanting to have things both ways. He was determined to preserve his independence whilst craving the security that less independence might bring him. Even in his final weeks, the trustees would be vainly trying to adjudicate disputed scholarship contributions between him and the masters.

****

The boys knew nothing of all this. They sensed that 'The Man' (as this last generation of pupils referred to him) had mellowed somewhat and that being sent to him for punishment often resulted in merely being told off and sent away. The more perceptive ones surmised that he judged his power of personality enough to reform them without any sanction. Some boys found him 'old, distinguished and rather remote'.

Even so, he could still inspire awe and terror. He was furious when a classical picture on the schoolroom wall was defaced. He punished two boys who ignored a ban on carving their names on some new desks – not by a caning, but making them spend a whole afternoon in the woodwork shop inscribing their names on the hardest piece of wood he could find. When a group of boys aimed their peashooters from windows at members of a travelling circus parading through the streets in costume, he held an emergency assembly, dismissing everyone with the words: 'Now go back to your kennels, you dogs!' His 'jaws' (lectures) about behaviour became very long and he resorted to mass 'gatings' (boys being kept in) even more than in the past, still believing that the whole community must take responsibility for the sins of the few.

Although some of his friends thought his preaching powers were in decline,[2] one young boy wrote in his diary of the strong impression made by a sermon in 1883 on 'the presence of God amongst us here in chapel. We only seem to believe what we see, as the telescope shows us wonders

---

[1] Confirmed by a letter to Parkin from Sarah, who by then was managing the domestic side of Thring's house for Marie.

[2] Courthope H Bowen: 'He was neither very audible, intelligible, nor very interesting. It must have been very wearing to the boys, probably because he tried to explain and argue, [whereas] his real strength lay in pleading, exhorting or denouncing – in the region of the emotions rather than intellect'. For Bowen, see chs. 19 and 23.

in the stars, so one day God will reveal the wonders of the spirit world'. In the classroom he relied increasingly on his reputation and experience. His age increased the frustrating barrier between him and younger boys who saw him as a grandfather-figure and at whom he threw increasingly baffling questions.[1]

He still loved teaching the older boys, but his teaching changed little from year to year except in one respect: his new enthusiasm for visual stimuli. He credited Ruskin with 'having put me into a new world of observation, beauty, power, and progressive thought, which amounted to a new world'.[2] His classroom became decorated with autotypes (large photographs) showing great men from history, learning or science; views of the Alps or modern Rome; illustrations of animals and birds. He insisted to colleagues that pictures were important in 'giving honour to lessons' and he developed different subject themes – Roman, Greek and English – in each classroom as well as displaying photographs in the house dining hall.

He was very moved by expressions of affection and appreciation, and at a leavers' supper it was 'almost touching to hear my upper sixth telling me how happy they had been here, especially in my division (sic), scarcely able to speak for coming tears. When I think how I slang them sometimes I feel half inclined to laugh, half to cry, at their affection'. The effect of his one-to-one 'paternals' remained powerful[3] – as when one nervous new boy was greeted with the words: 'Do you dare to beard the lion in his den?' It would be surprising if the older boys universally enjoyed these encounters, because they could be highly emotional occasions. After he gave a fierce telling-off to a boy caught lying:

---

[1] This had always been a tendency of his, but he was now taking it to extremes – see example at the end of ch. 21.

[2] He met Ruskin only once, because he gave up Ben Place before Ruskin started spending much time in the Lake District. When they met, he thanked Ruskin for his 'noble' book on modern painters and thus 'for having put me into a new world of observation, beauty, power, and progressive thought'.

[3] These have to be seen in the context of their time. Manliness did not preclude displays of emotion. There was no repression of physical contact; crying was seen as no disgrace. See Hyam, Ronald: *Empire and Sexuality: the British Experience* (1990) p.72: 'Early Victorian men walked about arm-in-arm... they accepted romantic, non-sexual attachment in youth as part of the natural order of things [but later] there was a marked shift to a cult of the emphatically physical... Manliness moved first from chapel to changing-room... the qualities most unsparingly disparaged by late-Victorians were sentimentalism and a lack of sexual self-control...'

'On my shaking hands he fell on my neck weeping and kissed me, and I him. Now it is a glorious thing that wielding the power I do as the Head of this great school, and being such a potentate, the hearts of the little boys in the school should some of them feel towards me lovingly as to do this. I thank God for this sign that my work and life touch their hearts'.

Boys who came up to see him in less emotionally-charged circumstances at teatime were often offered a large chunk of cake, with another to take back for a friend. At other times he seemed increasingly distant from the realities of life. He was deeply depressed as he looked back on having broken the rule of a lifetime by striking a boy in anger: it had left him unusually torn between his natural inclination to see boisterous fun from a boy's point of view and his duty to set standards of orderliness for the community:

'To-night I caught five of my house making a row in their bedroom. I struck two of them, I believe, for the first time in my life, not that I was particularly angry, but to show my contempt and indignation at what they were doing. I am rather puzzled what to do to-morrow with them, as it is a very bad discipline offence, but one of them, indeed two, are very good boys generally, and it was but a lark after all, though if the house was in good order it would not be thought a lark'.

Whilst worrying over this apparent decline in good order, he was greatly perplexed about homosexuality: what he termed 'indecency crimes – a strange mysterious horror'. He had once believed that the school was virtually free of them: it is hard to know whether he was wrong; whether such incidents were now on the increase; whether contemporary definitions of manliness had changed or whether they just loomed larger in his mind. He preached increasingly fiercely against sexual incontinence in all its forms and he caned a number of boys for it as well as expelling four more in 1880.[1] In 1883 he gave the whole school 'a furious jaw about fellows watching [other boys] at the baths: called us a set of homos etc and said he would like to lash us like hounds', causing resentment from those who noted that the perpetrators had mostly been in his own house.[2]

---

[1] The sixth form petitioned against the expulsions. Parkin implies that he relented, having extracted a promise from the entire school that they would act against indecency, and stating that he would expel future offenders.

[2] Throughout the 1880s he warned that any boy found corrupting another or behaving indecently would be expelled. In 1886 four boys were punished for having 'an indecent photograph', and three more left after a master intercepted 'an indecent note'. The situation worsened in schools during his successor's time.

Yet he had not lost his sense of humour. When he gave away the Lower School prizes the youngest winner was so small that Thring saw him coming only when the boy's head suddenly appeared across the schoolroom table – at which point he became completely convulsed with laughter. He loved unexpected visits from Old Boys, weeping copiously at the arrival of a visitor (1881) who had left the school under a cloud many years earlier:

> 'He is now a clergyman, and he came to say he had often written to me, but always torn up the letters, and now he did not know how to speak. I told him he need not speak: it was written on his face that he had risen to higher things... When he got up to go, he stood with tears in his eyes, and said he owed his life to me, and all he had hoped for and [now] was'.

Another returner was given a less easy time. Long ago, as a boy in Thring's house he had flung a hockey stick out of his study window, accidentally killing Thring's tomcat which often sat yowling horribly on top of the wall outside. Thring launched an enquiry whereupon the boy owned up, stammering out the first excuse that came into his head: 'Please sir, the cat killed my s-siskin!' It was the only bird he could think of and Thring ordered him to return that evening with the body. The boy managed to buy a live siskin somewhere in the town; wrung its neck and stored it in his cold study. When he eventually presented it, Thring looked at it for a long time and then told him to go and bury it.

Now, revisiting the school for the first time in many years, this former cat-murderer found himself next to Thring on the first XI boundary. He re-introduced himself, suggesting that Thring would not remember him. 'Of course I do', replied Thring, shaking his hand, 'you killed my cat!' He then prodded his visitor in the ribs, asking: 'Tell me – *did* my cat kill your siskin?' The man owned up. Thring stared hard at him and chuckled: 'I *thought* that was it. My cat would hardly have wrung the bird's neck, but I admired the lie!'

Thring's fictional *alter ego* appeared 25 years after his death when E W Hornung (best-known as the creator of the *Raffles* stories) published his school novel *Fathers of Men* (1912). Much less celebrated than Rugby's *Tom Brown's Schooldays,* it was closely based on Uppingham where Hornung had spent the first three years of the 1880s. He admitted that its legendary headmaster, Jerry Thrale, bore a close resemblance to the sixty-year-old Thring, as 'the little man with the imperious air grew into a giant in his marble pulpit [with] a transfigured face and a voice both stern and tender':

'Plainest in his pulpit — no longer a little old man, but majestic, noble, and austere; or limping down the street — frock-coat flapping, top-hat inclined to the back of his head, a snowy spread of tie and whiskers joining in his wide, radiant, out-door smile; or jabbing a copy of elegiacs with his formidable pencil, or looking cold steel at the morning's offenders, one blue-veined hand in rest upon his awful armoury of canes. He really was a flogging judge'.[1]

At one point, Hornung's fictional hero, the misunderstood schoolboy Jan Rutter, gets into trouble and is sent to be questioned by the great man:

'Jan was left alone in the presence, and that instant became ashamed to find he was already trembling. He had not trembled on the platform before the whole school; his blood had been frozen then, now it was bubbling in his veins. He was being looked at. That was all. He was receiving such a look as he had never met before, a look from wide blue eyes with hidden fires in them, and dilated nostrils underneath, and under them a mouth that looked as though it would never, never open'.

When Thrale finally speaks, Rutter is accused of being a rebel, and is told that all rebels deserve to be shot, while sulky rebels are the worst of all: 'Some rebels are good men gone wrong; there's some stuff in then; but a sulky rebel is neither man nor devil, but carrion food for powder'. Rutter struggles to explain: 'Oh, sir, I know I speak all wrong – you see...' Then he breaks down. 'Yet already the hard old man was on his feet again, and with one gesture he had cleared the throng from the diamond-paned windows, and laid a tender hand upon Jan's heaving shoulder: "I do see," he said gently. "But so must you, Rutter – but so must you"'.

As with the rowdy boys in Thring's house, in this fictional picture the headmaster's empathy with the young is in conflict with the disciplinary expectations demanded by his role. Hornung admitted that if he had stayed on into the sixth form, he might have seen Thring's softer side.

However, for some Uppingham pupils in Thring's final years (especially those in other houses), Hornung's picture of Thrale was very similar to how they recalled Thring: memorable in chapel or during the big set-piece occasions of school life; able to turn on a terrifying persona

---

[1] Hornung (1866-1921) was Conan Doyle's brother in law. His Uppingham career was blighted by asthma, preventing him from making any contribution to sport. It led to his leaving at the age of 17. Many of the heroes in his books became armchair cricket experts and statisticians. See *Fathers of Men* p.vi: Boys remembered in the headmaster that 'where the noun was, the adjective was never far away and together the two rolled out like noble thunder'.

when dispensing justice at noon each day, but essentially remote. Many boys still venerated him, but mostly from a distance.[1]

****

Thus Thring moved towards his final years, his bouts of peacefulness and contentment punctuated by anger or frustration. He was increasingly the victim of his anxiety and conscious of the limited time still left to him. His poetry became more introspective and nostalgic:

'And age is winter. I am growing old;
Grey hairs have long since straggled into place,
And feet, once winged jests, that laughed to race,
Plod slow and halting, like a tale ill-told.
What though the frost upon the roof lay hold,
T'is a poor house whose battered frame the wind
Can whistle through at will, and roomage find,
Whose bankrupt tenant all his goods hath sold!
But warm and bright Old Christmas sits at home,
Keeps mirthful house with noise of dance and jest,
Or silence sweeter still, when feet that roam
Meet round his hearth once more, and gather rest.
Let thriftless summer lightly come and go,
Old age hath steadier fires at his command that glow',

Shortly before the Tercentenary he wrote a poem describing how, over three centuries, the school buildings had watched and listened as boys went to and fro, and comparing nature's unchanging annual cycle with the remorseless progression of human existence from youth to old age:

'Still like a mountain rivulet
Clasped in its strong bed,
The old school; hears from hour to hour
The schoolboy's rippling tread.
And youth and age still love to meet
Round summer's mystic well,
Where age grows young, and youth rings out
A joyous passing bell'.

---

[1] *Spectator:* 10 February 1912 pp.239-240: 'Whether [Hornung's account] is a faithful picture of Uppingham in the last years of Thring's regime it is impossible for anyone who is not an Uppinghamian to decide... [but] the scene in chapel [and] the fragment of the headmaster's sermon... bring to a fitting close a story which is at once a fine tribute to a great school and a great headmaster'.

Even in his final years he drew pleasure and strength from the encounter of age with youth and he was still developing new interests. He and Gale instructed local children in the mysteries of botany[1] and he began a museum to house the boys' collections of grasses, stones and sea-shells brought back from Borth.

He was also overheard saying that a boy who did not know the note of a chiffchaff was not properly educated.[2] In a letter to Godfrey he described his new absorbing passion:

'You would be immensely pleased with our aviary in the school gardens, a bank enclosed for thirty feet by twenty in fine wire... with plants and grass and bushes, and a large aquarium in it. The birds are so tame and interesting; the siskins run up and down... and curious to relate, I believe we are the only people in the world who know the habits of the common blackbird, and one of its notes. We have linnets, redpoles, greenfinches, a robin, sparrows, hedge-sparrows, bullfinch, goldfinch, two Australian paroquets, blackbirds, thrushes, siskins, and a plover, and it is very interesting watching them, especially now they are beginning to sing'.

---

[1] Leyel, Hilda: *'A Modern Herbal'* (1931): 'That famous headmaster, Edward Thring, taught me botany in the school house garden and Uppingham fields. I still remember the pride when he strapped the black japanned tin lined with green on to my tiny back, and though I was only four and much too young to enjoy searching in the heat for rare plants... their names were impressed, like the dates of English kings, on my mind so vividly that it has been impossible for me ever to forget them'. Her father, E B Wauton, was a master (1881-1908).

[2] A small, olive-brown warbler.

CHAPTER EIGHTEEN

REACHING OUT

FROM Thring's very first years in Uppingham, as soon as his reputation began to grow, visitors from other schools started to beat a path to his door. One of the first was the twenty-six-year-old John Mitchinson in 1859, as he prepared for his elevation from day-school assistant master at Merchant Taylors' School, Northwood to boarding headmaster at King's Canterbury. The Dean of Peterborough had recommended him to consult Thring, 'the best of fellows'. Mitchinson walked the three miles from Manton Junction to Uppingham, where he received a warm welcome and an extended tour of the school with Thring expounding his philosophy as if Mitchinson was a prospective parent.[1]

He found Thring 'abstract and somewhat paradoxical' but he acknowledged how much he had learned from the visit: information which proved useful as he tried to persuade the Canterbury chapter to build new classrooms and dormitories. He returned to Uppingham for the first HMC Conference in 1869, and again in 1881 (by then, Bishop of Barbados), to tell Thring's boys how much that first visit had influenced his life.

The visit also prompted Mitchinson to send a copy of Thring's *Statement* to Charles Wright Hankin of Cheltenham College, who included it with his successful application to be headmaster of King Edward VI School, Southampton.[2] A year later (1860) Thring was consulted by a prominent Bristolian and a governor of the proposed new Clifton College in Bristol, Mr. Wasbrough. Thring took this as a great compliment;[3] his visitor reported back very positively on Uppingham and the local bishop was soon telling Archdeacon Fitzgerald (Thring's

---

[1] The visit took place five years before Mitchinson reviewed *Education and School* (see ch. 7) and a decade before they worked together to establish HMC. Merchant Taylors was largely a day school. Mitchinson spoke later of 'the cordial, sympathetic manner in which [Thring] welcomed me as a brother of the craft, and [sent] me away greatly helped, and encouraged. [He spoke] with authority [and] gave me willingly of his wisdom and experience'.

[2] Hankin provided Thring with 'the most frightful account of the immorality, connivance and crime' at Cheltenham. It was the year in which Marlborough declined to investigate the Fowler case evidence.

[3] 1860: 'They will found a really fine school on our system... I feel greatly strengthened by such a tribute'. Clifton had spent £13,000 on its site and planned to spend at least £100,000 in all.

Somerset brother-in-law), 'that the Bristol people were going to adopt my system as the best of all the public schools'.[1]

Thring made a point of showing Wasbrough's report to his own governing body, commenting waspishly on the large sum that Clifton had spent on its site and claiming that it proposed to build just the sort of schoolroom which at that time he wanted for Uppingham: 'Could not help feeling bitterly... about the proposed Bristol scheme, at the zeal and liberality there contrasted with everything mean, petty, and obstructive here'. He felt similarly peeved about the lavish plans of the trustees of the new Fettes College in Scotland who arrived for advice soon afterwards: 'I showed them everything... they had no principle to guide them, and I gave them one'.

Some years after being consulted over the foundation of Wellington College (1859) he discovered that Philip Kempthorne, one of his early pupils, had become a housemaster there. Kempthorne too came to see him and was warned of the dangers of cutting corners over staff, curriculum and domestic arrangements.[2] Thring took particular pleasure in the four hours spent with the Catholic Oscott School's president, Dr. Northcote, another former Ilminster pupil: 'A good man and thoughtful. I am glad to find an opening with the Romanists, and prize exceedingly any opportunity of showing Christian love and friendship. Hate is of the devil'. Even in his final months he was 'indoctrinating Walters, who is headmaster of the College in the Isle of Man, with sundry things'.

He could be very caustic whenever his work was used as a false example. Those who opposed Shrewsbury's possible move into the countryside (1872) cited Uppingham as an example of how a good school could flourish within a town. He icily referred them to his comment in *Education and School* that 'a boarding school in a large city is as admirable an arrangement as a poultry yard in a fox cove'.

Despite this flattering attention he remained something of an outsider and accepted himself as such. Possibly this stemmed from his self-consciousness at not having a doctorate. After one headmaster visited him (1862) wearing a doctor of divinity's top hat, Thring made much out of a claim that several masters and wives implored him never to acquire either

---

[1] It was Clifton's interest, more than any other event, which softened Thring's father's attitude towards Uppingham – probably because John Gale would have known some of the Bristol's leading figures.

[2] 'I think the visit did us both good'. Later (1879) he did not relish going back to meet the Commissioners of the Wellington Enquiry: 'I suppose something is gained, but I confess I feel some disgust at being sucked time after time, and then flung, like the gay young chafer, flat into a corner'.

the degree or the hat: to do so would be 'a mock dignity... utterly uncongenial with the spirit of this place'. The incident harked back to a suspicion of brainpower without morality which he had acquired during his Cambridge days, when his notebook included the idea that 'an overgrown intellect is as much a disease in human nature as an enlarged liver in the body'. It was also consistent with what he wrote in *Life-Science* and in a later paper entitled 'Education or Idolatry?' that 'many men are mere human maggots, crawling lengths of masticated books, swollen out to an unwieldy size'. He much preferred the Platonic harmony of work and play - in body and soul as well as intellect.

****

The Headmasters' Conference, which had begun its life with such a defined (albeit defensive) purpose, turned after 1869 to more mundane issues: its own constitution and membership; arrangements for examinations and inspection; its relationships with government and, as the decline of classical pre-eminence in schools and universities gathered pace, many hours of debate about standards of Latin grammars and correct Latin pronunciation.[1]

Thring missed only two of the first twelve conferences, serving on HMC's executive committee for six years in total.[2] At Sherborne, where 43 headmasters met in 1870, he spoke in the Latin debates; criticised schools which offered closed scholarships to preparatory school boys; supported a review of qualifications for university matriculation and argued that it was better if Oxford and Cambridge universities established an examination board than for the government to do so.[3] In that year's curriculum debate he described Uppingham's method of teaching English, with its coloured sentence maps to highlight the grammatical structure and value of each clause. He emphasised that learning the syntax of their own language helped boys to master classics. He thought science should be an

---

[1] There had previously been no consensus over pronunciation, which caused difficulty to pupils changing schools. Debates about compulsory Greek and the niceties of Latin pronunciation would preoccupy HMC headmasters for many years after Thring's time: see Witheridge: *Fletcher* pp.187-192.

[2] 1870-3 and, after a mandatory minimum three-year break, again in 1876-9.

[3] He had been consulted earlier by the new Oxford Delegacy (1857), and he attended an Oxford and Cambridge Schools' Examination Board Conference (1882) to consider state scholarships for top candidates in its examinations to attend universities. Like the Taunton Commission's more extreme proposals, this scheme fell foul of fears of excessive state control. Such a scheme started in 1920, but was small-scale at first. Student grants began as late as 1962.

extra subject rather than compulsory: it was costly to provide and some pupils derived little benefit from it. He returned home pleased that 'everyone felt the gain of the social intercourse. The [Clarendon] school delusion broken up. Winchester and Shrewsbury there; Eton has joined since. A great power is certainly started'.

When the Conference met at Highgate in 1871 with numbers grown to 50, he took the lead on constitutional and membership issues, asserting that meetings should be annual, in locations chosen by ballot and not confined to any one part of the country. He remained keen that HMC should not be exclusive: its membership should be defined by a school's work and not by its historical, legal or social character. Thus headmasters from 'the highest schools' (i.e. those preparing candidates for university) should be eligible for membership - whether those schools were public, endowed or proprietary. He failed to gain rights of attendance at most conference sessions for assistant masters, although the principle was accepted. To his relief, a rival proposal to admit assistant master delegates drawn exclusively from the Clarendon schools was quickly voted down.

Once home he wrote two articles for the new *Quarterly Journal of Education*. One was a report of the Conference itself; the other to inform the public of how HMC was breaking down geographical and other barriers between schools.[1] He spelt out his vision for its future, not as a closed elite but as a body to reform, oversee and nurture the entire profession.[2] It must make the public aware that no profession was so much at the mercy of 'external tinkering' by government, whose constant cry was for more subjects, or for all teachers to be 'professional' (i.e. certificated and registered). England's biggest problem was not the untaught poor but the 'ill-taught rich': those in positions of power who chose not to see this fact were 'the gilded hogs of society, the prancing cart-horses, [men with] foreheads like a brick wall'. If schools cheated their boys by providing over-large classes or lessons only suitable for the ablest, the boys would grow up with a cheating mentality: it was something that England could not afford.[3]

At King Edward's, Birmingham in 1872 he was in full flow, supporting the twin virtues of excellence and independence. He had

---

[1] It was 'the first time in history [that] common action has been taken by the great English schools... each school has been a separate world, and the chief workers have stood apart, absolutely cut off from one another'.

[2] Politicians and educationalists still wrestled with this issue 140 years later, after the demise of the GTC.

[3] 'If a thousand boys are to have shoes, one pair to every ten boys is not enough... If a boy is sent to school he is sent to be taught himself, however stupid he may be, and not merely to see clever boys learn'.

softened his attitude to the registration of teachers, but he was withering about the idea that teacher training might be offered by universities. They were quite unsuited to the role because, for all their academic expertise, they knew little of 'the study of the little boy heart and mind'. Yet universities *should* be responsible for inspecting schools, because anything was better than the government doing it, owing to politicians' 'fondness for statistics and for power'. He opposed pupils being forced to leave school when they reached 18 because he remembered how little time he had been able to find for reading during his adult years; he would not want the next generation to suffer a similar fate if it could 'lay up intellectual capital for later life' before being sent out to work.

A year later at Winchester (the conference where he first met Parkin) he declared that Sunday should be treasured as 'a day of rest and happiness'. In a swipe at the philathletes he warned against giving sportsmen excessive prizes, special training and special diet. He reminded his colleagues of his long-held views about the need for machinery, rather than relying merely on a headmaster's personality, linking this to his concern for curriculum variety: 'It is useless to talk of personal influence unless you can find [make] every boy [feel] he has self-respect and is respected... I have in mind sundry boys whom the gymnasium has absolutely saved, and others who in the carpentry shop have found the place they wanted'. It led to a debate on 'how best to counteract in schools the injurious influence of excessive amusements and luxurious habits', during which he described Uppingham's facilities one by one; workshops; gardens; aviary; gymnasium – and the Mission. He wanted more scientific and literary societies; school gardens, libraries and museums, and individual studies: 'For every boy a place for the sole of his foot'.

In 1874 at Dulwich there was a motion of sympathy for his absence after his father's death. Members debated a motion to remove a three consecutive year limit on membership of the committee, and his well-known opposition to its removal was cited by those who feared an over-powerful and ossified leadership. Despite his typhoid battles in 1875, in December he was at the gathering at Clifton where he heard a vote of support for him after the recent epidemic. In a partial reversal of his earlier stance he supported discussions with the Charity Commissioners on to how to create and publicise additional scholarships for poor boys.[1] During his low-point at Borth in December 1876 he joined his colleagues at Rugby – perhaps sensing that the change of scene would do him good.

---

[1] He also supported action against those who failed to pay conference fees; again condemned university-based teacher training and suggested 2-yearly conferences alternating with an 'educational congress' with assistant masters.

There he affirmed the need for teachers' pensions and recommended historical novels, and Latin verse for teaching English grammar. He warned that permitting universities to set school examinations should not allow them to dictate syllabuses too: it would erode schoolmasters' independence as 'the trustees of education in England'.

He repeatedly warned the Conference that it must tolerate no cliques or power groups. At Marlborough in 1877, with members worried about excessive time spent away from their schools, he wondered whether they should meet biennially. After his two-year struggle with epidemic disease and its fall-out he was invited to lead a special session on what he had learned from it: he recommended parental health certificates and the appointment of sanitary officers.

During the 1870s the public saw HMC as his creation and other Conference members recognised him as its founder. The frequency, length and range of topics on which he spoke confirm that he was the dominant figure, as well as the keeper of its conscience. However, he had begun to move away from the centre of its affairs, and the 1877 gathering was the last at which he was unquestionably *primus inter pares*.

After hosting the heady inaugural meeting he had inevitably found later ones an anticlimax. Never a natural committee man, he became frustrated as the headmasters came to realise how much their new-found friends were also their rivals; as they grew warier of sharing ideas so freely (and became keener to score points over each other), and as more fixed groupings and alliances emerged within the Conference. Borth had changed his priorities: he now had other writing projects and other interests. He no doubt perceived familiar issues coming round again, and new headmasters probably now looked suspiciously young.

As within Uppingham, his increasing age made him more irascible about HMC. The first signs of his disaffection appeared in 1878. No conference was planned for that year, so the committee was authorised to deal with any pressing issues. In its agenda papers he discovered a proposal to suggest to Oxford University that Greek be made optional in some of its examinations. He convinced himself that this somehow threatened the freedom of every school to decide its own curriculum. If the committee persisted with it, he would resign from the Conference itself. Although not a lone voice at the committee, he was outvoted, and he carried out his threat. He then awaited the reaction with interest:

'I am, of course, very sorry, but for years I have made up my mind never to sit in company with men engaged in work on a false basis... Much of the harm of the world has been done by men continuing to give their presence to things they are powerless to stop. No doubt I shall be soundly abused by some, but it will test how far the Committee is disposed to go... for the Conference may resent an action which turned me out without appeal to them'.

He was especially incensed by William Fearon, the recently-appointed headmaster of Winchester, a school with an immense classical tradition, who suggested that not all public schoolboys needed to learn Greek but who had no intention of reducing the time devoted to studying it by his own boys. Jex-Blake of Rugby (who had supported Thring in the vote) tried to persuade him to change his mind about resignation, which Thring saw as 'typically honourable and thoughtful'. Others suggested compromises. The issue became so contentious that a meeting of the interested members was hastily arranged after all at Harrow, but Thring did not go. Discussion of the question there proved inconclusive, but the Conference declined to accept his resignation, diplomatically passing a resolution that he had been 'The Founder'. Many wrote privately to him, asserting their personal loyalty and respect for him and urging him 'to come back in, and strengthen the opponents of hasty change'.

Once it became clear that the Greek question would not be put to any vote, he relented and returned to the executive committee. Quite why he had reacted so explosively is a mystery,[1] but he had become more conservative on other issues, too. Now, instead of arguing *for* assistant masters to have rights of attendance at the Conference, he was preoccupied with arguing *against* their admission as full members, on the grounds that they had no direct accountability to their school's governors.

Aware of the risk of retaining his HMC membership purely out of sentiment, he admitted to Jex-Blake his wider disillusionment:

'I am not general carpenter of the universe, with a roving commission to timber up all the holes that are made. Year by year I have felt the

---

[1] Maybe it reminded him of Sidgwick's attack on *Education and School*. The retreat of classics had begun some decades earlier: see Richardson, Edmund: *Classical Victorians: scholars, scoundrels and generals in pursuit of antiquity* (2013) p.4: 'Victorian England stumbled through a doubtful, painful and insecure relationship with the ancient world'. However, the Conference had discussed such questions before without incident, and the Greek proposal was already under discussion in Oxford itself. See also Goldhill: *Who Needs Greek?* p.208: 'Thring's exemplary conservative defence (in *Education and School*) of classics... had already been overtaken by... political trendies and their pamphlets'; p.212: The extreme assaults on classics had the effect of making total support for the status quo seem quickly out of date... Thring could only seem a dinosaur'.

downward slide more and more without being able to see how to avoid it... I determined never to be in this predicament... I cannot be present at such meetings. My whole soul revolts from attacking other men and their work. I think it wrong'.

He felt that the idealism of HMC's founding fathers had seeped away and that its members were now interested only in producing a 'marketable article'. Despite paying lip-service to the individual boy, they were becoming slaves to the cults of cricket and the army corps. It all testified to 'lack of ambition': the headmasters were 'short-sighted and octopus-like... I think that the man or nation who will not fight at the right moment will have to fight twice later on'. He feared that many of his colleagues secretly wanted to copy the Clarendon schools as a sign of status. Privately he accused Harper and others of 'funking' the classics issue.

It was inevitable that younger and newer HMC members, who had probably never read *Education and School*, saw him as an old-fashioned stickler for classics and increasingly out of touch with the changing world. However, he attended the 1879 conference, now 140-strong, held at Eton with all its memories for him. The hospitality of the Provost, his one-time tutor Charles Goodford, was sumptuous, and in one of the conference sessions Thring made what turned out to be a valedictory speech.

The government had again produced proposals for examining and registering teachers. These included an Educational Council, which revived all his memories of the full-blown proposals by the Endowed Schools' Commissioners. He completely rejected any parallel with the recently introduced registration in the medical profession, arguing that although it was the government's duty to protect the public from fraudulent or incompetent doctors, registration arrangements for teachers would destroy individuality and originality. It would produce state-approved, stereotype teachers 'drilled in certain methods [and excluding] the men who were best fitted to find their way to a boy's heart and least inclined to subject themselves to government tests'. The nation's education would become submerged in government statistics and politicians' ignorance. No nation could prosper if it 'went on allowing hands to be laid on the heart and life of the highest profession in the land'.

He spoke as passionately and lengthily as ever, but it is likely that other members felt that they had heard all this before. Some saw merit in teacher-registration if it led to enhanced professional status. The educational press criticised his 'most eccentric and violent utterances' against registration as inconsistent with his aim to promote the science of teaching. The once radical innovator was now seen as living in a world that had passed.

He served on HMC's executive committee again in 1881-3, complaining about business which members had been given too little time to consider, and about examination boards barring teachers from reading candidates' answers before sending them to examiners.[1] He continued to support moves to protect impoverished schoolmasters and their families. By now the Conference had become biennial, and in 1883 he suggested that it should meet only every three years unless sudden government legislation demanded otherwise.[2] After that, he did not appear again. One cruel journalist suggested that he was now seen by his colleagues 'as the Emperor of Brazil is regarded by the crowned heads of Europe: a king among outlandish folk, an ideologue to be treated with all true deference, but in international politics a negligible quantity', and that even Thring himself had recognised that his colleagues viewed him as 'an old fogey'.

There was a paradox in his break with HMC. At the moment when he was becoming ever-more disillusioned with the schools most similar to his own, his educational ideas had begin to attract interest further afield – both nationally and internationally. In 1879 Lajos Felmeri, a professor at the University of Kolozsvar (now Cluj) in Roumania, was sent to study English schools. Thring was delighted with Felmeri's summary of Uppingham principles in his report (1881) and later in the government policy blue book (1884).[3] It strengthened his resolve to write the book about teaching that had been taking shape in his mind for some time.

****

Thring had turned down several publishing approaches during the 1870s. *Thoughts on Life-Science* had received mixed reviews and *Education and School* had sold poorly. Some of his privately printed works had lost money; others reprinted for friends and admirers had merely increased his debts. With so many other concerns he preferred to believe that 'God's

---

[1] In 1884 he threatened not to use such examinations at all. One of his colleagues thought that although he had supported the establishment of the Oxford and Cambridge Joint Board, 'he was disappointed by the outcome in practice'. He also supported allowing dictionaries and lexicons in scholarship examinations.

[2] It remained so until 1894 when it became annual once again.

[3] See http://www.staff.u-szeged.hu/~comenius/hist.htm. Szeged University through Felmeri held out against Hebartianism: 'a narrow intellectual understanding of education' favoured in Budapest. Felmeri (1840-94) 'showed a vivid interest in psychological factors and attributed huge importance to the results of contemporary experimental and child psychology'. Others portrayed Thring's views less accurately: a French writer suggested that he was an austere Puritan in the mould of Bunyan and Wesley.

ways are living work and quiet, patient doing; in His own good time He will bring fruit'. He therefore confined his writing to his collection of *Borth Lyrics* (1881) and some *Notes on Teaching:* privately printed guidance for new masters which was reproduced in articles in the *Journal of Education* in 1882.

In that year he was urged by a notable educational commentator, the Revd. R H Quick, to write another book. Quick had long admired his ideas and he pointed to the increasing interest in education being taken by government and the public, as well as Thring's own high public profile. Thring replied cautiously, citing pressure of work and previous poor sales, and stating that publishers were now concerned more with profit than truth. After his customary side-swipe at government's educational 'amateurs [and] intellectual Goliaths who have never taught', he concluded that 'the hour has not yet come'.

Quick persevered and Thring relented. The book that resulted was his *Theory and Practice of Teaching*, published by the Cambridge University Press in 1883.[1] Whereas *Education and School* had been concerned with the nature of a good boarding school, this book discussed how teaching should be carried out within the entire profession. Some of its key ideas had appeared in earlier *Journal of Education* articles, but many of them still seemed strikingly original, and in later decades they would be considered way ahead of their time, feeding into mainstream thinking about child-centred education.

He began with some familiar themes: the bewildering speed of technological change and the frantic educational activity that came in its wake; new school subjects; examinations and inspection. He described how 'droves of children are driven in everywhere; there is much boasting of the money being spent in schools… much rushing to and fro, much confident action… authority busy at work'. He espoused the cause of 'skilled workmen' (teachers) pitted against 'general carpenters of the universe' and 'amateurs in perpetuity' (government officials). Whilst conceding that reform to ancient endowments had been overdue and that good schools did not come cheaply, he questioned the capability of officialdom to spend large budgets wisely and the wisdom of making the taxpayer responsible for funding educational opportunity for all.

In tones reminiscent of his final HMC speech he insisted that inspections and examinations were no reliable judge of success. They

---

[1] Quick's Essays on Educational Reformers (1868) were neglected in Britain but read widely in America. He gave the first lectures on the history of education in Cambridge and had taught at Cranleigh and Harrow. CUP's publication was one of a series, including educational treatises by Milton and Locke.

merely encouraged 'mental gymnastics', testing only whether schools were 'cut to the state pattern'. They pushed schools into a uniform mould in which originality perished. Ceaseless external regulation therefore degraded the schoolmaster. He could not comprehend how officials who had never taught a child in their life could regard themselves as authorities on teaching, yet the country was full of new authorities: 'an omniscient Babel'. Few politicians bothered to consult teachers and nobody tried to define the essential ingredients of proper education or good teaching.[1]

Returning to his ideas in *Education and School* about the difference between teaching and lecturing, he argued for more focus on the individual child. Young minds had to be made strong and not merely full. Education did not consist in pushing facts into a child's brain but in drawing out latent powers. Far too many people wanted to do the former, but this merely caused confusion and gave children no idea of the relative importance of anything. There was no point in trying to fill a kettle whose lid is still on: 'No skill can reach a boy who hates what he is set to do; who does not believe in the value of it; who does not believe that he can get it even if it is valuable'.

Teaching must therefore be concerned with much more than training for work beyond school. It involved observing a young mind's workings; getting inside it intuitively; identifying the child's distinctive mindset and (once having made it receptive) leading it into new fields of knowledge and a love of learning. He believed that 'the boy's mind must be *got at* somehow or other', and that success in doing so was tantamount to 'the winning of love by love'. As so often, his rhetoric became mystical: knowledge of lasting value was transmitted across the generations only when a child's 'high and refined powers of heart and head combined meet on terms of equality [with] the royal minds of old, wed them, and become in turn parents of glorious births of mind'. It was important that 'mind must touch mind'; that teaching was not a 'burglar intellect' in which the intruder forced himself into the home uninvited. The recent introduction of compulsory schooling made these issues all the more urgent.

He re-defined *True Life* as the difference between 'instrumental power' and 'living power': the 'market' value of education as opposed to its 'true' value. He challenged the nation's parents – the funders and

---

[1] 'They are eaten up with the idea that knowledge is power, and that through its schooling the state must promote "efficient life", without defining what constitutes proper teaching'. See also Hoppen K T: '*The Mid-Victorian Generation*' (1998) p.47: 'One government minister in this period likened the notion of consulting teachers about what should be taught to 'asking chickens with which sauce they would be served'.

vicarious consumers of education – to ask themselves why their schoolboy sons did not make more progress or seem more enthusiastic; why, having once grasped the essentials of reading and writing, some boys would 'not budge another inch' during fifteen years at school. He supplied the answer through a comparison of the education given to the modern English schoolboy and to Plato's young Athenian: 'Plato was dealing with the minds of his audience; schools [merely] deal now with the books they use'. Real education stimulated powers of observation, accuracy and an appreciation of beauty: through them the spirit and ideals of Plato's schoolboy could be re-born.

He had not changed his views about the importance of studying classical language and literature: it was 'the foundation of much of the spoken language of modern Europe, even though the briar patch can be uncomfortable at first'. Non-spoken languages instilled analytical powers because they made it impossible 'to substitute the glibness of an elaborate parrot, and an infantile familiarity with the sounds, for a real knowledge of the language'. Geography and other subjects had their uses, though not as mind-trainers. He again condemned the 'fetiche-worship' of concentrating only on the academically brilliant, noting that Socrates, widely thought of as the world's greatest teacher, had described himself 'as a man-midwife for mind. [He] created a science of questioning: he imparted no knowledge at all'. He added that Socrates would have starved in the England of the 1880s, with its endless manuals and 'grammars bristling with technical terms [and] labels for everything', because Socrates would have failed its unimaginative examinations.[1]

The metaphors proliferated. Good teaching strengthened the mind just as gymnastics strengthened the body. Teachers were 'a very artistic product': they did not grow 'like mustard and cress on a bottle' or by government decree. 'No true schoolmaster can produce the minds of his class as specimens on a board, with a pin stuck through them, like a collection of beetles': if he would only dispense with his grammars and rule-books, it would constitute the difference 'between doing lessons and having a teacher... between working blindfold and in chains and being guided through a glorious country'. Above all, a good teacher was 'a master in the kingdom of life... his life [existing] in living beings, not in printer's ink'. He should never let 'a single life of those put into his hands be spoiled, or wasted, or flung aside through neglect or scorn... he has as his study life and mind [and he is] the helper and friend of the weak'.

---

[1] 'Extensive knowledge can never be the possession of the many; excellent power of doing skilled work can'. Socrates 'sent a plough into the hearts of men and broke up the ground [with] a latent germinating power'.

The schoolboy was 'a frolicking puppy, always in motion, restless, but never in the same position two minutes together when really awake'. He must be taught the difference between poring over books at length and doing effective work. He should never turn his back on the master and never construe with his hand in his pocket, because correct attitude was all-important. Boys had good memories but limited powers of reasoning, a short attention span and little power to master a subject thoroughly. Therefore no lesson should be more than 45 minutes long, because 'inattention is a master's sin: a weed which above all others grows on badly farmed ground'.[1]

Whilst recognising the importance of individuality of mind, the teacher must also be guardian of the highest standards. No teacher should allow a boy to correct himself or to make wild guesses: 'There is a rigour in having to try to get things right first time'. The teacher must be uncompromising with sleepiness, inattention or disorder; his classroom furniture should be arranged to emphasise his own dominant presence.

Rules for their own sake were anathema: 'Rigid, formulated, square statements cannot find their way into the... little mind'.Words were 'the every-day messengers of common life', making it important to teach sentence analysis. Reading aloud had great value, and the teacher should not be afraid to demonstrate it before the boys tried it. He should insist on 'producing the final syllable of each word firmly, distinctly and unmistakably... To allow anything else dulls a sense of accuracy and is a recipe for confusion and indecision'.[2] Reflecting an increasing enthusiasm for visual observation, he maintained that lessons in drawing helped children's sense of perspective.

Parents did not teach enough general knowledge to their children, who needed to learn about England's 'travellers, colonies, great men, great deeds'. They should be taught to observe the wonders of nature, but it was no use giving them translations about animals (dolphins, whales etc) if they had no idea what those animals looked like. Imaginative teaching material was 'a gift to the young': children should be encouraged to look for modern parallels; to create mental pictures for themselves; to describe a scene from every point of view. He cited the biblical story of Jairus'

---

[1] Thring seems to have been won over by Candler's views on this: see p.142.
[2] 'Let us suppose a book in which every final syllable was left out, or blurred, and this too in a foreign language. What would be [its] value?' His idea contrasts powerfully with contemporary 'estuary English'.

daughter: pupils should be told to describe the reactions not only of the central characters but also the onlookers.[1]

He then returned to the idea that knowing *how* to learn represented the beginning of true knowledge. If pupils could learn how to work intelligently, it would be 'a wondrous advance'. Classes must be small enough to allow all participants to contribute. If the teacher could find in each pupil's mind a *Where do I stand,* the educational possibilities for that child would become infinite. The teacher's first maxim should be: 'If the boys don't learn, it's my fault', and he should take as his comforting mantra an idea that Thring had been repeating regularly since his days in Gloucester: 'The worse the material, the greater the skill of the worker'. He must 'try to find a chink here, to scrap open a little rift there, for a ray of light to get in... He endeavours to meet the boy on his own ground and to lead him on to conquest... a dull boy's mind is a wise man's problem'. He emphasised that teachers should never make 'the nauseous demand for higher work' (i.e. to teach only the abler classes).

All teachers should prepare lessons scrupulously, noting down the successful ones in detail for future re-use. The notes should include not just the material itself but how different children had reacted to it.[2] It was pointless to correct every single mistake that a child made, and better to concentrate on the most important or frequent errors, building up vocabulary gradually so that children were not overwhelmed. He suggested that 'five minutes in recapping dropped stitches would work wonders'.

A master should talk about his own hobbies, 'to fire the imagination and show his human side'. Demonstrating this empathy was essential because the difference between teaching and lecturing was not merely one of activity, but of character: 'The teacher must be full of human sympathy, inwardly exhaustless in kindness and patience, willing to bear anything but [a boy's] refusal to be taught'. Even then, he should be ready with as many resources as possible to counter that refusal. The successful lecturer (or crammer, or pumper-in of facts) had 'book-sympathy' like his teacher-counterpart, but a lecturer's sympathy went no further: he might be 'intensely alive to the writings he deals with, but intolerant to the last degree of slow humanity and blundering helplessness. It is not part of his

---

[1] Jairus' daughter was miraculously healed by Jesus: Mark 5: 21-43, Matthew 9: 18-26, Luke 8: 40-56.

[2] The teacher should 'make a scheme in his mind, and enter it into his private memorandum book [by]which he works day by day... keep to the path [or] his pupils will rush off, scattering in brainless confusion'.

business to succour the weak... [whereas] the low class is the teacher's pride and the pumper's dismay'.

Finally, 'the attitude of masters ought not to be slovenly'. They must be punctual; their classrooms must be tidy; they should never themselves have a 'careless or sleepy posture'; they should respect their pupils, and make sure that everyone treated the classroom fabric well. They must take pre-emptive steps against bad behaviour, nipping it in the bud quickly if it appeared. He advised them to 'honour the work and the work will honour you'.

He repeated principles from *Education and School* about sanctions. All punishments should have an educational value; if not, they merely made situations worse by destroying a boy's self-confidence.[1] He used an eccentric piece of imaginary classroom dialogue to demonstrate his conviction that the good teacher showed boys what they *did* know, not what they were ignorant about. He rounded off this section with a flourish:

'It is impossible to overrate the importance of giving confidence. Very much of what is called idleness and inattention is only utter bewilderment, produced by the way in which the swarm of novelties has been thrust on the beginner [in an unsystematic way]... till drenched, eyes and nose full, blinking and dazed, he is left the fortunate owner of a few answers by rote to the more familiar questions, as the reward for hours of disgust and toil'.

All through the book the ideas came tumbling out: like *Education and School* it was more a stream of consciousness than a rigorously organised polemic. Thring explained to Parkin: 'The pent-up feelings of forty years came with a sense of relief to the point of the pen'. He elaborated his thoughts with characteristically vivid and eclectic imagery: cathedrals and wheat-fields; St Augustine's golden key (another idea first formed in Gloucester); the genius of Mozart compared with the humble tom-tom player; cabbage butterflies and wasps; kettles and pumps; Chinese foot-bandages; the paintings of Turner; analogies between teaching and cricket.

****

---

[1] It should not cause extra work to the master; it must be quick and certain. A wise teacher chose carefully what to punish and what not to: 'A little judicious blindness and deafness is a great virtue in a wise teacher'. It was absurd to punish those who were struggling with their work by setting them more. See ch. 7.

Reviews in the English press were mixed. The *Leeds Mercury* believed that 'there is probably no abler work in the English language'. The *Journal of Education*, whilst agreeing on the importance of training teachers and praising the book's originality, criticised factual errors in some of the imagery. More significantly it claimed that there was a deep contradiction between Thring's belief in the dominance of classics in a narrow core curriculum and his vision of a broad education for all.[1] There was much greater enthusiasm for the book across the Atlantic: 'It is full of life', wrote the *New York Evening Post*, 'it comes fresh from the busy workshop of a teacher at once practical and enthusiastic, [with] the conviction of almost passionate earnestness'.

Thring warned Parkin before publication that the book might suffer the same fate as *Education and School* in being born before its time, although he felt that it had 'life' in it. In fact it proved to be well-timed: universal elementary education, introduced in England in 1870, had precipitated a widespread public debate about schools and the teaching profession was expanding rapidly. Beyond his home country it sold especially well in Hungary and Germany, and in Canada and the USA where Parkin did much to publicise it. Thring wrote of appreciative letters coming 'from various points in the United States, Indiana, Pennsylvania, the Rocky mountains, Boston, and some other places'. There were seventeen reprints by 1912, representing over 25,000 copies in all, many of them bought by school and training college libraries.

He dedicated the first edition to Quick, who had worked hard to persuade him to write it, and later ones 'to my wife, and partner in school-life; to whose courage and help I owe so much of life'. He felt elated by the book's success. Even if government made 'true teaching impossible', the book had changed his career. He told Quick that 'I am quoted everywhere... and know that the seed is being sown'.[2] He moved from gloom that it was 'useless to speak' (written in his preface to the first

---

[1] 'Except for a commendation of drawing, and a proviso that no child should learn any language but his own before the age of ten, there is no recognition of any other subject. Mr. Thring's cure for ignorance of common facts – a belief in carnivorous stags and four-footed whales – is an afternoon lecture in the winter term...' This review also lambasted HMC for not promoting teacher training in its schools: 'How is it that not a single master in a public school holds a certificate?' - a charge which Thring disputed, pointing to several conference resolutions in the 1870s, and claiming that lectures on teaching were established in Cambridge University as a result of them.

[2] 1885: 'Correspondence with the United States, Canada, New Zealand, Hungary, Germany... A curious change has come over the educational world... a religious silence [used to be] kept about Uppingham'.

edition) to being 'well pleased at obtaining a hearing' (in the second), and exultant that 'nothing is so wonderful in modern times as the marvellous communion and circulation' of ideas (in the third).

All the main ideas which had shaped his work had now been brought together in one publication: the teacher as skilled craftsman; firing up rather than merely filling young minds; teaching the less able as well as the quickest brains; the pupil learning how to learn and loving learning for its own sake; the importance of observation and experience; the role of the teacher in observing and learning the distinctive ways in which children thought and responded to new ideas and activities.

For a brief time he thought himself 'about to begin a new life instead of being at the close of one. I have been so much struck lately with the contrast of my early years and now in prophecy. I am *Laetus sorte mea* (happy with my lot), however heavy-hearted at times or surface-sad. My heart is wonderfully at rest'. *Laetus sorte mea* was a phrase which had recently been much in his mind. It reflected something more than his pleasure in his recent career success. He had adopted it as his mantra as the result of a friendship which had grown out of another great passion of his later years: letter-writing.

CHAPTER NINETEEN

A LIFE OF LETTERS

THRING was always a compulsive – and impulsive – letter-writer. He loved receiving letters too, especially after his circle of admirers grew dramatically in his final years and as travel became more of an effort. It is easy to imagine him tearing open the envelopes after the town post came and went twice a day and once on Sundays, for he described his correspondence to Charles Kingsley's widow in 1886 as 'a spiritual telegraph forever sending messages through the world from heart to heart... a communion of the goodly fellowship of the prophets'.[1]

His own letters in term-time were mostly dashed off in spare moments. Often terse and breathless, they cover tiny sheets of notepaper from top to bottom with the ends of messages curling up the side margins. He was frequently interrupted in full flow, as when he wrote to his old friend Thomas Powell[2] as the Christmas term ended in 1863: 'I am a Radical Conservative, [wanting] quietly to change everything, but slowly. I must shut up. The bell has sounded'. Letters written in the holidays were often on larger paper: slightly tidier; more reflective; longer; often abstruse, his butterfly mind lurching between big political or educational matters and gossipy snippets about colleagues or family.

Like his diaries the letters helped him to relieve pressure by venting (and sometimes over-stating) his true feelings, which is why Parkin generously described his judgements on individuals as 'singularly epigrammatic and picturesque'. At the same time they confirm the impression of a man often prone to self-pity and to feeling misunderstood by opponents whom he judged to be 'blind to the truth', full of 'miscalculation and blunder' or showing 'flat treason and treachery'. He castigated those who crossed him (even on minor issues) as 'specious', 'blind' or 'ostriches', who indulged in 'disgusting behaviour'. One close associate was 'like a wet cloak that will wrinkle in any direction it is flung'; another had 'an unhappy trick of somewhat hair-splitting, and considering a good sentence as powerful as a good fact'; as for a third,

---

[1] See introduction. Thring regarded Kingsley as 'a true pioneer' and told his widow (1886): 'Your thinking me worthy of your personal confidence, and telling me about your sons and yourself, is very delightful to me'. Most of the surviving letters come from his later years, but earlier ones are still being discovered.

[2] Vicar of Bisham, and father of Edgar and George: see ch. 10.

'his weak points are fear and flattery... he loves the winning side, and smells it afar off'.

Of people generally he felt that '[those] who are squeezable when they ought to be firm, will be firm when they ought to be squeezable. That is the law of incompetency', and that 'many men, like dead thorns, have no life in them, but much scratching'. When he was crossed: 'Argument is like an air-cushion; the clever manipulator has only to give a little more or less pressure to the windbag, and it takes what shape he pleases'. Frustrated whilst at Borth, he described the trustees 'sitting in conclave, playing with other peoples' lives, totally ignorant'; the RSA as 'instruments of oppression', and Rector Wales as 'out of his depth with his nose full of water'.

The letter to Mrs. Kingsley stated that he felt imprisoned by work.[1] Yet at other times he wrote of God working through him, and his joy in it. He included reminders to himself: 'Truth is giving your best always, never cheating God or man or yourself of time or work due'. He showed a scorn (tinged with awe) for academics, admitting that they thought him light-weight but feeling 'disinclined to mix with their follies' because they lived protected and over-glorified lives with little work or responsibility.[2]

When comparing his experience of parish and school work he concluded that whereas the parish priest had to be on call to deal with matters of life and death but was otherwise left largely to his own devices, the schoolmaster had to contend 'daily with every petty vexation and wearing responsibility and is compelled to do a hard day's work spread over a number of hours, and day by day at a given moment, well or ill, to be at his post, whether he pleases or not'.

For a man so often negative about his own lot, he loved passing on positive advice to others. He wrote hundreds of letters of encouragement to former pupils at home or abroad: Nettleship regarded them as 'like the blast of a trumpet, breathing strength and courage', even after the two men took contrasting spiritual paths. To another former pupil Thring was 'the only man on earth to whom I cared to go for advice [and] to whom I practically owed everything'.

---

[1] To another friend: 'For thirty years the only thing I really longed for was bed. It sounds mean, but it is true'.

[2] In 1886, to Professor J Churton Collins, literary critic and later Professor of English literature at Birmingham University (1904). They both admired Ruskin's belief in power of visual imagery: 'My name and experience [are not] worth much in the university world, and [I] am disinclined to mix myself up with their follies'. Thring told Birley: 'A college tutor lives in a place where his whole life is as shielded from care, and is as glorified as it possibly can be; he has very little compulsory work, and vacations long enough to sweeten even slavery'.

He frequently gave guidance on how to seek and interpret God's will. When Lionel Cholmondeley contemplated the mission field in Japan or China, Thring firstly cautioned him against a hasty decision: 'Glitter and possibilities' might be a temptation rather than a call from God. Eight months later and with Cholmondeley resolved to go, Thring encouraged him: he would be working amongst civilised people who valued education highly, and for women as well as men.[1] When he urged other Old Boys to do mission work at home, it was because 'there is no missionary like a schoolmaster', although he cautioned them against setting up their own schools because his own health had been undermined by financial worry. He shared his frustrations about the Uppingham trustees with Edward Miller, like himself a former Gloucester curate, but now running a school in Ceylon, who had run into difficulties with his own governors.[2]

For nearly twenty years he corresponded with Alfred Boucher, another Old Boy who became a young curate. In 1867 he encouraged Boucher to start a choir and discouraged the idea that a clergyman should become involved in politics. Three years later he explained how he had modelled Uppingham on what Eton *should* have been like, but said that he regretted the public perception that his own school was un-'intellectual'. This had dogged him all through his career:

'I do not think the idea of making a better school than Eton was ever consciously in my thoughts... It rather was a set determination to do true work, and act honestly by each boy, with a deep sense of the value of life... I would not have got up from my chair to make a few better scholars only; to make every boy a good and happy man, if possible, that I hold to be worth many lives. But it was very trying to find our own success acting against us. I know one important private tutor where the delicate or stupid boys are sent to us, as the only place where real care is taken, and the clever and promising [are sent] elsewhere. This is a compliment one could sometimes dispense with'.

He advised Boucher not to take up his family's comfortable church living until he had gained experience in a big-city parish. He regretted not having had such experience himself and, remembering his father's dominance, advised that it was 'impossible to develop freely at home'.

---

[1] Thring arranged a farewell service for Cholmondley in the chapel before he left for the Far East (see ch. 21). He returned after five years.

[2] Miller had taught at Highgate. Thring told him: 'In spite of all its trials, school life is full of life and blessing. You cannot think how much your telling me that my letter gave you courage gave me courage too...'

In repeated correspondence with Thomas Powell he discussed the proper limits of central government power. Thring disliked the way in which successive – especially Liberal – administrations were extending their work into spheres previously left to self-help and voluntary charity. Not surprisingly he supported public health initiatives but he feared that welfare legislation to help the poor would result in 'bread and treacle to the babies that squall loudest'. He could not see why the law should force a man to support his neighbour's illegitimate children: 'Why should I maintain [them]? Many people are in the world who have no right to be: the fruit of the sin, self-indulgence, and improvidence of their parents, who have broken the laws of nature'.

The experience of history showed that men should work and that they should not have to subsidise the drink or lust of others: higher taxation would be tantamount to picking men's pockets. In other letters, however, he conceded that taxes should be levied to protect the most vulnerable in society and to protect citizens against attack. To modern eyes his views often seem narrow, dogmatic and not always consistent or thought through, although he held firmly to the belief that being rich or poor should never be seen as coterminous with good and evil. Virtue depended on a willingness to work and to practise a degree of self-help, and as he grew older he often cited the principle: '*Help as much as you like, but never give all*'.[1]

Thring and Powell discussed education too. Thring did not like the prospect of schools funded by private initiative being squeezed out by politicians. The school Boards were 'an excellent example of public robbery'.[2] He told Courthope Bowen, who consulted him about professional training for maintained sector teachers: 'If free education, with its locust band of inspection and examination, is to come up over the land, farewell teaching, farewell liberty, farewell life'.[3]

---

[1] 1883: 'I do not mean to say that the rich are good and the poor bad, but that as a class the men who maintain themselves by work are good, and as a class the men who cannot maintain themselves by work are bad...'

[2] The Boards were set up by the 1870 Education Act to provide elementary education for children aged 5–12.

[3] Bowen was one of the founders of the Finsbury Training College for Teachers, set up by some members of HMC in 1883 to train men to teach in secondary schools. It collapsed in 1891 because so few had enrolled. Thring supported the scheme, but although they had become good friends (see ch. 23) the two men disagreed over his insistence on the importance of classics. Bowen also believed that while Thring *claimed* to believe in teacher-training, he wanted it only for elementary school teachers and insisted on his own particular definition of it.

Edward White, a free-church minister from London, came to him as a prospective parent. In their subsequent letters Thring expounded the virtues of 'machinery' and the benefits of boarding schools: they provided 'independence and self-government within limits' which was the best possible preparation for adult life. Boys from 'good' homes always thrived in them, although 'the majority of homes with which we have to deal are of a far lower type than our school life, and the boys are greatly raised by coming into our atmosphere'. He explained the financial struggle that his commitment to boarding education entailed: he was sending his own two sons through Uppingham, but under another housemaster and on full fees even though they could easily have lived under his own roof.[1] He was convinced that working in boarding schools offered young men more opportunity to improve the world than entering the church. He wrote glowingly of Alington's achievements in Woolwich and even wondered whether he might one day do similar work himself, although the prospect of retirement still seemed far away (1870).

Most of his surviving letters were written to those to whom he could issue advice as the superior party, but to three people – two at home and one abroad – he revealed his deeper self and the extent of his vulnerabilities.

****

Only a few letters to Thring's immediate family survive, nearly all of them judiciously edited by Parkin. They include a handful to his sons and one to his mother (1880) with his post-Borth euphoria still strong as he described his plans for a chapel extension and a swimming bath. There are, however, over 120 to his favourite brother Godfrey, the sensitive Somerset country clergyman. They span nearly half a century from Thring's Cambridge days until just before his death.

To Godfrey he poured out his struggles to interpret God's will, admitting his faults including 'my great trial': an inability to take advice. In middle age he shared his passion for woodwork, his plans for the Mission and for HMC. Later he enthused about the autotypes (photographic prints) in his classroom; the new stained glass windows in the school room and the reredos in the chapel; his new-found love of bowls and croquet; his delight at acquiring a recreation ground for the town; his enjoyment of his aquarium and his delight in confounding the

---

[1] 'So much do I think of this (i.e. the value of boarding away from home), that though headmaster here, I put my own two boys out of my own house into a master's and pay for them just as if they were strangers'.

sceptics about boys' enthusiasm for gardens, as no fewer than 77 of his pupils took plots on land next to his newly-built aviary.

The two brothers exchanged draft sermons and drawings of their respective inventions (Thring's fire-grate and Godfrey's distinctive stile-gate). He consulted Godfrey over most of his books, especially *Life-Science,* which he described as a vital project in the 'deadly struggle going on between Thought and Knowledge'.[1] In return he encouraged Godfrey's hymn-writing and poetry and was thrilled by the success of Godfrey's *Church of England Hymnbook* (1879-82). They shared their admiration of Tennyson, Coleridge and Ruskin, and their suspicion of Gladstone ('made drunk with popular applause'). They exchanged gossip about school and church promotions.[2]

During the Fowler and Jackson affairs they exchanged letters almost daily. Thring complained bitterly about the hostile press but assured Godfrey that 'liquid manure is a fine thing for a strong plant'. He wrote regularly about growing school numbers; his disappointments with masters; Nettleship's successes at Oxford; the governors' indifference to the schoolroom plans ('they are too lazy actually to be noxious'); the 'dreadful mess' of the Endowed Schools' Commission and the huge demands on his time from the New Scheme. He vented his fury when the *Guardian* described Uppingham as 'a remarkable instance of a little school starting to reach a level with Harrow'.

He confided concerns about his own health and much greater worries about Marie's anxiety, along with his fears about debt and his family's future if he suddenly died. When Godfrey became engaged he was delighted, but 'courtship is bilious work, and ecstasy is nonsense: I think you are likely to have the sober joy of a <u>helpmeet</u> (sic) for you'. He offered advice about where the couple might honeymoon in Italy, and playfully suggested that as Godfrey was known as 'Goo' within the family, he (Thring) might call Godfrey's wife Lilla 'Gooletta'. When Godfrey was seriously ill in 1877, Thring bombarded Lilla with advice from his own doctor-friends.

He used Godfrey as a go-between with other members of his sceptical family and during several robust disagreements with Henry. Letters during his long altercation with Charles and Lydia contain frequent references to

---

[1] 1871: 'Knowledge has it all its own way, and no-one wants to read a book which they cannot produce in little pellets or knowing conversation [or] the trouble of thinking instead of the much less task of remembering'.

[2] 1879: Thring considered Godfrey's hymnbook vastly superior to the 'audacity and blindness' of *Hymns Ancient and Modern.* Henry disagreed with them both over Gladstone, to whom he owed much in his career.

'open rebellion', whilst also showing the extent of his desolation. They include one (1864), heavily marked 'Private, to be burned directly' which asked Godfrey to help their mother understand that the falling-out with Charles was not all his fault and petulantly accused the independent-minded Lydia of being 'an awful woman'. When his Fitzgerald brother-in–law complained about Uppingham's poor teaching of Oxford candidates it was 'astounding cheek', but again he sought Godfrey's advice.[1] Even at Borth he found time to write regularly about his family's makeshift existence in the Cambrian Hotel: 'Rather a squeeze [but] it is a pretty sight on a fine night to see [the boys] all out on the beach...'[2]

It was a lifelong friendship on both sides. When he wrote something which annoyed Godfrey, he apologised abjectly: '[I] beg your pardon for anything annoying, with all my heart'.[3] Five days before he died his final letter was signed as always 'Your affectionate brother'. Godfrey subsequently added in red crayon: 'His last letter to me, alas, alas!'

****

Early in 1863 Thring's mother sent her five-year-old grand-daughter Margaret a popular children's story book: *Aunt Judy's Tales,* by Margaret Gatty. Thring became captivated by it and a year later, when he suggested in *Education and School* that boys should be sent away to school to broaden their horizons he borrowed one of Mrs. Gatty's images, crediting her in a footnote. This was the idea that a boy's home represented a 'pod' (shell, or plant husk) which protected him but also restricted his growth.[4]

Mrs. Gatty – a curate's wife in Sheffield, mother of eight and another victim of a youthful nervous breakdown – had originally developed a passion for marine biology. Her *Parables of Nature,* which Thring described as 'the most beautiful book in its way in the English language', combined good storytelling with a scientific knowledge of plants, especially seaweeds. She then began writing fairy stories based on her contribution to her own children's education which had included games,

---

[1] The rift with Charles was largely healed by the time of Thring's death, although Thring remained much closer to Godfrey. Maurice Fitzgerald was the son of their sister Theresa and the Archdeacon of Wells. Thring gave reduced-fee places to him and his brother. He won an Oxford scholarship.

[2] 'My dining room is at the end of a passage curtained off at the top of the stairs: if the boys come up and down too much one can come out on them like a giant spider, not to invite them into one's parlour though'.

[3] 1862: the issue is not known.

[4] See p.93.

theatricals, and a family magazine. *Aunt Judy's Tales* (1859) originated in nursery entertainments led by her favourite daughter Juliana (Julie). It was followed by collections of *Aunt Judy's Letters* (1862) and *Aunt Judy's Magazine* (1866-82).

Aunt Judy's Magazine was hugely popular. Its first edition told parents that they 'need not fear an overflowing of mere amusement. They will find things to be remembered in each month – and these will comprise facts and anecdotes, historical, biographical, or otherwise, deserving a niche in the brain-temple of the young'. Julie (now Mrs. Ewing) assumed an increasing role in the magazine, writing serial stories for it with well-crafted plots and strong narratives. It extolled the virtues of cleanliness, never being bored and never complaining about one's lot. It inspired children to acts of generosity: tiny sums of money flooded in to endow Aunt Judy's cots in the Hospital for Sick Children in Great Ormond Street.

Thring saw the magazine as manna from heaven for his children. When Margaret complained that the latest edition contained no story by Mrs. Ewing, he helped Margaret to write to her. She replied with a short story written specially for Margaret, whereupon he began himself to write to her even though they had never met. He believed that she and her mother had 'opened a new world of thought and feeling for mankind' through their portrayals of happy family life and the idealisation of a rural childhood so similar to his Alford memories.[1] Her praise for traditional military values contrasted with what he saw as a materialistic and selfish civilian world. When her characters died (often, and often young), they did so bravely and heroically. She did not talk down to children or moralise directly and – like Thring – she believed that there was a child inside every adult, regardless of age. Above all, she seemed able to enter the mental world of the young, with all its distinctive sensations and perceptions.

---

[1] Mrs. Ewing's admirers included E Nesbit (who later wrote *The Railway Children*). Rudyard Kipling admitted what he owed her, and her book *The Brownies and Other Tales* (1879) provided the characters from which later came the junior branch of the Girl Guide Association. See Avery, G: *Mrs. Ewing* (1961) p.66, describing another of Mrs. Ewing's books, *Our Field*: 'She manages to convey that blissful sense of losing oneself in play, that satiation with happiness... which it is impossible to find after the age of ten or so. She records, too, the craving that all children know – for a place of their own. The children play all summer, uninterrupted. The field has everything, a brook with fresh-water shrimps; bluebells...' Their yearning for a special space of their own parallels Thring's views on the importance of a boy's study as a place of refuge.

Juliana Ewing married an army officer and lived for a time in Canada (coincidentally, very close to Parkin) and then Aldershot. When her always fragile health deteriorated she settled in Somerset in 1879, the same year in which her best-loved story *Jackanapes* appeared, describing the unselfish heroism of a soldier in the recent Zulu Wars. By now she had a nephew at Uppingham and Thring sent her an early copy of *Theory and Practice of Teaching*, telling her that in his home she was called 'the Queen of Storytellers'. To his great joy she sent him a copy of *Jackanapes*, a 'perfect' gift which he acknowledged by return, telling her that its talented illustrator (Randolph Caldecott) had once used the birds in the Uppingham aviary as models for another of his books.[1]

Thring's correspondence with Mrs. Ewing reveals much about his deep need for affirmative friendship – from women as well as men. Julie was a woman whom he sensed could appreciate his fears for the future of education and who, through her own health problems, could empathise with his periodic battles with depression. He told her: 'I catch glimpses from time to time of far-off openings into light, as I doubt not, with all your fits of despondency, you do at times'. She replied appreciatively: 'No one is likely to say kinder things than you... there is no one to whom I am more glad to say that [*Jackanapes*] is doing well'. Indeed it was: 19,000 copies had been sold, including fifty which Thring ordered the school bookshop to put right across its window, after telling the whole school that if only he had the power he would make them all buy it.

They made several plans to meet, but her deteriorating health led to repeated postponements. Finally at Easter 1885, two decades after their first contact, he broke a journey to Somerset to call on her in Bath:

'She was very ill, but I was admitted, and I shall never forget her. I held it the honour of my life to have been received by her as a very dear friend, though she had never seen me before. She lay so wasted and so pale... but as soon as she looked up the great eyes filled with light. We had a few minutes of happy talk, and she asked me to say the Lord's Prayer, which I did, with her wasted hands in mine, and then I left her. I thank God for having allowed me the privilege of seeing her and comforting her'.

---

[1] *Jackanapes* tells the story of the orphaned son of a cavalry officer who had served at Waterloo. He joins the army and eventually dies in battle saving the life of his childhood friend... 'Leave you? To save my skin? No, Tony, not to save my soul'. Caldecott (1846-1886) was a notable book illustrator, recognised by the Royal Academy. He married the sister of one of Thring's pupils.

He visited her again a few days later. Their two meetings gave great joy to them both, although Thring knew that she was dying and tried to console her. Her sister (Mrs. Eden) noted that Thring 'gave great consolation by his unravelling of the mystery of suffering [in his own life], and its sanctifying power'.[1] On his return home, he and his daughters collected and despatched spring flowers and Marie's favourite lilies of the valley.

Julie died a month later, aged only 43. Thring was quite desolate: 'My queen is dead... the sweet voice is stilled on earth forever. Yet it speaks on forever too. What a light has gone out'. Her family asked him to return to Somerset to take the burial service and despite his own infirmity he made the long return trip. Major Ewing's military colleagues carried her body out of the church on a beautiful morning and Thring recalled how 'the grave was lined with moss and lovely flowers, fit for a life crowned... I read the service from the lesson to the end'.

The memory still overwhelmed him a week later. He turned for comfort to her last book, entitled *Laetus sorte mea* (Happy with my lot), published just before she died: 'My whole life rises at the thought of being associated with her last earthly hours... my lower heart is heavy, whilst my higher heart is full of a new faith and peace'. Next evening: 'I have not gathered my senses... I began reading again tonight, and at first could scarcely get on through the mist of tears, but I was strangely comforted as I read'. After another week he was still 'striving to be *Laetus sorte mea*, and to have no more repinings (discontentedness) or fear or disappoint-ment. Airs of Paradise are nearer than ever before. I am *Laetus*'.[2]

His awe-struck friendship with Mrs. Ewing confirms how he, the commanding yet vulnerable figurehead, could also be whimsical and child-like, compassionate, generous-spirited and deeply spiritual. In the

---

[1] Rigby: 'The idea of finding heaven here on earth and living its life on earth was the spiritual discovery of Thring's later years. He saw that heaven was not a posthumous reward, not a separate existence after death, but an eternal experience beginning in the here and now. '

[2] The book appeared four days before her death, with the title *Story of a Short Life*. It had been written during a remission in 1882 and published in *Aunt Judy's Magazine* under the title *Laetus sorte mea*. Again its military hero is mortally wounded in battle, and dies after joyful endurance of inglorious suffering in the barracks hospital, listening to 'Fight the Good Fight' being sung in a nearby tin chapel. Thring considered it 'a message from the world of truth sent us for blessings [by] the pure and inspired prophetess of God's life to men'. Her sister, Mrs. Eden, wrote that 'she certainly practised... the virtue of being *laetus sorte mea*... I never knew her fail to find happiness wherever she was placed, and good in whomsoever she came across'.

struggles of his final years her last book would become his mantra. She was his patron saint: a storyteller who 'turned dust to diamonds'; a 'mystic light'. He included a tribute to her in his *Poems and Translations* (1887):

'All in the dusty camp she stood, a queen by queenly right;
The sunbeams made her diadem, her parted lips breathed light...
So passed she, but the mystic light so far, so near shines on, shines on
From Paradise, where she is gone, where she is gone'.

He wrote to one of her friends whom he met at her home: 'I did not know till quite lately for how many, many years first her mother, and then herself, had been the central ideal in my heart of *gracious womanhood*'. However idealised his memory of her became, these two words reflected a new preoccupation of his final years: women's education.[1]

****

Thring also corresponded over many years with the young Canadian headmaster, George Parkin. During the mid 1870s they met only briefly – in Winchester, Uppingham and Ben Place. A large difference in age separated them, together with the breadth of the Atlantic Ocean. Nevertheless they developed a strong, multi-faceted friendship.

In personal terms Thring and his family provided encouragement to Parkin and his young wife, both of whom were similarly prone to depression. Parkin could be just as wholehearted as Thring when a cause caught his imagination and Thring, no doubt remembering Gloucester, urged his protégé to pace himself.[2] When Parkin's father died in 1881 Thring drew on his own experience seven years earlier: 'There is the sense of being left behind with no barrier between oneself and one's own departure. Too often also the last link is snapped which bound the family together'.

---

[1] See ch. 20. He was so affected by Mrs. Ewing's suffering, that in *Poems and Translations* he removed all reference to the idea of 'The lost battle won'. June 1885: 'I am in a new world and a higher world... All day long *Laetus sorte mea* is in my thought'. This deep impression was a symptom of, and a spur to, his growing interest in women's education.

[2] 1884: Thring was candid about his own experience, except that he claimed to have beaten the problem: 'All illness has disappeared, [but only] after 16 or 17 years of more or less invalidism'. He told Parkin to be careful: 'Use your holidays well... A breakdown is an illness, and a great amount of gradual waste and wear of tissue and guts and brain'.

At other times he could seem strikingly insensitive. When Parkin's young family was suffering from scarlet fever he wrote that even the most resistant patient must be forced to take food in order to avoid death, and that a child might be at risk for weeks after seeming better. He added briskly: 'We had [the illness] terribly once both in family and school'. When two of Parkin's children later died in infancy, Thring's strong sense of suffering being good for the soul (together, perhaps, with the fact that he had never lost a child of his own) led him to hope that their deaths might prove to be 'a purifying source [to] the work in which you are engaged'. He pointed out that God's promises in the Old Testament could not be fulfilled until Isaac was sacrificed, so 'gather strength my dear fellow and march on... Warriors must be wounded if they are to be warriors indeed'.

On a professional level he could identify with Parkin's career frustrations in trying to establish high-quality boarding houses in his school at Fredericton, New Brunswick. Pupils and funds were scarce and local opinion was sceptical. Thring tried to encourage him by recalling how things had changed since his own early years: 'I almost marvel now how I lived through the humiliation'. He bombarded Parkin with advice: 'Brook no dissent. Bide your time. Never force circumstances. Remember, no compromise is possible with a principle, [but] in details it is different. A fine piece of work must be perfect or it is nothing'.[1] He reiterated his passionate belief in boarding schools, asserting that 'taking the young Plutocrat out of his feather bed... teaching the boy to live alone, and feel himself a responsible being... is a priceless boon, especially to the wealthy'. He was sure that every Englishman would opt for this path if only he could afford it, and then 'school life [would become] an important factor in the social world'.[2] He included advice from *Education and School* about trust and punishment; the significance of individual studies and the need for close supervision during evening prep.

In other letters he enthused about his sixth form teaching successes; the town tennis club; his Borth Lyrics; his friendship with Mrs. Ewing;

---

[1] 1881: Above all: 'Stick to your early principles. Don't sell your success. The temptation will come to grasp the crown by ever so little betrayal of the good old beginning. "Get thee behind me, Satan," be on your tongue, ready when the time comes'.

[2] 'Learning to be responsible, to bear pain, to play games, to drop rank, wealth and home luxury, is a priceless boon... it has made the English an adventurous race. The public schools are the cause of this manliness'. In 1877 Parkin rented the large house in Canada once lived in by the Ewings, but boarding at Fredericton did not last for long. Parkin met with greater success with it when he moved on to Upper Canada College, Toronto (1895-1902).

paintings done by his daughters; how, in mid-winter, apples picked in Scotland the previous summer seemed like 'the fruit of the Tree of Life'. He sent Parkin his latest invention: 'A card which every boy in the school has, and instead of saying fiercely or mournfully "I told you this a thousand times" now I calmly say "Read rule 4, 5 etc", as the case may be'. Marie and Sarah added advice on boarding house domestic matters such as food, laundry and servants.

Parkin dutifully and gratefully absorbed Thring's advice, along with his customary scorn for utilitarian theories of education and payment by results and his belief in the need to resist the sterile uniformity so beloved by examiners and bureaucrats. His mentor also provided guidance about career progression and the mysteries of Providence: when Parkin considered applying for a more prestigious headship, Thring thought him 'reserved for better things'. When he was invited to become organiser of the Imperial Federation League (1887), Thring cautioned him (as he had Cholmondeley) against 'temptation and glitter'. When Parkin's dream for boarding at Fredericton ultimately failed, his gloomy reaction could easily have been Thring's own: 'True Education was never so dead in this province as at present: all the satisfaction that I get now is what I find face to face with my own classes'.

Their correspondence sustained both men. Having an impressionable protégé confirmed Thring's desire to do God's work amongst the next generation of teachers. Parkin was far away and could keep confidences, and Thring was becoming increasingly interested in the wider world as more of his Old Boys began working abroad: more than twenty of them in India alone by 1875. Like other mid-Victorians he saw the empire in a new light: no longer as a mere chain of trading posts but as an expanding moral responsibility.

He had become especially interested in North America and in the 1870s he spoke of crossing the Atlantic himself some day. However, he was scathing about the morality of American politics, foreseeing 'fearful troubles and misery' before the United States ever became a great country because it had made four great mistakes. The first was in assuming that all men were equal. This was wrong in itself, and also hypocritical, because of the second: its abominable treatment of negro slaves. The third was the love of 'the glitter of power and the greed of money', coupled with the fourth: the failure to separate the two, proven by the way in which Americans 'put up their country for sale every four years (i.e. at presidential election time) and turn the nation into a set of swindling adventurers'.

Despite this he saw great hope for American education. After half a century of public education provision in the pioneer states, teacher training colleges had developed a great interest in educational method. Education in neighbouring Canada seemed to offer even greater opportunities, but Canada must not make England's mistake in letting government dictate to teachers. He suggested that Parkin should promote the idea of 'a council or councils composed of schoolmasters, lawyers, and men of authority in equal proportions... who should have power to issue new regulations, subject to parliament'.[1]

The two men discovered a shared interest in the idea of Imperial Federation: a loose union of like-minded states which might ultimately supersede the existing British Empire. Thring saw this as a natural development which reflected his fascination with the impact of railways, telegraphs and electricity. These inventions would lead to the development of larger communities, just as roads had caused Britain to evolve from the Anglo-Saxon heptarchy: 'The only question is who will reap the benefit... Few pause to consider how Europe even now, with all its bitter hostilities, is nevertheless to a vast extent a Federal Government and conducting three-fourths of its business by federation'.

The English-speaking race was (Thring believed) 'by nature master of the world'. Thus England itself was ideally placed to lead an expanded empire of states responsible for their own defence: possibly with a small imperial army to guarantee their protection and a federal parliament for matters of empire-wide interest.[2] States would do business with each other on the basis of free trade, although there might initially need to be some protective tariffs because 'greenhouses are sometimes needed to bring things on'. Young countries might need temporary Protection 'just as a gardener shelters his cuttings'. Above all, the time was right: Englishmen had begun to recognise both the possibilities and responsibilities of empire, and sports (especially cricket and rowing) were uniting the English-speaking world.

Those who saw Imperial Federation as a disguised attempt by the mother country to regain control of its colonies, or who argued that Canada should develop closer ties with the USA must be resisted. Canada could play a key role in such a Federation, because British public opinion

---

[1] There was plenty of demand for good training in North America. The best colleges paid far more attention than English ones to educational method: good theoretical textbooks like Thring's were eagerly sought.

[2] 'Especially when combined with the only other colonising power, Germany, its kinsfolk'. Mangan, J A: *'Manufactured' Masculinity: Making Imperial Manliness, Morality and Militarism* (2013) p.340 perhaps tells only part of the story when it cites Thring as an example of how 'headmasters espoused British imperialism with a simple-minded, single-minded fervour'.

was very positive towards her.[1] Besides, anyone who believed that Canada and the USA could unite was a fool: 'No power on earth can hold together [such] discordant parts... I look on Canada as the only permanent power on the American continent'.

Thring described how his vision had been inspired by visiting the 1886 Colonial Exhibition, adding that 'even Gladstone couldn't ruin such a wonderful sight'. He saw the Prime Minister (re-elected in 1880) as the symbol of all that he disliked: excessive government activity at home combined with a limited, 'blind Radical' vision abroad which was confirmed by the Liberals' treacherous support for Irish home rule. He variously described Gladstone as 'our great Liberal!!'(sic); one of 'the great criminals of the world'; 'the weakest and most contemptible of men, a painted windbag' and 'a jellyfish: all movement and no bone'. Gladstone's greatest crime was to have been 'MOG': the murderer of General Gordon.[2]

By the mid 1880s Parkin had something significant to offer Thring in return. Recognising that his headship was poorly paid, Fredericton's governors allowed him to supplement his income through freelance journalism. This included a review for *The Nation,* an influential New York periodical, of Thring's *Theory and Practice of Teaching.* In it Parkin described Thring as 'my master' and 'a great teacher', warmly praising his mentor's innovations, his abhorrence of government bureaucracy and his intuitive understanding of the child's mind. He also arranged for a selection of Thring's speeches and pamphlets to be reprinted and widely distributed in North America. Thring was soon reporting with gratitude that it had led to enquiries from educational authorities in Pennsylvania.

The two men then hit on the idea of a long, illustrated profile of Uppingham for *The Century Magazine,* another New York based publication, which numbered its readership in hundreds of thousands. It would enhance Parkin's journalistic reputation whilst bringing Thring useful publicity in advance of a final battle that he saw looming with the Uppingham trustees. Parkin proposed that the article should be titled 'An

---

[1] 1879. Canada had recently offered Britain troops in the event of a Russian war.

[2] 'MOG' was a parody of Gladstone's nickname as 'The GOM' (Grand Old Man), although his great political opponent, Disraeli, claimed that the letters stood for 'God's Only Mistake'. Thring believed that it was government incompetence that had failed to save Gordon from the siege of Khartoum in 1885; Gladstone was 'engaged in disgracing England in every possible way at home and abroad'. In wars in Africa he 'shed torrents of blood in wars with no policy in which every death was a murder'; in Ireland there was 'bread and treacle coaxing of murder which so disgraces the present government'; in Europe, there was 'the silly French alliance'.

277

Ideal Public School' or 'An Ancient School worked on Modern Methods'. It would describe Thring's work in Uppingham and the principal ideas in his two major books about the value of good boarding schools, the nature of skilled teaching and the threat posed by encroaching bureaucracy.

Parkin felt sure that North America badly needed these messages, and he told the magazine's editor in very Thringian terms that 'in nine cases out of ten the homes of the wealthy are unfit places for the work of Education'. Such work could (he said) be done only superficially in day schools: the remedy was boarding education, as Uppingham was already showing in England.

The article was finally accepted in November 1886. Thring was elated and his family was thrilled that it meant that Parkin was likely to visit them again. He urged Parkin to stay as long as he could. The knowledge that the article would soon be published helped to sustain him through all the other problems that he would face in 1886-7.[1]

****

Thanks to Parkin's reviews of *Theory and Practice,* letters to Thring now flooded in from all parts of North America. The State Reading Circle of Minnesota adopted the book as a set text for 5,000 new teachers because 'we feel that the names and the thoughts of Quick, and Thring and Dr. Arnold of Rugby, belong to us as well as to England'.

It invited him to write an address to its members, in which he made a rallying call for the sharing of good teaching practice across the English-speaking world. This exchange was necessary because teachers were 'the most living creators of life that is to be'. He shared with them his belief in observation and visualising skills and his scorn for excessive emphasis on examinable knowledge. 'Smash up the idolatry of knowledge', he told them, 'your business is to train athletes, not to fatten geese'.

He added a new ingredient in defining a school's success: its 'Almighty Wall'. This represented an extension of his concept of 'machinery', affirming the importance of attractive buildings to give a boarding community a psychological and emotional focus, with the chapel at its heart. 'Make sure of your system [and] structure', he told the

---

[1] The magazine's editor asked Parkin to make it light and readable, and limited him to 3,000-4,000 words. He received only $100 for it, but felt that he had a foot in the door; it justified a visit to England to compile it. Thring offered to pay Parkin's expenses and to pay for off-prints 'to show my power to my insolent oppressors' (i.e. the trustees). The article was eventually delayed until 1888, after Thring's death: its illustrations were unfortunately very poor.

Minnesotan teachers, 'athletes are not bred in pastry-cooks' shops, or free men in prisons'.[1]

In a tribute to the state's large army of women teachers he praised nations which gave high respect to female workers. Women had a 'unique power to undermine and discredit force; to make work lovely; to present a living example [of] gentleness and helpfulness'. He called on *all* teachers armed with his ideas (female as well as male) to shape the future of their own profession. In a flourish reminiscent of Moses (peering towards the Promised Land from a distance, but himself destined not to enter it) he declared: 'I am only looking through the keyholes of the doors which I am trying to open for you. I see glimpses of the landscape, and the path and the light on the path, and all the life of it; I hope you will enter in and make it your own'.

He could not deliver the address in person but Parkin arranged for off-prints. It led to a request to write a song for Minnesotan pupils which he duly met. Invitations followed to write for or speak in New York and New Jersey; a stream of transatlantic visitors came to see him in England.[2] He received other letters from Australia and New Zealand, often from those who had read his recent book. To most of them too he repeated his warnings about 'government despotism' and his vision for teachers to form 'a confederation of skilled workmen all around the world'.

At the same time he corresponded about proposed American free schools. As in his letters to Powell he emphasised the virtues of self-help, questioning 'how far law can rightly interfere with private duty' and maintaining his high Tory position that 'free' education was a misnomer because it was paid for by taxation. Any education that was entirely free would be a dangerous road for America because it would kill any national feeling of brotherhood: 'Those who thrive give their tax and wash their hands of brotherhood. Those who receive it claim it as a right because it is law; hate it because it soon becomes a pittance, and are at war with those above them for not giving more. Brotherhood vanishes'. He pursued his

---

[1] It harked back to his early idea of how technological advance had 'annihilated space'. He congratulated Minnesota on its institutes and conferences for trainee teachers; he stressed the teaching power of photographs.

[2] The address (1886) was also read at the first gathering of the Imperial Institute in London (later the Commonwealth Institute). The New York invitation was from the New York Industrial Association; it came on a day when two of his former pupils gained Oxford Firsts. He also agreed to write a monograph on *Education and Idolatry* for the Education Association of New York City. Visitors included the father of William Wolsey Johnson, a mathematics professor; a Dr. Wayland of Pennsylvania and a Mr. West from Minnesota, an educationalist whom Thring regarded as 'a living link, and a visible ambassador' for that state.

argument to greater extremes than in earlier years as he suggested that those without children should not be expected to subsidise those who had them.[1] He was also convinced of a direct link between state-provided education and the exam and inspection-driven narrowness which he despised so much: it dealt a 'deadly injury to schools: death becomes a mere question of time. The life goes out of them'.

On one issue he had moderated his earlier thinking. He would now support the use of school endowments to provide 'four or five' competitive scholarships for each school's most promising pupils to transfer to a 'higher' school or to attend university, and to give schools a way to recruit and support a small number of 'needy boys whose brains do not make them prize-winners, but whose merits make them deserving'. These endowments should be placed in the hands of teachers, with oversight by external authorities ('interference by the ignorant') only to prevent fraud. Beyond that idea, however, 'the very poor should have just the elementary teaching of reading and writing provided for them *gratis* in a humble way, so as not to compete with any paying school'.

His long correspondence with Parkin had also made up his mind on another matter. As he awaited publication of the *Century Magazine* article in August 1887 he wrote to Parkin to give him 'a kind of last will and testament bequest: the task of writing my life'. 'I want a *man* to write it'. Possibly he thought that the commission might produce useful income for Parkin but the decision was also a condemnation of others, especially Skrine: 'I am sick of the half-gelded characters who cannot see practical truth'.

---

[1] '[Excessive taxation] is dishonest... it is deadly for law to interfere...The right to live is limited, [and] it shall not be exercised by preying on the life of others... Every tax in principle is the same... No law (to tax people) has any right when a man has been industrious, thrifty, restrained his passions, and married late, to take his money in order to pay for the support of the children of his idle, thriftless, dissolute neighbour, who seduced, or married some unhappy woman because of his lust... But this is done by every law which taxes those who have to pay for the children of those who have not... The moment the consequences of a man's idleness or evil deeds are taken off him, his power of idling and doing evil deeds is increased in proportion to the relief given. If the drunkard's children are brought up by the State, the State is paying for the drunkenness of the father, and practically is buying his beer for him'.

CHAPTER TWENTY

CELEBRITY AND ANXIETY

AFTER his lecture at the University College of Wales whilst preparing to leave Borth, Thring did little public speaking for several years. Then, gratified by the success of *Theory and Practice* he embarked in the mid 1880s on a round of stimulating but physically demanding public appearances. In his presidential address to the Education Society in May 1885 he portrayed himself as 'a workman fresh from his workshop and his forge', and reviewed his life in schools right back to Ilminster days.[1]

He affirmed the importance of child-centred education as opposed to the 'piteous sight of the good slow boy laboriously kneading himself into stupidity'. He hoped his audience would strive to be 'teachers, not hearers of lessons... making minds strong, not full; having mercy on the slow, the ignorant, the weak and encouraging them to improve'. Education was not just for the academic elite: 'Racing stables and a crack winner or two will not do'. The address repeated his long-held views on the importance of grammar, vocabulary, poetry, reading aloud, and Socratic questioning backed up by interesting information books.

He added other things too: his growing conviction of the importance of observational powers and of making full use of children's eyes and ears, whether in walking down a road or studying botany through a microscope. They must note down the date when each new flower appeared each spring; the colour and texture of different leaves on trees; the changing of the seasons and the migration patterns of the various birds; the rise and fall of rivers.

The *Journal of Education's* review of this address was much friendlier than its earlier assessment of *Theory and Practice*. Thring was 'a Head who believes in the science of education, [who has] himself served an apprenticeship in the art and knows how to communicate both his science and his skill to his staff'. It noted that reading was much better taught in America than England because teachers there had to ensure that children understood what they were reading. It praised 'the full share of (university) scholarships and honours gained by Uppingham as an extraordinary testament to Mr. Thring's method and ability, considering

---

[1] Thring's role with this national body reflects his growing fame, and the growth in the importance of the profession, as universal education became established. The *Journal of Education* first appeared in 1874.

that the school was handicapped as no other public school in England is by admitting all comers, whether stupid or clever, and never sending away a single boy except for some grave moral offence'. To illustrate Thring's concern for late developers it cited a long list of notable writers including Dryden, Swift, Goldsmith, Walter Scott, and Gibbon, all of whom (it claimed) would have stood little chance 'in any public school of today except Uppingham'.

Nearly a year later he suggested to an adult audience in St Albans that children's education had two complementary components: general knowledge and 'particular perceptions'. Pupils needed to be 'Jack-of-all-trades and masters of one': the former to develop skills of selection in accumulating their knowledge; the latter to train their minds in rigour and because every good runner thrived on 'the special challenge of the last ten or twenty yards of a race'. He again urged that classrooms be well ordered and full of pictures.

He returned in this lecture to the question of the increasingly crowded curriculum:[1] 'Not a letter is written to *The Times*, not a cabinet minister speaks, who does not toss into the school cauldron some half-dozen new indispensable subjects'. No child could learn everything; the pursuit of omniscience had to be given up in favour of 'a clear perception of necessary ignorance'. A subject had no value if it 'kicked out' a more valuable one.

He placed more emphasis than in the past on mathematics and science but he was concerned that 'we must get rid forever of the idea that painting, music, architecture and sculpture are less noble as mind-power, [just] because we may not put them into our hard-work time' (i.e. the mornings). He longed for more young people to learn how to appreciate 'great ear-languages': among them music ('the song of birds; the voice of winds and the waters shouting in joy') and word language' ('the sacred gift of conversing with the great minds and glorious thinkers of all time').

Children must be trained for leisure: it was 'the hinge on which true education turns'. They needed to know what constituted a healthy life and diet. There should be carpentry and metalwork for boys and needlework for girls. Uppingham's gardens were examples of how teachers should 'give God's great picture-book a chance... all nature is God's thought put

---

[1] April 1886: 'No one has asked the simple question... [is it] possible under existing conditions to teach every boy? Large sums are being lavished, and for the first time in English history a despotic power is laying down railroads for the minds of men, and insisting that all shall travel by their lines. What is education? – the making of mind full, or the making of mind strong? Is teaching the putting in of facts, or drawing out and practising latent powers?'

in shape for us to see or hear'. Country walks were important as well as compulsory games.

In autumn 1886 at the prize-giving at the Leamington High School for Girls his main theme was that character was better than prizes. Ambition and competitiveness alone were not enough, for 'we are to be trained for the battle of life'. It was natural for honest merit to be rewarded in this world – as it would be in the next. However, if prizes simply made the weak and stupid feel looked down on ('how I hate the very word "stupid" as bearing witness to contemptuous feeling'), he would abolish them. Then, reviving the notion of 'The lost battle won' which he had briefly put aside after Mrs. Ewing's death, he spoke to the girls about how defeat could be as glorious as victory. Setbacks were a good preparation for life, which was 'no summer day's holiday'. Girls (like boys) had to be 'trained for the battle of life, [for] if there is no battle practice, no drill, what sort of soldiers shall we be?' He praised Moses' faith in answering the call to go into the wilderness.[1]

In May 1887 at the Teachers' Guild[2] he concentrated on the value of visual skills and mental pictures. Perspective gave children a heightened sense of meaning. He described his classical pictures and friezes and looked forward to a time when 'every village school in the land shall have its decorations... maps and portraits' to assist memory and understanding. Teachers using them were on 'a voyage of discovery, a band of pioneers, yet certain of our promised land'.[3]

His audience was receptive, but it included one strong doubter: a reviewer for the *Journal of Education* who believed that Thring was too little concerned with mathematics and theoretical science, and that he was inconsistent in promoting lessons in natural history largely through allowing a boy to gain 'all his knowledge of dolphins and stags and boars through Ovid'.

The reviewer walked downstairs with Thring after the lecture and suggested that pictorial education was only the first stage of teaching, whereas the second was to guide pupils from the concrete to the abstract

---

[1] 'If I glory prize giving, far more would I glorify defeat. To be defeated, and to go on being defeated, is the highest thing that can happen to man... For the lost battle is always the victory of life later on. Be happy, then, you who are defeated... [because] character is better than prizes'.

[2] The Teachers' Guild was formed in 1883 as a central professional body to promote the welfare, independence and mutal support of teachers across the profession.

[3] 'The difference between knowledge of a fact, and a mental picture of a fact, is stupendous'. Knowledge alone was no use: humans needed to be taught to think in shape: thus the 'teacher can breathe life over the wall'.

and to dispense with the pictures altogether. Thring strongly disagreed, whereupon his interrogator asked: 'How would you then propose to teach algebra pictorially?' Thring replied, perhaps rather too casually: 'I have not thought it out, but I am sure it could be done'. It was a rare example of him being challenged on a matter of teaching technique, and his trite reply would be quoted against him after his death.[1]

All through 1887 the invitations came steadily in: to speak at the Mansion House and to preach in Westminster Abbey. His fable *Dreamland* was to be reissued; Cassell was to publish five more lectures; Fisher Unwin would produce a compilation of seven of his addresses, which he dedicated to his aged mother. Even so, his greatest source of pleasure was being described in that year's edition of the reference book *Men of the Time* as 'the brother of Godfrey Thring, the notable hymn writer'. He felt that recognition for Godfrey had been long overdue.[2]

****

In Uppingham Thring's final years were dominated by two great sources of anxiety – one personal and one financial. The first of them took him by surprise and threatened to destroy the very heart of his family life.

In December 1878 he and Marie had celebrated their silver wedding. It was a significant milestone in their happy marriage and his children organised a surprise party, decorating the house with wreaths of orange blossoms and giving them a silver tea service. Thring commemorated the event with a sonnet, ending with the lines:

> 'In God's dear presence man and maiden stand
> And heavenly alchemy its secret tries
> The silver wedding first, as Time takes hold
> With Love; and fifty years bring back the gold'.

Outside term-time the family's pattern of life had changed little over the years. Christmas was still a major event, from which Thring was absent only in 1883 when his mother was seriously ill at Alford. At New

---

[1] It was quoted anonymously in 1890 in a *Journal of Education* review of Skrine's book that included the reference to Thring as equivalent to 'the Emperor of Brazil' (see ch. 18).

[2] The Dean of Westminster was George Granville Bradley, once Master of Marlborough College (1858-1870). The *Schoolmistress* urged every teacher who 'aspires to the high rank of an educator', to read Thring's recently published volume of *Addresses*. Thring's brother, Henry, came to predict that Edward's and Godfrey's achievements would be better remembered than his.

Year and Easter the family mostly visited relatives in Somerset or acquaintances all round England. The children went to London periodically – with Marie, or as she grew older, with Anna or Thring himself, to stay with Henry and to meet friends. They enjoyed Henry's box at concerts in the Royal Albert Hall; visited the Colonial Exhibition in 1886 and joined the crowds at Queen Victoria's Golden Jubilee Day celebrations a year later. After Thring's Borth debts put an end to holidays at Ben Place, parents and daughters spent an entire summer in 1882 visiting friends. Thring had expected the absence of a proper holiday to be 'like cutting the light out of my day', but afterwards he declared it to have been 'the pleasantest holiday we have ever had'. They spent most other years between 1878 and 1884 at Borth, occasionally joined by Gale and Bertie. Margaret would go sketching; Sarah and Grace collected shells and Thring himself entertained his old Eton friend, Bishop Mackarness of Oxford, or presided over the local Eisteddfod. In 1879 he revised *Life-Science* and opened the new Borth path with its commemorative stone seats. Two years later he stayed for seven weeks, but in 1884 after the Tercentenary he could find time for only three.[1]

In summers from 1885 the family headed instead for central Scotland, travelling from Rugby to Pitlochry over two days in a private railway carriage. For Thring, holidays still offered escape, but rain, remoteness, fewer visitors, and only occasional walks and outings to Killiecrankie or the Birnam Highland games meant that Sarah (now 29), Margaret (27) and Grace (19) were desperately bored. They missed their pets, the aviary birds and their two brothers who now spent summers elsewhere with their friends. Thring took three hours' rest in the middle of the day and was always in bed by 10.30pm: 'Under no circumstances do I break through the extreme regularity of my daily routine'. He was also increasingly rigid about his diet.

Many years earlier in his *Index Rerum* he had included the maxim 'Remember if you have children, not to treat them as children after they are grown up', but he found it hard to live up to the advice. When Godfrey once dared to suggest that the girls led an over-sheltered life, Thring was

---

[1] September 1878 to Parkin: his stomach tightened up as he returned to Uppingham: 'I am feeling very cowardly and mean just at present, having had to go back to prison and the chains again... It is not the school work that I dread but the dull, poisonous atmosphere... with a heavy local authority round about...' The stone seats at Borth still remain.

very defensive: 'Besides our great school parties they go out at the Lakes and in one way and another see more society than most people'.[1]

All three had been educated by governesses, including the German-speaking Swiss Miss Heutschy whom, much later, they were allowed to visit in Switzerland. In term-time they were tutored in a range of useful activities but, significantly, dancing was not included.[2] There were visits and picnics with young ladies of their own age – notably Paul David's daughter, Lottie. They were allowed to attend house concerts, the end of term party celebrations (including musical chairs) and other school events with their parents, but there was no socialising with the boys. Their life beyond the school centred on the Mutual Improvement Society's activities for ladies. Ring-fenced from boys and masters except under strict supervision, they had little opportunity to seek other male company.

Marie still officially oversaw the domestic side of the house, but by 1885 her advancing age and anxiety meant that the efficient Sarah had effectively taken it over. Anna remained Thring's secretary and increasingly she became his memory. The family's own housekeeping now devolved on to Grace, whose cooking skills extended little further than the daily breakfast egg on which Thring insisted. Along with Bertie, she was the most intelligent and intellectually curious of Thring's children, with a strong sense of fun. Her hobbies included reading and music, animals, birds and botany, but she often regretted that she had no opportunity for practical science. Her daily routine beyond her housekeeping was hardly challenging: late-morning reading; music lessons and practice; the town choral society; walks and visiting friends; being allowed to take lunch with the boys, escorted by two carefully selected seniors.[3] Her career ambition extended no further than being her mother's secretary.

Margaret, the middle daughter, had an artist's independent mind and a dry sense of humour. She was an avid painter who had begun to exhibit her work and she loved the family's occasional visits to the National

---

[1] Possibly Godfrey saw Thring's failure to provide formal education for his daughters as a contrast with the opportunities provided by their brother Charles - and Lydia - for their own five daughters.

[2] Dancing had to wait until a visit to London. Even then, the lessons were limited in scope: described by Marie as 'more callisthenics, and for carriage and deportment, than actual classes'. Marie revealed her limited ambitions for her daughters' education in describing these lessons as 'the only thing they do not learn in Uppingham'.

[3] 'One is called Smith – a nephew of Mrs. Ewing's' (and thus presumably seen as 'safe'). 1886: 'My fixed hours are few... Reading is the pleasantest occupation...' but she wrote of falling asleep in her hammock whilst doing it.

Gallery, but she suffered recurrent bouts of scarlet fever and other illnesses and her parents insisted that she did not exert herself too much.

She managed one brief flirtation – with Dr. Christopher Childs, Thring's former pupil who had been sanitary officer at Borth. Thring had been happy to keep Childs on his staff after the school returned (not surprisingly, given Childs' popularity, his Oxford First in science and his athletic skills), but he disapproved of the match. This may have been because of the couple's twelve-year age-gap, or perhaps because he could not face the prospect of his daughters fleeing the nest. He and Marie thought the friendship a temporary infatuation and he made Childs promise not to court Margaret, but before long they were discovered together in the garden and Thring summarily dismissed him. There would be no further suitors for any of the girls.[1]

Gale and Bertie had more leeway, as boarders away from Thring's own house. After leaving the school they continued to take advantage of its wider social life: Old Boys' gatherings in term-time and the bachelor masters' dances during the holidays. After Cambridge Gale worked for a time at Bromsgrove School as a boarding supervisor for minimal payment and he briefly acquired a fiancée whom the family greatly liked.[2] Although no great intellectual he was a good sportsman and popular with his friends, but Thring openly saw his elder son as a disappointment. He took Gale on to his staff in 1881 but sensed that he might be accused of nepotism and that it was a risky decision: 'I told him he would have to take the lowest class as private pupils... May God make him a son in spirit as well as in the flesh'.[3]

Thring's doubts were well-founded. As his son's employer Thring found Gale 'a fine impractical fidgetty swell still' and he turned down Gale's requests for additional salary. Father and son co-existed uneasily thereafter because Gale (supported by Bertie) began to ask how much of the family's money Thring had committed to the school. Even if he had known the answer Thring would have been reluctant to give it, but worse

---

[1] Childs posed a problem for Thring because after Borth Dr. Bell became obsessed that Child was trying to steal his patients. Margaret was only a baby when Childs was in her father's house. Matthews suggested in *By God's Grace* that Thring thought Childs socially inferior – although he later became Lecturer in Public Health at UCL, and a school trustee. In old age Margaret described how, when forced to give Childs up, she put on a stout pair of boots and went for a long walk to get him out of her system.

[2] Marie thought her personable and intelligent: Helen Constance Overbury – but she and Gale did not marry.

[3] 1880: 'I knew the danger he could be, either a great help or a great pain, and there would be many lies told'.

quickly followed as he furiously objected to Gale's support for Bertie in what became the great sorrow of his final two years.

Bertie too had found Thring a heavy-handed father. Thring's twentieth birthday message to him in 1879 urged him to 'work and live so that every year may bring the feeling of life richer, better, purer, and more unselfish'. Subsequent letters urged him 'every day and night to read from ten to thirty verses of the Gospels carefully, and so go through them quietly and begin again', and 'to bear yourself in God's world true and faithful ever'. After Bertie's graduation Thring wrote again: 'Have you ever really, seriously, considered how you can most truly put out your talents for your Lord?'

This was the sort of question which he regularly asked pupils during 'paternals' but it was unlikely to go down well with his own son – especially as it was not at all what Bertie wanted to hear. After school he had gone to Oxford, but had done little work. He received a poor degree in 1882 which greatly upset Thring and seemed to rule out a teaching career. As Bertie graduated, Thring turned remorselessly to more questions about his future: 'Have you ever really, seriously, considered whether you would take... Holy Orders? The common atmosphere of "How can I get on?" so pervades the whole world'.

Keen now to be the one member of his immediate family to make any money – preferably away from Uppingham – Bertie sought Parkin's advice about a career in the timber trade or stockbroking in Canada. When he then began to talk of moving to Texas, Thring was horrified. He wrote Bertie a grim letter, spelling out (as he had to Parkin) his concern about America's 'glitter and greed'. He grieved at the thought 'that child of mine should abjure the name of Englishman'. Bertie backed off.

In 1883 Bertie told Parkin: 'I am at a tutorship in Dorsetshire', teaching the stupid but honest son of an army major. He complained of not much to do there – but he was allowed to go hunting once a week. By 1884 he was working for stockbrokers in London, bemoaning the fact that Saturday work denied him the chance to play cricket and football. He had fallen in love with an Italian, Sybil Linati, but with little money and uncertain prospects he seemed in no position to marry quickly. Thring had never met her, and he instinctively believed that her Catholicism made her unsuitable. He could do little to prevent the engagement but he asked Henry to make discreet enquiries about her family.

To his parents' acute dismay Bertie then suddenly married Sybil. Marie agonised innocently about the cause of such precipitate action and Thring declared that 'it clouded our whole lives'. He ordered that none of the girls should meet Bertie, although they could write to him if they must. Grace told Parkin by letter that her father had made it a head-on test of loyalty: 'He hoped we were at one with him in this. We said that we were, and so the matter ended'.

Bertie's subsequent visit to his parents was a very tense affair. Marie met him but Thring declined to, sending a message that 'it was not for want of love'. Frustrated by his father over many years, Bertie countered by launching a barrage of letters reproaching both his parents for their rejection of him and his wife.[1] Thring's suppressed resentment at what he saw as the disappointing careers of both his sons now boiled over. He had never experienced such defiance before and he was furious at any questioning of his financial decisions: 'God help us all. When have these two unhappy boys with their grievances ever given me... any reason to rejoice in their work?' Even when Bertie wrote to thank them for his birthday parcel, Thring remained clear about what the family's attitude must be: 'To show we are still affectionate, but to be as hard as the nether mill until he makes some amends for the fearful wrong he has done; also not to admit her (Sybil) amongst our daughters till we really know something about her... When the conventional safeguards of society are cast aside, on what a trackless wilderness one is let loose'.

Christmas 1886 was unusually subdued with the family's usual celebrations cancelled. Thring admitted to his diary that 'Herbert's treason has broken up the loving home and shaken the whole of our family world to its centre', and he rehearsed in its pages a conversation with his wayward sons: 'Hold your tongues, redeem your lost years before you dare speak. I gave you a start: you refused to train for it. Be successful before you open your lips to me'. He knew that delivering such a tirade would achieve nothing but 'I am absolutely horrified at their rejection of [my] work for Christ here, and putting their own self-seeking above the greater cause'.

By now Bertie was in desperate financial straits, even asking for permission to pawn his silver birthday spoons. When former school-friends sympathised with his plight and simultaneously Gale criticised their father for not supporting Bertie financially (whilst again asking for a salary increase for himself), Thring saw it all as an Old Boy-inspired plot. His anger and sorrow knew no bounds: 'I do not know why God has afflicted me and my wife. I grope in thick darkness and can only pray'.

---

[1] Thring: 'A blind and insolent letter... Gale and Herbert think they have grievances against me because after their idle wasted lives at school and college they have not at once got position and the power of marrying. Poor wretches, they must be unhappy if they feed on such poisonous fancies'. He was especially upset by their claims that his work had deprived his children of their inheritance.

In March 1887, less than eight months after Bertie's hurried marriage, the reason for it became all too clear. Thring was overwhelmed with sorrow: 'The unwelcome news this morning that I am a grandfather. May God [save] my unhappy boy from the pain he has brought on us. [We] have done all we could to make our children happy... I fear we must have been grievously wrong. Yet not [for] want of kindness, God knows'. He took especially hard Bertie's claim that the baby had been born prematurely: defiance was bad, but lying was far worse: 'He has severed all ties, poor wretch'. The stand-off continued and by August as he prepared to go on holiday, he was physically exhausted with worry:

'That unhappy boy Herbert's poison working in the family. Gale going to meet him in Town by appointment, independent of us. Gale not trustworthy, bitter himself with lies about our life. Marie at me to tell all which is going on. A great mistake, gone to bed upset... Very far from well, with very heavy work on'.

He was deeply concerned about Marie. She was much less resilient than in the past and months of worry had affected her even more than Thring himself. Recently she had steeled herself to remind Gale that everything that he and his brother had taken for granted since childhood resulted from Thring's work for the school.[1] All through 1887 he fretted about her peace of mind. In February she was 'ill... and with all sorts of ideas... which are very difficult to deal with'; a month later 'she comes and asks advice and won't take it, and goes on haggling over the whole matter... then when she has worried me out of my very life she says I won't let her speak and consult &c'. Early in April: 'I cannot get [her] to stop writing and leave matters alone'. He worried too about the impact on his daughters and his wider family: Anna and Godfrey were Bertie's godparents. Anna was equally ground down, certain that Sybil was 'not a good influence' and (despite being normally so calm) suffering from confusion, headaches and sleepless nights.

Thring's daughters (especially Margaret) largely stuck by him but Sarah noted how much the trauma had aged both parents. As the months went by she and Grace had increasing doubts about Thring's intransigence. Grace told Parkin that 'we girls think it a great mistake'.

---

[1] Thring: '[She asked] if I had remained a clergyman what would have been his (Gale's) fate for these thirty years and Herbert's too, that they had had splendid advantages all these years, and were living on my daily work now, that we had begun with nothing and by the toil they grudged had gained the money which they enjoyed and grumbled over'. Bertie sought Henry's advice: Henry was open-minded, if not actively sympathetic.

They had not been in contact with Bertie since (months earlier) being allowed to send him a Christmas hamper and now Thring was demanding that they write Bertie no more letters for a year: 'How we are to begin again after that long silence I cannot say. It is a miserable business'.

By August 1887 the three sisters had all but given up hope. They did not even know the five month-old baby's name and Gale, who went to see Bertie in London, returned tight-lipped. Grace began 'slowly accustoming myself to the fact that the old life with [Bertie] is over'. Thring remained devastated and helpless: the affair had challenged so many of his assumptions and he felt 'a sense of dread [as if tossed] in a boat on a stormy sea... During all these dreadful years of struggling, we did what we could for our children, I am sure we did all we could. I think now it was a mistake putting them at this school but I [believed] it best'.

****

Thring's other, simultaneous source of worry was the question of his own future. Before the Tercentenary he confided in Parkin that if he retired, although he would not be homeless he would certainly be 'very poor'.[1] He had a touching belief that 'having given up money and fortune for truth's sake', God would somehow protect him and his family, but he was increasingly conscious that, unlike the other housemasters, he owned neither his boarding house (which was held by the Trust) nor any property elsewhere. Ben Place had been the nearest to a home to him but it had long since gone out of his life.

His thoughts about the future moved rapidly to and fro. Apart from a few months in 1874-5, between briefly clearing his debts thanks to a legacy in his father's will and the first outbreak of typhoid, financial concern had always been 'the fox gnawing at my vitals'. He was acutely aware of the contrast between the school's restored numbers and prosperity since the return from Borth and his own need to economise, and also of his advancing age. As he began his thirtieth school year in 1882 he wrote of preparing for 'the squaring up my accounts and making all things ready for a decent exit'. Eighteen months later he was still

---

[1] 1882-3 to Parkin: 'I want to retire, and *can't* till I clear my bank book. I know not where to turn'. He was £3,000 in debt and had spent another £2,000 on the school. He estimated his total contributions to the school as £80,000, as well as providing £40,000-worth p.a. for masters' salaries. '£14,000 a year of this was legally my private property before the New Scheme... I have never launched out into any personal luxuries... I have given to the nation by my zests and pain and work... If one was unmarried and had no family [it] would be very different...'

'thinking of resigning before very long... I do not mean to hang on till younger men say that I am old fashioned and past my prime'.

He must also have been conscious that many leading HMC members had received educational or church preferment.[1] When Eton looked for a new provost in 1883, one journal suggested that 'everyone would be delighted to see it given to Mr. Thring as the too long delayed reward of a most distinguished career'. Another declared that 'only one man would satisfy all conditions: Etonian, clergyman, re-founder of a great school, distinguished writer on education'.[2] In many ways, however, he was far from the obvious candidate and nothing came of it.

When Thring had threatened to leave the Conference over the Greek question, Jex-Blake of Rugby put out discreet feelers about possibilities for him elsewhere, concerned that he was working himself into an early grave.[3] Bishop Fraser wrote to Gladstone suggesting that he would make a good cathedral dean, or a canon at Canterbury: 'The fire of his generous nature burns in him vigorously still'. Neither approach produced anything: Thring was unaware of them and he would probably have been both gratified and horrified, had he known.

On holiday in Borth in 1884 and with the Tercentenary over, he again speculated to Parkin about retirement, aware as he grew older that he had actually begun to enjoy times of idleness and that he no longer needed ceaseless activity to stop him worrying. In the autumn he told Marie that he might retire in the following summer. Soon afterwards he changed his mind, preoccupied with being '63½ [but] with [only] a small pittance ready (saved up)' and conscious that he still had a family to support. He was basking in the success of *Theory and Practice* and reluctant to give up the professional platform which enabled him to capitalise on the book's success. At the end of the year he consulted his principal supporters amongst the trustees and was heartened that they urged him to stay on.

---

[1] Amongst these, Harper (Sherborne) was Head of an Oxford College; Mitchinson (King's Canterbury) was Bishop of Barbados; Ridding (Winchester, who had introduced him to Parkin) was the first Bishop of Southwell. Thring's Eton friend Mackarness was Bishop of Oxford. Goodwin was Bishop of Carlisle. Benson, (Wellington) was Archbishop of Canterbury, with considerable church patronage at his disposal. There were several other former-headmaster bishops.

[2] The Provost was resident chairman of governors. Ironically this journal suggested that Gladstone would approve. It seems possible, but unlikely, that Bertie's troubles affected the outcome.

[3] Jex-Blake to Parkin (1888): 'Mr. Thring was a man of great energy and sincerity; and I was very desirous that he should have some promotion in time to save his valuable life'.

With no national pension scheme for teachers and only his book sales to fall back on, any retirement plans depended on the trustees' goodwill. During 1885 this issue became an increasing obsession for him. His greatest opponent, Wales, had left the Board yet Thring's closest allies, Jacob and Birley, remained. The Oxford University representative trustee was now Hugo Harper, formerly headmaster of Sherborne and now Principal of Jesus College, Oxford, who had helped him to set up HMC. Hodgkinson had also recently become a trustee: they had had their recent differences but surely Hodgkinson was too honourable a man to deny him on this matter. For all these reasons he felt cause to be hopeful and, acknowledging what the trustees had done for him in buying back the Elizabethan schoolroom,[1] he asked them to award him a retirement pension or to guarantee to protect his family if he were to die in harness.

Unfortunately for him, his future was not the most pressing issue on the trustees' minds at that moment. The recent rise in their income through the increased tuition fee and their newly-acquired ownership of the sanatorium and the Elizabethan schoolroom had given them an appetite for new capital projects. Ironically, Thring had himself suggested some possible developments in his post-Borth *Statement,* including the replacement of his own boarding house on a site on the far (west) side of the chapel. The trustees had subsequently added a proposal for a quadrangle of new classrooms.

Matters came to a head in October 1886. The trustees may well have sensed that the school was losing momentum towards the end of Thring's three and a half decades in office.[2] If so, they saw Harper as the best person to send on a visit to Thring to test the water over how long he meant to remain in post. As a former headmaster and a governor of several schools, he was better placed than any other trustee to appreciate the issues involved in calculating any retirement agreement.

Harper duly called on Thring during that month to ask about his future plans. It was a cordial meeting, yet within weeks something caused Thring to write in his diary of the 'meanness and injustice' of the pension being offered. He began to rail against having Harper (whom he saw as having run a 'lesser' school) and Hodgkinson (a mere former assistant master) deciding his fate.

---

[1] See p.236.

[2] A lukewarm examiner's report less than two years after Thring's death (even about the teaching of divinity) suggests that the criticisms had validity: Oakham fared better in the same report. The trustees may also have been mindful of other headmasters who had hung on too long: see Tyerman: *Harrow* p.353 for Thring's old friend Butler in this respect.

By now he was taking procedural and legal advice from a former parent, Sir George Couper, who advised him in November 1886 to ask for more detail about the settlement that the trustees proposed. Thring thought that a lump sum of £18-20,000 had been mentioned: a sizeable amount offering the prospect of a good income if well invested, although far less than what Thring had himself spent on buildings and salaries for additional masters over the years. He was glad that an offer had been made, but felt that the sum was inadequate. On Couper's advice he asked for further clarification.[1]

In January 1887 the trustees sent an initial response to Couper's questions, but adopted their usual stance of setting up a committee to consider details *and* 'the pressing want for classrooms'. This greatly angered Thring who now was 'tired of being trodden on by [these] snobs'. However, his unavoidable absence from the next finance committee meeting may have helped to produce constructive discussion of an annuity and a pension, both of which would continue after his death, and his mood briefly changed for the better. It was a proposal that he declared he would accept, and he was assured by Birley that the Board would agree to it.

Unfortunately the trustees then had second thoughts, and a week later Thring was again writing of 'hated trustees' meetings' and of how Harper had deserted him. Early in March he was optimistic once more, after an olive branch from Jacob – but this too was withdrawn as the other trustees forced Jacob back into line. Thring then inveighed against Jacob too – although even as he was complaining about how 'my friends are treating me like a fourth form boy, to be patronised if they are favourable, to be snubbed if not', he was again committing large sums of his own money to the school for workshop equipment.[2]

Around this time Hardie Rawnsley wrote enquiring as to whether his godfather and old friend was interested in looking for new work. Rawnsley did not specify what or where it might be, but Thring sensed that it might finally be God's sign that it was time to move on.[3] He replied that he would jump at the chance: there were only 'three of the men and

---

[1] 'It is sad having to play the gladiator but one may get a little fun out of [making Harper try to explain] it'.

[2] The trustees' minute book suggests that their second proposal would have saved c£1,000. Harper greatly offended him by seeming to suggest an annuity after all, at a reduced figure. Thring: 'I am unfeignedly sorry for what [Jacob] has done... dropping to the level of the pettifogging trustee'. The equipment was bought from a bigamous master (see ch. 21). He still found time to give moral support to a headmaster in Staffordshire who had recently been dismissed by his governors.

[3] Rawnsley was now a vicar in the Lake District: he may have intended to approach Bishop Goodwin of Carlisle over opportunities for Thring.

four or five of the women' at the school whom he would really miss, and 'how gladly would I shake the dust off my feet'. Desperately needing advice that he could trust, he confided in Sam Haslam, one of his most loyal and longstanding housemasters. Haslam was appalled at any thought of Thring resigning and strongly urged him to sit tight: he thought the retirement proposal unfair and he was sure that the trustees would be forced to pay a new headmaster far more than they had ever given Thring.

From this conversation came a remarkable show of solidarity from the housemasters as a body. They sent the trustees a strongly-worded petition listing all Thring's achievements over three decades and demanding that all his financial worries be removed forthwith. He had 'devoted to the school his whole powers' and shown 'indomitable perseverance and energy' in the face of every conceivable difficulty. They had complete confidence in him, and hoped that he might continue for a considerable time. Furthermore if the trustees thought that a change of face would automatically be for the better, they should remember what they would be losing: Thring had 'more than any other living man defended and promoted the cause of education in England [and] he occupies a position which none of his successors for centuries to come can occupy'.

Unmoved by this act of defiance, the trustees stood firm. At their mid-June meeting in 1887 they moved only about a quarter of the way towards Thring's financial aspirations. His bitterness was unconfined at this 'betrayal' by his key allies, all of whom had been absent from the meeting. He deeply resented the Board's new-found enthusiasm for extra buildings: he felt that he knew the school's needs far better than they. Besides, the school had waited three hundred years for classrooms, so surely it could wait another five or six until, in the natural course of time, he had left the stage. The meeting ended acrimoniously as he refused to act on a resolution about scholarships.

****

After so many years of damning the trustees for *not* wanting extra buildings it was deeply paradoxical that Thring was now the one opposing a plan to provide them. It would be easy to see to see this dispute as purely a pension issue, or a straightforward battle of wills between Thring and the trustees (as he and the housemasters did), and the trustees as the sole villains: ungrateful and indecisive in failing to achieve a quick and amicable parting of the ways, and exploiting the fact that Thring's best years all too evidently lay behind him.

The reality is more complicated, and clues to it lie in Thring's denunciation of Harper and Hodgkinson – and in the Charity Commission papers in the National Archives. The work of the Endowed School Commissioners and the detailed provisions in the New Scheme had returned to haunt him.

Within the pension discussions a contentious secondary issue had emerged: the basis on which the figures might be worked out. The New Scheme (by then in existence for over a decade) included clauses guaranteeing Thring capitation payments of between 1/6 and 1/4 of the tuition fees, the precise fraction to be approved by the trustees.[1] However, when the Charity Commissioners agreed to the 33% tuition fee increase after Borth, they and the trustees both failed to appreciate how much this would also increase the capitation payments which Thring received in addition to his stipend, admission fees and boarding fees. The charity commission returns show that these capitation payments had reached nearly £2,500 p.a. by 1886.

Both sides accepted the New Scheme's provision for such fees in principle, but whereas Thring wanted any pension or lump sum to be calculated on the basis of the higher fraction and the high pupil numbers and increased tuition fee charged during his final years, the trustees understandably argued for a calculation based on a lower fraction, average pupil numbers throughout his 34-year tenure, and fees at the New Scheme's original (i.e. pre-Borth) fee level. All this helps to explain why Thring referred to the trustees' pension proposal as 'the Jacob dodge'.

This financial disagreement reflected another change over the previous decade, whose significance Thring had failed to appreciate. The trustees were now using the Scheme exactly as the Endowed School Commissioners had originally intended: as a manual for how to oversee the school. This in turn had now fundamentally altered the relationship between them and the Charity Commission.

The increased tuition fee was far from the only issue on which the trustees had asked for guidance from London over the previous few years. Since Borth they had sought permission from the Commission before making the sanatorium and Elizabethan schoolroom acquisitions, building the new swimming bath and making several small land and property purchases. They had done so too before granting Earle's pension. They would now follow precedent and do the same in Thring's case: after all, the sums involved in any settlement for Thring were much greater.

Harper made several approaches to the Commission on the trustees' behalf during 1887, explaining the competing demands of Thring's

---

[1] According to the Charity Commission papers, Thring had been granted an increase from the 1/6 to 1/4 of these fees for a two-year period from 1884. He had now asked that this be extended until he retired.

pension and the plans for new classrooms, but making it clear he had little sympathy with Thring's demands. He believed that Thring's formula for calculating his pension broke the spirit, if not the letter, of the earlier agreement to increase the tuition fee, and that his capitation fees were far greater than those in force at other comparable schools.[1] He also asserted that after Thring's claims over Borth had been settled several years earlier, any extra revenue should have been used to build up the school's reserve fund. Hodgkinson wrote too, at pains to ask that his letter should be private and unofficial, but denying Thring's long-held claim that money of his own spent on the school should be seen as a donation to the Trust.

It is possible to see both Harper's and Hodgkinson's actions as less than generous, but it is not the only interpretation that can be placed on them. Thring's longstanding reluctance to engage with the trustees on financial matters, coupled with the size of the capitation fees that he was now receiving, may have caused them greatly to underestimate how much money he was injecting annually into the school. They may therefore have felt that he needed a far smaller pension than he was demanding. They may also have feared that in the reformed climate of opinion about how a school's endowments should be used, presenting any proposal which the Commissioners could regard as unreasonable might cause them to reject the idea of a pension altogether.

Whatever the reason, seeing now that he could not win, Thring lashed out in all directions. Harper had been brought on to the trustee body purely to thwart him; Jacob was a turncoat and Birley was in Jacob's pocket.[2] The Board was playing a devious game: posing as forward-thinking in its desire for new classrooms, whilst in fact cheating him. He briefly threatened to expose the trustees' years of mismanagement through the press, but he eventually chose to vent his frustration on their chairman, the hereditary trustee Augustus Charles Johnson, instead.[3]

It must have been a poignant encounter as Johnson, fifteen years his junior, let the tired old man bluster on, wisely declining to be drawn into a re-run of age-old arguments. Thring accused the trustees of behaving like

---

[1] See ch. 22.

[2] Thring's and Harper's assocation went back for two decades, but Harper was also heavily involved in Oxford University matters, as treasurer of the Radcliffe Hospital, and was a member of four other school governing bodies. Both a parent and governor of Sherborne, he gave his hapless successor a difficult time. When (like Hodgkinson five years earlier), Harper wrote to Thring seeking for a job for his son, Thring's refusal letter began with the cold words: 'Dear Mr. Trustee'.

[3] Born in 1837, he was the son of General Johnson, Thring's early supporter who died in 1863.

shopkeepers and treating him as one, and he claimed that his own family was equal in rank to any of them. He repeated Haslam's view that his successor would be paid far more.

Only once did Johnson break in, gently pointing out that times – and needs – had changed. This only provoked a new tirade from Thring: 'One thing does not change here: the school being full. If you hunt me from the place, you may find it difficult to find a man who in these days will keep the numbers up'. Having fulminated for some time, he then pleaded for understanding: 'Old as I am, though with plenty of work in me yet, I am not young enough to begin life again fresh'. He and Johnson parted politely but still at odds and when term ended in July 1887 the issue remained unresolved.

In that month, after what he described as 'one of the severest terms that I have ever passed', Thring again wrote to Godfrey. Describing his life as one of 'ceaseless toil, anxiety, calumny and misrepresentation' he harked back across the decades to his struggles with Charles and Lydia. He resented how often he had been 'spoken to like a baby' by Henry. He envisaged dying in a debtor's prison with his wife and children. He begged Godfrey's pardon for such gloom, but few other people would understand. There would be only one more letter between them.

CHAPTER TWENTY-ONE

FINAL YEAR

THRING began what would prove to be the final volume of his diary in October 1886 to mark his forthcoming 65th birthday. Along with his two great concerns that year there had been a succession of other troubles which took a cumulative toll on him and Marie: a chimney fire which damaged the private side of the house; the theft of Marie's jewellery by a burglar, caught red-handed but subsequently acquitted by what Thring grimly described as 'a Rutland jury'; the death of two family dogs both thought to have been poisoned.[1] As her daughters took turns to read to Marie each evening they worried that her rheumatism and anxiety were increasing and that her short-sightedness might be a prelude to going blind altogether. Anna had neuralgia, made worse by overwork.

Like Thring's 1850s' diary, this volume has survived in full and it shows how much he was now living in two parallel worlds. Celebrated beyond Uppingham by Old Boys, teachers and in the press, in his own domain he was withdrawing into himself: increasingly protective of his health; too often riled by boys or colleagues; angry with past enemies real or imagined.

In the last weeks of 1886 he had to deal with a difficult case of a master's lack of classroom competence. Soon afterwards two others were involved in different sexual indiscretions: one had committed bigamy and the story briefly surfaced in the national press. After a pair of boys had a minor fight in the house he tore into a 'sulky fellow' who came to dispute his punishment, sending him away 'humbled and repentant'. In the classroom 'half my class today quietly shirked, either from carelessness or wilfulness'.

He unaccountably banned a debate on political issues and, unprecedentedly, he used the excuse of a slight cold and stormy weather to miss a concert performed in another house. Even the school performance of Handel's *Judas Maccabeus* failed to enthuse him: 'Things

---

[1] One was his; the other, Gale's. It was the first time in years the family had no dogs, but he would not replace them - a special blow to a man who once suggested for his tombstone: 'He was beloved by children and dogs'.

299

went off all right, though the words are such nonsense'.[1] Before the bachelor masters' end of term ball he was fretting about catching a cold. A week later he was relieved to be past the shortest day, but fearful of what the New Year would bring and wishing that he could call off his visit to Somerset. There was acute frost, and Margaret had scarlet fever again.

The January term was no better. 'Catapulting cads' from the town threw stones at school buildings for the first time in many years, breaking a window in the schoolroom. His confirmation class was 'ignorant beyond belief'. In the summer there was more rowdiness and 'indecency in Skrine's house'. His 'jaws' about bad behaviour grew in length, and he declined to give any English prizes to his class in the end of year examinations: 'Disgraceful: no prize exercises worth looking. The worst year I have ever had'.

Housemasters who reported boys for bad work were 'disagreeable' and those who came to see him were given increasingly short shrift: 'Half the day was poisoned [when] Campbell came in after breakfast with some trifles... this intrusion for nothing is intolerable'. At the weekly masters' meeting his decisions were being challenged, with objections to lessons being cancelled for a special service to mark the departure of the Old Boy Lionel Cholmondeley for the mission field.[2] He viewed queries about contractual arrangements with the local doctors as 'petty rebellion'; he told everyone present that they had never understood Socratic questioning methods and (after a housemaster went behind his back to the trustees over a minor issue about scholarship payments)[3] he launched into a long diatribe about disloyalty at Borth, saying that he was 'sick of the whole of their captious controversies'. Then he walked out, declaring: 'I have had enough of it, and never [mean] to confer with them again if I can help it'.

He also took exception to the new Rector raising questions about standards in the town's elementary school and, seemingly oblivious to the fact that it was now four decades since his experiences in Gloucester, he told him very forcibly: 'I have taught a good deal in National Schools', adding in his diary: 'He is an ass'. When one of Holden's former pupils wrote in the visitors' book at Borth that Holden had paved the way for Thring, he again sounded off about his poor inheritance. He re-ran his arguments with the Commissioners in the 1860s; with Rector Wales in the

---

[1] Thring complained of 'the great falling off in the singing and responding and common prayer in this chapel. A meaner heart seems to be in the place. A lower generation, I suppose, has succeeded to those of old...'

[2] Sarah and Grace had heard of the objection, and they alerted him. The service went ahead, and Thring preached.

[3] 'I cannot stand his jaw... full of quibbles'. Scholarships were a Trust matter.

70s; with Old Boys who had recently supported Bertie; with his German sister-in-law Louise who (he claimed) was sending him begging letters. He was bitter that Walter Earle, a former colleague, could afford to buy a large house and garden elsewhere to start a new preparatory school.[1]

There were still occasional glimpses of his old self, however: his sermon declaring that where reputations were concerned, true manliness came before cricket; his pleasure at the fine mosaics taking shape on the chapel reredos as a memorial to Alington[2]; his enthusiasm for new arrivals in the aviary; the first aconites and crocuses after a hard winter; a housemaster telling him how much the younger boys liked his lessons. Above all, he still valued his pastoral work and his paternals. He was deeply moved when two brothers, recently sent to the school from India, came to see him. They were unable to read their father's letter and asked him to help them. He thought it was 'the most honourable, touching and prettiest thing, I believe that ever happened to me... To think that these boys should come to me (they not in my house) is something glorious'.[3]

****

In contrast to his troubles, in June 1887 he presided over a happy and notable event: the Conference of the Association of Headmistresses whom he had invited to meet in Uppingham that year. It marked the culmination of ideas which he had developed over several years and which can first be clearly seen in his support for the new Cambridge Teacher Training Syndicate (1879) which encouraged initial and postgraduate teacher training for women as well as men.

Two years later (1881) he addressed a hundred shop-girls in Brighton. He was far from the obvious person to do it, but friends had pressed him and it confirmed his dawning interest in education and career prospects for girls. This ran in parallel with his concern that young men had too little respect for women – which formed the theme of his paper to the Carlisle Church Congress entitled 'The Best Means of Raising the Standard of Public Morality' (1884). Drawing on his experience of Gloucester and Woolwich, he spelt out the difficulties for anyone of living a chaste life in slum housing: 'Men and women, who have no earthly pleasure save sex and beer, cannot be chaste'. Those who merely talked

---

[1] Louise Ulrike (Koch) Breusing, was the sister of Marie and Anna. Walter Earle was on Thring's staff 1864-73: brother of William Earle, the Usher.

[2] See footnote p.225.

[3] Two sons of Michael Joseph Brind, an Old Boy 1863-6 and now Director of Telegraphs in India.

religion or gave money for new churches but did nothing to address urban squalor were humbugs.[1]

In this and several later addresses he drew on his friendships with women such as Frances Kingsley and Julie Ewing and on the influence of staff wives within the school to assert the role that God had intended for women. He declared a 'reverence for womanhood [because] the saving power in this present world is in women and God meant it to be so'. He saw woman as 'the helpmeet for man and the partner for life' (sic). He was convinced that 'the heathen idea of sex in the medieval and modern world must be rooted out. Honour to women: that is the key to all life'.

In 1885 he spoke at St Paul's Church, Knightsbridge during *The London Mission to Public School Men*. It was one of seven lectures by well-known church and school figures to promote the work of the new public-school missions, and he took as his text Genesis 2: 7 ('God formed man of the dust of the ground and breathed into his nostrils the fire of life'). He defined life as a gift and sacred trust from God, and he spelt out the importance of purity and self-control for married and non-married alike – surely surprising his audience of young men by the explicit way in which he declared that 'life, work and sex [are] the basis of human action'. Sex was 'part of the blessing on perfect work... God has willed that his sacred act in giving life should be carried on by the union of a man and a woman. Sexual intercourse in marriage is thus nearest to God, the most sacred of all acts... a direct continuance of God's command of His gift of life'.[2]

He went on to spell out a 'Charter of Life', emphasising community responsibility: 'Begin with something people understand... Teach happiness. How can those, whose only possible pleasures are beer and lust, be Christians? Make them human beings first... Let mission rooms, and attractive teaching, and attractive amusements, and life, [persuade] them. Music will reach everybody: teach it. Get [them] clothed and in their right mind, [and only] then preach to them'. He added an imperative

---

[1] He called for less humbug about 'purity' and 'continence': 'Whole families pigging it in one room cannot, in a civilized country, be chaste... We talk of divine truths, and build churches, when we ought to be going around with a scavenger's cart and a navvy's pickaxe, carting off filth and making sewers... I hold the man who provides good amusement for the poor, and teaches them to enjoy it, to be pre-eminently a man of God'.

[2] Victorian headmasters frequently praised essentially feminine virtues. See Nelson, Claudia: 'Sex and the Single Boy: Ideals of Manliness and Sexuality in Victorian Literature for Boys', *Victorian Studies* 32:4 (1989) pp.525-550, and *Invisible Men: Fatherhood in Victorian Periodicals 1850-1910* (1995).

borrowed from Charles Kingsley's *The Water-Babies*: 'Do as you would be done by'.

By now he was convinced that the distinctive moral and practical qualities of women gave them a right to career opportunities. His 1885 Minnesota address asserted 'that nation to be highest in the world which gives the highest place to women as workers'. He congratulated his former pupil Mitchell[1] (who had once enquired about fives courts) on promoting women's education in his northern parish. As he enjoyed the success of *Theory and Practice* the references to 'the boy' in his books and lectures had begun to shift more towards 'the child'. The 1886 lecture in St Albans (in which he spoke of general and particular levels of knowledge) was given to supporters of female higher education, and in it he celebrated the role of mothers as 'real' teachers, explaining the complementary nature of the two genders.

Many years earlier in *Education and School* he had suggested that the second decade of a child's life was of prime importance. Now he appeared to assign that significance to the *first* ten years – which constituted the time when children were shaped by their mother. If she did her task well, the child would be like Plato's true learner, accumulating skill and knowledge 'smoothly, without stumbling'. Thus, he declared, 'the real rulers of the world for good or evil must be those who have [a child's] first ten years in their hands... The sovereignty of woman is a fact. Those ten years make it so'.

Later that year (1886) his prize-giving speech at the Leamington High School for Girls came about because its headmistress was the Kingsleys' elder daughter. With memories of his meeting with Mrs. Ewing still fresh in his mind, he travelled there with Sarah and visited Frances Kingsley (now an invalid): it was an experience which confirmed to him that life was enriched by 'holy and gifted women'. If the Leamington girls were baffled by his tortuous views on prizes, they must also have struggled with his broader messages about a woman's role in life as a helpmeet. Although they could not match a man in physical strength, the Fall showed that they could exemplify 'the intense power of loveable weakness when it does right, [and] the irresistible victoriousness of helplessness and beauty when it is enlisted on the side of truth'. He was clearer in his assertion that in future mothers should be properly educated, not fobbed off with 'accomplishments', a fate which horrified him:

'You will all have professional work... [some] as teachers, nurses, managers of various kinds, [others as] daughters or wives with household

---

[1] See p.227.

duties. You should make yourselves mistresses of everything you have to manage, and this involves proper training... I rejoice that for the first time in the history of the world, an attempt is being made to put women... on the great platform of true workers. As for the ornament theory [of a woman's role], all I can say is, I believe it to be of the devil'.

In March 1887 he was invited to speak to young women at Newnham College, Cambridge about the importance of teaching as a career. It reminded him of 'how Mrs. Ewing's life and memory has set me going on all this woman's work' and of all that he owed to the women in his life: in particular his mother, Marie and Anna. His address, entitled 'A Workman's Hints on Teaching Work', was largely a re-working of old ideas (child-centredness; the value of words; recognition of the teaching profession; the needs of the slower learner) and even by his standards it was rich and varied in analogy: sheep and shepherds; architects creating lasting edifices; men not being made fishermen simply by buying fish at the fishmonger's shop.[1]

The visit itself was more important to him than the address. Briefly he rolled back the years, feeling that his stay in Cambridge was 'the most successful two days I think I have ever spent', and he saw the electrifying effect that the University had on his own daughter. With Marie too frail to go with him, instead he took twenty-one-year-old Grace. She described her experience in vivid detail in a twelve-page letter to Parkin shortly afterwards: staying with the Vice Chancellor in St John's; exploring the city and the Backs; visiting King's College Chapel; being entertained by various Heads of House. Permitted to dine in Trinity with some young men while her father was on High Table, she marvelled at the College's silver and its paintings. Her letter ended with a flourish: 'Everything went off swimmingly. They have elected him one of the university preachers for next year, so I hope I shall go again, if not before'.

Possibly Grace's enthusiasm brought home to Thring the limited opportunities he had given his daughters compared with his sons –

---

[1] Newnham, founded in 1871, was Cambridge's second women's college. Henry Sidgwick played a leading role in its inception, marrying Eleanor Balfour, one of its earliest students who later became its principal: see Heffer. Simon: *High Minds: The Victorians and the Birth of Modern Britain* (2013) pp.550-5. Thring's lecture included familiar distinctions between teaching and lecturing; mind and memory; knowledge and skill – and more side-swipes against examiners and governors: 'the dragons that guard the fountains of youth'. He showed his concern for diet and exercise with sporting metaphors to stress the importance of 'pre-working', too: food, sleep and exercise must all be regulated *before* the runner comes to the starting post.

especially when he remembered that the Headmistresses' Conference was now only a few weeks away.

Two decades earlier another witness to the Taunton Commission, Frances Mary Buss, the first principal of the North London Collegiate School, had shown that girls' schools had woefully meagre endowments compared with those for boys. Since then local initiatives had created many new girls' schools, together with an emphasis on formalised training for those who taught in them. This was very much in line with Thring's declared aim to promote teaching as a science and a noble profession. Out of this development had emerged the Association of Headmistresses, devised in 1874 by Miss Buss and Dorothea Beale, principal of Cheltenham Ladies' College. It had collaborative aims very similar to those of HMC five years earlier. The headmistresses' work made a profound impression on Thring, and in 1885, a month after Mrs. Ewing's death, he invited them to hold their 1887 gathering at Uppingham.

During the Easter holidays after his Cambridge visit he called on both headmistresses, telling their staff that women must 'do something to reform our wretched Education (so called)'. Once the summer term began, he and Anna started to prepare the details. Masters offered to escort the visitors from local railway stations; families would provide accommodation and praepostors would guide them around the school.

A few days before their arrival he spoke to the boys 'about the ladies coming'; telling them with a smile that 'they would have the most shrewd critics of character [and] behaviour here that they would probably ever meet in their lives'. He suspected that some of the boys had been making jokes about it all, but on the day (10 June) they rose to the occasion:

'It was a grand day... We put all the [visitors] up, feted them, gave them a concert, and entertained them as royally as we could. It was [their] first official recognition... They were a delightful company, entirely free from all nonsense; not a trace of "woman's rights" about them, but most sensible, sober-minded workers and thinkers... I believe [it] to be one of the most important things we have ever done; a landmark in the history of Education, a turning point'.

Fifty-nine headmistresses came. In his address of welcome Thring compared their struggles for recognition with his own battles with the Commission and explained his vision for women in the new educational order. They would have 'the divine privilege of being helpers, making good the deficiencies of the world of man'. He spoke of how 'man is intended to do the rough work of the world, while it is the divine mission of women to follow on his work, to put the finishing touches, to help, and

305

bind up, and soothe, and cheer, and throw a halo of gentler life round this hard, warring, daily contest of good and evil'. He pointedly compared them very favourably with their male counterparts in HMC:

'The hope of teaching lies in you. You are fresh, and enthusiastic, and comparatively untrammelled, whilst we are weighted down by tradition, cast, like iron, in the rigid moulds of the past... We want (i.e. need) something new; life, not human museums. And we have it. For are not we ourselves to-day a sort of parable, and a prophecy? Very few years ago how utterly wild the idea would have appeared of this distinguished company of lady teachers meeting in the great schoolroom of this public school during term time. What a bit of pictorial teaching this is! How plainly it puts before our eyes the change that has already taken place. It speaks of a new present; it prophesies a still greater coming age; you cannot help seeing how welcome you are; how you honour us by being here'.

The conference photograph became a striking memorial for a man who saw pictorial images as such an important support for a teacher's work.[1] One headmistress told him as she departed that 'other schools may be bodies corporate, but Uppingham has a soul', and her colleagues wrote to thank him for inspiring them, one adding that *Theory and Practice* had altered her whole life. Mrs. Kingsley read his address and wrote to congratulate him. Miss Buss, the Conference president that year, sent him a decorated edition of Ruskin's works, offering to take Margaret with her on a winter visit to view art in Rome. Miss Beale invited the Thring girls to Cheltenham.

Only a few months later and shortly after Thring's death, Miss Beale and Miss Buss each reflected on their visit. Miss Beale believed of Thring that 'never... has there been a life more devoted to the work of education in its highest sense'. For Miss Buss:

'[It] marked a new era in the career of the public schools for girls. It is not easy to express the appreciation that we all feel here of Mr. Thring's invitation to our members to hold the Conference at one of the most distinguished public schools for boys in the country. We shall not soon forget that he was the first of the great headmasters thus to recognise the sister education movement which we represent – nor his genial inspiring influence among us'.

****

---

[1] See photograph in second plate section.

Briefly Thring felt released from his worries elsewhere and that he was 'moving in a sort of dream': the Conference success; Rawnsley's intriguing letter about future possibilities; the forthcoming article in *The Century Magazine*. They 'filled the air with a magic and a glamour full of prophetic throbbing and thrills whilst day by day the [routine] work goes on'. Yet he also knew that he was driving himself too hard. His rheumatism was advancing and his colds were more frequent. He rejoiced that his laburnum tree was still in full bloom at the end of June for the first time in 34 years, but within a fortnight he was feeling the heat and longing for rain and the holidays: 'Rather shaky still, but I hope to get on'.[1] Exhausted, and suffering from nervous sickness again every day, on 27 July (the last day of term) he 'worked 12 hours and felt very ill, but my breakfast stuck, and I got through. Tonight all is over, and quiet and stillness reigns'.

Earlier that year he had altered his will, leaving his diaries to Marie and most of his books to the girls: 'Please God this may be some help to them'.[2] He thanked Anna for leaving him small reminder slips on his desk blotter: 'I don't know what I should do without you; you are my memory now'. She reckoned that the last year had taken a great deal out of him but she told him that many parents had praised his stirring end-of-term speech:

'He had always liked me to tell him what I thought of his speeches and sermons, so I said to him "Oh, Eddy, I liked your speech so much, it was excellent", and he answered "I'm glad you liked it: I felt very down this morning, but when I got into the schoolroom I felt I had a message to deliver and the strength was given to me"'.

Other visitors were impressed too. One was Ellis Gilman, who had been a pupil for just two years (1857-9) when pupil numbers were still very small. He had seen Thring only twice since then, but he returned as a prospective parent that summer and Thring took father and son round his transformed school. Gilman later described his impressions of Thring's 'striking countenance':[3]

---

[1] There was measles in the school, and the concert at Poplar might be cancelled – but he did venture out to baptise the baby daughter of a housemaster.

[2] Later he added the volumes of Ruskin which he had recently received from the headmistresses.

[3] The son started in May 1888, by which time Thring was dead, but the meeting left a big impression on him and his father.

'I never saw its like. It was indeed a speaking face. When dwelling in eager tones upon absorbing questions of work, it would kindle and grow, and then almost suddenly as he ceased to speak, there would come over it a perfectly still, calm, solemn look, the eyes fixed ahead, wrapt in thought, and far away from present surroundings... He had a great delight in showing us the plants, and the birds in the aviary, calling them individually and feeding them almonds from his pocket.

I think I understood while at school and afterwards his greatness and power, but till I had [that] last interview with him I never appreciated his wonderful tender hearted love and sympathy for the boys who had passed year after year under his rule'.

Near the end of term a Mr. Wilson came to examine Thring's form. He had not met Thring before, but for him too it was a time that he would never forget: 'I learnt more from my week in Mr. Thring's company than I had done from whole years in ordinary society: he seemed to give one new aims and aspirations... It is not easy to express the feeling produced by his mere presence. It was as if virtue went out of him to help and heal'.

****

With term over, parents and daughters again headed for Scotland. The sisters knew that time would hang heavily for them: a year earlier Grace had described the Highlands as 'that benighted hole: Father and Mother asleep in front of the fire: he with *The Times* and she with her sewing'.

They were only too right; the 1887 holiday was no more platable for Thring's daughters than 1886 had been. After Thring objected to Grace drawing faces on his blotting paper, she passed the time as best she could: improving her French; brushing up her botany with the aid of a small microscope; pressing flowers. Sarah helped her father with a compilation of his recent poems and addresses and she attempted translations of her own out of a German novel. Margaret sketched – and noticed that Marie seemed starved of company: 'She lights up when people come, but they make no effort to see new people'. They all noted how much both parents had aged and how they now took only short walks. Even Thring thought their holiday 'rather dull'.

He returned to Uppingham in the final week of September and term began. Well-rested, he considered his new class 'the nicest by far that I have had for years'. He was working on another article for New York, and in Canada Parkin had negotiated further reprints of his writings. The *Addresses* needed some final touches. He had plans for a second book of school songs and a new edition of *Agamemnon*. There was a lecture to prepare on 'The Body: its Life and Teaching', emphasising the need for healthy exercise.[1]

All through the summer he had lived with 'the trustee nightmare', especially after his latest expenses claim for repairs to his house had been extensively picked over. He had admitted some small mistakes in it but was horrified to be treated in such a 'blackguard way'. As the trustees fleshed out their plans for the new classrooms whilst leaving his pension issue unresolved, he decided that he would engage with them as little as possible.[2] The offer of an honorary canonry by the Bishop of Peterborough did little to cheer him: it required him to give an annual sermon, but carried no financial reward. He thought the Bishop meant well, but after 34 years in post it seemed an insult. A further hint from an influential friend of a pre-retirement post briefly gave him hope.[3]

On 4 October Grace accompanied him all the way to Worcester, where he preached to 2,000 people in the cathedral and spoke at the recently opened High School for Girls run by Alice Ottley. He was worried about being away from Marie, and they returned home to find her deeply depressed: Gale had been minding the house and they had again quarrelled over Bertie.[4] Next day he cheered up and went for a long walk with Skrine, who later recalled him grinning at the boys who passed them on the road and walking back with the sun full on his face.

By the following week he had a slight cold, although he spent a happy evening with his daughters sharing out some African curios sent by an Old Boy, but keeping none for himself because (he said) he already had plenty of possessions. On Friday several masters commented that he looked ill, but he went to off to tea with a group of housemasters' wives, one of whom was helping him with yet another project for publication. She later said that he seemed cheerful until it was time to go. Then, unusually, he did not insist on her staying in the warm drawing room rather than seeing him out. At the front door he whispered to her that he was very worried, but he gave no details. As she helped him on with his coat he laughingly

---

[1] The manuscript sent to Parkin sank with the *SS Oregon* (off New York in a collision in 1886), but a second copy arrived safely. He was cheered that a Grantham local paper printed a glowing article by an American visitor to Uppingham. He was sure that the songs would be 'much better than Harrow's'.

[2] 'What a relief it is to be at open hostility with these tyrants and not compelled to mince my words any more'.

[3] Lady Portsmouth: its nature is not known.

[4] 'It troubles me greatly as I cannot help her... it is a sad home to come to in spite of its many blessings'.

buttoned it around his throat saying: 'You don't know how good and obedient I am getting'.

On Saturday evening (15 October) he seemed full of fun at family dinner. Later he set aside his article for New York to write the sermon that he planned to preach the next evening and to make his regular diary entry:

> 'A most cheering letter from an assistant schoolmistress about the *Addresses* negotiations going on with Fisher Unwin. My article for New York is getting into shape... Anna has gone to [friends at] Eton... Grace and perhaps Margaret are soon going to visit Miss Beale at Cheltenham: I am glad of that. It puts them in with a new and powerful world, and may be of great service to them. And now to bed, sermon finished, and a blessed feeling of Sunday coming'

The final full stop remained unwritten. On the Sunday morning, although far from well, he went to chapel as usual. A third of the way through the service he signalled to the chaplain to carry on. Refusing help, he then walked quietly out through the rows of kneeling boys, with Gale following close behind. He insisted on taking lunch with the boys but he spent most of the day asleep, huddled by the fire.

Despite 24-hour medical attention over the next few days he developed a heavy cold followed by fever and lung congestion.[1] On the Wednesday he insisted that Sarah and Grace go on an architectural visit with the Mutual Improvement Society, but as he became increasingly drowsy his mind began to wander. His hand movements often suggested that he wanted to write something down and he tried periodically to speak to Gale about the trustees' meeting due that Friday. When Friday came Marie, sitting with him, called out urgently for Sarah to come. He had suddenly sat up in bed, pushing her aside and shouting: 'You must not stop me. It is school business!' Then he gradually slipped into a coma and died peacefully at 8am on a sunny autumn Saturday morning with his family at his bedside.

Skrine, who had spent the previous night trying to sleep on a sofa downstairs, wrote the letters announcing his death. Between the blotting sheets on the desk lay his diary, along with his unused sermon from the previous weekend entitled 'Knowing Good from Evil'. It included the words: 'How completely God's plan is carried out in the plan of a school like this. What opportunities for manliness and self-denial there are in the work... How your life together calls for gentleness and forbearance with one another'.

---

[1] Dr. Bell, several nurses, Marie and Sarah took turns to watch him. Two specialists came later that week.

Godfrey and Lilla arrived soon afterwards, and Anna quickly returned from Eton. Bertie came too, distressed that they had not been able to find him earlier. Sarah, writing to Parkin, described the whirr of letters, telegrams and funeral plans over the next few days: staff wives helping to run the house and comforting them all; Marie 'wonderfully calm'.

On Sunday the family gathered round the bedside and Gale read prayers: 'It was a lovely sunny day. He looked so calm and quiet; we could not grieve for him'. After chapel, masters and wives came to pay their respects. Grace, impressively self-possessed, received them all in the drawing room and some went upstairs to view the body. Two days later the family visited his open coffin surrounded by flowers, and on Wednesday evening a group of masters carried it into the chapel. There were white flowers and his favourite violets; wreaths and crosses had arrived from far and wide – including one from 'the women of Borth'.

During those days school life had gone on much as usual. Members of his house were given a sequence of written bulletins posted on the door into the boys' side which prepared them for the worst. One of the youngest, Ned Lidderdale, wrote a series of letters to his father. On Friday: 'The "Old Man" is pretty bad: he has been in bed since Sunday. A Dr. Beal (sic) came to see him yesterday.[1] There is a trustees' meeting on Saturday. The weather is much warmer'. Later that day: 'P.S. The "Old Man" is very bad. He has three doctors and three nurses. The whole house is awfully quiet. It has gone to his chest'. Saturday morning: 'P.P.S. We have just heard that the "Old Man" is dead'.

On Sunday: 'The whole house has crape (sic) around their hats. Campbell is [temporary] headmaster. Between 9 and 10 [yesterday] the post office was simply crammed with fellows telegraphing or sending letters home. The house is left entirely to its own devices. Everyone comes to call-over of his own accord, no bell being rung. There is to be a collection for a wreath: we are all meant to give 2/6d... Nothing seems right without the "Old Man". All games are stopped for the present'.

At 2pm on Thursday the funeral took place in the chapel. Sarah wrote later to Parkin that she would never forget the sight: a dark and stormy day with the chapel gas lamps clearly lighting up the coffin; wreaths of bay leaves denoting the victor's crown and masses of flowers. After the service Old Boys carried the coffin in the pouring rain across the square to the churchyard as the watching crowds sang the hymn *Oh God our Help in Ages Past.*

Bertie had been apprehensive about how old friends would react to meeting him after all his recent family difficulties, but he found their

---

[1] Dr. Lionel Beale: Thring's old friend from Marlow days – see ch. 2.

warmth so unbearable that he was relieved to return to London that evening. Grace, who had spent so much time with Thring on his travels that year, was bereft: 'I could only feel glad for him, I could not pray for his recovery, he so wanted rest, and he is so happy now. I think of him as living without pain or care, for his life was one long service to his Master and now he has gone to him forever'. The family was overwhelmed with letters and offers of help, but they found it hard to meet people.

Master Lidderdale was more restrained: 'Thurs 27 Oct: The "Old Man" was buried today, but in what weather!!! Rain the whole time with a cold wind. I was glad we were given extra clothes'.

A member of another house, Henry Walker, remembered it slightly differently. A diffident small boy who had arrived only a year earlier in the Lower School, he had been a member of a class visited by Thring. There, he had been the hapless recipient of one of the 'Old Man's' increasingly eccentric, scattergun questions: 'What is Marlborough?' After a long silence from the scared and tongue-tied youngster, Thring had chuckled and provided his own perplexing answer: 'Why, the thought of the cook, of course!'

Now, young Henry found himself in the driving wind and rain, standing with other boys eight abreast as they waited the coffin to leave the chapel. Wearing two pairs of drawers, two additional vests and an overcoat, and with the crêpe tied tightly round his cap, he 'felt like a trussed chicken'.

CHAPTER TWENTY-TWO

RECKONING

THERE was little time or privacy for Thring's family to reflect upon their loss. Sarah wrote to Parkin of 'the great sorrow that it has pleased God to send us', telling him that with Gale overseeing the house for the rest of term it seemed as if her father 'had just gone off to lecture somewhere... waking in the mornings we wondered if it was all a bad dream'.

The trustees expressed formal condolences, agreeing that Marie should receive the full term's fees but making it clear that she must be out of the house by Christmas. The family had no plans: she wanted to remain near Gale who would continue to work at the school, although Margaret favoured the rest of them leaving Uppingham. On what would have been Thring's sixty-sixth birthday (29 November), Marie addressed the sixth form, thanking them for their wreaths and other gestures of sympathy. She told them how much Thring had specially loved those in his house and his sixth form classes, and of the messages she had received from Old Boys across the world. Margaret found 'the last day of term very strange'. They all moved into a small school property only a few hundred yards away, given to them rent-free on the assumption that they were unlikely to stay in Uppingham for long.[1]

The trustees moved fast, appointing senior housemaster William Campbell to oversee the school until the end of term. Four days after Thring's death Harper wrote urgently to the Charity Commission admitting that 'we have got into a mess at Uppingham' over capitation payments and citing fifteen comparable schools where they were much lower than Thring's 'excessive' stipend. Within a month the Commission agreed to amend the New Scheme to give the trustees discretion to lower the new headmaster's entitlement – by which time the Board had appointed Revd. Edward Selwyn as Thring's successor: a choice possibly prompted by the powerful Old Boys on Merseyside. Aged only 34 and already the successful headmaster of Liverpool College he was able to

---

[1] Marie's letters suggest that briefly she thought she might live in part of the house for a time after Selwyn arrived. His wife, a grand-daughter of Thomas Arnold, was expecting a baby and would not be able to join him immediately.

take up the post in January 1888, quickly proving to be a vigorous new broom.[1]

Selwyn's brief included working with the trustees to change the school's arcane financial structure: something that more entrenched masters found hard to accept. He had very different priorities from Thring's. Numbers rose to well over 400 and studies became shared. There was less supervision of praepostors and more emphasis on high-flyers. Compulsory Greek ceased. Conformity and manliness were the order of the day, with more individual activities squeezed out. Rugby became the winter game within a year and team games prospered; a rifle corps was introduced. Selwyn regarded music merely as 'a refining influence for good in the zone of manners, without [any] moral power'.

Having Thring's family living so close to the school was difficult for Selwyn – and for them. Former colleagues passed on gossip or asked for advice. Ten masters left within two years, three of them dismissed. Sarah warned Parkin that 'it will be very painful for you coming to us, all is so different'. It was especially hard for Anna, who lost not only her home but her job as secretary. Her last task was to box up Thring's papers because Marie could not face doing it. Thring had always been her father-figure and Anna felt that her life was now purposeless. As for Selwyn (she claimed): 'He is not liked by anyone'. Godfrey scorned Selwyn, calling him a man driven by notions of payment by results: 'It would have broken [my brother's] heart to watch his life's work being undone'.[2]

Marie coped with moving house better than her children had feared; Godfrey thought she bore up 'wonderfully well' but all this – together with the prospect of a greatly reduced style of life – cannot have been easy. She was absent from the 100th birthday celebrations for Thring's mother in Somerset in 1891 although all three of her daughters attended.

---

[1] Under the New Scheme's amendment, the contentious fraction of between 1/6 and 1/4 of the tuition fee given to the headmaster as capitation fees (see ch. 20) was replaced by payments of between £4 and £7 per boy: effectively only 1/10 to 1/6 of the tuition fee, and breaking the direct link between the two fees. Selwyn's appointment and arrival were very rapid compared with modern practice (especially considering that he was headmaster of another school), suggesting that the trustees may have had him in mind as Thring's successor for some time.

[2] J P Graham was a boy under Selwyn; later a master and trustee: 'Whereas Selwyn's great aim was to make masters as well as boys think for themselves, some, but not all, of Thring's staff were content to let Thring do the thinking for them, nor was the great man himself apparently averse from this attitude'. Margaret remembered that 'we did not have a pleasant time during Mr. Selwyn's headmastership'. According to Godfrey, 'the new headmaster, though a gentleman, seems singularly deficient in reverence for the past'.

She also stayed away from the ceremonial unveiling of a fine memorial statue of Thring at a large gathering of visitors in the chapel a year later.[1]

****

During Thring's lifetime his family had been largely shielded from financial matters. Marie shared his faith that the future would take care of itself, and Anna, although his book-keeper as well as his secretary, appears to have been too loyal to question his belief that God would somehow provide for them all. Gale's financial naivety would soon become apparent and the three daughters knew nothing of business beyond the day-to-day running of the house. Only Bertie with his London stock-broking experience appreciated the family's parlous situation.[2]

Although Thring's family was unaware of it, Harper's recent approach to the Charity Commission had shown scant sympathy for Marie's plight: 'From what we hear, [Thring] seems to have been very badly off, although no-one has the least idea how he spent his earnings. We do not believe that he has spent much upon the school, although he had convinced himself that such was the fact, and as he has raised the school enormously... maybe we can acknowledge this via a small pension'.

If, however, the trustees suspected that Thring was wealthier than he claimed, they were wrong. The assessment of his estate in 1888 revealed how much his own finances had become tangled up with the school's over the years - and the full extent of his contribution to Uppingham's development. This document listed total assets of over £17,000, but that figure mostly consisted of the notional value of various pieces of land and property which the school had used for many years. Thus, for the school, possession proved to be nine-tenths of the law, because although these items were registered in Thring's name, even if Marie had wished to claim them, doing so would have seemed like an assault on Thring's memory.

All the other school properties appear to have been registered in the name of the Trust,[3] giving Thring's family no rights over them. After brief negotiations through solicitors it must have been apparent to Marie and

---

[1] Thring's mother died in 1891 aged nearly 102, two days before her eldest son, Theodore. They had a joint funeral. The (Galilee chapel) extension was designed by A E Street, son of the architect of the original building. Thring's statue sited within it was unveiled by Sarah. It was designed by Thomas Brock RA and paid for by public subscription.

[2] 'We are left very badly off... I have nothing at all. My mother and the sisters will have about £400 p.a.'

[3] Apart from the housemasters' ownership of their houses – but Thring's house was the Trust's property.

her children that any action might involve fighting the Charity Commissioners as well as the trustees. Even if it were successful, the legal fees incurred might prove greater than any compensation.

She and her daughters (along with Anna) therefore relied on the goodwill of the trustees, who had no legal obligation to compensate or protect them. The Board was committed to new classrooms and the Trust itself still had limited funds. After lengthy negotiation with the Commissioners the trustees agreed in 1889 to pay into Thring's estate just over £2,000 for the workshops (which he had owned himself) and some furniture and equipment around the school. This sum represented less than 2% of what he often claimed to have invested in new school buildings with his colleagues over the years and it took no account of any salaries or other expenses that he had underwritten. Anna, who had periodically loaned him money, had a charge on one-sixth of his estate and after funeral expenses, outstanding debts, and un-repaid loans to his two sons had been taken into account, Marie received a £300 bequest and a small income from what remained.[1]

****

Meanwhile there was still the thorny question of who would be Thring's literary executor. The discovery that Thring had chosen Parkin for this role came as a surprise to his family - and a crushing blow to Skrine, coming so soon after the loss of his childhood idol and professional mentor. He had thought of himself as Thring's closest confidant and he had already written the account of the school's time at Borth. More recently he had made little secret of his ambition to be Thring's successor, a hope which he thought Marie privately shared.

However, jealous colleagues had long considered Skrine to be much too close to Thring. They shared the trustees' desire for a fresh pair of eyes, and in the highly-charged atmosphere around Thring's funeral Skrine played into their hands. He circulated a memorandum describing the school's 'singular history and separate character' and suggested that no headmaster from outside could ever appreciate it. This backfired: a movement to stop him quickly developed and, once rejected, he immediately announced that he would be leaving the school at Christmas,

---

[1] The £2,000 sum took account of the recently-purchased workshop equipment, but not the purchase or improvement of the Fairfield land which included the aviary. Thring left Marie £300, and he had advanced just over £200 to Gale and Bertie. His funeral cost £90. He owed various creditors £6,000, a third of it to Anna.

now only a few weeks away.[1] On the final Sunday of term he preached in chapel on the theme 'This Thy School', in which he pointedly made a challenge to those whom he would be leaving behind: 'The past is ours: never let it go'.

Thring had first considered who should edit his papers as early as 1859, even before Skrine entered the school as a boy. Then, after many bouts of indecision, in the 1880s he had taken against his protégé for the role because of Skrine's high-churchmanship, ingratiating manner and occasional carping criticism. Alternately grateful for the younger man's devotion and irritated by his 'ludicrous' attentiveness, Thring became further convinced early in 1887 that 'Skrine must not deal with my troubles. Someone of strength and backbone, who has suffered must deal with it, or let there be silence'.

Marie knew how much Thring had relied on Skrine in his later years and she was grateful for all Skrine's help during the fraught days after her husband's death. Yet after her initial shock on discovering Thring's instruction that the task should be taken on by Parkin, she also recalled her husband's annoyance late in life that Skrine had written *Uppingham by the Sea* like 'a cheap novelette'.[2] She decided to respect Thring's wishes.

Skrine, however, would not let matters rest. Since their first meeting in the early 1870s he and Parkin had exchanged occasional letters on educational questions. Now, while Marie was making her farewell address to the sixth form boys on the anniversary of Thring's birthday, Skrine pointedly used the date to write to Canada urging Parkin to withdraw. He described his crushing sense of rejection and how he had hoped to do for Thring what Dean Stanley's biography had done for Arnold:

---

[1] Skrine had narrowly missed securing the Repton headship just before Thring's death. Now he declared: 'I recognise the defeat of the principle for which I stood. I came to Uppingham fourteen years ago with the desire of being a reconciler. I remained, refusing offers of more valuable (i.e. better-paid) and important masterships for the sake of the duty which I recognised here as mine... I now wish to leave without one word which would shame my purpose'. After some travelling in Europe, he was appointed Warden of Glenalmond.

[2] Thring's diary (1859): 'Let no one write Latin humbug or English over my bones. No word of praise or blame if they love me.' A year later: 'If any of this is ever published let it not be by any child of mine but by some good impartial man'. Skrine was still a child then, but when Thring reconsidered the question many years later he stuck to his original criteria, realising that Skrine did not fit them: 'Neither Nettleship nor Skrine must do it. For different reasons they do not understand'. He also wrote: '[Despite] all his merits, [Skrine] is a bad teacher, not decisive; the boys want sharp outlines and strong impressions'. He told Marie that Skrine lacked 'ballast in some way, and had not suffered enough'.

'I was beyond any question [Thring's] favourite pupil. I came to him through a marriage connection of our families... I did not think that he would have wanted another biographer... I do not believe that anyone can do it except myself... The English public insofar as they know Uppingham will look to me to do it'.[1]

Hardie Rawnsley, Thring's godson, weighed in too, suggesting that Parkin had no time for such a huge task and that Skrine should at least be asked to help. Rawnsley mischievously challenged the Canadian: 'What would you have said if a Britisher had written the life of A(braham) Lincoln?' Skrine immediately followed up Rawnsley's letter with another of his own, emphasising his rich range of contacts and stating that having left Uppingham he could now give the work the time that it deserved. He suggested a partnership: he would write about Thring's years in Uppingham while Parkin could concentrate on his 'wider influence'.

Parkin stood his ground, encouraged by a letter from Grace who since childhood had regarded him as a hero: it was 'wonderful' that Parkin intended to fulfil her father's dearest wish. Skrine then changed tack, wishing Parkin well but re-asserting his duty to write a book of his own. Skrine's *A Memory of Edward Thring* appeared as early as 1890: it was more an affectionate tribute than an objective study but its anecdotes and first-hand experiences painted a vivid and widely-praised picture of his mentor.

By then, Parkin had barely begun work. He visited England three times between 1888 and 1895[2] and at times seemed overwhelmed by Thring's papers which were far more extensive than he had realised. Living outside Britain and moving to a larger school in Canada in 1895 impeded him too: both his publisher (Macmillan) and Thring's family began to wonder if the project would ever be completed.

---

[1] 'I was a boy in his house, and... his pupil in the sixth form. From the very first I had a passion of admiration for him, and he certainly returned it with a very visible affection. One day as he looked over an English poem of mine (I was then 17) he turned round to me and said with deep feeling in his voice: "Skrine, you shall write my epitaph". ... In a remarkable letter he actually called me "his son"'. Skrine saw the book he proposed to write as 'from my dearest friend: equivalent to a command'. He believed it would attract significant public interest.

[2] Other than his wife, Parkin had no secretarial assistance because the advance was so small. He had to transcribe documents by hand. He also turned down much more lucrative offers, including one from the Cambridge University Press to write a history of Canada, and his other writing subsidised the Thring project. He used the time between leaving Fredericton and taking up his new post at Upper Canada College to visit England for the whole summer of 1895.

Nor did it prove easy to steer a course between historical accuracy and the conflicting sensitivities of Thring's family, trustees, staff and friends. Within the family Marie, Anna, Henry and Godfrey all helped Parkin: especially Anna, who used her many years of working closely with Thring to provide contact names and details of Old Boys and to introduce Parkin to Macmillan. She remembered her brother-in-law as Godfrey did: 'A true hero and lover of truth: original, tender, with a childlike simplicity and only angry in the face of injustice', whereas Henry seemed to recall only the 'difficult and disappointing antagonisms'.

Reading Thring's diaries and letters produced another shock for Marie and her children. They feared that, even with careful editing, Thring's vision and achievements would be obscured by his frequently-expressed gloom and frustration. Margaret would later criticise Parkin in this respect: 'My Father noted down his troubles and worries in his diaries, and far too much mention has been made in his biography of his debts, of which his family knew nothing. His nature was essentially genial, buoyant and optimistic'. Marie eventually determined that the diaries should be destroyed as soon as Parkin had completed his work.[1]

Parkin had to work through a mountain of newspaper obituaries from around the world: a few critical, but most of them like the *Spectator's,* which highlighted Thring's conviction that 'Every boy is good for something'[2]. Old Boys wrote effusively and in huge numbers, presenting him with further difficult decisions about whom to quote and whom to omit. Their many questions saddled him with yet more correspondence.[3] Friends and associates, some of whom had met Thring only once, sent testimonies of his powerful personality but others wrote long, complex analyses of his weaknesses: descriptions which were hard to gather into a coherent whole. Thring's former HMC contemporaries were divided too: one thought his work 'unique in our generation' but others were more guarded.

---

[1] In fact, the first and last diaries were rescued, probably by Sarah. See Matthews: *By God's Grace* p.114.

[2] 'If he cannot write iambics or excel in Latin prose, he has at least eyes, and a hand, and ears. Turn him into the carpenter's shop, make him a botanist or a chemist, encourage him to express himself in music and if he fails all round here, at least he shall learn to read in public clearly his mother-tongue, and write thoughtfully an English essay. One thing from first to last Thring taught and wrought for: the boys he dealt with should be dealt with as individuals, and not as masses... He denied himself the privileges and convenience of a large house; he refused... that the school should exceed a certain numerical limit'.

[3] Macmillan acted as a collection point for many additional unsolicited letters.

Of his former housemasters, Earle generously praised how Thring had personified 'True Life' but others puzzled over why 'he closed up like an oyster to some men who could not see eye to eye with him'. Candler made a wry observation about the prospects for Parkin's book: 'There will be a lot to contradict!'

Parkin sought to steer a careful path between all these judgements, judiciously expunging all personal or family details. His two-volume work finally appeared in 1898, eleven years after Thring's death. Macmillan's first print run was modest, reflecting their lowered expectations for its sales figures after years of delay, but the first edition quickly sold out and the book became widely circulated across the Empire.[1]

The reviews of the book included a new round of opinions about Thring himself: understandably more qualified and reflective than the obituary articles a decade earlier. The *Guardian* thought his diaries 'extraordinarily interesting [as] a remarkable record of heroic perseverance [but] absolutely unreadable' and *The Times* tired of him 'constantly representing himself as a victim of adversity'. To a Leicester newspaper: 'With all [his] limitations, crotchetiness, extravagance, positiveness, religious mania, and lack of mental perspective, it is impossible not to be moved [by] a vehement and great-souled man'. The *Daily News* pointed out that he had never seen Uppingham as a stepping stone to preferment but added a barbed comment, reminiscent of *Punch's* verdict in the Jackson case many years earlier: 'If ever there was a strong man, it was Thring. [He had] a will which no accumulation of misfortune could baffle: Governors, masters, boys – he beat them all'.[2]

With so many compromises to make, Parkin had found it hard to capture Thring's essence. Some critics described the book as a dull but worthy labour of love, with too little about his family life or his strong belief in music. In retrospect Parkin admitted being over-sensitive in what he omitted, and he conceded that Skrine's book (and another by Hardie Rawnsley's brother, Willingham) had already used the best anecdotes.

Inevitably, Skrine wrote to Parkin again. He stated how well Parkin had carried out his 'extraordinarily difficult' task but chided him for his 'unfortunate' failure to repeat Skrine's own best material and his failure to do justice to the 'hero-worship' of Thring by his early pupils. Skrine also

---

[1] The two-volume edition sold 1,250 copies. The single-volume edition (1900, reprinted 1904) sold 2,500. The Parkin archive in Ottawa contains nearly 200 reviews, many from Canadian and American city newspapers. Several felt that the single-volume was 'half the length and twice as readable'. Not surprisingly, the Canadian reviews were among the most positive.

[2] See ch. 4: 'We don't know whether Mr. Thring trains the boys' minds; but he makes them mind their trains'.

felt that Parkin had given too 'stern' an impression of Thring's relationship with his masters.

Skrine could claim first-hand authority on all these issues, but his comments would surely have been better left unsaid. With his letter he sent a modest cheque from the proceeds of his own book. It may have been what it claimed: recognition that Parkin had done so much work for so little reward. In the circumstances in which he received it, however, Parkin decided merely to pass it on to his publishers. They too declined it.

****

Parkin's many difficulties were compounded by one other issue which was elusive but far from negligible: comparisons of Thring with the great Thomas Arnold. Some were made by obituary writers and Parkin's own reviewers, the most dismissive of whom deemed Thring's reforms merely to be 'the small change of Arnold's grander plans'.[1]

Thring was always sensitive about the great Doctor. He recognised Arnold's many successes, achieved in an era of much less public interest in education than his own. However, when his reputation began to grow he resented the fact that Arnold's saintly legend seemed to increase even faster, especially after the publication of *Tom Brown's Schooldays* in 1857, fifteen years after Arnold's death and in his own fourth year at Uppingham. He then began to criticise Arnold, often exaggerating their differences: '[Arnold] sent his failures away: if a boy was dull, naturally stupid or idle, he got rid of him. I cannot and will not do that. The blockhead and the dullard have a claim on us as strong as the clever and bright boy'.

As early as 1858 he criticised Arnold's indifference to 'machinery':

'Dr. Arnold was a very great man but a bad schoolmaster... What personal influence could do, he did. What wise and thoughtful application of means should have done, he did not. He dealt with his

---

[1] Rigby believed this article was written by Edmond Warre, Head Master of Eton (1884-1905). It claimed *inter alia* that Thring was a disciple of Arnold. *The Times* review of Parkin's book claimed that Thring's diaries had an 'almost total absence of any reference to literature [or] matters intellectual: here is one of the differences between Thring and Arnold'. This review also criticised the low intellectual level of the Uppingham sixth form and Thring's teaching methods, claiming that he was 'profoundly ignorant' of mathematics and theoretical science throughout his life.

school as a great and truthful individual, not as a great and truthful governor and legislator. He left no constructive memorial of himself'.[1]

Given Rugby's continuing success the final sentence smacked of jealousy. Much later in 1886 as Parkin prepared his article for *The Century Magazine* Thring repeated the charge – claiming that Arnold was a 'power-worshipper and idolater... spare me Arnold as much as you can'. When Parkin stuck to his guns and *did* mention Arnold, Thring wrote again: 'God forbid anything I have done should have been in his spirit'.

Arnold's public reputation was helped by the fact that no fewer than 23 of his assistants became headmasters of other (mostly well-known) schools between 1842 and 1899. Ironically, the later ones were able to take advantage of the expansion of the very demand that Thring's success had helped to create. To Thring, however, Arnold's reputation appeared to rest largely on *Tom Brown's Schooldays* and on Dean Stanley's *Life of Arnold*. He regarded *Tom Brown* as the 'bitterest satire' ever written on education, and he reckoned that Stanley too had written 'a novel': he was 'the most mischievous man in England [because] he gave the impression to the world that Arnold was a great schoolmaster and Rugby a nearly perfect school'.[2]

Nevertheless, Thring was fighting a losing battle. Parkin could never hope to have the same impact as Hughes or Stanley, given all the difficulties he faced and the prevailing climate of militarism and philathleticism in the 1890s. Thring's own fictional portrayal as 'Jerry Thrale' in E W Hornung's novel *Fathers of Men* never enjoyed the same popularity as *Tom Brown* nor that of Hornung's own *Raffles* books. Moreover, his book was based only on the diminished *persona* of Thring's final years.

Thring and Arnold also had much in common - including their belief in the school as a moral community with the chapel at its centre and the sixth form as its embodiment. Both had bouts of introspection and a love

---

[1] Thring (1858): 'A school may enshrine the individual in their hearts, but it ought to have a monument of him in its system. There are times when a man must build his ship, as well as be able to command her...'

[2] Stanley, A P: *The Life and Correspondence of Thomas Arnold, D.D.,* 2 vols (1845). Stanley's book appeared very soon after Arnold's death. Thring died well before a fierce attack on Arnold by Lytton Strachey. For discussion of Arnold's biographers, see Copley, Terence: *Black Tom: Arnold of Rugby: The Myth and the Man* (2002) pp.1-16, and Simon Heffer's defence of Arnold in *High Minds* (pp.1-10), in which he states: 'His ethos came to suffuse the public school system... for the rest of the century'.

of walking in the Lake District.[1] Both believed in smaller dormitories, individual studies and careful supervision. Both held to the paramount value of classics in teaching English, saw a role for mathematics and modern languages as important additional subjects, and favoured Socratic teaching methods. Both could inspire fear in their pupils; both had a special horror of boys telling lies, and expelled older boys and caned younger ones for breaches of trust. Both held a strong belief in a headmaster's independence, although Thring faced greater opposition from his governors.[2] Both supported social justice, and had great misgivings about America.

However, they existed in different generations and worked in very different circumstances. Arnold's death (1842) coincided with the start of the huge new demand for his type of boarding school (thus cementing his fame) whereas Thring left the scene just as the harsher brand of manly values that he had resisted for so long became unstoppable. Arnold's time at Rugby was well under half Thring's span at Uppingham and Arnold reinvigorated an already well-established and famous school. It can be argued that Arnold worked skilfully within an existing system, achieving significant reforms without revolution and handling his assistants more skilfully.[3]

Thring had to re-invent a very small school: it had no obstructive traditions but also very few resources. Even Stanley acknowledged that Arnold owed much to his housemasters: he established their role, but not the 'family' style of the Uppingham houses that prompted Canon Robinson to observe to his fellow-Commissioners that 'at Rugby the school made the houses and at Uppingham the houses made the school'.

Arnold set greater store by intellectual knowledge and his teaching was without histrionics. Thring was ambivalent about 'knowledge-worship' and in the classroom he loved playing to an audience. Arnold concentrated much of his energy and intellectual ambition on the adult world – unsurprisingly, given that he was much the more systematic and

---

[1] Arnold took pupils to his house there (Fox Howe) after an epidemic, but on a much smaller scale than Borth.

[2] Arnold was rarely challenged by his governors, but he came close to resignation when they divided equally on a censure motion of him in 1836 after he wrote a controversial article criticising the Tractarians.

[3] McCrum, M: *Thomas Arnold Head Master: A Re-assessment* (1989): 'Arnold added few new buildings apart from moving the library... while he altered many old customs... most of his changes were slight shifts in emphasis... the adaptation of traditional practices to new and worthwhile ends.' Stanley described Arnold as 'an emperor not afraid to delegate his authority to viceroys'.

incisive thinker. Thring was a schoolmaster to his fingertips: more a doer than a writer. His writings were merely a means to an end.[1]

It is in their attitude to their pupils that the two men reveal their greatest difference. For those who believed that Thring was essentially a 'King of Boys' this was sometimes a belittling epithet, but for others it was the essence of his greatness. Certainly there was something of the boy in Thring: a character facet that the young Arnold once had but seemed later to lose. Arnold tended to pronounce confident judgments that labelled a child as good or evil and he was impatient with the less attractive side of adolescence. Thring was much more concerned with unlocking every boy's potential, however limited – and with trusting him. The *Journal of Education* summed it up:

> 'Arnold regarded boyhood from the Calvinistic point of view as a dangerous age [and] riper years [as] the time when the real life of a man began. Thring looked on boyhood not only as a precious seedtime, but as having a beauty and value of its own, and capable, if passed in a healthy atmosphere and congenial surroundings of being the happiest portion of a man's life. Arnold first taught that a public school is a Christian commonwealth. Thring taught the no less vital truth that each individual has a soul to be saved'.[2]

The same idea can be seen in the verdict of the historian of HMC many decades later: 'Arnold may well be said to have changed the *heart* of English education, but it was Thring who changed its *face*'.[3]

****

---

[1] Despite his Cambridge successes and his writing, it is impossible to imagine Thring as the Professor of Modern History that Arnold became, or producing Arnold's works of scholarship. Simon and Bradley: *The Victorian Public School* p.71: 'Beside [Arnold], his nearest rivals pale into insignificance. Thring was almost a nonentity in his narrowness'. Arnold crossed the Channel twelve times between 1815 and 1842. Thring went on his European tour, but thereafter only on occasional foreign visits, mostly to his wife's family in Germany.

[2] Stanley quoted Bonamy Price, a pupil of the young Arnold's at Laleham, on how he took delight in playing with boys in the garden or swimming in the Thames with them, and his 'gleeful high spirits'. Castle: *Moral Education* pp.286-7 takes a different view, believing that 'Arnold so feared the capacity of small boys for evil that when two or three were gathered together, he was apt to see the Devil in their midst... If he could have had his way with his Creator, he would have abolished adolescence altogether... it showed a man more intent on improving the world than on shepherding the young'.

[3] Percival: *Origins* p.21.

The Old Boys who swamped Parkin with their tributes also revealed how much Thring had influenced their later lives. He was not unique amongst headmasters in this respect, and one must assume that those who took the trouble to write were amongst his strongest admirers, but his influence was seen in the proportion of his pupils who took up church, educational and social work both at home and abroad: significantly greater than in many comparable schools. Many took holy orders at a time when an increasing number of their contemporaries preferred the armed forces, the law, administration or politics. This reflected both the ethos of the Mission and Thring's belief in Christianity expressed through actions rather than words.

Abroad, Old Boys worked as missionaries in many parts of the world, often receiving financial support from the school or Thring personally. One wrote to him in 1870 of working amongst the black population in South Carolina, describing 'the hunger for learning among some so old that they can hardly see their books, and some so young they can hardly speak'. Thring was proud of them all, noting their names meticulously in his diary and adding the words 'Glory be to God' in Greek each time. After his death his former pupils included a pioneer of the boys' club movement on Merseyside and a Warden of Toynbee Hall in London – where his erstwhile colleague, mathematician and timetabler, Howard Candler, taught after his retirement from Uppingham.

Thring's belief in music for the many rather than merely for the few found later expression in the careers of men like Cecil Sharp, sent to Uppingham by parents who thought Thring the only headmaster who took music seriously, and who himself became a teacher, composer and principal of the Hampstead Conservatoire. (Sir) Arthur Somervell moved on to King's College, Cambridge, and later became chief inspector of music to the Board of Education.[1] Paul David gave help to other schools - and to musical societies right across the Midlands which resulted in his receiving a Cambridge honorary degree. Former members of Thring's staff, George Howson of Greshams and Walter Earle at Bilton Grange preparatory school, became headmasters who gave musical opportunities to the next generation including composers such as Sir Arthur Bliss.

While a handful of Thring's colleagues became headmasters (along with at least three former pupils and two nephews) more than twenty others secured teaching posts in schools and universities throughout the

---

[1] Sir William Ellis, described by Rigby as 'once a very average boy', acquired a love of music at school which lasted him all his life. He repaid the debt to Uppingham in 1951 by presenting it with a new organ.

United Kingdom and abroad.[1] However, the *Journal of Eucation* asserted that his true disciples were thousands of classroom teachers throughout the English-speaking world who treasured the memory of 'the man who himself honoured the profession of teaching'.[2] The shoal of letters that Parkin received from them showed how widely Thring's name had become known.

An administrator in India wrote that Thring stood out as the most powerful and practical exponent of educational truth of his generation. The inaugural address for a Natal branch of the Teachers' Guild had the simple title: *Mr. Thring*.[3] Other schools adopted his ideas: William Lee Cushing, founding headmaster of Westminster College, Connecticut, read Thring's books and built his school on Uppingham's ethos.[4] In Australia Thring's maxim 'Honour the work and the work will honour you' inspired the motto and school song of Melbourne High School. Parkin himself led two schools in Canada on Thringian principles before devoting his life to the Empire as the first Secretary of the Rhodes Trust scholarship programme. Both of the leading Canadian authorities on Parkin recognise Thring as one of the greatest – if not *the* greatest influence on his life.[5]

---

[1] Former-colleague headmasters included Blakiston, Stokoe, Rowe, Howson and Skrine; in prep schools W F Rawnsley and Walter Earle. Old Boys who became headmasters included John Millington Sing (OU 1877-81), Warden of St Edward's, Oxford, who was nearly a Lower School fatality in the typhoid epidemic of 1875; Frederick Tracey (1872-3), All Saints' College, Bathurst, New South Wales; Jacob Reynolds (1868-71), Havelock School, New Zealand; also a prep school Head, Charles Freeman (1864-69). Oswald Powell (1881-6) took Thring's insistence on machinery to Bedales as its Second Master. Two of Charles Thring's sons became headmasters: Lionel at Dunstable Grammar School (where, unusually in a grammar school at that time, he promoted arts and music) and Llewellyn at Brunswick House, Churchill's former prep school.

[2] Rigby gives extensive details of Old Boys teaching in over a dozen schools across the country: Bedford Modern, Blundells, Charterhouse, Downside, Epsom, Eton, Harrow, Lancing, Rossall, The Leys, Rugby, Tonbridge, Trent College, Wellington and Westminster. Arthur Hassall became history tutor at Christ Church, Oxford. Two Old Boys became HMIs. Thring also influenced the boarding house system begun at a leading girls' school, St Leonard's Fife.

[3] Frances Cobbe (1822-1904), an Irish writer, social reformer, anti-vivisection activist, and leading suffragette described Thring as 'one of the ablest and most far-sighted of teachers'.

[4] Cushing copied the Uppingham bell to call pupils to lessons. The school has a 'Thring (fundraising) Society'.

[5] Terry Cook: 'Apostle of Empire: Sir George Parkin and Imperial Federation' (Queen's University, Kingston, Ontario Ph.D. thesis 1977) p.90; William Christian: *Parkin: Canada's Most Forgotten Man* (2008): p.32.

It was a view which Parkin himself did much to reinforce. Speaking at Uppingham in 1921 to celebrate the centenary of Thring's birth, he claimed to know the colleges and universities across the Empire (and their leaders) better than anyone and he recalled hearing an Australian Minister of Education describe Thring as 'the hero of the schoolmaster world'.

****

With Thring's estate determined and Skrine gone, Marie's temporary home in Uppingham became permanent until her death in 1906 at the age of 86 (five years before Anna's). She, her sister and her two younger daughters lived off the capital and income left to them in Thring's estate. Parkin visited her several times to borrow more papers and they corresponded for years over enquiries from Old Boys and much more. She asked him repeatedly but to no avail to find school work in Canada for Gale, of whom she remained fiercely protective.

Gale stayed on at the school, posing an increasingly difficult problem for Selwyn. Headmaster and colleagues were surely all too aware of his limitations but he had a network of Old Boy friends and for a while his name protected him.[1] He took on a small boarding house and in 1896 built a larger one (Farleigh, named after a favourite house in the Lake District). Ostensibly he was a bachelor master with Sarah keeping house for him, but it transpired that he had secretly married a cook in Peterborough and, knowing she would be deemed socially unsuitable as a housemaster's wife, he kept her and their daughter out of sight there. His financial skills were poor and tradesmen threatened to cut off supplies to the house. Eventually he became bankrupt, and in 1909 the trustees approved his dismissal. He and Sarah now had no income and the Charity Commissioners rejected an application to give the Thring daughters any grant from school funds.[2]

---

[1] His obituarist in *The Times* believed that 'he found the changes [to] his father's cherished aims hard to bear'. Conversations between Rigby and those who remembered Gale included the view was that he was 'too easy-going' and that he was 'totally unfit to be a schoolmaster'. He had a reputation as 'a bit of a lad', who at one time kept two horses. He had sometimes left his class to fend for itself while he went off to do some gardening.

[2] The trustees had been prepared to give Thring's daughters £1 per week (probably between them) – but only if the Charity Commission agreed. An approach was made on their behalf to Prime Minister Asquith in 1907, but it too was rejected, because too much time had elapsed since Thring's death, and because Henry and other relatives were well able to support them. Possibly Asquith (a Liberal) knew of Thring's views on Gladstone.

In declining health, Gale then ran a fishing lodge in Ireland until hostility to the British at the time of the Easter Rising forced his return to England – which prompted the Commissioners to relent, allowing the trustees to grant him a small pension until his death in 1920.[1] His daughter Mollie was later befriended by Sarah and Margaret but she appears to have inherited psychological problems from her mother. After many years in care she died in 1998.

Bertie's baby son, the cause of so much heartache, died within a few weeks of Thring. Reconciled with his mother and siblings, Bertie was the only one of the five children to achieve anything like financial stability, eventually becoming Secretary of the Incorporated Society of Authors, and editor of *The Author* for 37 years. After Gale's bankruptcy Sarah went to live in a small bungalow in the Lake District which held so many childhood memories. By 1940 she had been joined in Ambleside by Margaret – and by Bertie, now long estranged from Sybil. His death occurred a year later[2] and the two sisters battled against increasing infirmity until Sarah died in 1946 and Margaret three years later.[3]

Grace, the free spirit of Thring's children, was 21 when she lost her father. Cooped up in a small house with an anxious mother who often interrupted her attempts to study, her letters to Parkin reveal her desolation: Uppingham was 'empty, a feeling of some strong presence missing'. She hoped to gain her independence by becoming a qualified teacher; she spoke of wanting to go to Oxford like Bertie and even of an academic career. However, Marie was very protective, fearing that Grace might overstretch herself mentally.[4] Eventually she was allowed some

---

[1] The trustees rejected an Old Boys' offer to give a grant from their own funds towards a pension for Gale. His will shows that he died with minimal possessions, having acquired a new 'companion' (sic).

[2] Retirement and Sybil must have eaten away at Bertie's capital. Some years after his burial, the Society of Authors discovered that there had been no money to pay for a tombstone in Ambleside churchyard: it donated one.

[3] Margaret was forced to leave her home in 1931, when its site was needed for a new boarding house (West Deyne). She found another house nearby, and visited School House each year after the Borth Commemoration service to drink a glass of port and to reminisce. In the late 1940s the school received pleas on Margaret's behalf for financial help, possibly with nursing home fees, which was given in the final year of her life. Martin Lloyd (headmaster 1944-65) advised against a trustees' grant to Sybil – as had his predecessor, Wolfenden.

[4] 'Mother... objected to our leaving her for even a visit of ten days' duration. Work is the thing I desire above all else now... I do not know if you have any experience of a nervous invalid in your house... there is *nothing* so wearing as mental anxiety'. Marie would not let Grace live with Gale and Sarah at Farleigh.

pre-university tuition in Cheltenham and in 1888 she started a degree course at Newnham College, Cambridge which she had visited with such enthusiasm just before Thring's death. Sadly, her mother's fears for her proved right: following a breakdown she withdrew from her course and returned home for good. During a visit to Italy in 1912 she discovered that she had cancer, from which she died in March 1914.

Thus Edward Thring's branch of the family died out. Despite his faith that (in the words of hopes expressed by one Old Boy's letter to Parkin after Thring's death) 'his children would not suffer from his own unworldliness', the final settlement of his estate four years after Marie's demise resulted in each of their children receiving the princely sum of just over £111. It suggests that Thring had put far, far more capital into his school than he realised or ever admitted.

Sarah and Margaret bore their reduced circumstances with dignity and stoicism, although in old age they once observed that their father had sunk £100,000 of his own money into the school (nearly £10m at 2014 values) and that he received nothing but trouble from the trustees for his pains. Given what can be pieced together about Thring's finances and the school's costs, the claim seems understandable, even credible. Even if it was an over-estimate, it helps to explain the resentment of him in the mid 1880s by Gale and Bertie. It also confirms that those closest to Thring paid a very high price for his determination to keep his independence, come what may.

CHAPTER TWENTY-THREE

LEGACY

IN 1913 the *Uppingham Magazine* published an anonymous letter:

> 'Dear Sir, I wish to draw attention to the fact that the statue of Edward Thring, at the west end of the chapel, is, and has been for a long time, covered with cobwebs and dust. Would it not be possible for this statue to be kept clean, in view both of the excellence of the sculpture and the greatness of the subject represented? A little water is all that is required'.

For well over half a century after 1887 events did Thring's reputation no favours. Selwyn had no scruples about manipulating the past to his advantage, harking back not to Thring's innovations but to a disciplinary policy which (Selwyn claimed) had 'smashed, bruised, and removed out of the place' those who fell foul of it. Far-reaching changes began as the trustees gradually assumed financial responsibility for the school, rapidly building the new classrooms to which Thring had objected so much, along with a handsome new boarding house for his successors. The first bursar was appointed in 1910 and a decade later the trustees began buying up every boarding house. New housemasters would no longer have to purchase them from their predecessors and from 1946 they no longer drew profits from their houses but were paid a salary instead.[1]

Beyond Uppingham (and to some extent, within it) Thring's ideas went profoundly out of fashion as the Great War approached. Headmasters were far more pre-occupied with conformity than individuality. *The Public School Magazine* claimed that Thring's school had lost its distinctiveness: his legacy was now to be found not in the 'unlivening commonplaces' of Uppingham, but in schools such as Loretto.[2] Few headmasters dared to stand out against the philathletic tide: when one brave HMC member proposed the motion 'that the worship of athletics has increased... and ought to be diminished', it ran into an awkward silence.[3] After 1918 schoolmasters returning from the war to a world that had changed so much were determined that their schools should change as little as possible.

---

[1] Schools where housemasters still ran for-profit enterprises generally made these changes between 1919 and 1945. See (e.g.) Tyerman: *Harrow* p.392.

[2] Loretto's H H Almond was headmaster for 41 years (1862-1903).

[3] Culley of Monmouth. Only Lyttelton of Haileybury gave Culley any real support.

In those post-war years (as in many schools) the focus of remembrance turned to honouring the 450 Old Boys killed in the recent conflict, although Uppingham's memorial Hall (1924) was consistent with Thring's insistence on a secular building large enough to hold the entire school. Other opportunities to expand his 'Almighty Wall' of facilities were then constrained by prolonged economic depression, the 1939-45 war and the age of austerity which followed it. Ironically, the most imaginative and reforming headmaster of that era, John (later Lord) Wolfenden (1934-44), was the one whose tenure coincided with the time of greatest economic stricture.

Thring's name appeared sporadically during this period in educational histories and government reports. His passion for a broad education without neglecting formal learning skills can be seen in the Hadow Report (1926) on *The Education of the Adolescent* and the Spens Report (1938) on *Secondary Education.* However, although the writer of his entry in the *Dictionary of National Biography* in 1900 had called him 'a pioneer of educational improvement', those who still remembered him noted with surprise how rarely he was quoted – and how inaccurately,[1] especially by zealots who claimed him as a conventional supporter of muscular Christianity. Even so, his memory never entirely died. A fifty-year retrospective article in *The Times Educational Supplement* in 1937 suggested that all prophets suffer from their principles becoming commonplace, but that Thring 'would be remembered in the heritage of English education for his unceasing insistence on the worth of each individual boy, stupid or clever, famous or obscure'.

After 1945 the growing demand for university places – and the increasing number of grammar school boys beating their public school counterparts in the competition for state scholarships to university – reduced the emphasis in schools on sporting success and re-affirmed academic and other achievements.

Thring's greatest advocate in the immediate post-war period was Sir Cyril Norwood, one of the architects of the 1944 Education Act. Norwood recognised Thring's originality and how he saw 'the value of music, the bad effect of ugly surroundings, and the necessity of making educational buildings suitable for their purpose'. He admired Thring's emphasis on effective education for all abilities and his opposition to turning tests and

---

[1] E.g. the maxim: 'For boys, only the best is good enough'. Rigby ascribed this to Sir Arthur Somervell (see ch. 22). Others cite it as a phrase used by Paul David (see ch. 5). However, Thring would surely have agreed with its sentiments.

examinations into an obsession.[1] The greatest written tribute to Thring in that period appeared in Professor E B Castle's book *Moral Education in Christian Times* (1958).[2]

A generation after Norwood, Sir Alec Clegg, the innovative chief education officer of the West Riding of Yorkshire,[3] drew inspiration from Thring's belief in the infinite possibilities within children and how their creative powers must be encouraged. Thring was also acknowledged by two successive directors of education in Leicestershire: Stewart Mason, a pupil at Uppingham when his father taught music there in the 1920s,[4] and Andrew Fairbairn who championed child-centredness, independence for Heads, innovative buildings, creative arts and music. The development of thinking about the value of child-centred education for younger children (as in the 1967 Plowden Report) re-focused attention on Thring's idea of 'every boy being good at something'. In the 1970s there was a reassessment of his views on school sport which confounded earlier claims that he was an uncritical supporter of team games for all.[5]

In 1960s Uppingham, despite the school's organisational reforms the essence of Thring's creation still remained. Many buildings had barely changed externally. The 'little commonwealths' of boarding houses were still spread across the town; still with smaller numbers than houses in many other schools, and with their catering arrangements surviving several aborted proposals for a central dining hall. The school still set a high priority by teaching boys of a wide variety of abilities as well as the academic elite.

---

[1] Norwood (1875-1956) was headmaster of Bristol Grammar School, Master of Marlborough College, Head Master of Harrow and President of St John's, Oxford. In his book *The English Tradition of Education* (1929) he cited Thring's views about boarding, and praised the Mission, describing him as 'one of the greatest teachers that the nineteenth century produced'. Norwood's report led to the tripartite schools system of 1944.

[2] Castle was headmaster of Leighton Park School and later Professor of Education, University College, Hull.

[3] Sir Alec Clegg (1909-1986): CEO 1945-74. In *Making the Whole World Wonder* (1972), he praised teachers who believed that that there is good in every child, and quoted the 'great' Thring at length.

[4] Recorded as 'Stewart' in the *School Roll* and elsewhere, but occasionally spelt 'Stuart'. See Jones, Donald K: *Stewart Mason: The Art of Education* (1988) pp.21-2: 'Mason developed a lifelong aversion to ball-games – but also never forgot Uppingham's musical facilities or the choral events in which he took part'.

[5] See the works of Malcolm Tozer in particular, cited in the bibliography. Wolfenden's government report on sport in the community (1960) was by then leading to the development of sports centres.

As more prosperous economic times returned, many schools began to add to their 'machinery'. In the maintained sector this was accelerated by the move to comprehensive schools (1965) and the raising of the school leaving age (1972). For the independent sector it reflected both educational conviction and the increased competition between rival schools as, in Uppingham and elsewhere, a succession of ambitious new art, design and science buildings, theatres, sports centres and music schools made possible a reinterpretation of Thring's vision of giving every pupil a chance to excel. New boarding houses were created, some converted from huge sanatoriums no longer needed after advances in medicine had eliminated the threat of Victorian-style epidemics. Pupil numbers grew as traditional boys' schools increasingly admitted girls: co-education in Uppingham might even be claimed as a belated memorial to the unfulfilled ambitions of Thring's daughter, Grace.[1] Though he was no supporter of study-bedrooms, their existence in many schools can be seen as a re-invention of the 'little refuge' studies which he valued so much.

****

150 years after the publication of *Education and School,* how should Thring be remembered? There is an uncanny similarity between many of the issues which confronted him and those which schools wrestle with nowadays: encouraging inspirational teaching and developing learning skills rather than teaching to the demands of examinations and inspectors; the remorseless tide of regulation and compliance from government; mandatory teacher-training; cost controls; questions of access and of charitable objects; local town-school relationships.

Immediately after his death there was a lively debate over whether Thring had really changed English education or merely created one school that was distinctive for a few decades. Some have argued since then that in his work both for Uppingham and for HMC he simply found himself in the right place at the right time; that his school grabbed a slice of the available market and that he devised an educational philosophy to fit it; that in his passion for independence he was little more than a fanatical upholder of the headmaster's autocratic rights.

Beyond Uppingham, Thring - who spent his life in a boys' secondary boarding school and who travelled comparatively little - arguably had most influence on the professional careers of women teachers, and those working in day-primary schools, many of them beyond Britain. Yet far from belittling him, this highlights the extraordinary reach of his ideas and

---

[1] Sixth form girls in 1975 and full co-education from 2001.

the concentric circles of his legacy: to his school; to ideas about independent education; to the wider teaching profession *and* to a modern understanding of child-centred education. His ideas in *Education and School* were later adopted by Heads and governors elsewhere, as others sought to emulate or learn from what he had created in his re-formed Uppingham. The readership of *Theory and Practice* included many teachers, both primary and secondary, and plenty of parents.

He can be defended for the consistency, or criticised for the repetitiveness and intransigence, of some of his views: for example, on government, inspection and examinations. In other areas such as visual perception or the education of women, his ideas developed significantly during his career. Sometimes he held contradictory views – insisting on the right to dismiss staff whilst allowing his health and finances to suffer by failing to exercise it. The enthusiastic supporter of educational opportunity in Woolwich, Queensland or Japan showed surprisingly little interest in helping Uppingham day boys or (until his final few years) in scholarship opportunities for school or university aspirants. He lived by – and financially almost perished through – his belief in independence, an issue on which he can be accused of being over-proud or naive.

Some see him as hostile to, or fearful of, the working class, denouncing free elementary education as theft and unable to see that good education depended on an active role for the state[1] – a role that he vigorously demanded in public health matters. Yet he also showed great compassion and belief in the value of individuals regardless of status. His 'King of Boys' character made him unsuited to be headmaster of one of the traditional 'great' schools even if he had wished it – or to be involved in the politics of a cathedral close or the collegial government of an Oxbridge college. It also exacerbated problems with some colleagues, yet it did not stop them supporting him over the major crisis points in his life.

He had none of the sources of income enjoyed by many other schools. His governors/trustees were supine as he faced the Commissioners and they did little to help his fight to moderate the New Scheme. He had few allies against philathleticism. It is paradoxical that he has been described as 'an unyielding pioneer, with the missionary, but a touch of the

---

[1] Apart from exceptions such as Matthew Arnold, the Victorians had a far more minimalist view of the state than modern generations. Contrast the attitude to the police in Summerscale, Kate: *Suspicions of Mr. Wicher* with Adonis: *Education,* (2012) p.xvii: 'The crux issue for progressive reformers today is not whether the state matters and needs to command significant resources – of course it does – but how it translates its social and educational duties into institutions which work and promote a successful common life... the state works best when it works with and through strong autonomous institutions in a strong civil society'.

fanatical, temperament of a Livingstone or a Gordon', because it was no mean feat to bring the first members of HMC together. As its historian (Alicia Percival) stated, they were unaccustomed and temperamentally unsuited to collective action: 'They needed a great man to lead them'.

Above all, through courage, organisation and improvisation he triumphed over typhoid and at Borth. Despite the declining powers and the difficulties of his final years he deserved better than the mountain of concerns that he had to face. He never lost his belief in music, or trust, or Platonic manliness and his Mission in Woolwich provided a template for many other schools. His passion for the opportunities offered to pupils of varying abilities by a good boarding education never dimmed, either: he always believed in high-quality houses and in central-school buildings erected, maintained and decorated in a style which would encourage pupils to respect the value of what they were being taught.

Though Thring was not the first campaigner for 'new' subjects he devoted far more time and money to curriculum innovation and breadth than most other headmasters of his time. Some of them shared parts of his vision, yet no one (especially in the grammar schools) was so active in delivering so much. Percival included Thring among her cast of *Very Superior Men* because 'so much of what is now taken for granted was pioneered by Thring: the gymnasium, the athletics field, the fives court, the carpentry shop, the school gardens, the swimming bath and the concert hall'. Moreover, the reformers were the exception rather than the rule: many other schools continued to provide poor rote learning in classics for up to 80% of the timetable even in the 1870s, resisting science and vocational subjects as fit only for the socially inferior and associated with vulgar 'industry'.[1]

Some writers have argued that in his demands for a broad, varied and imaginative curriculum he should have been more radical: that he never reconciled his protection for the classics with his concern for the average boy who found them so impenetrable. His awareness of a boy's limited attention span should have led him to embrace earlier Candler's belief in a

---

[1] Thring was not the first campaigner for 'new' subjects: Butler of Shrewsbury (1798-1836) provided teaching in English, geography, algebra, Euclid and English history and Arnold was enthusiastic for modern history and German. Farrar (Marlborough) lectured to the Royal Institution as early as 1859 on the neglect of science: other science enthusiasts included Frederick Temple, Mitchinson and Harper, and Thring's old foe Stokoe (Richmond, Yorkshire). Temple believed that 'a boy ought not to be ignorant of this earth on which God has placed him, and ought therefore to be well acquainted with geography (and botany and chemistry)'. Heffer's *High Minds* (p.449) cites examples of mathematics and modern languages in the 'Nine' (Clarendon) schools by 1850.

timetable of more, shorter lessons. However, he could not have allocated more prime time to 'new' areas of education without appearing to ignore the traditional education that many prospective parents wanted.[1]

In his vision for childhood his consistent aspiration was that children should be seen as individuals, distinct from adults and not merely a smaller version of them.[2] To him, childhood was a life-form in its own right. Getting inside the child's mind and seeing things as a child saw them in order to 'unlock' the budding intellect was a far cry from the top-down attitude of many well-meaning academics who went into school teaching at that time. These ideas, and his concern to give children self-respect, self-confidence and happiness, are a commonplace nowadays but in Thring's time they were 'not only unacceptable but incomprehensible'.[3]

Through these aspirations he can be seen as a link in an ideological chain from Rousseau, Froebel and Pestalozzi through to John Dewey, and Maria Montessori.[4] The progressive schools which began in the 1890s (some of which included agriculture and gardening in their curriculum) took a stage further his belief that every pupil could do something well and supported his view that the schools' system should not be geared

---

[1] Some see *Education and School* (p.103) where Thring states that it is 'absolutely impossible' to devise a curriculum which provides both for professional education and 'mental and bodily training', as another example of how Victorian headmasters disliked the advance of science and vocational studies into time previously devoted to classics. See Green, Andy: *English Education and the Liberal State* (1990) p.285; Wiener, Martin: *English Culture and the Decline of the Industrial Spirit 1985-1980* p.19; Reader, W J: *Professional Men: The Rise of the Professional Classes in Nineteenth-Century England* (1966) pp.105-115.

[2] He was arguably ahead of his time. See Abrams, Fran: *Songs of Innocence: the Story of British Childhood* (2012): The twentieth century was 'the one in which the child took on its own identity [and] childhood became not just a prelude to adulthood but a crucial, formative period... The Edwardians were pre-occupied about the distinctive importance of childishness and opportunities for play: for the first time children became central to England's sense of self'.

[3] Percival: *Very Superior Men* pp.194-5: 'Fathers, when they sent their sons away to school, paid their money for them to be taught the recognised curriculum [which] took them to the University. Or else, like Tom Brown's father, they sent him to acquire from his fellows and through the school discipline a code and habits for living'.

[4] See Stewart, W A C: *The Educational Innovators Vol. II: Progressive Schools 1881-1967* (1968); Skidelsky, Robert: *English Progressive Schools* (1969). Dewey championed the idea that children learned through experience and that a good education wakened their latent powers; Maria Montessori used her work with young slum children in Rome in the early twentieth century to develop a child-centred, scientific teaching method to develop the senses and the intellect.

exclusively to the top scholar or athlete.[1] Thorold Coade was headmaster of Bryanston from 1932-59, putting a strong emphasis on the idea that freedom and self-development implied self-discipline. Echoing Thring, Coade believed that education's purpose was 'the widening and deepening of the experience of life'. Significantly, one of his last housemasters was John Royds, headmaster of Uppingham for ten years from mid-1960s, a decade when the end of austerity finally allowed a re-interpretation of Thring's ideals through a succession of striking new projects in art and design, sport and drama – and an extension to the chapel.

On top of all the demands on him within his schoool he chose to devote great energy to championing the work and status of the teaching profession at a time when others sought to demean it, and he was well ahead of his time in highlighting the technical importance of good classroom practice. His repeated distinction between the teacher and the hammerer has strong overtones of the twenty-first century's desire to promote independent learning. Through these ideas he established his credentials as *The Teachers' Teacher.*[2] If his books are sometimes tortuous and eclectic, they are also alive with vivid analogies, images and maxims to back up his ideas – devised more rapidly than he could ever logically write them down.

No one could doubt his courage or his pride in the 'different' school that he constantly talked about. In the words of one modern writer:

'All that is best in English education could be found at Thring's Uppingham... attractive surroundings and a homely atmosphere; Christian teaching and moral guidance; intellectual training and a broad general knowledge; a well-planned physical education programme and real attention to arts and music; a sense of communal responsibility and a spirit of individual freedom – all these comprised an education in manliness. The education of the whole man and the attention to the individual child are the two central legacies that Thring has left...'[3]

---

[1] The progressive movement in fee-charging independent schools had three phases: the 1880s-90s (Abbotsholme, Bedales and King Alfred's); the 1920s (Summerhill, Dartington and Kilquhanity) and the 1960s (Gordonstoun and Atlantic College). At Greshams Howson (who worked for Thring in 1886-7) promoted closer staff-pupil relationships – as did (e.g.) Reddie (who founded Abbotsholme), Almond (Loretto), Jacks (Mill Hill). The Platonic ideals were taken up by Kurt Hahn at Gordonstoun from 1934.

[2] Rigby's intended title for the book he never completed.

[3] Tozer, Malcolm: *Manliness: The Evolution of a Victorian ideal* (University of Leicester Ph.D. 1978) p.555.

Few forgot the light in his eye when he first met them or his total sense of engagement with them in conversation. Some thought him convinced that God kept a permanent watch over his work; others that he was 'a Shakespearean man' or 'a great and good man with the fire and enthusiasm of an Old Testament prophet'.[1] His view of himself as doing the Lord's work and of any opponents as the enemies of the Lord round about him made him always prone to seeing issues in black and white: it fed his sense of persecution but it stemmed from the deep religious faith that also nourished his optimism, as he explained in 1866 to a friend:[2]

> 'I believe and know a Lord and Giver of Life. I feel Him working in and with me. I understand the world plan. I read the past and see the happy progress, whatever backwaters or eddies there may be in Life's great river. I see the future, and know what our own times mean, and in the rough what is coming, and whatever backwaters or eddies there may be whirling individuals or nations backward for a time in life's great river, I see the great river sweeping all on equally to a happy end'.

Shortly after Thring's death Parkin received a perceptive letter from Courthope Bowen, whose efforts Thring had supported to found a men's teacher training college. Bowen had been frustrated by Thring's eclectic writing style and had often disagreed with him (not least about the centrality in the curriculum of classics) but he admired Thring's 'keen sympathy with dunces [which] decisively cut him off from the old type of schoolmasters', and the vital intensity and personal magnetism which left such an impression on many whom he encountered:

> 'To meet [Thring] and to talk with him was an experience never to be forgotten. His emotion was not violent; it was deep and intense: every fibre of his being seemed to vibrate with it; it moved in his eyes: it trembled in his voice; it set him pacing up and down. It did not result in weakness, but in strong desire for activity. It seemed rather a spur than a hindrance to his intellect – except that it made his mind work as it were by flashes, without emotional sequence, in striking metaphors, which though oftenest brilliant at times hurt more than helped the effect of his words.

> But whether his fashion of speech was mainly happy or not, it left an impression on one unlike anything else. Right or wrong, hasty, fantastic

---

[1] Skrine admitted: '[Thring] brought not peace, but a sword... as an organiser who could be frustrated and betrayed. [He] felt that persons who got in the way... of genius did not have the right to do so'.
[2] J Churton Collins: see ch. 19.

or keen-sighted, he made one feel that he was veritably in earnest; that he was not speaking of a mere hobby or as a specialist, but was telling you what to him were vital truths...

He holds with unrivalled fervour that the school exists for the boy and not the boy for the school, he has a keen sympathy with dunces, and he sees the immense value of a boy's being successful in something... He has beautiful feelings about boys and education – a splendid earnestness and enthusiasm for both. But he has no reasoned principles about either – no scientific knowledge of them... His writings on education are exhilarating and stimulating as those of very few educationalists are – but his views want reasoning out, co-ordinating, organising.

But I will not go on. It is painful to me to point out his failures and shortcomings – for I loved the man'.

In the same year (1888) another, very different man spoke much more directly of his respect for Thring. 'Skelly' had been the Uppingham school porter for many years. He encountered a new boy who, nearly half a century later, described the scene[1]:

'Being a stout and ponderous old man, he was naturally always called "Skelly", which was, I imagine, a shortened form of "skeleton". Knowing that to him Mr. Thring was the greatest man that had ever lived, I timidly asked him what manner of man [Thring had been].

"Skelly" shifted the tight woollen comforter around his neck as though to free his throat for some portentous pronouncement, and looking down scornfully at me, he replied: "It's a good thing Mr. Thring never lived to set eyes on the likes of you!"'

---

[1] J P Graham *Forty Years of Uppingham* (1932) p.87.

APPENDIX 1

TIMELINE

APPENDIX 2

HOUSEMASTERS AND THEIR HOUSES DURING THRING'S TIME

THRING'S PRINTED WORKS

(listed in chronological order, with first date of publication):

A Few Remarks on the Present System of Degrees at King's College, Cambridge (1846: anon).

The Elements of Grammar Taught in English: with questions (1851).

The Child's Grammar: being the substance of 'The Elements of Grammar Taught in English': adapted for the use of junior classes (1852).

A Construing Book (1855).

School Songs (1855).

Translations and Songs (1855).

Two Letters and Axioms on Education (for private circulation: no date).

Three Letters and Axioms on Education (1858).

School Songs: A Collection of Original and other Pieces (1858).

Sermons Delivered at Uppingham School (1858).

Uppingham School. The Statement of the Rev. Edward Thring. Head Master, respecting the Organisation of the School; and the Decree of the Governors in October, 1859 (revised 1872).

School Delusions. Essays by the Sixth Form. Intro by Rev. E. Thring (1860).

Truth in Schools (1862).

A Latin Gradual. A First Latin Construing Book for Beginners (1863).

Education and School (1864).

Commemoration Sermon, preached in Uppingham School Chapel on April 27, 1866 the First Anniversary of the Chapel Opening (1866).

A Manual of Mood Construction (1867).

The Agamemnon of Aeschylus (translation, 1867).

Exercises in Grammatical Analysis (1868).

On the Principles of Grammar (1868).

Thoughts on Life-Science by Benjamin Place (1869).

Boarding Schools: Their Theory and Classification (1869: anonymous).

'The Enchanted Wood', in *Uppingham School Magazine* (Christmas, 1871).

'The Conference of Head Masters', in *The Quarterly Journal of Education*, 1 (1872).

An Address delivered to the Students of the University College of Wales; March 28th, 1877.

The Petition of Edward Thring, M.A., Head Master of Uppingham School to the Charity Commissioners (1878).

Borth Commemoration Sermon (1880).

Borth Lyrics, with illustrations by C. Rossiter (1881). Edition with music (1881).

Four Choral songs for Public Schools. The words written by Rev. E. Thring. The Music composed by the Music-Master of Uppingham School and edited by Paul David. No.1 Cricket song; No. 2 Football Song; No. 3 Fives Song; No. 4 Farewell! (n.d.).

Uppingham School Songs with Music (1881).

'Notes on Teaching' (first privately printed: 1882), in *Journal of Education.* (March and May, 1882).

Theory and Practice of Teaching (1883).

'The Best Means of Raising the Standard of Public Morality': a paper read at the Carlisle Church Congress (1884).

Address on 'Sex and Purity' (typescript: 1884).

Speech at the Tercentenary Celebrations, June 26, 1884.

An Address delivered before the Education Society by the President, the Rev. Edward Thring: May 1st, 1885.

'The Charter of Life', in *The School of Life, edited by C.J. Vaughan, D.D. Seven Addresses delivered to the London Mission 1885 in St. Paul's Church, Knightsbridge, to Public School Men, by late and present Head Masters* (1885).

Speech on the Allotment Question on Saturday October 31, 1885.

Sermons preached at Uppingham School: 2 vols: (1886).

An Address to the Teachers of Minnesota, U.S.A. (1886).

A Speech delivered at the Prize-giving at the High School for Girls, Leamington (1886).

'Thinking in Shape and Pictorial Teaching': *Journal of Education* (1887).

A Sermon for the Nineteenth Sunday after Trinity, October 16th, 1887, in Uppingham School Chapel.

Addresses (1887).

Poems and Translations (1887).

SELECT BIBLIOGRAPHY

PRIMARY AND LOCAL SOURCES, listed by location

Uppingham School Archive

Bell, T.,	Letterbook.
Field, R.,	*Report to the Sanitary Authority* 6 January 1876.
Haviland, A.,	*Report on the Late Outbreak of Enteric Fever in Archdeacon Johnson's School, Uppingham, Rutland: June-November 1875.* (1875).
James, W.P.,	Thring and Uppingham (typescript). Lingfield mss: Letters between Edward and Godfrey Thring.
Rawlinson, R.,	*Uppingham: Town and School Reports* 1876.
Rigby, C.,	Unpublished manuscript of a book on Edward Thring.
Rome, R.C.,	Uppingham: The story of a School 1584-1948 (typescript).
Rowe, The Revd. T.B.,	The (Uppingham) School Guide Book (1872).
Skrine, J.H.,	Diary (undated extract).
Tarbotton, M.O.,	*Report to the Trustees and Headmaster of Uppingham School January 1876.*
Thring, M.,	Unpublished memoirs.
Thring, E.,	Diaries: 2 vols – 1854-62 and 1886-7.
	Index Rerum.
	Sermons (boxed).
Uppingham School	*Magazine* 1853-1887 (bound volumes).
Uppingham School	*Roll:* Sixth issue (1932).
Uppingham School	Trustees' Minute Books
Wolfenden, J.F.	Speech at the Thring Centenary 1853-1953 by J.F. Wolfenden, C.B.E.,Vice-Chancellor of Reading University, July 25th, 1953.

The archive also holds financial statements and many individual letters written by Thring.

Headmasters' and Headmistresses' Conference, Market Harborough
HMC holds electronic copies of the minutes of its early meetings.

National Archive, Ottawa, Canada
Sir George Parkin's Papers. These are spread across many boxes, catalogued as MG30 D44.
The Archive has compiled an extensive finding aid, including individual letters.
See also boxes of scrapbook material, Thring's obituaries and reviews of Parkin's books.

The National Archives, Kew
Local Government Board papers: The Uppingham Poor Law Union 1860-1882
MH12/9812-7.
Charity Commission papers ED 27/3932-40.

Record Office of Leicestershire, Leicester and Rutland
Census Return for Uppingham (1871) RG10/3301-2.
Kelly's *Directory for Leicester and Rutland* (1876).

Somerset Record Office, Taunton
Thring Papers. SRO Box No 8. DD/THG.

SECONDARY SOURCES

Abrams, F.,   *Songs of Innocence: the Story of British Childhood* (2012).

Adonis, A.,   *Education, Education, Education* (2012).

Anon. (Rawnsley, W.F.,) *Early Days at Uppingham under Edward Thring by an Old Boy* (1904).

Archer, R.L.,   *Secondary Education in the Nineteenth Century* (1921).

Avery, G.,   *Mrs. Ewing* (1961).

Ballance, S.,   *A Town called Eton* (1982).

Balls F.E.,   'The Origins of the Endowed Schools Act 1869' (Cambridge Ph.D., 1964).

Bamford, T.W.,   'Public School Town in the Nineteenth Century', *British Journal of Education Studies* (1957): pp. 25-36.

Bamford, T.W.,   *Rise of the Public Schools: A Study of Boys' Public Boarding Schools in England and Wales from 1837 to the Present Day* (1967).

Barber, J.,   *The Story of Oakham School* (1983).

Baron, G.,   'The Origins and Early History of the Headmasters' Conference, 1869-1914', *Educational Review,* viii (1955) pp. 223-234.

Benson, S.G.,   *I Will Plant Me a Tree: An Illustrated History of Gresham's School* (2002).

Bonney, T.G.,   *Memories of a Long Life* (1921).

Bristed, C.A.,   *Five Years in an English University* (1852).

Candler, H.,   *Help to Arithmetic* (1868).

Card, T.,   *Eton Established* (2001).

Carpenter, H.,   *Secret Gardens: a Study of the Golden Age of Children's Literature* (1985).

Carroll, L.,   *Through the Looking-Glass* (1872).

Castle, E.B.,   *Moral Education in Christian Times* (1958).

Christian, W.,   *Parkin: Canada's Most Forgotten Man* (2008).

Clegg, A.,	'Making the whole world wonder': a speech at Bingley College of Education (1972). http://www.educationengland.org.uk/documents/speeches/1972clegg.html
Cook, T.,	'Apostle of Empire: Sir George Parkin and Imperial Federation' (Queen's University, Kingston, Ontario Ph.D., 1977).
Copley, T.,	*Black Tom: Arnold of Rugby: The Myth and the Man:* (2002).
Curtis, S.J., and Boultwood, M.E.A.,	*An Introductory History of English Education since 1800* (1960).
Cust, L.,	*A History of Eton College* (1899).
Cutting, S.M.,	'Howard Candler, MA, FRSL (1838-1916), Schoolmaster, Educationalist and Polymath', *Camden History Review* 32 (2008), pp. 25-9
Darwin, B.,	*The English Public School* (1929).
Darwin C.R.,	*The Descent of Man, and Selection in Relation to Sex,* (1871).
Darwin, C.R.,	*On the Origin of Species* (1859).
Daunton, M., (ed),	*The Organisation of Knowledge in Victorian Britain,* (2005).
Douglas, N.,	*Looking Back: An Autobiographical Excursion,* 2 vols (1933).
Eden, H.K.F.,	*Juliana Horatia Ewing and Her Books* (1896).
Ewing, J.H.,	*Jackanapes* (1884).
Erdozain, D.,	*The Problem of Pleasure: Sport, Recreation and the Crisis of Victorian Religion* (2010).
Farrar F.W.,	*Life of Christ* (1874).
Felmeri, L.,	*Az iskolazas jelene Angolorszagban,* two vols (1881).
Fitch, J.G.,	*Notes on American Schools and Colleges* (1890).
Fitch, J.G.,	*Educational Aims and Methods,* (1900).
Fletcher, S.,	*Feminists and Bureaucrats: A Study in the Development of Girls' Education in the Nineteenth Century* (1980).
Garland, M.M.,	*Cambridge before Darwin: The Idea of a Liberal Education, 1800-1860* (1980).
Gardner, B.,	*The Public Schools: an Historical Survey* (1973).
Gathorne-Hardy, J.,	*The Public School Phenomenon (1977).*
Gatty, M.,	*Parables from Nature with a memoir of the author by her daughter Juliana Horatia Ewing* (1899).
Goldhill, S.,	*Victorian Culture and Classical Antiquity: art, opera, fiction, and the proclamation of modernity* (2011).
Goldhill, S.,	*Who Needs Greek?: contests in the cultural history of Hellenism* (2002).
Gourlay, A.B.,	*A History of Sherborne School* (1951).
Graham, B.T., *et al:*	*Ilminster Grammar School 1549-1949* (1949).

Graham, J.P.,   *Forty Years of Uppingham* (1932).

Graves, C.L.,   *The Life and Letters of Alexander Macmillan* (1910).

Green, A.,   *English Education and the Liberal State* (1990).

Grayling, A.C.,   *Cultural Olympians: Rugby School's Intellectual and Spiritual leaders* (2013).

H. and M.P. (ed).,   *Teaching, Learning and Life. Thoughts from the Writings of Edward Thring of Uppingham* (1913).

Harford-Battersby, C.F., *Pilkington of Uganda: with an Introductory Chapter by Rev, J.H. Skrine* (1899).

Harrod, R.F.,   *The Life of John Maynard Keynes* (1951).

Hay, I.,   *The Lighter Side of School Life* (1914).

Heffer, S.,   *High Minds: The Victorians and the Birth of Modern Britain* (2013).

Hinchliff, P.,   *Frederick Temple, Archbishop of Canterbury: A Life* (1998).

Honey, J.R. de S.,   *Tom Brown's Universe: The Development of the Victorian Public School* (1977).

Hoppen, K.T.,   *The Mid-Victorian Generation 1846-1886* (1998).

Hornung, E.W.,   *Fathers of Men* (1912).

Hoyland, G.,   *The Man Who Made a School: Thring of Uppingham* (1946).

Hughes, T.,   *Memoir of Daniel Macmillan* (1882).

Hughes, T.,   *Tom Brown's Schooldays* (1857).

Hyam, R.,   *Empire and Sexuality: the British Experience* (1990).

Jones, D.K.,   *Stewart Mason: The Art of Education* (1988).

Jones, D.K.,   *The Making of the Education System 1851-81* (1977).

Kegan Paul, C.,   *Memories* (1899).

Kingsley, C.,   *The Water Babies, A Fairy Tale for a Land Baby* (1863).

Lawrence, P.S.H.,   *The Encouragement of Learning* (1980).

Lawson, J, and Silver, H., *A Social History of Education in England* (1975).

Leedham-Green, E.,   *A Concise History of the University of Cambridge* (1996).

Leigh, A.A.,   *King's College* (1899).

Leese. J.,   *Personalities and Power in English Education* (1950).

Lester-Garland, L.V.,   *A Memoir of Hugo Daniel Harper, D.D.* (1896).

Leinster-Mackay, D.,   *The Educational World of Edward Thring: A Centenary Study* (1987).

Leinster-Mackay D.,   *The Rise of the English Prep School* (1984).

Leyel, H.,   *A Modern Herbal* (1931).

McConnell, J.,   *Eton: How it Works* (1967).

McCrum, M.,   *Thomas Arnold: Head Master – A Reassessment* (1989).

McCulloch, G.,   'Cyril Norwood and the English tradition of education': *Oxford Review of Education* 32: 1 (2006) pp. 55-69.

354

Mack, E.C.,   *Public Schools and British Opinion 1780 to 1860* (1938).

Macmillan, G.A., (ed),   *Letters of Alexander Macmillan* (1908).

Mangan, J.A.,   *Athleticism in the Victorian and Edwardian Public School* (1981).

Mangan, J.A.,   *The Games Ethic and Imperialism* (1985).

Mangan, J.A.,   *'Manufactured' Masculinity: Making Imperial Manliness, Morality and Militarism* (2013).

Matthews, B.,   *By God's Grace: A History of Uppingham School* (1984).

Maxwell, C.,   *Mrs. Gatty and Mrs. Ewing* (1949).

Morgan, C.,   *The House of Macmillan 1843-1943* (1943).

Moore, J.R.,   *The Post-Darwinian Controversies: A Study of the Protestant Struggle to Come To Terms with Darwin in Great Britain And America, 1870-1900* (1979).

Nelson, C.,   'Sex and the Single Boy: Ideals of Manliness and Sexuality in Victorian Literature for Boys', *Victorian Studies* 32:4 (1989) pp. 525-535.

Nelson, C.,   *Invisible Men: Fatherhood in Victorian Periodicals 1850-1910* (1995).

Newsome, D.,   *A History of Wellington College 1859-1959* (1959).

Newsome, D.,   *Godliness & Good Learning: Four Studies on a Victorian Ideal* (1961).

Norwood, C.,   *The English Educational System* (1928).

Norwood, C.,   *The English Tradition of Education* (1929).

Old Colleger, An,   *Eton in the Forties* (1896).

Parker, J.W., (ed),   *Essays and Reviews* (1860).

Parkin, G.R., (ed),   *Edward Thring, Headmaster of Uppingham School: Life, Diary and Letters,* 2 vols (1898); single volume (1900).

Parkin G.R.,   'Uppingham: An ancient school worked on modern ideas', *The Century Magazine* XXXVI: 5 (1888): pp. 643-657.

Pattenden, P,) and Thomson, A.,)   The Snuffing of Sanitary Smith: Fellow and Senior Bursar', *Peterhouse Annual Record 2002-3* (2005) pp. 43-56.

Patterson, W.S.   *Sixty Years of Uppingham Cricket* (1909).

Percival, A.,   *Very Superior Men: Some Early Public School Headmasters and their Achievements* (1973).

Percival, A.,   *The Origins of the Headmasters' Conference* (1969).

Peterson, A.D.C.,   *A Hundred Years of Education* (1952).

Potter, J,   *Headmaster: The Life of John Percival, Radical Aristocrat* (1997).

Protherough, R.,   'Shaping the Image of the Great Headmaster', *British Journal of Educational Studies* Vol. XXXII No 3 (1984) pp. 239-249.

Quick, R.H., *Essays on Educational Reformers* (1868).
Rawnsley E.F., *Canon Rawnsley: an account of his life* (1923).
Rawnsley, H.D., *Edward Thring: Teacher and Poet* (1899).
Rawnsley, W.F., *Edward Thring: Maker of Uppingham School, Headmaster 1853-1887* (1926).
Reader, W.J., *Professional Men: the Rise of the Professional Classes in Nineteenth-Century England* (1966).
Richardson, E., *Classical Victorians: scholars, scoundrels and generals in pursuit of antiquity (2013).*
Richardson, N., *Typhoid in Uppingham: Analysis of a Victorian Town and School in crisis* (2008).
Rigby, C., 'The Life and Influence of Edward Thring' (Oxford, D.Phil.,1968).
Rowcroft, C., *Confessions of an Etonian* (1852).
Ruskin J., *The Seven Lamps of Architecture* (1849).
Russell, G.W.E., *Fifteen chapters of autobiography* (1912).
Saltmarsh, J., *King's College: A Short History* (1958).
Sargant, W.L., *The Book of Oakham School* (1928).
Sidgwick, H., *The Method of Ethics* (1874).
Simon, B., *Studies in the History of Education*: 1780-1870 (1960).
Simon, B. and Bradley, I., *The Victorian Public School: Studies in the Development of an Educational Institution* (1975).
Simpson, J.H., *Howson of Holt* (1925).
Skidelsky, R., *English Progressive Schools* (1969).
Skrine, J.H., *A Memory of Edward Thring* (1890).
Skrine, J.H., *Uppingham by the Sea* (1878).
Somervell D.C., *A History of Tonbridge School* (1947).
Stanley, A.P., *The Life and Correspondence of Thomas Arnold, D.D.,* 2 vols (1845).
Stansky, P., 'Lyttelton and Thring: a study in Nineteenth Century Education': *Victorian Studies* (V), No 5. (1962): pp. 205-225.
Stewart, W.A.C., *The Educational Innovators Vol. II: Progressive Schools 1881-1967* (1968).
Strachey, L., *Eminent Victorians* (1918).
Stray, C., *Classics Transformed: Schools, Universities and Society in England, 1830-1960* (1998).
Summerscale, K., *The Suspicions of Mr. Whicher* (2008).
Thompson, I., *The English Lakes: A History* (2010)
Thomson, A., *'A Study of Roles and Relationships in a Rutland Village in the Mid Victorian Period: Glaston c1860-90'* (Leicester M.A. in English Local History, 1999).
Thring, S., *Victorian Grandmothers* (2008).
Tozer, M., 'A perfect pattern of manly power: coming to manhood at mid-Victorian Uppingham School': *Rutland Record* 32 (2012) pp. 79-85.

Tozer, M.,	'Cricket, School and Empire: E.W. Hornung and his Young Guard': *The International Journal of the History of Sport* 6:2 (1989) pp. 156-171.
Tozer, M.,	'Education for True Life: A Review of Thring's Educational Aims and Methods': *History of Education Society Bulletin* 39 (1987) pp. 24-31.
Tozer, M.,	'Education in Manliness: Idealist, ideal and exemplar': *Religion* 17:1 (1987) pp. 63-80
Tozer, M.,	'Happy Gains: Edward Thring's Obligations to Literature – A Centenary Essay', *Journal of Education Administration and History*, 19:2, (1987) pp. 26-35.
Tozer, M.,	'H.H. Stephenson: The first of the great school coaches' *The Sports Historian* 15:1 (1995) pp. 54-64.
Tozer, M.,	'Manliness: The Evolution of a Victorian ideal': (Leicester, Ph.D., 1978).
Tozer, M.,	*Physical Education at Thring's Uppingham* (1976).
Tozer. M.,	'The Great Educational Experiment: Edward Thring at Uppingham School' *Rutland Record* 12 (1992) pp. 58-65.
Tozer, M.,	'The readiest hand and the most open heart': Uppingham's first missions to the poor': *Journal of the History of Education Society* 18:4 (1989) pp. 323-333.
Tozer, M.,	'Thring at Uppingham-by-the-Sea: The Lessons of the Borth Sermons': *History of Education Society Bulletin* 36 (1985) pp. 39-44.
Tyerman, C.,	*A History of Harrow School* (2000).
Uppingham Local) History Studies Group)	*Uppingham in 1851: A Night in the Life of a Thriving Town* (2001).
Vaughan, H.,	*Squires of South Wales* (1926).
Walston, C., (ed),	*With a Fine Disregard: a Portrait of Rugby School* (2006).
Wiener, M.,	*English Culture and the Decline of the Industrial Spirit 1985-1980* (1981).
Wilkinson, L.P.,	*A Century of King's 1873-1972* (1980).
Willison, J.,	*Sir George Parkin* (1929).
Winstanley, D.A.,	*Early Victorian Cambridge* (1940).
Witheridge, J.,	*Frank Fletcher 1870-1954: A Formidable Headmaster* (2005).

There are extensive bibliographies in Rigby's manuscript and dissertation of the sources which he consulted, and in Richardson, N., *Typhoid* of sources relating to the events of 1875-7 in Uppingham and Borth.

INDEX

www.ingramcontent.com/pod-product-compliance
Lightning Source LLC
Chambersburg PA
CBHW020341100426
42812CB00029B/3211/J